P9-CQP-528

The What, Where, When, How & Why
Of Gardening In Illinois

Illinois GARDENER'S GUIDE

JAMES A. FIZZELL

COOL
SPRINGS
PRESS

Copyright© 1997 James A. Fizzell

All rights reserved. No part of this book may be reproduced or transmitted in any form or by any means, electronic or mechanical, including photocopying, recording, or by any information storage and retrieval system, without permission in writing from the publisher.

Fizzell, James A.
    Illinois Gardener's Guide: the what, where, when, how & why of gardening in Illinois / James A. Fizzell

    p.   cm.
    Includes bibliographical references (p.) and index.
    ISBN 1-888-608-41-2
    1. Landscape plants --Illinois 2. Landscape gardening -- Illinois.
    3. Gardening -- Illinois I. Title.
635.9--dc20
Fiz

Cool Springs Press, Inc.
206 Bridge Street
Franklin, Tennessee 37064

First printing 1997
Printed in the United States of America
10 9 8 7 6 5 4 3 2

Horticultural Nomenclature Editor: Floyd Swink

On the cover (clockwise from top left): Maple, Lilac, Astilbe, Floribunda Rose

Map (p.11) provided by Agricultural Research Service, USDA

Visit the Cool Springs Press website at: www.coolspringspress.com

DEDICATION

THIS BOOK IS DEDICATED to John R. Culbert, Professor of Horticulture (retired), University of Illinois.

ACKNOWLEDGMENTS

*T*HREE PEOPLE HAVE BEEN ESPECIALLY HELPFUL in preparation of the manuscript for the *Illinois Gardener's Guide*. Special thanks goes to Floyd Swink, botanist of international reputation and friend, for horticulture editing of the manuscript and for technical advice. Gregory R. Stack, University of Illinois Extension horticulturist and colleague, provided resources and moral support. My wife and business partner, A. Jane Fizzell, has provided hours of proofreading, many miles of travel in picking up and delivering materials for editing, as well as days of support as we prepared the manuscript.

CONTENTS

5

The Joy of Illinois Gardening

ELCOME TO ILLINOIS GARDENING, where horticulture is an art—an art that is learned by doing! We make our mistakes, and we have our successes. We correct our mistakes and go on. As I work with the folks who grow gardens and care for landscape plantings, and as fellow gardeners tell us of their problems at shows and on the air during my radio programs, I realize what tremendous interest there is in plants and how they grow. The questions we were asked a decade or two ago can now be answered by nearly every gardener. The questions today are complicated, showing a high level of expertise by Illinois gardeners.

But don't let that discourage you if you are a beginner. Plant people are different! Instead of trying to keep their secrets, they will go out of their way to tell them to you. Just because a gardener isn't "schooled" doesn't mean you can ignore the information. Those of us who have been at it a long time have made many mistakes and have profited from them. If the comments in this book are helpful to you, it is because I, along with my friends who helped put it together, have been where you are. We have had the question and found the answer. I thank all those unselfish gardeners who taught me, and I hope you can profit from our collective knowledge.

ILLINOIS GARDENING: HISTORY AND TRADITIONS

Settlers found flatlands and prairies when they reached Illinois. The land was quite a change from the hills and dense forests through which they had cut trails, and in which they had carved out farms. There were tall grasses as far as the eye could see, as high as a horse's head. The soil was flat and fertile, and there was enough wood from forest-bordering rivers and streams to build their homes. The rivers provided good transportation to other settlements, to the Mississippi on the West and to the shores of Lake Michigan and the little community of Chicago up north.

Farming consisted of trying to grow some row crops and enough feed for the horses and livestock. That was man's work. The garden

Introduction

was next to the house, and women were in charge there. The garden was easily accessible to the kitchen and fenced to keep out wandering livestock. Anne Grant in her *Memoirs of an American Lady* (1808) wrote:

> On working farms, hollyhocks and sunflowers frequently shared space with cabbages in the vegetable patch. Here, under the housewife's watchful eye, were all the herbs she needed for making medicine, flavoring foods, freshening the air, dying cloth, and repelling bugs and vermin. Here also grew the vegetables, greens, and herbs she needed for meals. And here grew flowers. . . just for their beauty and fragrance, and for the little joy a few on the dinner table brought to an otherwise hard life. These gardens that combined herbs, vegetables, and flowers persisted in the expanding towns until the Civil War.

> In towns, everyone had a garden. Kidney beans, asparagus, celery, a great variety of salads, cucumbers, etc., were only admitted into the garden into which no foot of man intruded . . . A woman in very easy circumstances, and abundantly gentle in form and manners, would sow, and plant, and rake incessantly. These fair gardeners, too, were great florists, and did indeed produce "Flowers worthy of Paradise."

The fifty years between the Civil War and World War I were a time of tremendous change. Illinois grew from a strictly rural state to an industrialized state, with Chicago, Peoria, Galena, and Decatur developing a privileged class who had the time and resources for landscaping and gardening. At the same time, the nation was experiencing a gardening revolution that led to burgeoning seed companies, nurseries, and horticulturists. Explorers were bringing in all kinds of plants from every part of the temperate world. The Orient was a particularly fruitful source, and many of the plants we grow today were introduced during those fertile years.

There were scores of gardening books published, and horticultural societies were founded. Landscape architects, among them Frederick Law Olmsted, who was the first to use that title, were busily planning the great gardens and conservatories. Daniel Burnham was planning the 1893 World Colombian Exposition in Chicago, and convincing the people there to preserve some of the rapidly diminishing vacant land. He enlisted Olmsted to plan the grounds for the Exposition, and many of those gardens and parks along the shores of Lake Michigan are still there. The forest preserves of the northern Illinois counties, the great estate gardens, and the Chicago motto, *Urbs in Horto* (City in a Garden) are all results of the inspiration of these two "plant people."

The flower gardens of prairie homesteads eventually moved to the city, as the plants and flowers familiar to Grandmother became incorporated into increasingly sophisticated landscapes on the estates of industrial giants of that era. Large gardens were planted with the new kinds of trees and shrubs, as well as with the familiar native plants.

As increasing numbers of Illinois families moved from the farm to town, the little gardens went with them. The sunflowers and coneflowers, the goldenrod and phlox, the hollyhocks and cosmos, the lilacs and mock oranges . . . all moved to the city. Flowers grew in the backyards of small homes in the cities, and along the front entrywalks. Shrubs and trees were planted to soften the harsh lines of the cities. Large plant nurseries and greenhouses for growing flowers and plants were built and planted all over the state.

Following the Depression and World War II, the cities moved to suburbia. In these last fifty years, landscape and gardening have become a passion for folks in Illinois. Horticulture courses are taught at state colleges and universities, and there are garden clubs in every town. Arboreta and botanic gardens display plantings of the kinds of plants that will grow in this wonderful state, and they offer classes as well.

Introduction

What Makes Gardening Unique in Illinois?

THE SEASONS

Illinois has a moist, temperate, continental climate. Spring is often cool and wet, with snow common until mid-April. The weather can be quite changeable, with high temperatures in the 70s in March, followed by highs in the 30s a day or two later. Spring can be so wet that planting is delayed, and so cool that the emergence of leaves can be delayed until the end of April. Often spring has a hard time arriving.

In addition to the normal weather patterns, the nearness of Lake Michigan keeps areas in the northeast corner of the state cool. An on-shore breeze develops when air over the land warms and rises, pulling in the cold air off the lake.

Summers are warm with temperatures in the 80s and 90s, reaching 100 degrees Fahrenheit on occasion. A succession of low and high pressure systems produces alternating warm and cool weather and provides summer rains, mostly as thunderstorms as the lows pull humid air northward from the Gulf of Mexico.

Rainfall averages about three inches per month throughout the summer. There are periods, however, when the normal movement of fronts is interrupted and droughts lasting as long as three or four weeks can occur. Conversely, there are seasons that have excess rainfall, and thunderstorms can produce localized or even general flooding.

Fall can be the most beautiful season of the year in Illinois. Temperatures are generally moderate, in the 60s and 70s in early fall, with daytime highs falling to the upper 30s by late November. October days can be clear and bright. Rainfall generally becomes more frequent, although extended drought is not uncommon. Late fall, from mid-November on, can be dark and cloudy. The first measurable snow can appear by mid-October. The first 3-inch snowfall can be expected by Thanksgiving.

Introduction

Winter weather is often quite variable. Some years there is little snow, and temperatures remain moderate. Normally, however, there are about three feet of snow, and temperatures will fall to as low as minus 10 degrees Fahrenheit at least once during the season. Extreme low temperatures of minus 25 to minus 30 degrees have been recorded.

The progression of low- and high-pressure weather systems that dominates the weather the rest of the year also affects winter weather. The lows bring precipitation, usually snow in normal years. The high-pressure systems originate in the polar regions and usher in very cold air. Rapid changes in temperature are common.

In winter the moderating effect of Lake Michigan is felt, with temperatures usually warmer because of the warm lake waters. In years when the lake freezes over, or during exceptionally cold weather with strong west winds, this lake effect is nullified.

The growing season is from about 150 days in the northern part of the state to about 205 days far south. The average date of last frost is around April 5 near the Ohio River, May 5 in the Chicago area, and may be as late as May 25 far northwest. The average date of first frost is October 20. The earliest frost has occurred around Labor Day, the latest usually around Halloween.

WEATHER AND PLANT HARDINESS

Plant hardiness is affected by several factors, including low temperatures. The ability of a species or cultivar to tolerate the lowest temperatures it will experience in its location is usually what is meant by "plant hardiness." But hardiness is also affected by high temperatures, how fast the temperatures change, wind, shade, humidity, and soil conditions. And plants are often found growing well outside their suggested hardiness range where they are protected, or where extra care is provided.

There are two hardiness rating maps in general use. These zones are based on the average minimum temperatures that can be expected in a particular part of the continent. According to the United States Department of Agriculture (USDA) (see page 11),

USDA HARDINESS
ZONE MAP

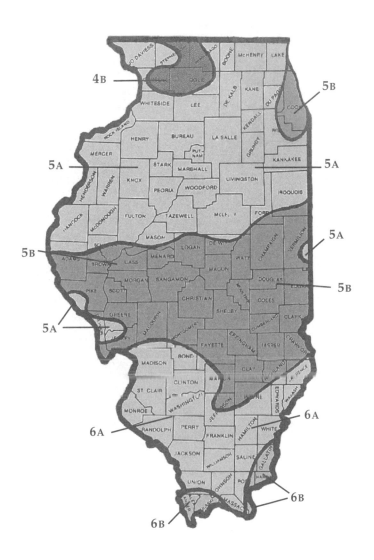

AVERAGE ANNUAL MINIMUM TEMPERATURE

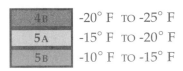

4B	-20° F TO -25° F
5A	-15° F TO -20° F
5B	-10° F TO -15° F

6A	-5° F TO -10° F
6B	0° F TO -5° F

Introduction

Illinois is in Plant Hardiness Zones 4B, 5, and 6. The Arnold Arboretum map indicates Illinois is in Zones 4, 5, and 6. Be sure to notice which rating system is being used for any plants you purchase.

It is more common for the Arnold Arboretum system to be used in the nursery industry. In the gardening community, the USDA system is more common. There is a third system developed by the Garden Writers Association, but it is not in general use at this time. We follow the USDA system in this book.

There are some things you can do to help your plants tolerate extremes in temperatures; plants can be treated so that they become acclimated to a particular environment. Plants treated this way are referred to as "hardened off." In spring, if plants are moved gradually from the greenhouse to the cold outdoors, they will tolerate frost. Plants moved directly into the cold will freeze. Houseplants moved from the cool shade indoors into outdoor full sun will be sunburned and cooked. If they are moved gradually into outdoor shade, then filtered sun, and then full sun, they will survive quite nicely. Hardening off is promoted by use of fertilizers high in potassium.

Plants can be protected from adverse temperatures or weather for short periods. In spring or fall, tender plants can be covered with blankets until temperatures moderate. Plants on the south side of a building may be warmer because of the "Dutch Oven" effect. The effect may even last overnight, protecting otherwise sensitive plants. In summer, plants can be moved into the shade on particularly hot days, or some kind of shade cover can be provided.

Mulches can protect roots from temporary high or low temperatures. Water helps plants tolerate high or low temperatures. Water loss (transpiration) cools plant tissues, and water, as long as it doesn't freeze, can keep plant tissues from freezing. Commercial growers often use sprinklers to apply a mist of water over tender plants to protect them from a freeze. Be sure plants entering stressful periods are well watered. Wilted plants are much more sensitive to extreme temperatures.

Introduction

Microclimates can affect the survival of plants. These effects can be regional or localized. Bodies of water affect plants near them, the larger the body, the larger the affected area. The moderating effect of Lake Michigan is mentioned above. Temperatures in urbanized areas tend to stay above those in surrounding areas; buildings and pavement warm up in the sun and keep the heat all night.

Wooded areas tend to stay cooler in summer and warmer in winter. Drive into a forest preserve on a hot summer day, and the change will be apparent. Shade and transpiration from leaves of the trees are responsible for most of this natural air-conditioning.

There can be big differences in microclimates within a garden. The shaded north side of the home may be cooler and moister than the south side. Trees provide shade and air conditioning the same as those in the forest preserve. A fence can direct summer breezes and moderate winter winds. The south side of a building will stay warmer in winter, and plants like spring bulbs will bloom earlier than those planted elsewhere.

Deciduous trees planted on the south side will shade the home in summer but allow the sun to warm it in winter. Evergreens on the south side will provide summer shade but will shade the home in winter, preventing warming by the sun, keeping snow from melting from walks, steps, or roof. It is best to plan carefully before planting trees so they serve the purposes intended for them.

UNDERSTANDING SOILS

The foundation of all agriculture, including gardening, is the soil. The most productive parts of the world are blessed with good, fertile soils. This country developed first as an agricultural society. The expansion west took place when soils wore out and farmers moved on to better land. We are fortunate to have some of the best soils in the world in Illinois. We need to understand why, and to know how to handle these soils to make the best use of them.

Soils are formed by the weathering of rock. They can form in place, or they may be moved by water or wind from their original locations. About 80 percent of the soils in Illinois are loess. This is material that was formed by the grinding down of rock by glaciers, deposited in river beds as glaciers retreated, then picked up by winds and carried east. Most of our soil material came from the Mississippi/Missouri river valleys. The soils tend to be coarser near those rivers, finer to the east. Loess soils are mostly loams.

The dust bowl days of the 1930s were nothing new; they were a continuation of the mechanism that created our productive land. Most of Illinois was covered by glaciers except for the northwest corner, a little piece along the Mississippi river, and the far southern tip. The Wisconsin was the last glacier, and it went as far south as Shelbyville. It left the hills called the Shelbyville Moraine as it receded.

Soils are made of solids (mineral and organic), air, and water. Productive soils are about 50 percent solids and 50 percent pore space. Ideally, half the pore space will be filled with air, half with water. In reality, this pore space is full of water following rainfall or watering and full of air when soils are dry.

Soils are named according to the kinds of solids in them: sands, silts, or clays. The names describe the soils and identify their characteristics.

Sands have large particles; their grains are big enough to be seen without a hand lens. Spaces between the grains are relatively large, too. Water moves easily through sandy soils, so they are described as well drained. Managing sands is easy if there is enough water, and if fertilizer is applied to make up for the nutrients washed away by rains or watering.

The particles of silts are small, and you can't see them individually. Spaces between the particles are tiny and easily filled by capillary water, leaving no room for air. Silts drain poorly and are hard to handle.

Clay particles are very tiny, molecular in size, and visible only with an electron microscope. Clays can be very productive if handled right, or they can be impossible. The structure determines whether they will support plants or not. With good structure, clays

Introduction

are friable and well aerated, with enough water for plants. If structure is poor, they are like modeling clay, saturated when wet, hard and cracked when dry. The tiny pieces of clay are made up of layers. Water gets between the layers, causing them to expand. When the soil dries out, the water moves from between the layers and the clay particles shrink. That is what makes clays crack when they get dry. Some clays move so much when they get wet and then dry out that they will move the buildings set on them. Sometimes a concrete patio will move away from the house several inches as the clay moves. This force is so strong that it can crack foundations and cause bricks to fall off houses.

Loams are soils that have the correct amounts of sand, silt, and clay. Loams are the best garden soils because they have the good features of each kind of soil. In Illinois the soils are mostly loams.

THE VALUE OF ORGANIC MATTER

Organic matter comes from things that were alive: grass clippings, dead garden plants, leaves, peat moss, straw, compost, manure . . . and lots of other things. The microorganisms in the soil break down organic matter and release the nutrients so plants can reuse them. They also help cement soil particles together to make aggregates.

Coarse organic matter opens the soil so air can get in. This is beneficial in heavy clay soils. Organic matter pieces are like sponges and hold lots of water, so they improve light sandy soils, too.

Lots of organic matter is essential for a healthy, productive garden soil. Try to add as much organic matter as you can to your soils. There is no need to throw any away.

SOIL ACIDITY/ALKALINITY (pH)

The soil pH measures soil acidity or alkalinity. At a pH of 7.0, the soil is neutral. Most plants prefer acidic conditions; a pH of 6.0 to 7.0 is ideal. Soils throughout Illinois, however, are often quite alkaline; a pH of 8.0 is not rare. Thus it is important to select plant material that will tolerate alkalinity (soils with a high pH are notoriously difficult to change).

Introduction

Applications of lime (calcium carbonate) and gypsum (calcium sulfate) are often recommended for garden soils. You must test Illinois soils before adding lime or gypsum. Excess calcium adds to alkalinity and to the deficiency of other nutrient elements. Sulfur that lowers the pH is sometimes better in our soils.

SOLUBLE SALTS

Soluble salts are minerals dissolved in the soil. All fertilizers and minerals from water, soil acids, or anything else in solution add to the total soluble salts. If the amount of soluble salts is too high, it will keep plants from getting enough water and can damage plants. This is more common with pot plants. Unless these plants are leached as they are watered, the minerals will collect in the soil. Thorough leaching or repotting with fresh soil will reduce the salt levels.

Salt used for melting ice in winter can cause excess salts in the lawn or shrub beds. Sometimes spring rains correct the situation, but removing and replacing the layer of salty soil might be necessary before plants such as grass will grow.

UNDERSTANDING FERTILIZERS

Fertilizers provide essential elements for plants. The elements used in the greatest amounts by plants are nitrogen, phosphorus, and potassium. Fertilizers usually contain some or all of these elements; the amounts of each in the particular fertilizer material are shown in the analysis on the label.

The analysis shows the amounts by weight of the Nitrogen (N), Phosphate (P), and Potash (K), always in that order. A fertilizer with an analysis of 10-6-4 contains 10 percent nitrogen, 6 percent phosphate, and 4 percent potash. This is a complete fertilizer containing all three of the major elements. A complete fertilizer containing all three elements in equal amounts is called a balanced fertilizer. An analysis of 16-16-16 is balanced.

Some fertilizer materials provide one or two of the major elements. Mono-ammonium phosphate has an analysis of about

16

12-48-0. Potassium nitrate is 14-0-46. Some single-element carriers are ammonium nitrate (33-0-0), muriate of potash (0-0-60), and superphosphate (0-45-0). These materials are used alone to correct deficiencies, or are used in blends to make a particular analysis.

Generally, unless a soil test has been done and specific recommendations are made, garden fertilizers are used based on the amount of nitrogen in them. The standard rate is 1 pound of actual nitrogen per 1000 square feet of lawn or garden. If you use the 10-6-4 fertilizer, with its 10 percent nitrogen, you will need 10 pounds of fertilizer to apply a pound of nitrogen. If you use a 16-16-16, you will need to spread $6^1/6$ pounds over 1000 square feet. The phosphorus and potassium go along for the ride, usually just for insurance in case there is a deficiency of either one.

SOIL PREPARATION

The first step in preparing soil is to make sure the surface is graded so water runs off in the direction you want it to go. It must run away from the house or any other structure, and away from the garden.

Second, take the time to get rid of all vegetation. Spraying with a non selective herbicide such as glyphosate according to label directions kills all existing vegetation, including underground parts, but it will not kill seeds that might germinate the next day. So let the soil lie dormant for a couple of weeks, and treat anything else that grows. For a perennial garden or groundcover bed, a third treatment may be worthwhile.

Next, check the drainage. Dig a hole a foot wide and deep and fill it with water. After it drains, fill it again. Do it a third time. If the hole drains out in 12 hours, the drainage is good. If it does not, install tiles or build raised beds. Some plants will tolerate slow drainage; other plants will deteriorate and eventually die.

Rototilling the soil is fine for annuals, and for some shallowly rooted perennials and groundcovers. For deeply rooted plants, especially some perennials, spading to two or three spade depths is necessary. These procedures are called double-digging and trenching.

To double-dig the garden, remove the soil one spade deep across part of the garden. I try to start with an area two or three rows across and 5 or 6 feet wide. Stack the soil up to be used later. Add organic matter to the second layer, and spade it over. Move to an adjacent area of the garden, cover it with organic matter, and turn it into the area first vacated. This will open the second level for another few rows. Add organic matter and turn over. Work your way down the garden to the end. This will leave an open area into which you can dump the soil from the first rows you opened. Trenching is the same type of procedure, but 3 spades deep. This is a lot of work, but it is essential for plants like delphiniums and lupines. You do not need to do the whole garden, just the places where you intend to put these demanding plants. Take your time. You don't need to complete the job all at once.

SOIL MECHANICS
Where two different soil materials meet abruptly, they cause an interface that prevents the movement of air or water, and the development of roots. Planting a sand-grown shrub in a clay soil, peat-grown sod over clay soil, or a light, artificial soil mix in garden soil creates interfaces. Prevent them by buying plants grown in the same kind of soil as you have in your garden, or mixing the two kinds of soil going back into the planting hole to cause a gradual change from one to the other. Soil incompatibility is the most common problem preventing successful transplanting of garden plants.

INSECT AND DISEASE PROBLEMS
Most plants are affected by some pests. Sooner or later the pest problem will arise, and you will scramble to find out what to do about it. The first step is to identify the problem; until you know what it is, you won't know if it is necessary to treat it or whether it will go away on its own. When certain problems are common in a particular plant, we have tried to identify them in the plant descriptions.

The next line of defense is your neighborhood garden center. Often the folks there will have a troubleshooting guide on hand. If

Introduction

that is not sufficient help, there are University of Illinois Extension Offices in many counties where horticulturists or master gardeners are available to help. Community colleges and any of the four-year universities teaching horticulture courses have horticulturists on staff who are knowledgeable and helpful, and the Chicago Botanic Garden, Morton Arboretum, and the Klehm Arboretum have plant information offices to provide these kinds of services.

Don't overlook consulting an experienced gardener in your neighborhood. Such people have seen most of the neighborhood gardening problems before. Even if they can't exactly identify a particular problem, they may have found a way to contend with it.

For best growing results, plants need to be placed where they will receive the proper amount of light. The amount of light suitable for each plant's growing requirements is indicated in each profile. The following symbols indicate full sun, partial sun, and shade.

Full Sun   Partial   Shade
        Sun

HOW TO USE THIS BOOK

I have divided the plants into the following chapters: Annuals, Bulbs, Groundcovers, Ornamental Grasses, Perennials, Roses, Shrubs, Trees, Turfgrasses, Vines, and Wildflowers. The plants that I have selected are proven performers in Illinois—plants with which I have had years of successful growing experience. Each entry contains the information you will need to plant and then maintain healthy plants.

The tallgrass prairie hardly exists in Illinois any more, but our land can still grow flowers. The chapters in this book present the various kinds of plants that make gardening exciting in Illinois, and they tell how to get the most enjoyment from it. So let's get started!

CHAPTER ONE

Annuals

*I*F YOU WANT COLOR AND EXCITEMENT IN YOUR GARDEN, nothing can beat annuals—their flowers provide immediate color, and they last all summer long.

An annual is a plant that completes its life cycle in one season. It germinates from seed, grows, flowers, ripens new seed, and dies, all in one year. Garden flowers are not the only annuals—two other very familiar annuals are corn and soybeans. The seed from these plants is sown in spring, the plants flower in early summer, and the crop (seed) is harvested and in the bin by late fall.

Some plants grown as annuals in Illinois are actually tender perennials, plants that grow from seed one year and then live and flower for years. In truly mild climates with no frost these plants can go on year after year. Geraniums, for example, grow into huge plants in California; begonias can be kept as houseplants for years here in Illinois, but we usually let such plants freeze in fall, then start them over the next spring.

In addition to their season-long display of color, annuals have another distinct advantage: they begin the season in an empty garden, making it easy to till and improve the soil. Weeds can be eliminated before planting, using herbicides if necessary, as there will be no damage to flowers.

You can grow new annuals every year—no need to plant the same thing until bored stiff with it! And annuals are inexpensive. If they don't look good during the season, you can pull them out and plant something else.

STARTING ANNUALS

You can buy annuals at garden centers, supermarkets, hardware stores . . . any place that plants are sold. But if you find the choices too limited, try starting your own seeds indoors under lights. You will need a plant stand with fluorescent lights—a stand four feet long and two feet wide will accommodate four standard 10-inch by 20-inch flats. The lights can be a pair of shoplight fixtures, each holding two 40-watt cool white tubes. Attach the lights to chains or to ropes, pulleys, and weights so they can be adjusted above the plants. Use one of the commercial artificial soil mixes for the propagating soil. Buy a mix such as Jiffy Mix, Pro Mix, or any other brand composed of shredded brown peat and polystyrene beads or perlite. (Black "potting soil" is not satisfactory for starting annuals.) The seed may be sown in the 20-row seed-starting inserts sold to fit the 10- by 20-inch flats. Moisten the soil mix, sow the seeds, label them, and cover the container with clear plastic wrap to keep it from drying out. Set it on the plant stand and lower the lights to an inch or so above the surface. This will provide all the heat and light needed. We have indicated in the following plant profiles whether the seed needs light or dark to germinate. If a seed needs light, don't cover it with soil or propagating mix.

When the seedlings are big enough to handle, transplant them into plastic cell-packs, the kind commercial growers use, or into any other convenient container. Keep the lights just above the plant tops and fertilize the plants with liquid fertilizer after they start to grow. Set in the garden when there is no danger of frost.

USING ANNUALS IN THE GARDEN

Annuals can be used in many ways. The shorter ones can be used for edging or bedding, and the taller ones may be placed in the back of the garden. Use annuals as fillers in perennial beds where the flowers have died down, or in a cutting garden. Annuals can also be used in pots, windowboxes, or planters, and they can be plugged into any bare spot in the yard. Check the descriptions in this chapter to see which will grow in the shade and which require full sun.

Some of the best annuals are chosen each year by All-America Selections for special awards. The Fleuroselect awards are selections made by European judges. Such awards are given to varieties that have been tested and found to be superior in all respects.

Annuals are wonderful plants. Don't be afraid to try them in new and different ways. Enjoy them. Let your imagination run wild— and most of all, have fun!

Ageratum

Ageratum houstonianum

Other Name: Flossflower
Zones: All
Size: 6 to 15 inches tall and wide
Blooms: May to frost
Flower Colors: Blue, pink, white, lavender

Light Requirement:

*B*lue flowers with a long season of good show are difficult to find, but ageratum is one of the best. Clusters of tiny, fluffy blooms cover mound-shaped plants that are well suited for borders, edging, or masses of color. If you are looking for the blue for a red, white, and blue border, you'll find ageratum is perfect in combination with annuals such as white petunias and red salvia. Earlier seed strains of ageratum were rather uneven, with the same seed packet often producing both tall and short plants. The better algeratum strains were all vegetatively propagated. Now breeders of the seed strains have developed plants that produce better form and flowering, and they have extended the color range to pink, white, and lavender. The better low cultivars can be counted on to be covered with blooms from May to frost; taller cultivars tend to be more open in form and not as densely covered. Ageratum is adapted to a wide range of soils as long as you provide enough drainage and adequate water. Small plants are easily damaged by excess fertilizer, so fertilize with restraint until the plants are well established.

WHEN TO PLANT

Seeds are small, but they can be germinated easily indoors at 70 degrees Fahrenheit under lights. Sow in late February for nice-sized plants by May 15. Broadcast the seeds on the soil surface, or sow them in the 20-row seeding inserts that fit standard 10 x 20-inch flats. Moisten the propagating mix and cover the container with clear plastic wrap to maintain moisture. Transplant seedlings and continue to grow them at 60 degrees. Cuttings root without much trouble. Set out started plants when danger of frost has passed.

WHERE TO PLANT

Ageratum does best in full sun; in partial shade it may become leggy. In the southern part of the state, however, protection from full sun during the hottest part of the day is desirable.

How to Plant

Ageratums are usually sold as bedding plants, as blooming seedlings, or in 3- or 4-inch pots. Work up the soil by tilling or cultivating. Set the smaller, bedding types on 6- to 8-inch centers. Taller cultivars and plants for the cutting garden may be set up to 12 inches apart.

Care and Maintenance

Ageratum is basically free of problems. If plants become a little tired and leggy in mid-season, they can be cut back to about half their height, and they will respond with a flush of new blooms. Water when the plants wilt: apply an inch of water, then don't water again until the plants begin to wilt again. Go easy on the fertilizer— these plants burn easily, especially in transplant containers. Aphids and mildew are occasionally troublesome. Overfertilization and overwatering can result in plants rotting off at the soil line.

Additional Information

Ageratum is native to Belize, Guatemala, and Mexico. The genus name, *Ageratum*, is derived from *a*, meaning "not," and *geras*, which means "old." The color of the blooms does remain fresh for a long time. Some taller cultivars are suitable for cutting. Midday shade may be beneficial in hot, dry parts of the state.

Additional Species, Cultivars, or Varieties

Older, inbred strains of ageratum were rather uneven in height, and some were sparse bloomers. Most cultivars today are F1 hybrids, which are much improved. 'Adriatic', 'Blue Blazer', 'Blue Lagoon', and 'Blue Ribbon' are reliable in flower and have compact low form. 'Fine Wine' is burgundy in color and has a good compact habit. The 'Hawaii Hybrid' series includes blue, white, and royal colors and good low form. Flowers of 'Bavaria' and 'Capri' are blue with white centers. 'Blue Tango', which grows to 12 inches, is good for cutting.

Alyssum

Alyssum maritimum, Lobularia maritima

Other Name: Sweet Alyssum
Zones: All
Size: 4 to 8 inches tall, spreading 12 to
   18 inches
Blooms: Spring to frost
Flower Colors: White, lavender, pink

Light Requirement:

lyssum provides a true carpet of white, lavender, or pink blooms from late spring to frost. It is one of the most reliable edging plants and is at home in borders, masses, or rock gardens. Use it to hide the ripening foliage of spring bulbs, especially crocus, daffodil, and squill. In containers or hanging baskets, alyssum will develop into cascades of fragrant blooms. It is also fragrant when growing on the ground, but you will have to get on your hands and knees to smell it! Plant it in a windowbox or a raised planter next to your deck, and you will be able to enjoy it effortlessly.

WHEN TO PLANT

Seeds are easily germinated at 70 degrees Fahrenheit in the light. Broadcast them on the soil surface or sow them in the 20-row seeding inserts that fit standard 10 x 20-inch flats. Moisten the propagating mix and cover the container with clear plastic wrap to maintain moisture. Damping off can be troublesome, so be careful when watering. Plants may be set out after the average date of last frost. These plants are tolerant of soft frost.

WHERE TO PLANT

Alyssum does well in full sun or partial shade. In the hottest weather, flowering may be stalled; the plants will resume flowering with the return of cooler temperatures. Purple cultivars do better in cooler spots or in partial shade. Alyssum does well in light shade and is one of the annuals that can be recommended for shady gardens in the inner city. It tolerates a wide variety of soils, but it does best in soils with good drainage.

How to Plant

Alyssums are sold as bedding plants with several blooming plants per cell. When planted on 6- to 8-inch centers, they fill in rapidly. Set the plants shallowly, covering only the roots, and make sure the soil has good drainage. Water in the plants, then hold off further watering until they are near wilting. Deep planting and overwatering can result in damping off. You may choose instead to sow seed directly in the border after the danger of a hard freeze is past. Alyssum is a hardy annual and can stand a frost. Be sure to scatter the seed evenly. Planting from seed is probably best when interplanting with spent bulbs because this procedure will not disturb the existing plants.

Care and Maintenance

Alyssum is basically free of troubles. If the plants become leggy, they can be sheared back; they will respond with renewed growth and blooms. Syringing with a light spray of water in the hottest weather may keep them blooming—in other words, it may prevent them from taking a summer vacation.

Additional Information

Alyssum is native to the Mediterranean area. In some areas it is so aggressive that it becomes a weed. Here in Illinois, where it is strictly annual and eliminated by winter, its vigorous habit is truly an asset. In especially favorable spots, alyssum will reseed itself faithfully.

Additional Species, Cultivars, or Varieties

Little has been done (or maybe little can be done) to improve this popular plant. Additional colors have been introduced, and better heat tolerance has been sought. The 'Easter Basket' strain comes in Easter colors: white, pink, lavender, rose, and deep purple, as well as a mixture. The functional plants 'New Carpet of Snow' and 'Royal Carpet' do indeed have a carpet-like effect. 'Snow Crystals' seems to have better heat tolerance than the others.

Begonia

Begonia semperflorens-cultorum

Other Names: Fibrous-rooted Begonia,
   Wax Begonia
Zones: All
Size: 6 to 16 inches tall and wide
Blooms: Spring until frost; can be moved
   indoors
Flower Colors: White to shades of pink or red

Light Requirement:

For use in borders, as mass plantings, and in formal designs, begonias are nearly as popular as impatiens. They are equally well suited for planters, windowboxes, pots, and for the indoor landscape. Begonias are among the most reliable annuals in the garden, relatively trouble-free and blooming faithfully from spring until fall, even continuing to bloom after light frost. They do equally well in full sun or shade. All the commercial begonia cultivars are F1 hybrids. Leaves are glossy (waxy) in many shades of green to dark bronze-red, or in variegated green-white. The better cultivars hold their blooms well above the foliage and produce masses of color in the garden. This dependable performance is valuable where color and form need to be consistent all season. Begonias are tolerant of many soils as long as there is good drainage and enough moisture.

WHEN TO PLANT

The tiny, dust-like begonia seeds are sown indoors under lights in January. Grow the plants in pots or packs at 70 degrees Fahrenheit. Set them in the garden at the average date of last frost, usually about mid-May.

WHERE TO PLANT

Plant in full sun to fairly dense shade. In the southern part of the state, the plants may sunburn if set in full sun without adequate hardening. Move them gradually into full sun or protect with light shade until they are acclimated.

HOW TO PLANT

Begonias are sold as bedding plants in bloom, or in 3- or 4-inch pots. Set smaller cultivars on 9- to 12-inch centers. Large-leaf cultivars can be set 15 to 18 inches apart. If the plants are potbound, slice the ball vertically on 2 or 3 sides to encourage roots to grow into the surrounding soil. Set the plants at the same depth they grew in the containers.

CARE AND MAINTENANCE
Begonias require little care other than watering when needed. The flowers are tiny, so there is no need to deadhead the plants. If the plants become leggy in midseason, they can be cut back and restarted. Botrytis blight, mildew, leaf spots, and thrips are begonia's main pests, but they usually require no special treatment. During especially wet seasons, stem rot may result in some plant losses.

ADDITIONAL INFORMATION
Wax begonias are native to Brazil. They were named for Michel Begon, an avid botanist and Governor of French Canada during the 1600s. You may lift the garden plants, wash the soil from their roots, and pot them with soil mix for indoor bloom all winter. Cuttings root easily for additional plants. Let the kids root some cuttings during the winter, pot them, and give them as gifts for Mother's Day.

ADDITIONAL SPECIES, CULTIVARS, OR VARIETIES
It is futile to try to compile a complete list of begonia cultivars. Breeding is going on at such a fast pace that the long list is new each year. Spend some time perusing the garden catalogs in January to select some cultivars that look interesting. Order them immediately if you intend to grow your own seedlings. For 1997, the 'Ambassador' and 'Senate' series advertised the newest colors. 'Cocktail Hybrid' is sun-resistant; 'Pizzazz Hybrid' is recommended for potting in the fall.

Tuberous begonias, *Begonia × tuberhybrida*, can be used in the shade as bedding plants, or in pots, containers, and hanging baskets. Although they are usually treated as annuals, they are actually tender perennials growing from tubers and may be saved over winter. (Dig them up and store indoors.) The flowers are huge, from 3 inches to more than 7 inches in diameter, and brightly colored. White, yellow, orange, pink, and red blooms are borne in clusters of three, a male and two females. Try the 'Nonstop' tuberous cultivars, which are started from seed and produce 2^1/$_2$- to 3-inch blooms on 10- to 12-inch-tall plants. Sometimes said to perform well in full sun, they seem to do better if given at least light shade. 'Nonstop Apple Blossom' is new for 1997.

Browallia

Browallia speciosa

Other Name: Sapphire Flower
Zones: All
Size: 12 to 18 inches tall, with tidy, rounded habit
Blooms: Early to late summer
Flower Colors: Blue, lavender, or white

Light Requirement:

*M*asses of white, blue, or lavender star-shaped flowers with long, slender corolla tubes are borne on well-branched plants with attractive foliage. The neatly rounded form makes these plants ideal for planters, hanging baskets, or urns, as well as for the border. Tolerance for shade makes them good for flowering houseplants all winter. Browallia prefers a rich, well-drained soil. It is a native of the rain forest and needs plenty of water and humidity in the hottest weather.

WHEN TO PLANT

Sow seed under lights in February. Hold the temperature at 75 degrees Fahrenheit until germination occurs. Transplant to packs or pots, and pinch when about four inches tall to encourage branching. Cuttings taken in spring or fall root easily. These tender annuals cannot stand any frost, so don't be too hasty to get them out in spring. Memorial Day is fine for planting.

WHERE TO PLANT

Browallia does best in light shade, but it will stand full sun if kept watered. In dense shade it will bloom poorly and become leggy.

HOW TO PLANT

Plants are available from garden centers as bedding plants in bloom, in 3-inch pots, or in hanging baskets. Prepare the soil well, making sure there is good drainage. Space plants about 10 inches apart, or plant singly among other bedding plant cultivars for accent. Set the plants at the same depth they were growing in their containers; too-deep planting can result in rotting of the plants at the soil line.

CARE AND MAINTENANCE

As natives of the rain forest, these plants need warm moist conditions, but they resent wet soils. Good drainage is essential. Overwatering and overfertilizing will produce big, healthy plants, but few flowers. Potted plants and those in hanging baskets will benefit from daily misting to increase humidity. Few pests bother these plants, though whiteflies may become serious problems if brought into the garden on these or on other plants. If you want to try browallia as a houseplant, dig and pot up plants before the first frost, or take cuttings and bring them indoors for the winter. Set the plants on a bed of moist pea gravel and mist daily, especially during the heating season, to maintain humidity.

ADDITIONAL INFORMATION

Browallia is named in honor of an 18th-century bishop, Johan Browall. It is native to Columbian rain forests. Equally at home in sun or shade, browallia does best when protected from afternoon sun. It is especially good for adding a touch of blue to shaded spots. Browallia blooms faithfully from early until late summer.

ADDITIONAL SPECIES, CULTIVARS, OR VARIETIES

Most hybridizing of this plant has been done to improve form and compactness. 'Blue Bells Improved' is a dwarf strain that needs no pinching. Some white cultivars are available—'Silver Bells' and 'White Troll' have pure white blooms on compact plants—but there are plenty of other white flowers from which to choose, so I prefer the intense blues such as 'Blue Troll' or 'Marine Bells'.

Celosia

Celosia sp.

Other Name: Cockscomb
Zones: All
Size: 6 to 30 inches tall, spread depends
　　on type
Blooms: Summer
Flower Colors: Brilliant red, pink, yellow,
　　orange, gold

Light Requirement:

Celosias are especially notable for their intense colors. The blooms are of three types: crested, plume, and candle. The crested type, *C. cristata*, looks like a large convoluted rooster's comb. Plume types, *C. plumosa*, are softer and have been infused with some pastel colors. New are the candle types, *C. argentea spicata*. Old-time celosia cultivars, large and difficult to work into the border, were better suited to the cutting garden. Newer cultivars are available in various sizes suitable for edging, bedding, containers, and cut and dried flowers. Dried arrangements hold their color well.

WHEN TO PLANT

Sow indoors under lights eight weeks before the latest date of last frost. Cover the seeds lightly with soil, and hold at 75 degrees Fahrenheit until they germinate. Grow the plants under bright light, at no lower than 65 degrees. Celosias are able to stand a soft frost, but nothing is gained by setting them out while the soil is still cold. If the roots are chilled, the plants stop growing and take a long time to get started again.

WHERE TO PLANT

Celosias need full sun, and they can take the heat. Don't plant them in the shade unless you have no choice. Use shorter cultivars in borders or edgings. Tall cultivars are best at the back of the garden or as accents in urns.

HOW TO PLANT

Celosia can be direct-seeded in the garden after danger of frost is past and the soil is warm. If the soil feels warm to the touch, it is at about 75 degrees Fahrenheit, the right temperature for germination.

Celosias are available as bedding plants or potted from garden centers. Set plants or thin seedlings of smaller cultivars to about a foot apart, taller cultivars to about two feet. Tall cultivars may need staking.

CARE AND MAINTENANCE
Mites can be a problem, as can stem rot if the plants are kept too wet. Deadheading as flowers fade will prolong bloom, especially for the tall varieties.

ADDITIONAL INFORMATION
Celosias are natives of Equatorial Africa, Asia, and America. The name *Celosia* means "hot" in Greek. This word can describe both the color of the flowers and the ability of these plants to stand the heat.

ADDITIONAL SPECIES, CULTIVARS, OR VARIETIES
'Fireglow', a crested type with outstanding, 6-inch, scarlet-orange blooms, is an AAS Bronze winner. 'Prestige Scarlet', a 1997 AAS winner, produces a large central flower and many side branches each with a smaller bloom; it is one of the most floriferous in masses. The 'Castle' series of plume types includes scarlet, yellow, and a mixture, as well as 'Castle Pink', 1990 AAS winner. 'Castle Orange' is new for 1997. Bright orange 'Apricot Brandy' was an AAS winner in 1981. Candle (or wheat) types 'Purple Flamingo' and 'Pink Candle' are two of the hottest new flowers for commercial florists as well as for amateur flower arrangers.

Cleome

Cleome hassleriana

Other Name: Spider Flower
Zones: All
Size: 4 feet tall and wide
Blooms: Summer until frost
Flower Colors: Pink, rose, cherry, lavender, white

Light Requirement:

*C*leome is a wonderful plant for use in hot areas. I have seen it along the south side of houses next to blacktop driveways where it gets baked by the sun, and with a little water it continues to thrive and bloom faithfully all summer. Yet it does well enough in partial shade to be on our list of plants for shade gardens. The plants become leggy when grown in the shade and will need support. Airy, spider-like, 6-inch heads of delicate blooms are borne on large 4-foot-tall and -wide plants. The name "spider flower" is descriptive of the individual blooms, which have abnormally long, 2-inch stamens. Leaves of the cleome plant are palmately compound, not unlike those of cannabis. Older stems will develop thorns.

WHEN TO PLANT

Cleome grows true to form from collected seed. Chill at near freezing for a week before sowing. Germinate at 80 degrees. Set plants out after the frost-free date, about mid-May in central Illinois. Cleome will reseed itself with abundant seedlings. These can be picked out and transplanted or hoed or easily pulled. If the volunteer plants are not allowed to flower, no seed will be produced for the next season. Started seedlings, not usually in bloom, are sold at most garden centers.

WHERE TO PLANT

Cleomes are large plants. They belong at the back of the border or along the fence line where they will have room to grow. They make good temporary hedges, and they are great for cut flowers.

HOW TO PLANT
Thin seedlings or set out started plants at least 2 feet apart. These are large plants that need room. If crowded, they will become leggy and weak.

CARE AND MAINTENANCE
Little needs to be done to grow these plants. They prefer moist, well-drained soil, but they will tolerate drought. They prefer full sun, but they can stand partial shade. No diseases or insects bother them.

ADDITIONAL INFORMATION
The flowers are borne on indeterminate heads that keep elongating all season, leaving pods of seeds below. The dense plants and thorny stems make excellent temporary hedges and the blooms are attractive all summer long. These plants are native to Brazil and Argentina.

ADDITIONAL SPECIES, CULTIVARS, OR VARIETIES
There are few named cultivars. The 'Queen' series includes pink, white, cherry, violet, and a mixture. 'Helen Campbell' is white.

Coleus

Coleus × hybridus

Zones: All
Size: 9 to 16 inches tall and wide
Blooms: Summer; insignificant
Foliage Colors: Combinations of green, white,
   yellow, chartreuse, maroon, pink, or red,
   with as many as four colors in each leaf

Light Requirement:

Coleus is grown not for its flowers, but for the wonderful foliage colors it brings to the shady part of the garden. Leaves may be a combination of colors, with as many as four colors in each leaf. Breeders have produced a potpourri of every imaginable color and pattern, including pastels. Individual leaves may be a solid color with a contrasting border, or they may have several colors spreading out from the middle of the leaf. The leaves may be wide or narrow, smooth, scalloped, or toothed. A member of the mint family, coleus is vigorous, but it is not invasive in the garden. Plants are usually upright mounds, but some trailing kinds will cascade from hanging baskets. The plants are about as wide as they are tall, and have a coarse, rounded habit.

WHEN TO PLANT

Seed germinates easily when uncovered under lights at 70 degrees, but seedlings develop slowly. Sow in March for nice-sized plants by Memorial Day. Cuttings root easily any time. Cuttings can be rooted in a glass of water at room temperature or in containers of propagating mix. Don't rush these plants into the garden. Coleus is a tender annual and cannot stand frost. Plants will not grow much until the soil warms up, anyway.

WHERE TO PLANT

Coleus prefers well-drained, moist soil. It tolerates full sun, but it does best in light shade, where the colors develop most intensely. Use in edgings, borders, pots, planters, and hanging baskets. Uniform, single-color selections are well suited for floral carpets.

How to Plant

Plants are available as bedding plants or in pots from garden centers. Set plants with large leaves on 12-inch centers; smaller-leaved cultivars may be set closer together. Set plants shallowly in a well-prepared moist soil, covering only the roots to avoid damping off.

Care and Maintenance

Coleus is nearly maintenance-free: once established, the plants require little care other than watering in dry weather and removing flowers to prolong the season of color. If plants become leggy, pinching will renew them and keep new foliage developing. In unusually wet weather, leaf spots may develop. Several kinds of insects—whitefly, aphids, mealybugs, and mites—can become troublesome.

Additional Information

Coleus originated in Java. The name *Coleus* is derived from the Greek *Koleos*, meaning "sheath," and refers to the arrangements of the stamens in individual flowers. Propagation of these plants from cuttings is so easy that this can be a great first lesson in horticulture for children. As cold weather approaches in fall, lift a stock plant and have youngsters take cuttings, root them in water, and pot them up for holiday gift plants.

Additional Species, Cultivars, or Varieties

Usually listed as *C. blumei* in most gardening literature, modern cultivars are hybrids of several species and are more correctly listed as *C. × hybridus*. The list of cultivars seems endless; there are varieties of every color, shape, and pattern imaginable. The 'Carefree' and 'Fiji' series are self-branching and will cascade in hanging baskets. 'Fairway' and 'Jazz' strains are dwarf, about 8 inches tall, and they will spread; they do well as edging. The 'Wizard' series is taller, 12 to 14 inches, and has large leaves.

Cosmos

Cosmos sp.

Zones: All	**Light Requirement:**
Size: 18 to 36 inches tall and half as wide	
Blooms: Summer	
Flower Colors: Pastel, reddish, pink, rose, white, yellow, orange, or crimson	

osmos is an old-fashioned flower, much loved by Grandmother, who scattered seeds around the old water pump on the farm to add a bit of color. The warm pink shades were the colors of late summer memorialized in many a summer floral pattern, and reflected in the painting that still hangs in the family room. The plants were untidy, falling over if not supported, but they bloomed tirelessly. A tiny bouquet thoughtfully picked by small hands often graced the dinner table. These are large, feathery plants with daisy-like blooms, though newer selections are more tidy. The introduction of the sunny colors of *C. sulphureus* in the middle of this century have greatly improved this favorite. Cosmos needs full sun, but it isn't particular about soil. Too much fertilizer and water will mean extra-floppy plants and fewer blooms.

When to Plant

Seeds germinate easily at 70 degrees Fahrenheit under lights. Sow 8 weeks before the last frost date, covering lightly with soil. Transplant, then grow on at 65 degrees. Started plants are available from garden centers. Sow seed directly in the garden, or set plants when all danger of frost is past.

Where to Plant

Cosmos plants need plenty of room to grow. Put them at the back of a border or along a fence in full sun. Plant a row in the cutting garden if you want a ready source of blooms all summer long.

How to Plant

Seeds may be sown directly in the garden. Thin seedlings to 12 inches apart. The extras can be transplanted if care is used to avoid breaking off tiny roots. Set started plants 12 inches apart as well.

This is closer than would normally be recommended for plants of this size, but the close spacing allows the plants to weave together, which helps them to support each other.

CARE AND MAINTENANCE

Cosmos plants are virtually maintenance-free. They tolerate drought, and they resent overwatering and overfertilizing. Few insects or diseases bother them.

ADDITIONAL INFORMATION

Cosmos is native to Central and South America, from Mexico to Brazil. The name *cosmos* is from the Greek; it means "beautiful and orderly". These compound flowers are attractive to butterflies. They reseed easily enough to assure plants for the following year, but not so much as to be a nuisance. Smaller, seed-eating birds will be seen after a fall frost trying to get the last seeds from the old dry stems—so don't be too hasty to cut down the old plants in the fall!

ADDITIONAL SPECIES, CULTIVARS, OR VARIETIES

C. bipinnatus types, in the old-fashioned warm colors, have been bred to reduce height and increase flower size. The 'Sonata' series is advertised as only 2 feet tall with 3-inch flowers. 'Sonata White' is a Fleuroselect winner. The 'Versailles' series is about 3 feet tall and has large pink, blush-pink, red, or white flowers; it is a Japanese selection bred for commercial cut flower production. 'Sea Shells,' new in 1997, has tubular petals with fluted edges in carmine, rose, pink, and white. *C. sulphureus* types are naturally shorter. These are the yellow cultivars, and they include some AAS winners. 'Diablo', AAS 1974, has burnt-orange semi-double, 2-inch flowers on 24-inch stems. 'Sunny Red', AAS 1987, is a foot tall and produces bright red flowers with yellow centers; they are good for cutting and for mass plantings.

Dusty Miller

Senecio cineraria, (Cineraria maritima)

Other Names: *Chrysanthemum ptarmicaeflorum* and *Centaurea gymnocarpa*	**Light Requirement:**
Zones: All	
Size: 8 to 15 inches tall and wide	
Blooms: Late summer (grown for foliage, not blooms)	
Foliage: Wooly white, rather stiff	

*T*here is nothing like dusty miller. It is so interesting that it automatically qualifies for any list of annuals. Dusty miller is actually a common name for several different kinds of plants, and it refers to the looks of the foliage of these plants rather than to any taxonomic similarity among them. All are dusty-white, many with interesting lace-like foliage. They are grown for the color and texture of their leaves rather than for their flowers. Flowers are yellow and borne in clusters above the foliage, but most gardeners interested in the silver-white mass remove the flower stalks. Dusty miller is adapted to edging, borders, bedding, and containers. It is often mixed with other blooming annuals in planters for Mother's Day.

WHEN TO PLANT
Seed is easily germinated uncovered under lights at 75 degrees. ('Silver Lace' is better at 65 degrees.) Sow seed about the first of March. Damping off can be troublesome. Transplant into pots or cell-packs as soon as the plants are large enough to handle. Continue to grow at 60 to 65 degrees Fahrenheit, and set the started plants in the garden after danger of frost is past.

WHERE TO PLANT
Dusty miller does best in full sun. In shade it will become lanky and lose its characteristic compact form and rounded habit. It prefers dry soils rather than wet places, making it one of the more tolerant container plants.

HOW TO PLANT
Dusty miller plants are always available in spring at garden centers or any other place bedding plants are sold. Most of these outlets

don't really know which "dusty miller" they are selling. If you want to be sure you know which one you are growing, you will have to grow your own from seed. Plant dusty miller about 6 inches apart in the border or bed, closer together in containers. Set the plants no deeper than they grew in the container. Water in.

CARE AND MAINTENANCE

Dusty miller is nearly trouble-free once it is established. Stem and root rot can be problems, but these are due to improper watering practices. Constant application of small amounts of water will result in damping off of the plants. Remember to water thoroughly, then allow the plants to dry to the point of wilt before watering again. Overgrown plants can be sheared back about halfway and will respond with a flush of new growth.

ADDITIONAL INFORMATION

The name dusty miller refers to the dusty appearance of the plants. The name *cineraria* means *ash* in Latin. *Senecio* comes from the Latin *senex*, which means old, and refers to the look and form of the seed-heads. *Senecio* is native to the Mediterranean.

ADDITIONAL SPECIES, CULTIVARS, OR VARIETIES

Because of the confusion about dusty miller's botanical names, it is easier to discuss the more readily available varieties. 'Cirrus' is small, 6 to 8 inches, and silver. 'New Look' has white leaves, more oak-like than cut. 'Silver Lace' has the most delicately cut foliage. Look over the selection at your local supplier, select the one that suits you best, and buy it. Don't worry about its name.

Flowering Tobacco

Nicotiana alata

Other Names: Nicotiana, Ornamental Tobacco
Zones: All
Size: 12 to 24 inches tall and as wide
Blooms: Early summer to fall
Flower Colors: Red, white, pink, maroon, crimson, yellow, or green

Light Requirement:

*I*f you are interested in attracting hummingbirds or butterflies, there is nothing better than flowering tobacco. These plants, covered with trumpet-like blooms on upright stems, perfume the garden with a tuberose-like fragrance; and their bright colors beckon. Some of the older hybrids were bred for form and color, and the fragrance was lost. Newer hybrids have regained some of the fragrance. Grandma's garden had plants of tall, flowering tobacco (*Nicotiana sylvestris*), with white flowers fully 5 feet above the giant leaves. At dusk, the fragrance filled the air around the farmstead and hawk moths could be seen darting around the big white blooms. Somewhat loose and lanky, nicotiana is best used in a border or in the cutting garden where its untidy form won't be noticed.

WHEN TO PLANT

Seeds germinate at 70 degrees in the light. Don't cover them with propagating mix. Sow about ten weeks before the frost-free date, then set out in the garden when all danger of frost has passed.

WHERE TO PLANT

Nicotiana thrives in full sun, but it will stand some shade. Drainage is essential. Improved cultivars of nicotiana tolerate heat quite well.

HOW TO PLANT

Flowering tobacco is available from garden centers as bedding plants, in pots, or in containers. Space plants of compact cultivars about 15 inches apart in the garden. Taller varieties such as *N. sylvestris* will need to be spaced about 2 feet apart.

CARE AND MAINTENANCE

Once planted, nicotiana requires very little care. Water if the plants stay wilted overnight, but never overwater. Apply a balanced liquid fertilizer about mid-season if the foliage begins to go off color. Insects that affect tomatoes will sometimes invade nicotiana. Tomato hornworm is easily picked off, but flea beetles can make leaves look like they were hit with buckshot. Try Sevin insecticide to control these pests.

ADDITIONAL INFORMATION

Newer cultivars of flowering tobacco make a continuous show of fragrant blooms from early summer to frost. Nicotiana is related to commercial smoking tobacco, *Nicotiana tabacum*, and the leaves do contain nicotine, which can be poisonous if ingested. Nicotiana is named after Jean Nicot, French consul in the late 1500s.

ADDITIONAL SPECIES, CULTIVARS, OR VARIETIES

The 'Niki' series is probably the best known of the nicotiana hybrids, and includes rose red, pink, white, and mixed colors. 'Niki Red' is an AAS winner. More compact and earlier blooming are the 'Domino' hybrids, which include pink with white eye, lime green, and mixtures. 'Havana Red' and 'Havana Purple' are new for 1997. Also new for 1997 is 'Heaven Scent Mix', with an improved habit and great fragrance.

Four-O'Clock

Mirabilis jalapa

Zones: All **Size:** 36 inches tall and wide **Blooms:** Summer to frost **Flower Colors:** Pink, white, yellow, red, or striped	**Light Requirement:**

*T*here are several things that make this otherwise unassuming plant worth growing in the annual garden; one, its flowers open at four-o'clock in the afternoon (they may actually open before or after that, depending on the weather); two, they are very simple to grow; and three, there are flowers of various colors on the same plant, making them especially interesting to children. Four-o'clocks with their flowers that popped open late in the afternoon were intriguing to me as a youngster. We did not grow them, but we had friends who did. It was a treat to go to see these neat plants in their garden.

WHEN TO PLANT
The seeds are large and easy for children to handle. They can be seeded into an artificial soil in any kind of container. Cover them about 1/2 inch deep. They will be ready for the garden in about a month; set them out when danger of frost has passed.

WHERE TO PLANT
Four-o'clocks are undemanding. They can be planted in sun or shade and they tolerate just about any kind of soil. Places such as the narrow strip of ground between the house and driveway are fine for these plants. They are often used as temporary shrubs until permanent ones can be planted.

HOW TO PLANT
Four-o'clocks are rarely available at garden centers. They are so easy to grow from collected seed that it is not profitable to try to grow them for sale. Set started plants in the garden about 2 feet apart. These plants are not particular, but are best set about as deep as they

grew in the starter container. Seeding directly into the garden after danger of frost has passed will develop plants almost as fast as starting them ahead of time.

CARE AND MAINTENANCE

Few pests bother these plants. Provide water if the plants do not recover from wilting overnight. Soak the ground, then don't water again until the plants wilt again. Four-o'clocks will reseed vigorously. Hoe out the extra seedlings, or transplant them where they can be useful.

ADDITIONAL INFORMATION

These plants are well suited to an urban environment, as they tolerate dust, smoke, heat, and other kinds of pollution. They can stand hot, dry places in which other plants would die immediately. The plants usually bloom at four o'clock in the afternoon, hence their common name. The botanical name *Mirabilis* means *wonderful* in Latin, and it must describe the plant's colorful flowers.

ADDITIONAL SPECIES, CULTIVARS, OR VARIETIES

There is only one cultivar, 'Jingles', and it is better branched than the species. Colors of the flowers are striped red, yellow, rose, white, and pink.

Gaillardia

Gaillardia pulchella

Other Names: Annual Blanket Flower, Indian Blanket
Zones: All
Size: 18 to 24 inches tall and wide
Blooms: Summer and fall
Flower Colors: Combinations of red, bronze, orange, and yellow

Light Requirement:

*G*aillardia is a bright addition to the annual garden. Its composite blooms, often multi-colored with yellow tips on the petals, resemble Indian blankets—thus the common name. Best planted in mass plantings or borders, these flowers will also adapt to naturalized areas, and breeders have developed more compact kinds that are suited to containers and bedding. Longer-stemmed cultivars are excellent for cutting. Gaillardia will stand hot, dry conditions better than most garden flowers. Tolerant of poor soils, it needs little fertilizer. It may become weak and overly vegetative if it receives too much nitrogen.

WHEN TO PLANT

About six weeks before the last frost date, sow the seeds indoors on a moist planting medium; do not cover. The seeds need light and 70-degree temperatures (Fahreneheit) to germinate. Set the seedlings in the garden when all danger of frost has passed. Gaillardia also grows well from seeds sown directly in the garden after the last frost; plants are available at garden centers in cell-packs or blooming in pots.

WHERE TO PLANT

Remember that gaillardia is a plant for sunny, hot spots—if a spot is too hot and its soil too poor for most plants, gaillardia will probably find it to its liking!

HOW TO PLANT

Broadcast seed directly in the garden; thin seedlings to 12 inches apart. Home-grown or purchased plants should be set on 12- to 15-inch centers. Prepare poor soil by loosening it so the plants can get started; once established, they require little care. Deep planting or overwatering can result in root rot.

CARE AND MAINTENANCE

Gaillardia is essentially maintenance-free. Deadheading will prolong blooming, which continues until the plants are frozen off. Plants of taller cultivars may benefit from staking, but if closely planted, they will tend to support each other. Insects and diseases rarely cause problems.

ADDITIONAL INFORMATION

Gaillardia is a native North American plant. It is well adapted to our climate, especially our dry summers. It grows and produces colorful blooms in spots where nothing else seems to want to grow, and will reseed itself in some situations. Its mass of flowers and pattern of colors produce an effect like that of woven Indian blankets. Gaillardia has not become very popular among home gardeners, however. As a young child, I saw these plants around the edge of a Victory Garden and enjoyed their colors. Some of the nicest displays of these plants have been seen at the Cantigny Gardens and at the Chicago Botanic Garden, where they make beautiful masses of color all summer. The genus is named after M. Gaillard de Charentoneau, 18th-century patron of French botanists.

ADDITIONAL SPECIES, CULTIVARS, OR VARIETIES

Species gaillardias are still offered in wildflower mixes, but most commercial offerings for the garden trade are hybrids. Breeders have developed an improved, compact form with double flowers and single colors, making this plant better adapted to smaller gardens. 'Red Plume' (AAS winner) and 'Yellow Plume' are fully double on compact, 12-inch plants. They are fine for bedding or containers.

Garden Pinks

Dianthus chinensis

Other Name: China Pinks, Annual Pinks
Zones: All
Size: 6 to10 inches tall and wide
Blooms: Early summer to fall
Flower Colors: Red, pink, white, raspberry,
violet, or bicolor

Light Requirement:

*T*hese relatives of the florists' carnation, *D. caryophyllus*, prefer cooler temperatures, but they will do fine in full sun or partial shade. They are adapted to alkaline soils and will thrive at a pH near 8.0. Several related species are spring-flowering perennials, and the common Sweet William is a biennial member of the same family. All have a faint clove-like fragrance. The plants are tidy and excellent for borders, edging, or containers. Flowers are borne on neat mounds of foliage; they are especially suited for the rock garden. Breeders have taken an interest in these bright little plants, and they have improved their range of colors as well as their heat tolerance. Some hybridization of *D. chinensis* and other species has resulted in several All-America Selections winners.

WHEN TO PLANT

Sow seeds indoors about March 15, moistening and just barely covering them with propagating mix. Keep at 70 degrees Fahrenheit until the seeds have germinated. Transplant the seedlings to packs or pots. Set them into the garden after the last hard freeze, though pinks will stand a frost.

WHERE TO PLANT

Pinks prefer a cool place with bright sun and moist but well-drained soil. In the hottest part of the state they may go on vacation in mid-summer, but they will return with cooler weather.

HOW TO PLANT

Pinks are sold as bedding plants or in pots. Set them on 8- to 10-inch centers in borders or beds. If used in windowboxes or planters, they should be planted rather tightly to make a solid mass.

CARE AND MAINTENANCE

Pinks are trouble-free for the most part, though they are susceptible to rust in wet weather, and to crown rot if planted too deeply. Mites can be troublesome in hot weather. There is no need to deadhead these plants—the flowers are tiny enough to disappear on their own. Pinks resent too much nitrogen fertilizer; they will respond with tip-burn of the leaves, and will cease flowering. They can be allowed to run quite dry before watering, especially in cool weather.

ADDITIONAL INFORMATION

With a little protection or good snow cover, pinks will survive winter even in the Chicago area. Pinks are native to Europe and eastern Asia. The generic name, *Dianthus*, is from the Greek *dios* (*divine*) and *anthos* (*flower*, or *flower of Zeus*).

SPECIES, CULTIVARS, OR VARIETIES.

Some AAS winners are 'China Doll' (crimson red with white), 'Ideal Violet' (has a velvety look), 'Queen of Hearts' (scarlet-red on a bushy plant), and 'Snowfire' (white with cherry-red center). Varieties in the 'Parfait' series (Strawberry Parfait and Raspberry Parfait) and the 'Telstar' series have been recipients of Fleuroselect and AAS awards for early bloom and compact habits.

ANNUALS

47

Geranium

Pelargonium × hortorum

Other Name: Zonal Geranium
Zones: All
Size: 12 to 18 inches high with equal spread
Blooms: All summer
Flower Colors: Red, pink, salmon, or white

Light Requirement:

*T*wo-inch flowers are carried well above the foliage in large round clusters. Leaves are large, 3 to 5 inches across, round and scalloped, many with interesting zones or variegation. Geraniums are among the most popular plants. Whether used with just a few plants in a pot next to the front door, or in extensive beds, the brilliant flower colors contrast beautifully with the bright-green leaves. Geraniums have traditionally been sold as vegetatively propagated, 4-inch plants in pots, usually ready for Memorial Day. Buying a lot of them can be expensive. Today most geraniums are grown from seed and sold, in bloom, as bedding plants.

WHEN TO PLANT

Start seed geraniums under lights in January. Germination takes about 2 weeks at 75 degrees Fahrenheit. Transplant seedlings to pots or packs. Cuttings from older plants root easily; they can be rooted directly in pots. Plants can be set out after the threat of a freeze is past. They will stand a soft frost.

WHERE TO PLANT

Geraniums are best planted in full sun and a cool, moist soil, where they will develop the most intense colors. To avoid stem rot problems, make sure the soil is well drained. Most cultivars will tolerate light shade, but they tend to become leggy.

HOW TO PLANT

Geraniums are sold as bedding plants in bloom, or in 4- or 6-inch pots. If planting in beds, set them about 12 inches apart and only as deep as they were growing in the container. In planters, flowerboxes, urns, or hanging baskets, they are usually spaced plant-to-plant.

CARE AND MAINTENANCE

Geraniums are easily grown, but they do have some special needs. Remove large clusters of flowers and old, yellow leaves to keep the plants attractive and to stimulate continuing bloom. Expect mites, leaf spot, and gray mold in wet weather, as well as various caterpillars. Natural rainfall is seldom sufficient to keep containers watered, so check them daily. Water in hot dry weather when planted in beds.

ADDITIONAL INFORMATION

Geranium is from the Greek and means *a crane* (seedpods of these flowers resembled a crane's bill). The botanical name, *Pelargonium*, is also Greek; it means *stork*. Geraniums are tender perennials. They grow continuously in mild climates, becoming large plants. In our state, bring plants indoors for the winter, then set out again in spring. This can be done one of three ways: Lift entire plants, trim them back, pot, and grow indoors. With sufficient light, they will bloom all winter and can be moved out in spring. Or take cuttings from plants before they freeze; root, pot, and grow them through the winter to be planted in spring. A third way is Grandma's way: she kept geraniums over by lifting the best plants, shaking off the soil, and hanging them upside down in brown paper bags in the basement. In spring, the leaves had dried and fallen off, but the stems were still succulent, ready to grow. She potted the plants, cutting off the shriveled parts. In a few weeks leaves appeared, and the plants were ready for setting out. This system still works!

ADDITIONAL SPECIES, CULTIVARS, OR VARIETIES

There are so many cultivars of geraniums from which to choose that many garden centers sell by color, not by name. Today the 'Sprinter' series of seed-grown cultivars is the standard. 'Freckles' was a 1991 AAS winner. 'Orange Appeal', a true orange, received a 1991 Fleuroselect award. Smooth- and ivy-leaved geranium, *P. peltatum*, is used exclusively for hanging baskets or other containers. Colors include intense lavenders and purples. Species of scented geraniums are grown for their fragrance and foliage—a few common ones are 'Lemon', Nutmeg', 'Peppermint', and 'Citronella'. 'Citronella' is often grown around porches and decks where its crushed leaves can repel mosquitoes. Scented geraniums are usually started from cuttings.

Gerbera

Gerbera jamesonii

Other Name: Transvaal Daisy
Zones: All
Size: 18 to 24 inches tall; basal leaves spread
    12 to 18 inches
Blooms: Early summer to fall (may be moved
    indoors)
Flower Colors: Scarlet, orange, pink, crimson,
    rose, yellow, and white

Light Requirement:

Gerberas have been grown as commercial cut flowers for many years, often in greenhouses. They have been on the flower markets of Europe for decades, having been shipped from their native Transvaal. Older cultivars took a year to produce blooms from seeded plants; only recently have breeders developed cultivars that grow from seed fast enough to be useful as outdoor garden plants in the colder parts of the country. Large, brightly colored, daisy-like flowers, 4 inches across, are borne on straight, strong, 24-inch stems. The body of the plant is a rosette of long leaves as large as a foot and a half in diameter.

WHEN TO PLANT

Seeds are very expensive, as much as 60 cents apiece. They require light and germinate in 2 weeks at 70 degrees Fahreneheit; sow them in early February. Seedlings take up to three months before they are large enough to plant outside. Pot them as soon as they are large enough to handle; they may require repotting into larger pots as they grow. Unless you have a greenhouse or sophisticated indoor lighting system, it is better to buy plants from a garden center. Set started plants into the garden when frost danger has passed.

WHERE TO PLANT

Gerberas need a spot with full sun and excellent drainage.

HOW TO PLANT

Plants are available for sale in pots, often in bloom. If you intend to grow these plants for cut flowers, construct raised beds of a soil mix to assure necessary drainage. If the soil is wet, flower production will be poor, and the plants will have a tendency to rot off at the base. Set the started plants on 12-inch centers to allow enough room for their large leaves to extend fully. Set them no deeper than they were growing in the pot; deep planting will result in rotting of the crown at the base.

CARE AND MAINTENANCE
Once established, gerberas are relatively trouble-free. The most damaging problem is crown rot, which is invariably due to poor drainage or improper watering. Water only when the plants have dried to the point of wilting, then water thoroughly. Cut the flowers as they open, or deadhead if allowed to "die on the vine."

ADDITIONAL INFORMATION
Gerberas are wonderful cut flowers, and excellent houseplants if you have the right place for them. A greenhouse is best, but an artificial light setup can be made to work as well. One way of handling them is to grow them in pots which are plunged in the garden for the summer. Lift the pots and plants in fall to be moved indoors for the winter. Since these are actually tended perennials, they can be kept over easily. *Gerbera* is named for the German botanist Traugott Gerber.

ADDITIONAL SPECIES, CULTIVARS, OR VARIETIES
'Rainbow' gerberas are most commonly available. These are compact plants sold in mixtures or by separate colors. Catalogs list scarlet, orange, pink, crimson, rose, yellow, and white selections 'Happipot Mix' is selected for container use, and it is often grown in a greenhouse as a potted plant. Cut gerberas after they have been open for a few days. (When first open they have a tendency to close at night.) After cutting, keep the flowers straight up or the stems will bend; once bent, they are impossible to get straight again.

ANNUALS

Impatiens

Impatiens walleriana

Zones: All
Size: 8 to 16 inches high, 12 to 24 inches
  wide
Blooms: Early summer to frost
Flower Colors: Red, salmon, pink, orange,
  lavender, white, and bicolors

Light Requirement:

There is no question that impatiens is the number-one bedding plant in Illinois. Formerly considered a shade plant only, newer selections tolerate shade or full sun equally well, growing into mounds of succulent leaves and becoming covered with brilliant flowers. Even tiny plants flower, and the plantings are covered with blooms from spring until frost puts an end to the display. Impatiens have assumed the position held by petunias for so many years: they are the standards by which all others are judged. Impatiens is the most reliable and easiest to grow of all the common annuals. Plant it, water it, and forget it.

WHEN TO PLANT

Impatiens plants take a long time to start. If you want to set out plants in mid-May, you must sow seeds in late January. Do not cover them—the seeds need light to germinate. Germination takes about 2 weeks at 70 degrees Fahrenheit. Set started plants in the garden after danger of frost has passed.

WHERE TO PLANT

Impatiens plants are excellent in planters, pots, hanging baskets, and shade gardens, for edging or bedding, and around the bases of trees. Plant them in full or partial shade, or in full sun. Plants will wilt in full sun during the heat of the day, but they recover readily as the temperatures moderate. Soils must be moist but well drained.

HOW TO PLANT

Impatiens is available at all garden centers and wholesale nurseries, or anywhere plants are sold in spring. There should be no difficulty finding the colors and types to suit your needs. They are normally sold as bedding plants, in flats, or in hanging baskets. Flats hold 50 to 75 plants each. Space smaller cultivars 6 inches apart; taller culti-vars can be spaced as much as 1 foot apart and will fill in well. Set the plants no deeper than they were growing in the container. Water the plants after planting to settle the soil around the roots.

CARE AND MAINTENANCE

Water is essential for the maintainence of impatiens. If allowed to dry out they will lose their leaves, and they will take their time about recovering. Fertilizer is generally not needed; overfertilization will result in lanky, tall plants that will fall over. If plants become leggy in midsummer, cut them back to about 6 inches. They will regrow quickly into shorter, more compact plants. Thrips can cause injury to the leaves and flowers, but normally no treatment is necessary. Root rot due to poor drainage or improper watering is the most common problem.

ADDITIONAL INFORMATION

Impatiens walleriana is native to eastern Africa. The name *Impatiens* comes from a Latin word that describes the way the seedpods pop open and scatter seeds when they are ripe.

ADDITIONAL SPECIES, CULTIVARS, OR VARIETIES

The most common impatiens types are probably the 'Super Elfins'. A desirable feature of newer cultivars, in addition to their heat toler-ance and many colors, is their uniformity. New colors for 1997 are deep pink and melon. All the plants of a series such as 'Super Elfin' will grow to about the same size. The 'Pride' series is large flowered; it seems to be passing the 'Blitz' series, which has been the standard for container plants. So many new cultivars arrive each year that many growers have resorted to growing just one type in as many colors as possible, labeling the flats by color only. The related New · Guinea impatiens is a newcomer on the scene. The plants are large-flowered and brightly colored, and their foliage is colorful as well. They are grown mostly as pot plants, but the newer selections, which come true from seed, make excellent bedding plants. Garden balsam (also Sweet Sultan) is *I. balsamina*, another relative. The flow-ers of balsams tend to remain hidden beneath their leaves, but newer improved strains have been bred to avoid this undesirable characteristic.

Lobelia

Lobelia erinus

Zones: All
Size: 6 inches high, spreading 12 to 18 inches
Blooms: Spring to frost
Flower Colors: Crimson, lilac, rose, blue, white; some have a white eye in the center

Light Requirement:

*T*here are so few plants that have blue flowers. Lobelia is a lovely little plant that does well in borders and as edging. It is especially good in the partially shaded border or the rock garden, and in planters, hanging baskets, or windowboxes. The strap-like leaves are green or bronze. This is one of those plants that I learned to appreciate early in my gardening experiences. I saw it used extensively in winter gardens in Southern California, where its color was particularly appreciated. It is equally at home here in the Illinois summer.

WHEN TO PLANT

Sow seeds indoors under lights about mid-January. The seeds need light to germinate, so do not cover them with the medium. Keep the germinating medium moist by covering the container with clear plastic wrap. Set started plants in the garden when danger of frost has passed.

WHERE TO PLANT

In the hotter parts of the state, lobelia should be protected from full sun during the heat of the day. In the cooler areas, it can stand full sun as long as it has adequate water. It prefers soil with good drainage.

HOW TO PLANT

Lobelias are available in garden centers in spring as bedding plants, in hanging baskets, and in planters. Set plants about 12 inches apart in a border, planting no deeper than the plants were growing in their containers.

CARE AND MAINTENANCE
There are no serious problems with lobelia. If it gets too leggy, cut it back. It will regrow without difficulty.

ADDITIONAL INFORMATION
Lobelia erinus is native to the Cape of Good Hope in Southern Africa. It prefers a cooler climate, and it may stop blooming if the weather gets too hot; flowering will resume when temperatures moderate. This plant was named for Matthias de l'Obel, Flemish botanist and physician to James I of England.

ADDITIONAL SPECIES, CULTIVARS, OR VARIETIES
'Blue Moon' is a deep, cobalt blue. 'Crystal Palace' is dark blue with bronze foliage. 'Paper Moon' is white. 'Rosamund' is deep carmine. *Pendula* types include the 'Fountain' series with colors of crimson, lilac, rose, blue, white, and a mix.

Marigold

Tagetes sp.

Other Names: Dwarf French Marigold,
   African Marigold, Tall Marigold
Zones: All
Size: Dwarf French marigolds 8 to 12 inches
   tall, spreading to 18 inches; African or tall
   marigolds to 36 inches
Blooms: Early summer to frost
Flower Colors: Yellow, gold, orange, mahogany,
   and white

Light Requirement:

*M*arigolds are the workhorses of the flower garden. They are cheery flowers with bright colors and upturned faces. Once they begin blooming, they brighten any corner of the garden, and they seem to tolerate almost any situation. Marigolds have been hybridized vigorously, and type distinctions have become blurred. The African types were tall and had one bloom on a long stem. These are now called American marigolds, and most are now F-1 hybrids with large, fully double, 4-inch blooms in yellow, gold, orange, and white. They are best used in masses or for cutting. Dwarf French marigolds are shorter and have either single or double flowers in rust, mahogany, yellow, orange, or bicolors.

WHEN TO PLANT

Seeds germinate quickly under lights, in as short a time as 24 hours at 70 degrees Fahrenheit. Seed sown in April will develop into plants of sufficient size to plant in the garden by mid-May. Set plants in the garden when all danger of a freeze is past.

WHERE TO PLANT

Marigolds prefer full sun; they can stand the heat and they tolerate rather droughty soils.

HOW TO PLANT

Marigolds are sold as bedding plants, in flats, pots, planters, and hanging baskets. Plants of the shorter hybrids should be spaced about 12 inches apart. Tall American or African kinds should be spaced at 2 feet. Work up the soil by tilling or cultivating, and set the plants no deeper than they were growing in their containers.

CARE AND MAINTENANCE

There are pests that can wreak havoc on marigolds. Earwigs will make lace of the foliage—these nocturnal insects can destroy a planting overnight. You can protect them by applying Sevin insecticide to the plants when you set them out. Marigolds are also lightning rods for mites. Try insecticidal soap or just a hard shower from beneath to dislodge these pests. Aster yellows disease will turn the flowers green and prevent them from opening; pull out and destroy any infected plants immediately. Except for fighting these pests, marigolds require little care. Deadhead the larger kinds to promote continuing bloom. Apply water only when the soil is dry and the plants have started to wilt (overly wet soils will result in stem rot). Marigolds have acquired an undeserved reputation for discouraging pests with their odor. If they do discourage pests, it is not because of their odor, but because they can trap soil-borne nematodes, reducing the numbers of this type of pest.

ADDITIONAL INFORMATION

Marigolds are not French, nor are they African: they are natives of Mexico. *Tagetes* refers to Tages, a mythical grandson of Jupiter who sprang from the plowed earth as a boy and taught the Etruscans the meanings of natural phenomena. Among the easiest plants to start and grow, marigolds are excellent for teaching youngsters about plants. Marigolds were the favorite flowers of Illinois Senator Everett Dirksen from Tazewell County, who lobbied long and hard to make them the national flower.

ADDITIONAL SPECIES, CULTIVARS, OR VARIETIES

French marigolds include one of my favorites, 'Janie', now in many colors, but still displaying a good compact form. Triploids such as 'Zenith' don't set seed, so they are less likely to stall in the hottest weather; they have big flowers on compact plants. 'Discovery' and 'Inca' American types are reliable, large-flowered, and not as tall as many of the others. New for 1997 are 'Disco Mix' and 'Troubadour Yellow'.

Morning Glory

Ipomoea purpurea, (Convolvulus purpureus)

Zones: All
Size: Vines to 10 feet; spread 2 feet
Blooms: Summer
Flower Colors: Blue, pink, purple, white

Light Requirement:

Often a temporary screen is needed to cover a utility pole, the vacant side of a garage, or an unattractive fence. Morning glories perform that job well, and they look beautiful while doing it. They quickly cover a trellis. Where a west-facing porch is too hot for comfort on a summer afternoon, morning glories can be grown up strings to provide shade. The heart-shaped leaves of these attractive plants are bright green. Their flowers are trumpet-shaped, purple, blue, pink, or white. (I prefer the traditional purple ones that remind me of Grandma's garden.) These plants will grow to an amazing size in a couple of months, producing a lot of plant material that will need to be removed in the fall. They vine by encircling whatever they can find to grow on. I find it is easier to give them a temporary support than to try to unwind them. Use twine (try binder twine) or mesh that can be cut down and rolled up. Make sure the support is biodegradable, and you will be able to run all of it through your compost pile.

WHEN TO PLANT

Seeds can be started indoors; they will germinate in a week at 75 degrees Fahrenheit. But the plants grow so fast that starting seed indoors is probably an unnecessary exercise. Try sowing seeds outdoors directly where you want the plants to grow.

WHERE TO PLANT

Full sun is best. Morning glories will tolerate partial shade, but they will flower less. Plant them where they have room to grow and a strong support.

HOW TO PLANT

Morning glories are rarely offered for sale at garden centers or other plant outlets. Occasionally you will see them in containers growing up a small trellis. These plants can be set into the garden, but be careful not to disturb the roots or the plants will stop growing. Morning glories are best seeded directly where they are to grow. Morning glory seed coats are tough. Soak them overnight before you plant them, or nick the seed coat with a file. Work up the soil by tilling or spading and sow seeds in groups of threes. Push the seeds into the loosened soil about ¹/₂ inch deep and cover them with the soil.

CARE AND MAINTENANCE
Once they start growing, morning glories are just about trouble-free. It is possible to underestimate the weight of the vines; if you provide supports that do not have sufficient strength, the whole thing can come tumbling down. Make sure the supports are well fastened. If the vines do fall, they can be re-attached and will continue to grow. Heavy watering or fertilization will stimulate lots of leaves and vines, but flowering will be reduced.

ADDITIONAL INFORMATION
Ipomoea comes from the Greek word for "bindworm," *Ips*. It is a native of the tropics, where it can become weedy. Related to bindweed, that scourge of gardeners, morning glory is more civi-lized in the Northern climates. In some parts of the South it has become naturalized, and in some states it is not lawful to grow these plants. The name "morning glory" was given to this plant because its flowers open every morning.

ADDITIONAL SPECIES, CULTIVARS, OR VARIETIES
'Heavenly Blue' is the best of the cultivars. Seeds are available for red, white, blue, or mixed colors. 'Moon vine', *I. alba*, a related species, has large fragrant white flowers that pop open at sunset. New for 1997 is 'Tie Dye'. Its large, 6-inch flowers are sky-blue over-laid with swirls or stripes of navy.

Moss Rose

Portulaca grandiflora

Zones: All
Size: 6 to 8 inches high, spreading to
  12 inches
Blooms: All summer
Flower Colors: Red, rose, orange, pink, white,
  fuchsia

Light Requirement:

*M*oss rose will probably thrive in a spot in your garden where it is too hot and dry for anything else to grow. Well suited to harsh environments, moss rose is often used for roadside plantings where rain will not fall for months at a time. We use it in the area between our driveway and our neighbor's driveway where the sun bakes down all day. This is a spreading plant with succulent narrow leaves, and it is covered with brilliant blooms. With just a little water, these plants will flower faithfully all summer long. The blooms of older cultivars were sparse, but the newer selections are covered with fully double flowers in bright colors. They begin flowering when the plants are still so small as to be otherwise unnoticed.

WHEN TO PLANT

Moss rose seed can be started indoors under lights, germinating quickly at 70 degrees Fahrenheit. Seed sown directly in the garden germinates when soil temperatures have warmed sufficiently, usually about the middle of June.

WHERE TO PLANT

These tough little plants are suited for hot, dry, sunny places where other things refuse to grow. They are useful in a perennial bed where the foliage has died down and left a void.

HOW TO PLANT

Moss rose is available as bedding plants at garden centers. Sow seed or set plants out when soils have warmed. Seed can be broadcast and lightly raked into the soil. Set plants about 6 inches apart and plant them no deeper than they were growing in their containers. These plants need hot weather!

CARE AND MAINTENANCE

The foliage is a little thin on these plants as they are starting, and weeds, particularly purslane, can be troublesome. Pull the purslane and apply a little preemergent herbicide. Dacthal works fine for this purpose. Otherwise, the plants are tidy and require no care other than a little watering during extended droughts.

ADDITIONAL INFORMATION

Moss rose produces a lot of seed, and volunteer plants will come up every year where these plants are regularly grown. Unfortunately, since the better cultivars are hybrids, the seedlings may not be up to par. Rely on some of the seed, but also start new plants from seed or transplants every year. The botanical name *Portulaca* is derived from the Latin *Porto*, "to carry," and *lac*, "milk." some species have a milky sap. Annual moss rose is native to Brazil.

ADDITIONAL SPECIES, CULTIVARS, OR VARIETIES

Many of the newer cultivars are F2 hybrids. They are superior, and come in a great range of colors with continuous blooming. Try the 'Sundial' or 'Afternoon Delight' series. Colors range from red, rose, orange, and pink to white and a new fuchsia and mango.

Pansy

Viola × wittrockiana

Zones: All
Size: 4 to 8 inches high, spreading 12 inches
Blooms: Spring, early summer, fall
Flower Colors: Tri-colored, purple, yellow,
   white, blue, dark red, brown, and apricot
   in single colors or various combinations

Light Requirement:

Who doesn't enjoy the smiling faces and cheery colors of pansies? As soon as soils are dry enough to work, pansies appear wherever bedding plants are sold. The bright splashes of color in the garden are certainly welcome after a long, dreary Illinois winter. Even before soils are workable, you can set out a few plants in pots or planters, for these hardy little plants will stand a freeze and keep on blooming. They have been known to survive a Northern winter if they have adequate snow cover for protection. While not particularly fond of heat, some of the newer selections will bloom throughout the summer if protected from the midday sun. Longer-stemmed cultivars can be cut for a little color indoors during springtime. Plant pansies where late-developing perennials are expected, or in annual beds where they can be removed in time to plant the hot-weather kinds.

WHEN TO PLANT

If you would like pansy plants in March, the seed can be started indoors under lights at 60 degrees Fahrenheit in late December or January. Moisten the seed, and chill it for a week in the refrigerator. When starting, cover the seeds lightly with the propagating mix—they must be in the dark in order to germinate. Transplant them, and grow on at 55 degrees Fahrenheit. Set them out when the soils are dry enough to work in March.

WHERE TO PLANT

Pansies can be planted in full sun or partial shade. In the shade, they will flower all summer; in full sun, they tend to stall out. Soils should be cool, fertile, moist, and well drained.

How to Plant

Set plants on 6- to 8-inch centers for immediate effect. Plant them at the same depth they were growing in the containers, and water them in to settle the soil. Do not keep them constantly wet, or the stems will rot at the soil line.

Care and Maintenance

Pansies require little care. Water them if the weather is dry, and remove the spent blooms in order to keep the plants flowering. When the plants get long and straggly, cut them back; they will respond with renewed growth and flowering. Pansies are affected by the usual problems associated with plants grown in cool moist places. Slugs and earwigs will make lace out of the flowers. Use slug baits, and spray the plants with Sevin to control earwigs. Both pests are most easily controlled while they are still small, so start early.

Additional Information

Viola is the old Latin name for violet. Most modern cultivars are descendants of *V. tricolor*, the 'Heartsease' of the Elizabethan period. The common name comes from the French *pensee* which means "pansy," as well as "thought."

Additional Species, Cultivars, or Varieties

Most of the popular pansy cultivars are F1 hybrids. They are more vigorous, have larger flowers, flower earlier, and can stand the heat better than the inbred types, or even than the F2 hybrids. Much of the earlier hybridizing was done in Switzerland, which resulted in the large-flowered, Swiss hybrids of a generation ago. 'Majestic Giants' are large-flowered and early. Single colors are available; all have the familiar "faces." 'Padparadja', 1991 AAS winner, is named after the famous orange sapphire, and is the same color as the gem. For bedding plants, single-color cultivars with smaller flowers and no faces are preferred. They stand up better in rainstorms, and the colors are more uniform. There are many pansy strains, and growers generally produce the ones they have grown most successfully. Often pansies are sold as mixes, with no cultivar name indicated. If you want to be sure of the type of cultivar you are getting, buy the seed through a catalog and start your own plants.

Petunia

Petunia × hybrida

Zones: All	**Light Requirement:**
Size: 8 to 16 inches high, spreading about as wide; new carpet types spread up to 3 feet	
Blooms: Summer	
Flower Colors: Red, white, purple, pink, salmon, yellow, and with stripes or star-like marks	

For decades, petunias were the bedding plant of choice. Not until the advent of the improved impatiens was there any competition for these dependable plants. But breeders aren't done yet . . . the new groundcover types of petunias have renewed interest in these popular plants. For dependability and long season of bloom, nothing comes close to petunias. They have many flower forms, a wide range of colors, and a variety of growth habits, and they remain the most popular bedding plants for sunny locations.

WHEN TO PLANT

Petunias can be started from seed, but this does take time. Sow the seed indoors under lights in February, covering lightly with the propagating mix. Germination takes five days at 70 degrees Fahrenheit. Transplant, and continue to grow the seedlings at 60 to 70 degrees. Set them into the garden when all danger of a freeze is past. They will stand a frost if they are properly hardened off.

WHERE TO PLANT

Petunias are sun-loving plants. They will tolerate some shade at the expense of flower production. Good drainage is necessary to avoid stem rot.

HOW TO PLANT

Petunias are available as bedding plants, and in pots, hanging baskets, and planters. Space bedding types 12 inches apart; ground-cover types should be spaced about three feet. Work up the soil by tilling or cultivating, and set the plants no deeper than they were grown in their containers. After planting, water the plants thoroughly to settle the soil.

CARE AND MAINTENANCE

Petunias have their share of problems. Slugs and earwigs can make lace of flowers and leaves; protect the plants with slug bait and Sevin insecticide. Stem rot can be a major problem that is aggravated by poor drainage or poor watering practices. Water thoroughly to soak the soil, but always allow the plants to wilt before watering again. Avoid heavy mulches and frequent, light, shallow watering. Stem rot will show up on the lighter colors first. If you see this happen, reduce the watering and drench the bed with Banrot or a similar product. Deadhead spent blooms. Cut back overly-long, straggly plants about midsummer; they will respond with renewed growth and flowers.

ADDITIONAL INFORMATION

The name "petunia" comes from the Brazilian *petun* ("tobacco"). They are solanaceous plants that are related to tobacco, and they are native to South America.

ADDITIONAL SPECIES, CULTIVARS, OR VARIETIES

Petunias are grouped according to flower form. Multifloras generally have lots of single, 2- to 3- inch flowers, and there are double multifloras as well. Grandifloras have fewer, but larger, 5-inch blooms. Double grandifloras are huge and spectacular, better used for containers and pots. The blooms of double grandifloras are too heavy for the garden; with the first rain, they will end up in the mud. Cascade types may be either multifloras or grandifloras; they have longer, trailing stems and are best used in hanging baskets, windowboxes, and urns. The groundcover types are extra-vigorous cascade types that make 6-inch-high mats covered with blooms. 'Purple Wave', a 1994 AAS, was the first of these. In our trials it made a dense mat six feet across, and bloomed throughout a hot summer. 'Pink Wave' is reported to be less vigorous but equally floriferous. 'Fantasy' hybrids are in a new class called "millifloras" or "thousand-flowered" petunias. They form dense, 6-inch mounds covered with 1-inch flowers in pink, red, ivory, and blue. Mixes are also available.

Salvia

Salvia splendens

Other Name: Scarlet Sage
Zones: All
Size: 6- to 30-inch-tall plants, either upright or mound-shaped
Blooms: Summer to frost
Flower Colors: Red, white, violet, salmon, purple, burgundy

Light Requirement:

*B*right-red salvia is one of the flowers especially suited to red, white, and blue flower beds. A good combination is low-growing blue ageratum, medium-tall white petunias, and the taller, bright-red salvia with spikes held above its bright-green foliage. Red is still the most popular salvia color, but breeders have been developing other colors as well, and plant form and size have also undergone some changes. The strictly upright forms of the past are giving way to short, compact types covered with blooms and better suited to bedding. Colors range from the reds to salmon, burgundy, violet, purple, and white.

WHEN TO PLANT

Salvia can be started from seed indoors under lights. The seed does need light to germinate, so don't cover it with soil. Germination takes about 5 days at 70 degrees Fahrenheit. Transplant the seedlings, then grow them at 60 degrees. The tiny plants are easily injured by fertilizer, so use it sparingly. Try liquid fertilizers at 1/4 normal strength. Set the plants in the garden when all danger of frost has passed.

WHERE TO PLANT

Salvias do best and develop their most intense color in full sun. They can take a lot of heat, and they prefer moist but well-drained soil. In partial shade the plants will become leggy and may begin to fall over.

HOW TO PLANT

Salvia is available as bedding plants from local garden centers and other plant stores. Soil should be prepared by tilling or cultivating;

set started plants on 10- to 12-inch centers, planting no deeper than the plants were growing in their containers. Water thoroughly after planting to settle the soil. Pinching will hasten branching of the taller varieties. Newer, compact forms do not require pinching; they will branch themselves.

CARE AND MAINTENANCE

Salvia is relatively trouble-free. Stem rot can be a problem if the soil stays wet, or if the plants are watered too often. Soak the soil thoroughly, and let it dry until the plants begin to wilt before watering again. Some of the shorter cultivars will continue to bloom without deadheading. Taller cultivars should have spent flower spikes removed for continuing bloom.

ADDITIONAL INFORMATION

A mass of red salvia flowers against the plant's bright-green foliage is one of the more spectacular color combinations for the annual garden. It will overwhelm any other combination, so be sure to use it carefully. *Salvia* is from the Latin *salveo*, meaning "to heal." Pliny, an early Roman scientist, referred to the medicinal properties of some of the members of the genus. Red salvia is native to Brazil.

ADDITIONAL SPECIES, CULTIVARS, OR VARIETIES

Dwarf selections include 'Firecracker', 'Hot Stuff', and 'St. John's Fire'. Taller 'America' grows to 20 inches, 'Splendens Tall' to 30. The 'Hotline' series is short, 10 inches, and includes red, white, violet, burgundy, and mixed selections. 'Salsa Mix' includes new colors: burgundy, bicolor scarlet, and bicolor salmon, which is new in 1997. A related species is the blue salvia, *S. farinacea*, which is less showy, but excellent as a dried flower. 'Cirrus' (compact white) and 'Signum' (indigo blue dusted with white) are new for 1997. *Salvia officinalis* is common sage, the cultivar used for cooking.

Snapdragon

Antirrhinum majus

Other Names: Snap, Garden Snapdragon
Zones: All
Size: Bedding types from 6 to 30 inches
Blooms: Spring to fall
Flower Colors: White, pink, yellow, orange, lavender

Light Requirement:

*S*napdragons are among the plants that seem to be of special interest to children. I recall tales from my childhood in which snapdragons were villains, catching and holding those unfortunate enough to wander into the field. Even as children, no one really believed those stories, but it was fun pinching the blooms to make them snap open. Snapdragons were some of the first plants I grew. They did well even when I sowed them directly in the garden. As I recall, our gardens were usually pretty much in the shade, but the snapdragons grew anyway. Snaps in those days were tall and narrow, with blooms held upright on 20- to 30-inch stems; they belonged in the cutting garden or at the back of the border. The newer, more versatile, cultivars are short, with spikes of interesting, pastel-colored flowers borne on compact 6-inch plants.

WHEN TO PLANT

When the seeds are placed under lights at 70 degrees Fahrenheit, snapdragons will germinate in about 7 days. Sow the seed in early March. Transplant the seedlings, and grow them at 60 degrees. Snaps will tolerate frost, but set the started plants in the garden when freeze danger has passed. Seed can be sown directly in the garden as early as the soil can be worked in the spring.

WHERE TO PLANT

Plant snaps in full sun to partial shade. They need a moist but well-drained soil.

HOW TO PLANT

Snaps are sold at virtually every garden center and plant store as bedding plants. Space started plants of tall cultivars 12 inches apart, bedding cultivars on 6- to 8-inch centers. Prepare the soil by tilling or cultivating, and set the plants at the same depth they were growing in the containers. Deep planting can result in stem rot.

CARE AND MAINTENANCE

Bedding snaps need tending to assure continued flowering; remove the spent blooms. If the plants begin to get leggy in mid-season, cut them back to about six inches and they will respond with new foliage and blooms. Tall snapdragons need support. Stake them so the stems are straight for cutting. After removal of the first spike, tall snaps will rebloom with shorter side shoots. Spider mites can be troublesome in hot weather. Syringe them off with a stream of water, or try insecticidal soap. Stem rot can become serious if there is poor drainage or poor watering practices. Snaps would rather be dry than wet. Water them thoroughly, but do not water again until the plants begin to wilt. If plant losses remain severe, treat the soil with Banrot according to label directions.

ADDITIONAL INFORMATION

Snaps are cool-weather plants. The newer cultivars will tolerate heat, but the tall types will often stall. They will grow again when temperatures moderate. Tall snaps are excellent for flower arrangements. Cut them early in the day and plunge the stems into warm water. Set them in a cool place to harden off for five or six hours. They will last a week in an arrangement. My friend and adviser Floyd Swink says, "Let the fruits develop on some plants; I know it sounds impossible, but snapdragons have the most bizarre fruit of any plant in the entire world!" *Antirrhinum* is from the Greek *anti* ("like") and *rhinos* ("snout")—the flowers do have a curious shape. Snaps originated in the Mediterranean.

ADDITIONAL SPECIES, CULTIVARS, OR VARIETIES

Bedding types include early-flowering, heat-tolerant 'Tahiti', which comes in ten colors and a mixture. Medium-tall 'Lipstick Silver' has white flowers with red "lips." 'Little Darling', with mixed colors, was a 1971 AAS. 'Rocket' hybrid is the most common tall snap for cutting gardens. At its best, it rivals the greenhouse snaps grown for the florist trade.

Sunflower

Helianthus annuus

Zones: All
Size: 2 to more than 10 feet tall, spread
2 to 4 feet
Blooms: Summer
Flower Colors: Red to brown disc flowers
with yellow to orange ray flowers

Light Requirement:

*T*he name sunflower immediately brings to mind a huge, tree-like plant with a nodding head well beyond the reach of a child. I remember the first ones I grew as a child. They grew very tall, and then they fell down. Things have improved since those days. Even the tall cultivars have better stand-ability, and they usually don't get as tall as they did years ago. Sunflowers are grown as conversation pieces and for the birdseed they produce. The squirrels and birds often get the seed well before harvest time, however. Tall sunflowers are still very popular, but breeders have developed dwarf kinds that produce the same large heads and seeds, but on shorter plants. The bushy dwarfs are from four to six feet, still tall by most standards. These plants are not for the border, but where there is space, they are attractive additions to the flower garden.

WHEN TO PLANT

Sunflowers are seldom available as bedding plants. They can be started indoors in peat pots about four weeks before the frost-free date, or seeded directly into the garden when danger of frost has passed.

WHERE TO PLANT

Sunflowers are for the sun: plant them where they get full sun all day long. They tolerate dry soils, but for best seed production, give them plenty of water when their flowers are developing.

HOW TO PLANT

Sow seed directly in the garden, or transplant started seedlings. Cover seed with 1/2 inch of soil, and thin seedlings to about 2 feet. Set plants on 2-foot centers.

CARE AND MAINTENANCE

Sunflowers require very little care. Some overly tall plants may need support if you can find something tall enough. Birds and squirrels are the worst of the pests. To prevent them from stealing all the seed before it ripens, try covering the flowerheads with old pantyhose. It looks strange, but it works.

ADDITIONAL INFORMATION

Tall sunflowers are good planted at the back of the garden where they can provide screening. Morning glories can be planted to grow up the sunflowers; you can grow pole beans on them as well. The name *Helianthus* comes from the Greek *helios* ("sun") and *anthus* ("flower"). Some sunflowers have commercial importance as food crops; the tall sunflower is grown for seeds and oil. *H. tuberosus* is the Jerusalem artichoke. Sunflowers are native North American plants.

ADDITIONAL SPECIES, CULTIVARS, OR VARIETIES

Seed catalogs now show pages of sunflowers. 'Velvet Tapestry' is a cultivar that offers a mixture of crimsons, golds, and bicolors. Sunspot is a large-flowered dwarf with 12-inch flowers on 2-foot plants. 'Pacino' is new for 1997, with large flowers on 20-inch plants. Five-foot 'Sunshine Mix', also new for 1997, includes more colors: white, cream, lemon yellow, gold, orange, bronze, red, and burgundy. New cultivars appear every year. Check the seed catalogs for those that look good to you, and buy a little seed of several kinds. When you find one that suits your situation, stick with it.

Verbena

Verbena × hybrida, (Verbena × hortensis)

Zones: All, but does better in Zones 5 and 6
Size: 12 inches tall; upright, or spreading 18 to 24 inches
Blooms: Summer
Flower Colors: Bright red, white, blue, lavender, or purple with distinct white or yellow centers.

Light Requirement:

When I was a youngster working in a garden center after school hours, this cheery plant was fascinating to me. It was one of the first plants for which I learned the botanical name. (It wasn't hard since it is the same as the common name.) In a world of petunias and geraniums, this was a novelty plant. It impressed customers, and it helped start me on a fascinating journey with plants. Verbena is a "crisp" little plant. It makes a good groundcover, appearing brighter than most with its happy little flowers. It works well in rock gardens, beds, windowboxes, planters, and as edging. Full sun is preferred, and verbena also needs a moist, well-drained soil. During hot summers, it does better in the northern parts of the state. When temperatures are in the 90s day after day, blooming may stop. Watering is helpful at these times, as it tends to cool the plants, but a return to temperate conditions promotes renewed blooming.

WHEN TO PLANT

Verbena germinates with difficulty. Chill the sown seed in the refrigerator for about ten days to break its dormancy, then set out at 70 degrees Fahrenheit. Cover lightly with soil mix, as the seed germinates in the dark and is sensitive to moisture; keep it on the dry side. Germination will take five to fifteen days. As soon as the seed has germinated, lower the temperature to 60 degrees. Transplant when large enough to handle; you may set the plants in the garden when threat of a freeze is past. The plants will stand a frost if they have been properly hardened off.

WHERE TO PLANT

Plant in well-drained soil in full sun. These plants can stand a drought better than they can a flood!

How to Plant

Verbena is always available at garden centers and plant stores as bedding plants or in pots. Work up the soil by tilling or cultivating. If the area is poorly drained, raise it or provide drainage. Set started plants on 15-inch centers, no deeper than they were growing in their containers. Deep planting can result in damping off from stem rot.

Care and Maintenance

Verbena requires little care. If the weather is hot and dry, watering will help to stimulate flowering. Removal of spent blooms will prolong flowering. Damping off is the most serious problem, and this is due to excess moisture.

Additional Information

Verbena is thought to have come from the Latin word for the laurel branches carried by priests. Others believe the name is a corruption of the Celtic word *fervane*, a holy herb used to "cure certain ailments," to "protect from the bite of rabid animals," and to "avert antipathies." It was worn by heralds in ancient times as a badge of good faith. Annual verbenas are all hybrids that probably originated from European species.

Additional Species, Cultivars, or Varieties

Blooms of the heat-tolerant cultivar 'Peaches and Cream' are an unusual blend of salmon and apricot. In 1992 it won both AAS and Fleuroselect awards. 1993 AAS-winner 'Imagination' has lacy foliage and deep, magenta-blue flowers. My favorites are the scarlet-red 'Blaze' and the 'Amour' mix with its half-dozen colors. Related are the taller *V. rigida*, which is available only in purple, and *V. bonariensis*, which is 3 to 4 feet tall and has lavender blooms.

ANNUALS

Zinnia

Zinnia elegans

Zones: All
Size: 12 to 36 inches tall
Blooms: Summer
Flower Colors: Rose, red, white, yellow, green, orange, and violet

Light Requirement:

*Z*innias mean summertime! Few plants are as easy to grow, have as many colors and types, or are as fondly regarded as are zinnias. Old-fashioned gardens always had at least one row of zinnias for cutting, and they all grew tall in those days. "Victory gardens" were not complete without zinnias to brighten them, or to be cut for the dinner table. Summers were hot, and the blossoms were brilliant in the afternoon sun. These cheery flowers have been favorites for generations, and they remain so today. Zinnias are well adapted to our Midwest climate and soils. They are tolerant of our heat and drought, thriving in weather that sends other flowers into senescence. Hybridizing has been directed at developing smaller, bushier plants that have a greater color range and some disease resistance. Cultivars are classified according to their height. Flowers may be single or fully double; their forms may be dahlia-like, ruffled, or cactus (quilled) with brightly colored flowerheads as large as 6 inches across.

WHEN TO PLANT
Start zinnia seeds indoors under lights about 8 weeks before the last frost date. Seeds germinate quickly under lights, in as little as 24 hours at 75 to 80 degrees Fahrenheit. Seed sown in early April will develop into plants of sufficient size to plant in the garden by Memorial Day. Don't rush zinnias into the garden. These are hot-weather plants, and cold weather will set them back.

WHERE TO PLANT
Plant zinnias in full sun. They do best in hot, dry locations.

HOW TO PLANT
Seed can be sown directly in the garden, and this is the better way to grow the tall cultivars. Space the tall-growing kinds at 24 inches.

74

Dwarf zinnias are always available as bedding plants from garden centers; taller cultivars are harder to find. Set out started plants when soils have warmed. Space dwarf cultivars about a foot apart.

CARE AND MAINTENANCE

Zinnias don't require a lot of care. They don't mind dry soil, but they will flower better if given water when they are dry. To avoid mildew, water them early in the day so that the leaves will dry off before dusk. If mildew appears late in the season, spray the plants with sulfur or triforine. Remove spent blossoms to keep the plants flowering. Zinnias make excellent cut flowers, so keeping them cut for arrangements accomplishes the deadheading task. Tall cultivars may need staking.

ADDITIONAL INFORMATION

Zinnias are native to Mexico. The name *Zinnia* was given to the plant in honor of Johann Gottfried Zinn, an 18th-century botanist. Zinnias, among the easiest flowers to grow, are favorites of children. Give the children a little space to grow plants and some seeds. Help them scratch a seedbed and sow the seed. In a few days seedlings will be up, and in a matter of weeks there will be a profusion of blooms. This is a great way to get children interested in gardening at an early age.

ADDITIONAL SPECIES, CULTIVARS, OR VARIETIES

Small cultivars include 'Thumbelina', which is 6 inches tall and produces $1^1/2$-inch flowers. The medium-sized Cut-and Come-Again 'Peter Pan Hybrids' have won AAS awards; they are about a foot tall and have large, upward-facing blooms. The large-flowered ($3^1/2$ to 4 inches) 'Dreamland Mix' is improved for 1997 with additional colors. Another 12-inch-tall series is 'Pinwheel', which has large, upward-facing single flowers in pastel colors and good mildew resistance. Tall, giant-flowered cultivars include the 'Big Top' mixture with cactus-flowered blossoms, 'Tetra Hybrid', and 'Burpee's Zenith Hybrid'. These large plants fit most people's ideas of what zinnias should be. A related species, *Z. angustifolia* is a groundcover or border-type zinnia with narrow leaves and white or yellow flowers. *Z. a.* 'Crystal White' is a 1997 AAS winner.

$\mathscr{B}$ULBS PLAY AN IMPORTANT PART in the flower garden pageantry of spring and summer, and they can even move indoors for the winter. Crocuses break forth before the snow is quite gone and are followed by daffodils and majestic tulips. Then the summer bulbs take over with cannas, tuberous begonias, gladiolus, and stately lilies.

Plants that come from bulbs, tubers, or corms are among the easiest plants to grow. Their underground structures allow them to survive adverse conditions such as winter in the northern climates, excessive heat, or droughts. Bulbs are actually compressed underground buds, while tubers and corms are stems.

Inside a bulb is an embryonic plant complete with roots, stem, leaves, and flowers. If you cut an onion or a daffodil bulb in half lengthwise, you will be able to see all its parts just waiting for the right time to begin growing. Bulbs do not even require soil to grow. Stick a paper white narcissus bulb in a glass of water, and it will burst forth with a mass of blooms.

A true bulb consists of concentric layers which are bases of modified leaves. (These are called turnicated bulbs.) Daffodil or tulip bulbs are true bulbs. Lily bulbs consist of individual overlapping scales.

Tubers are swollen underground stems that store starch. The new plant—leaves, stems, and roots—grows from a single bud. Potatoes are tubers, and their eyes are the buds. Dahlias and tuberous begonias grow from tubers too. A corm is a short stem that has leaves and more stems growing from its pointed end, and roots growing from its bottom.

Irises and daylilies grow from rhizomes. Rhizomes are slender, root-like underground stems that store starch as well. We will talk about daylilies in the chapter on perennials.

Chapter Two

Now we have defined these terms, but are the definitions really important? For all practical purposes, these are all "bulbs," and we are most concerned with getting flowers from them.

Bulbs may be hardy or tender in our Illinois climate. Hardy bulbs stay in the ground, perfectly able to survive the winter. Because they will stay in place for many years, it is wise to take some time to plan their location and to prepare the ground for them.

Spring-flowering bulbs provide the best display if naturalized or if planted in masses. Planting them in straight rows like toy soldiers may show a lack of imagination! Plant a dozen or so in a mass where they will make a statement. Then plant another mass on the other side of the yard. Even if there is nothing in a bed later in the spring but the old leaves, a full bed of color will have created an image that will not be forgotten. Naturalized plantings of hundreds of squills or daffodils also create memorable sites (and sights!). Just scatter the bulbs and plant them where they fall. Be sure not to remove the leaves before they die, and these plantings will increase in size and color each year. Lilies are the aristocrats of the garden. With a little attention, their gorgeous blooms will faithfully appear at a time when their beauty is really appreciated.

Tender summer bulbs take over where the hardy spring bulbs leave off. You can plant them in the very beds vacated by the spring bulbs, among the perennials, in the cutting garden, or in a mass display for a striking effect. Tender bulbs should be lifted and stored for the winter and planted the following spring.

Bulbs of all kinds are sold in garden centers at the right times for planting. The best way to know what you are getting is to look at the pictures on the store display. Try a few that look good. If you like them when they grow in your garden, buy more the following year. One of the joys of gardening is experimentation. You never know what you will discover.

Bearded Iris

Iris hybrids

Zones: All
Size: Dwarfs under 15 inches, tall kinds
grow to 4 feet
Blooms: Late spring to early summer
Flower Colors: Blue, violet, purple, pink,
yellow, white, red

Light Requirement:

*B*earded irises are the most popular of the large class of perennial flowers known as Iris. Some irises grow from bulbs, but most, including the bearded iris, grow from strong rhizome systems. The familiar iris flower is divided into 6 segments. The center 3 segments, called standards, are upright; the outer 3 are called falls, and they have "beards" along their middles. Bearded irises are categorized according to height, as dwarf (under 15 inches), intermediate (15 to 28 inches), or tall (over 28 inches). Each of these categories may be subdivided, but that kind of subdivision can get too complicated, and unless you are showing irises, it really doesn't matter. (If you are showing irises, this profile is too simple for you anyway!) Irises are simple plants to grow. Few flowers reward you so well for so little work. They do best in full sun, and drainage is important so the fleshy roots and rhizomes don't rot. If you have a wet garden, there are other irises that will do just fine.

WHEN TO PLANT
Irises are planted in summer after the blooms have died down, usually in August. Plants in containers may be planted anytime during the season.

WHERE TO PLANT
Plant irises in full sun, in a good, well-drained garden soil. Irises are distinctive in the perennial border; they make a wonderful show in beds as well. Dwarfs are suitable for edging, and all of the irises can be naturalized in meadows. The taller kinds are excellent for cutting.

HOW TO PLANT
Irises are sold in 1-, 2-, and 6-gallon cans, or as divisions from mail-

order suppliers. Plants can be divided in midsummer. Prepare the soil by tilling or spading to a 6-inch depth, adding organic matter to improve the condition and drainage. Holes will have to be dug for the larger, container-grown plants, as deep and twice as wide as the plant ball. Set the plants at the same depth they were growing in the nursery. Space dwarfs 12 to 18 inches apart. Tall irises can be set 2 to 3 feet apart. Soak the plants thoroughly following planting to settle the soil around the roots.

CARE AND MAINTENANCE

Irises are relatively trouble-free. They have one pest that will destroy them if not controlled: iris borer, the larva of a night-flying moth. The borer's eggs are laid on the edges of the leaves about the time the plants are in flower. The borers tunnel through the edges of the leaves to the rhizomes, where they proceed to chew them to bits. A bacterial rot grows in the mess. Control the borer by spraying the plants just about the time the flower stalks appear in spring, using Cygon or Orthene. These systemic insecticides are absorbed by the leaves. Follow directions on the container very carefully. Irises will need to be divided when they become crowded. Lift the clumps and cut away any damaged parts. Separate the clumps into segments, each with a fan of leaves, a piece of rhizome, and several feeder roots. Extra pieces will be eagerly sought by your neighbors.

ADDITIONAL INFORMATION

Irises come in almost all the colors of the rainbow; the name means "rainbow" in Greek. Tall irises may tend to fall over, especially if growing in semi-shaded or windy areas. Stake the flower stalks, being careful not to injure the roots or rhizomes.

ADDITIONAL SPECIES, CULTIVARS, OR VARIETIES

There are literally hundreds of iris cultivars, and there are many other iris species. Japanese iris, *I. ensata*, has gorgeous big flowers that are flat instead of having standards and falls; they are plants of wet places, well adapted to pondside plantings. Blue flag, *I. virginica*, is a native wildflower found throughout the tallgrass prairie. Spend some winter evenings consulting garden catalogs from iris growers. You will find hundreds of cultivars and species listed.

Caladium

Caladium × hortulanum

Zones: All
Size: 1 to 2 feet tall and wide
Blooms: Not significant; plants grown for foliage
Foliage Colors: Many combinations of white, pink, red, and green, two or more colors in each leaf

Light Requirement:

*C*aladiums are unrivaled for creating a spectacular display in a shady, moist spot in the garden. The response from people who see ours for the first time is invariably: "Wow! What are those?" Caladiums are unusual and very colorful. These are tender perennials, tropical in origin, and they are not at all hardy in our state, requiring special care. In spite of the extra work, the tremendous display these plants provide makes the effort worthwhile. They grow from potato-like tubers that are actually swollen stems. Their leaves are large, heart-shaped, and richly colored. While coleus and hosta have deep, intense colors, the caladiums are mostly pastels with a lot of white, and their leaves are delicate. They are suited for growing in containers or for setting out into the garden, but they must be taken inside in fall before a freeze and stored indoors all winter. If you have a place to store them and don't mind a challenge, caladiums offer an unusually rewarding growing experience.

WHEN TO PLANT
Caladium tubers need to be started indoors about eight weeks before the last frost-free date. They should be potted and watered, and set in a warm (70 degrees Fahrenheit) place to develop. After all danger of frost is over, they may be moved outdoors.

WHERE TO PLANT
Caladiums can stand full sun if the humidity is quite high, but they are best suited to a shade border or to massing in a shade garden. Try to protect them from strong winds, which will tear the delicate leaves.

How to Plant

In a border or shade garden, started plants may be removed from their pots and planted on 12-inch centers in the garden, or the pots may be plunged. Plants grown for urns or planters may be handled either way as well, but they are usually set plant to plant.

Care and Maintenance

Caladiums need a moist but well-drained soil. If they stand in water, the tubers will rot. If there is a drainage problem, try raised beds. Though these plants need a lot of water, their roots need plenty of air. Eighty-degree temperatures and high humidity are ideal. If the humidity is low the plants will suffer, and misting might be necessary. Caladiums can handle temperatures in the 90s as long as they have adequate moisture. Lift the plants and move them indoors before a frost. Allowed to dry, they can be stored in their pots, or in boxes of peat moss. After a rest period of about 5 months, the plants can be started again. If new tubers have grown on the sides of the parent tuber, they may be removed to start additional plants. Caladiums have no serious pests.

Additional Information

Caladiums are quite unusual in Midwest gardens. We include them in this book because with a little care they can add an unexpected dimension to your garden.

Additional Species, Cultivars, or Varieties

There are many named cultivars of caladiums, but it is most important to pick out colors and patterns that appeal to you. It is best to select plants that have started so you can see the range of colors. Some of the more readily available selections are 'Carolyn Wharton', which is pink, red, and green; 'Frieda Hemple', which is solid red with green margins; 'Florida Sweetheart', which is white with red veins and green margins; and 'White Christmas', white with green veins. Most selections are the result of the efforts of amateur gardeners rather than of commercial efforts to develop new cultivars.

Canna

Canna sp.

Zones: All
Size: 1 to 6 feet tall, spread 1 to 3 feet
Flower Colors: Red, orange, pink, salmon, yellow

Light Requirement:

*I*f you're going for the spectacular, nothing can beat cannas. Their six-foot-tall spikes of blooms in masses are the centerpieces of summer floral gardens in Chicago's Lincoln Park each year; on that grand scale, anything less would be lost. If you have room, these plants can have the same magnificent effect in your garden. Strongly upright with banana-like foliage, these plants are topped with stalks of brightly colored gladiolus-like blooms from early summer until frost. They can be used as a screen or as the center of a formal bed. If you have less room, you may want to try the shorter cultivars; they also provide a spectacular display. Cannas aren't just for the garden; the newer cultivars, some just over a foot tall, are perfect for large urns or planters, or at the back of the border.

WHEN TO PLANT

Cannas are tender perennial plants that grow from fleshy rhizomes. Smaller cultivars may be handled as annuals and their seed sown indoors in January. Plant rhizomes or started plants in the garden after all danger of frost is past.

WHERE TO PLANT

Cannas perform best in full sun. They prefer a deeply prepared soil that has good drainage. If you are planting the larger cultivars, make sure there is enough room.

HOW TO PLANT

Work up the soil in the planting area by spading or tilling to a depth of 12 inches. Set started plants or rhizomes on 12-inch centers. The plants are unbranched and can be planted quite close together. Rhizomes should be planted at least 4 to 6 inches deep, while started plants should be set at the same depth they grew in their containers. Water thoroughly to settle the soil around the tubers.

CARE AND MAINTENANCE

Cannas require little care in the garden. The first fall freeze will kill back the foliage, and the tubers must be removed for storage indoors. Cut off the stems about 6 inches above ground; you will use them for handles to carry the clump. Store the clumps of rhizomes in damp peat moss in a dark room at 45 degrees Fahrenheit. In spring, separate the clumps into rhizomes, each with three eyes. Pot them, or place them in a box of sand to start the plants growing, before setting them back in the garden when danger of frost has passed.

ADDITIONAL INFORMATION

Cannas originated in Central and South America. There are several species from which the modern cultivars were developed. The origin of the name is not known.

ADDITIONAL SPECIES, CULTIVARS, OR VARIETIES

Giant canna cultivars include 'Red King Humbert', with red foliage and orange blooms; 'Richard Wallace', with yellow flowers and green leaves; and 'Rosamund Cole', which has green leaves and red flowers tipped with yellow. The 'Pfitzer' series of dwarf cannas includes a salmon pink and a yellow. The 'Seven Dwarfs' mix is a dwarf selection of several colors that grows from seed and is treated as an annual. This selection is often used in theme parks. Another seed strain is 'Tropical Rose', which is bright pink with deep-green leaves. It grows to 3 feet and is in bloom about three months after sowing the seed.

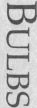

Daffodil

Narcissus species and hybrids

Zones: All
Size: 6 inches to 2 feet tall
Blooms: Spring
Flower Colors: Bright yellow, white, orange, pink, green, or bicolor
Deciduous: Foliage dies down in late spring after flowering

Light Requirement:

*B*right yellow daffodils are universal spring favorites. Even people who don't plant any other flowers will buy a dozen daffodil bulbs in the fall and plant them, anticipating a row of happy yellow blooms with the first warm days of spring. There are so many types of narcissi that they have been classified into 11 major divisions by the (British) Royal Horticultural Society. Most of the classifications are based on trumpet length and color. The daffodil is only one of these many narcissi, and the name usually refers to the types that have large yellow trumpet-like flowers.

WHEN TO PLANT

Daffodils are hardy spring-flowering bulbs, and they must be planted in the fall. Starting in September, bulbs are available in garden centers or wherever plants are sold.

WHERE TO PLANT

Daffodils can be planted in masses in the perennial border or naturalized throughout the lawn, garden, or wooded area. They are equally at home in sun or partial shade.

HOW TO PLANT

Like most bulbs, daffodils need good drainage. Wet soils will cause the bulbs to rot. Prepare the soil in beds by spading or tilling and add organic matter if the soil is particularly heavy. Plant the bulbs 6 to 12 inches apart and 6 inches deep. In sand or other light soils, plant them as deep as 8 to 10 inches. To naturalize, randomly scatter the bulbs over the area to be planted. With a trowel or bulb digger, plant them where they fall.

CARE AND MAINTENANCE

Once they are planted, daffodils require very little care. After the plants bloom in spring, their foliage should be left to replenish the bulbs for the following year (to improve their looks, they can be tied up with twist ties). Remove the foliage after it begins to turn yellow. Annuals can be planted between the ripening leaves to hide them; these annuals will be well established by the time the daffodil leaves are removed. When the bulbs have multiplied for a few years, their blooming will cease, and they will have to be dug up and divided.

ADDITIONAL INFORMATION

Narcissus is from the Greek word *narkeo*, which means "to stupefy" and the bulbs contain substances that do have a "stupefying" effect if they are eaten. Narcissus was a youth of Greek mythology who spent his days admiring his reflection in a pool. After rebuffing the advances of the beautiful nymph Echo he was punished, and was transformed into a daffodil growing beside the pool forever. Narcissi are native to the Mediterranean.

ADDITIONAL SPECIES, CULTIVARS, OR VARIETIES

There are over 10,000 named cultivars of narcissi. Most suppliers provide pictures of the flowers in their bulb displays. Viewing the pictures is the best way to be sure of what you are getting; the names of cultivars mean very little to the average gardener. One of the most popular is the paper-white narcissus that can be forced in a dish of water. This is a great project for children who are looking for an indoor activity in the fall. Other types of narcissi can be forced as well, but they require a long period of cold to prepare them to grow.

Flowering Onion

Allium sp.

Zones: All
Size: 1 to 5 feet tall with a basal rosette of leaves
Blooms: Late spring to early summer
Flower Colors: Purple, white, pink, or yellow
Deciduous: Leaves die down in summer after flowering

Light Requirement:

There are at least half a dozen species of ornamental onions that can be used as garden flowers. They range from the giant onion, 4 feet tall with a 6-inch ball of blooms, to Lily Leek, a foot tall with clusters of bright yellow blooms. Onion bulbs are fully hardy in Illinois. The period of bloom is only about 2 weeks, but during that time these flowers make a memorable show. Most make excellent cut flowers. The taller kinds must be relegated to the back of the garden, and they may need to be supported in windy areas. The shorter ones can mix nicely with other spring-flowering bulbs.

WHEN TO PLANT
Flowering onions are planted in fall.

WHERE TO PLANT
Plant in full sun in a well-drained soil. If planted in shade, the flower stalks will be weak and will fall over; poor drainage will result in bulb rot problems.

HOW TO PLANT
Prepare the soil by spading or tilling to a depth of at least 6 inches. Set the bulbs with at least 3 inches of soil above the tops.

CARE AND MAINTENANCE
Once established, flowering onions require little care. Remove the flower stalk after the blooms have faded. Plants may become crowded; they may be lifted after the foliage dies down and the bulblets that develop at the bases of larger bulbs can be removed. The large bulbs and the larger of these bulblets will flower the fol-

lowing year. Discard the small bulblets or give them to friends. Flowering onions are nearly pest-free. Thrips sometimes damage foliage. Bulb rot is a problem only in wet locations.

ADDITIONAL INFORMATION

The flowering onions are all related to the culinary onions, chives, leeks, and garlic. Each has its own distinctive aroma if bruised. While not generally grown as ornamentals, chives are attractive if allowed to go to bloom. *Allium* is the Latin name for garlic.

ADDITIONAL SPECIES, CULTIVARS, OR VARIETIES

Persian onion, *A. aflatunense*, makes a clump of wide, strap-shaped leaves. Its star-shaped flowers are purple in a 4-inch ball that is held held 2 feet above the leaves; it is good in the border and lasts 2 weeks as a cut flower. 'Purple Sensation' is dark purple and blooms in late spring. Giant onion, *A. giganteum*, produces a 6-inch ball of lilac-pink blooms on a 4-foot stalk. The blooms are excellent for fresh cut flower and dried flower arrangements. The tall inflorescences will have to be staked for support. It blooms in late spring through early summer. Turkestan onion is only a foot tall, but it produces a 6-inch ball of silver-lilac blooms, just above the characteristic pair of leaves. It is useful in the perennial border, blooming in late spring. Lily leek or golden garlic, *A. moly*, is a low-growing plant with loose clusters of bright yellow, star-like flowers a foot above the leaves. Excellent in the spring border, these plants will colonize well in the natural landscape, blooming mid- to late spring.

Gladiolus

Gladiolus × hortulanus

Other Name: Glads
Zones: All
Size: 2 to 4 feet tall, half as wide
Blooms: Summer
Flower Colors: Red, yellow, orange, purple,
    green, white, some with contrasting
    colored markings
	Light Requirement:

*G*lads are favorites of the florist trade, used extensively as cut flowers. They are garden favorites as well, easy and rewarding to grow. Above sword-shaped upright foliage, the spikes of lovely flowers, some 4 inches across, are spectacular. With successive plantings glads can be enjoyed from early summer until frost. These are summer-flowering tender perennials that grow from corms. While the large-flowered types are the most popular, there are dwarf forms as well. Butterfly types have flat flowers which are showy, but in my opinion lack the character of the standard types.

When to Plant

Glads are tender and will not stand a freeze. Set corms out starting at the average date of last frost. Plant additional corms every week to ten days until August for continuous bloom.

Where to Plant

Glads do best in full sun. The soil should be well drained.

How to Plant

Prepare the soil by spading or tilling to a depth of at least 6 inches. Plant individual corms pointed side up, 4 inches deep and about a foot apart.

Care and Maintenance

Glads require very little care as they grow. Thrips can be troublesome in some years, marking the blooms with tiny white trails. Use Orthene, insecticidal soap, or neem to control them. The corms must be dug before a hard freeze. Cut the tops to an inch or so, and spread out the corms to dry in a warm place. After drying, remove

the fresh new corms from the old top and mother corm, and store at just above freezing temperature in onion bags. Large corms will flower the next year. Tiny cormels will not bloom for several years and are best discarded. Discard any cormels that show signs of rotting.

ADDITIONAL INFORMATION

The name for *Gladiolus*, with its sword-shaped leaves, is derived from the Latin word *gladius* ("sword"). The species types were native to South Africa, although there are kinds growing wild in southern Europe and the Near East. Illinois has been a leading producer of glads. There is a glad festival every summer in Momence in Kankakee County, a center of glad production.

ADDITIONAL SPECIES, CULTIVARS, OR VARIETIES

The tall, large-flowered hybrid glads are vigorous growers and they come in many colors. These are the prized kinds that are grown for the commercial cut flower market. While most cultivars have names, the names may mean little to gardeners. Buy the colors and kinds that appeal to you when you look at the pictures on the bulb displays or in the catalogs. *G. primulinus* hybrids are somewhat less vigorous than the taller kinds, but they are more graceful, especially for use in arrangements. (The larger-flowered types are often too big for use in most homes.)

Lily

Lilium sp.

Zones: All
Size: 2 to 8 feet tall with slender, leafy stems
Blooms: Early to late summer.
Flower Colors: White, orange, yellow, rose,
    red, maroon, and bicolors

Light Requirement:

ilies are the undisputed aristocrats of flowers. They have been objects of art and symbols of honor and purity throughout history, and they were referred to in ancient literature including the Bible: "Not even Solomon in all his splendor was dressed like one of these." (These biblical "lilies" may not have been lilies as we know them . . . but it remains a story worth telling.) There are many types of lilies, and more hybrids are being developed every year. The traditional Easter lily, *L. longiflorum*, is the most familiar one, and it can be grown in gardens throughout Illinois. There are, however, many better lilies of varying colors and forms. Every garden should have at least one lily. Some are very easy to grow: plant them and forget them. Others require special care.

WHEN TO PLANT

Plant lilies in the fall. Bulbs are available at that time in garden stores or anywhere plants are sold, with the names and pictures of the flowers on display. Lilies also are sold potted and in bloom throughout the summer. You can knock these plants out of their pots and set them in the garden any time during the growing season.

WHERE TO PLANT

Lilies need full sun for best performance, though most will tolerate light shade. Tiger lilies will grow in full shade, and will even bloom well, but they will be tall and weak. Good drainage is always a must.

HOW TO PLANT

Lilies do best when the bulbs are deeply planted in deeply prepared soil. The plants make roots from the underground stems and from the bottoms of the bulbs. Spade the soil a foot deep, making sure there is good drainage. If drainage is poor, construct raised beds or install tiles. Plant the bulbs twice as deep as they are tall; for example, a 3-inch bulb should be planted 6 inches deep. Make an exception to this rule when you plant Madonna lilies—plant them one inch deep.

CARE AND MAINTENANCE

Most lilies require some care. Taller ones need support. Relegate them to the back of the garden where they can lean on a fence or be staked. Try planting tall lilies so they grow up through shorter plants that can support them. Deadheading keeps the plants looking attractive as remaining buds open. Many lilies are excellent as cut flowers. Intelligent fertilizing will improve the growth of these plants and increase the numbers of flowers. Apply a balanced fertilizer in spring as the plants begin to grow. Keep the fertilizer away from developing foliage. The soil needs to be moist and cool; shade from other lower-growing plants or mulch is helpful. Aphids and slugs can be troublesome. Insecticidal soap will keep aphids at bay. Use slug bait around the plants, starting early while the slugs are still small. Repeated baiting will be necessary. Some lilies are quite susceptible to a viral disease that can be very destructive. Others are seemingly unaffected by the same disease, and they grow on happily. Buy bulbs from reliable dealers to reduce the virus problem. If plants begin to show symptoms (malformed or spotted leaves), destroy them. Remove spent tops in the fall. Lilies grow from hardy bulbs, although some lily varieties are marginally hardy in northern Illinois. These marginally hardy plants will benefit from mulching with straw to prevent freezing and thawing.

ADDITIONAL INFORMATION

Lilium is the Latin name for the lily.

ADDITIONAL SPECIES, CULTIVARS, OR VARIETIES

Virtually all modern garden lilies are hybrids. They have been developed from species lilies collected all over the world. Species lily bulbs are still available, and many of these plants are quite unusual. There are far too many kinds of lilies to list them here. For a rather long listing and for other information on growing these magnificent plants, contact the North American Lily Society, Box 476, Waukee, IA 50263. My favorite lilies: regal, *L. regale*, for overall use and for cutting; tiger lily, *L. tigrinum*, for naturalizing and for tough situations; and a plethora of new hybrids for bedding.

Spring-Flowering Bulbs

Chionodoxa luciliae, Crocus vernus, Scilla sibirica, others

Zones: All **Size:** 6 to 12 inches tall and wide **Bloom:** March, April, May **Flower Colors:** White, purple, pink, yellow, striped **Foliage:** Deciduous; dies down following bloom	**Light Requirement:**

*T*he many kinds of spring-flowering bulbs are delightful harbingers of the season, reminding us that even after the toughest winter, there will be flowers. Tulips and daffodils are the most familiar, but there are many other kinds, commonly referred to as "minor" bulbs. These faithful little plants are all perfectly hardy. Once planted, there is little that needs to be done to them except to enjoy them. Glory of the snow, *Chionodoxa luciliae,* has blue star-shaped flowers with white centers, 6 or 8 per stem above a cluster of ribbon-like leaves. A pink cultivar is much rarer. It blooms just as the snow melts at 6 or 8 inches high. You may see crocuses, *Crocus vernus,* blooming sometimes before the snow has melted. Where protected on the south side of a house, they will bloom in early March. The first one is always a welcome sight. The leaves are grass-like and often striped down the center, and the plants themselves are about 5 inches tall. Their 3-inch flowers are purple, blue, white, yellow, and striped. They open on sunny days and may stay closed when it is cloudy. Squills, *Scilla sibirica,* are woodland plants that will tolerate quite a bit of shade. Their flowers are blue or white in clusters of 5 or 6 per stem, growing from a rosette of strap-shaped leaves. Squills certainly spread. There is a shady yard covered with them each spring near our home, and people plan to stop by to see them every year. Even though this lawn is mowed, the squills grow on and even increase in number.

WHEN TO PLANT

Plant spring-flowering bulbs in the fall. You can find them in garden centers shortly after Labor Day. The earlier you get them in the ground, the better they will flower the next spring.

WHERE TO PLANT

These are small plants. They all prefer full sun but will be quite happy in the partial shade of leafless, deciduous trees or full shade at the north side of the house. They can stand moist soils, but they don't want to be drowned all spring.

HOW TO PLANT

There is no need for any special soil preparation. These bulbs will grow in any garden soil where shrubs are growing, in natural areas, or where annuals will be planted. The bulbs are tiny. Plant them about 2 inches deep, using a trowel or bulb planter. In borders, plant them in groups of half a dozen, spaced 3 to 6 inches apart. For naturalizing in a lawn or a wooded area, scatter the bulbs at random and plant them where they fall.

CARE AND MAINTENANCE

Once they are growing, these plants need virtually no care. To replenish the bulbs, keep the foliage on as long as possible after the blooms die down. Squirrels and mice will try to dig up the bulbs. If this is a problem, cover with chicken wire after planting. The wire can be removed in spring as new leaves arise.

ADDITIONAL INFORMATION

If these bulbs are planted in the lawn, mowing may need to be delayed until the leaves have ripened. This may not bother someone who lives in a rural area, but fastidious gardeners in upscale neighborhoods may be a little uptight about it. Keep this in mind if you want to plant bulbs in the lawn. Your alternative is to be prepared to replant each fall. If some plants do survive, all the better.

ADDITIONAL SPECIES, CULTIVARS, OR VARIETIES

Other spring bulbs include: trout lilies, *Erythronium*, with 2 leaves spotted like a trout and a single yellow flower to 6 inches; grape hyacinth, *Muscari*, which has grape-like clusters of purple flowers to 6 inches; snowdrops, *Galanthus*, growing to 6 inches tall, with drooping pure-white blooms; and winter aconite, *Eranthis*, which has leaves immediately beneath yellow buttercup-like flowers on a 3- to 8-inch-tall plant.

Tuberous Begonia

Begonia × tuberhybrida

Zones: All
Size: 12 inches tall and wide
Blooms: All summer
Flower Colors: Red, orange, yellow, pink

Light Requirement:

---

*I*f you want color in shaded situations, the tuberous begonia is spectacular. It has huge, exquisite 6-inch camellia-like blooms in all colors except blues. While the newer cultivars are advertised to tolerate full sun, these are in reality shade plants. They are perfect for the patio or porch in containers or hanging baskets, and for shady spots in the garden, they can't be matched. Until recently, these plants were grown only from tubers that had been started from seed months before. All named cultivars were vegetatively propagated, placing them in the luxury category and limiting their use. Today the most popular cultivars are started from seed, and they perform just as well.

WHEN TO PLANT

Sow the fine, dust-like seed in December under lights at 70 degrees Fahrenheit, scattering it on top of moist propagating medium. Transplant the seedlings when large enough to handle into pots. Set out when all danger of frost has passed.

WHERE TO PLANT

Plant tuberous begonias where they will get filtered shade at least during the middle of the day. These plants are excellent for bedding on wooded properties, or you may use them in planters, pots, or hanging baskets.

HOW TO PLANT

Prepare the soil by spading or tilling to a depth of 6 inches. Good drainage is essential. Tuberous begonias prefer a fibrous organic soil, but they will tolerate any soil that is well prepared. Tubers and started plants are available from garden centers in spring. Plant tubers in the garden after danger of a freeze is past, setting them hollow side up so that the tip is an inch below the soil surface. Set started plants at the same depth they grew in the pots and about

12 inches apart. Another planting method is to plunge pots in spots in the garden where a little color is needed. Hanging baskets can be set out when there is no danger of frost.

CARE AND MAINTENANCE

Tuberous begonias are particular about water. Water them thoroughly and let them dry so the crowns and roots have a chance to get some air before watering again. Watering too much or too frequently will result in crown rot. The large flowers must be removed when they have faded. This will stimulate more blooms, and it will reduce the incidence of botrytis that sometimes affects plantings. Slugs can be troublesome, and earwigs may damage the blooms. Slug bait and Sevin insecticide are effective controls. The first freeze will kill the tops, after which the tubers must be dug up if the plants are to be saved. Allow the soil to dry, and shake the tubers loose. Store them in boxes of dry peat at about 45 degrees Fahrenheit for the winter. If grown in pots, the plants may be simply dried down and stored in the pots. Six weeks before the frost-free date, water the pots and set them in a warm place to begin growing. Tubers can be potted up or planted in the garden as described in the "How to Plant" paragraph.

ADDITIONAL INFORMATION

Tuberous begonias are native to South America. They were named for Michel Begon, an avid botanist and Governor of French Canada during the 1600s. If you have an especially good spot for plants, potted begonias can be moved in for the winter—or the garden plants can be lifted, the soil washed off roots, and potted with soil mix for indoor bloom.

ADDITIONAL SPECIES, CULTIVARS, OR VARIETIES

There are many named cultivars of tuberous begonias. Most of these names mean little to the average gardener; buy tubers according the pictures on the display or from garden catalogs. Started plants are usually in bloom so you will be able to see what you are buying. The exception to this is the 'Non-Stop' strain of seed-started plants. These are available in single colors or in a mix.

Tulip

Tulipa hybrids

Zones: All
Size: 6 to 36 inches tall, spread 12 inches
Bloom: March, April, May
Flower Colors: Red, orange, yellow, purple,
   pink, white, green, and blends
Type: Deciduous; dies down after blooming
   finishes

Light Requirement:

Tulips are probably the best-known and most loved of the garden flowers. These most colorful of spring flowers are almost indispensable parts of the landscape. Nearly anyone with a little piece of ground has planted a few of these undemanding flowers and been rewarded with their blooms. The history of these flowers is not like that of any other plant. Tulips were grown in Turkish gardens before 1550 when the first bulbs were brought to Europe. In Holland, their commercial value was quickly recognized, and the result was tremendous demand for any new and different variety. By 1620 speculators had driven up the prices of unusual bulbs to astronomical levels in a phenomenon known as "Tulipomania." Some of the highest-priced were striped or mottled kinds, which were later discovered to be infected with a virus that caused the unusual patterns. Tulipomania collapsed around 1637, and fortunes were lost. Holland is still the major producer of tulip bulbs. The auction at Aalsmeer is the number-one wholesale market for the cut blooms.

WHEN TO PLANT

Tulips are fully hardy spring-flowering bulbs, and they must be planted in the fall.

WHERE TO PLANT

Tulips do best in full sun, but they will tolerate the filtered shade of bare deciduous trees. They seem to prefer soils that are heavier than those preferred by other bulbs, but they do need good drainage or the bulbs will rot.

How to Plant

Spade the soil for tulips to a depth of at least 12 inches, making sure
the drainage is good. If necessary, consider raised beds or drain tiles.
Plant the bulbs 6 inches deep and 8 to 12 inches apart. These flowers
look best in masses, so don't be tempted to plant rows of them like
wooden soldiers. Plant groups of half a dozen or a dozen in one
place, or plant full beds of them. Species and shorter tulips can be
naturalized: scatter the bulbs, and plant them where they fall. Soak
the bulbs after planting. If planting is late, the bulbs may not have
time to make roots before the ground freezes. In that case, 4 inches
of straw will insulate the ground so that it doesn't freeze up quite
as fast.

Care and Maintenance

Tulips require very little care. Their major pests are mice, squirrels,
and rabbits that dig up the bulbs. If these pests become a problem,
cover the planting with chicken wire. Remove the wire in the spring
when leaves begin to grow through it. Tulips appreciate fertilizer
applied in spring as leaves develop. Remove spent blooms. Make
sure the leaves stay green as long as possible to replenish the bulbs.
Remember, if the tulips are in a lawn area, you won't be able to cut
the grass until the leaves ripen.

Additional Information

You can force tulips in pots for winter bloom. Choose forcing cultivars and pot them in bulb pans, using a soilless potting mix. Plant
them bulb to bulb with the tips just exposed. Moisten the mix, and
cover the pots with clear plastic wrap. Store them in the refrigerator
for 16 weeks to break their dormancy, and allow the infant flower
buds to develop. Bring a few out into a bright 60-degree (Fahrenheit) place every week or so for continuous bloom.

Additional Species, Cultivars, or Varieties

Tulips are classified according to their size, time of bloom, and
flower form. Early-season types include most of the species tulips
and some named varieties. Mid-season types include the Mendels,
Triumphs, and Darwin hybrids, which have the largest flowers.
Late-season types are the tallest: Cottage, Darwin, and Rembrandt.
If you plant a selection of cultivars, your tulip blooming period can
last from early spring until June.

CHAPTER THREE

Groundcovers

*G*ROUNDCOVERS ARE LOW-GROWING PLANTS that are
normally found in shady glens, on the banks of streams, on the
forest floor, or in open sunny meadows.

There is no question that a well-tended lawn sets off a landscape,
but lawns have a big problem: they require a tremendous amount
of consistent (and costly) maintenance. They must be mowed,
edged, cultivated, fertilized, and watered. Bugs, weeds, and diseases
must be controlled. Most gardeners are trying to find ways to avoid
such maintenance chores. Another problem with grass is that it
won't grow everywhere. I receive as many questions about what
to plant in those shaded areas where grass won't grow as we do
questions on any other single topic. Turfgrasses are not suitable in
shade, on slopes, in soggy spots, in borders, and in areas beneath
low trees or shrubs, and in these places maintenance is just about
impossible.

There is a whole group of plants that are more suitable to such
conditions than are the turfgrasses. Low woody plants, vines, and
herbaceous species can be found growing in just these conditions:
these are the *groundcovers*.

The woody groundcovers are often found at a forest edge where
they are exposed to shade and light. Sometimes they seem to strug-
gle for their existence. Others inhabit rocky outcroppings or areas at
the seashore with its constant sun and wind. Herbaceous groundcovers are often found in the open woodlands, and they get light at
certain times of the year or of the day. They may flower beautifully
early in the season while light still reaches the forest floor. The natural adaptations of all of these plants to variable conditions make
them perfect for the groundcover uses our landscapes require.

We can plant groundcovers in beds under trees where it is too
dark for grass. We can use them as facer plants between grass and
the shrub plantings. They may be planted at the tops of banks, over

Chapter Three

walls, and in places where it is too hot, too wet, or too small for anything else. Sometimes we plant them just so there won't be so much grass to mow. Most of the time we plant groundcovers because they add charm to our plantings—they are interesting and nice to look at.

Many groundcovers are capable of spreading. Some, such as cotoneaster and sumac, root where they touch the ground. The vines do the same. Herbaceous types, such as lily of the valley and sweet woodruff, spread by rhizomes. Ginger produces abundant seed and rhizomes, allowing it to survive in difficult circumstances. Most spreading groundcovers are so well suited to their circumstances that they will keep out weeds when used properly—but you may need to keep the groundcovers under control as well!

On the following pages are profiles of just a few of these delightful plants. To see other members of the group, visit one of the arboreta or botanic gardens. We are fortunate in our wonderful state to have several outstanding places where plants can be observed, including the University of Illinois at Urbana/Champaign; Southern Illinois University, Carbondale and Edwardsville; the Chicago Botanic Garden at Glencoe; Morton Arboretum in Lisle; and the Klehm Arboretum in Rockford. We can also visit the Missouri Botanic Gardens in neighboring St. Louis.

Ajuga

Ajuga reptans

Other Name: Bugleweed
Zones: All
Size: 6 to 10 inches high, spreading
Blooms: Spring
Flower Colors: Blue, sometimes red, white, purple
Type: Semi-evergreen or evergreen; green, bronze, or multi-colored pink, or creamy foliage

Light Requirement:

*A*juga is a fast-growing spreading groundcover, evergreen or semi-evergreen. It will grow in full sun, but it tends to die out in the hotter parts of the state. It prefers semi-shaded spots and moist soil. This groundcover is most attractive in spring when it is covered with flowers. At other times, it is rather unnoticeable. It is one of the lowest-growing groundcovers and it serves its function well. In the proper location it becomes aggressive and will compete with weeds. It will invade the lawn under shaded conditions. Where this aggressive trait is an advantage, ajuga is an excellent plant.

WHEN TO PLANT
Ajuga is available from nurseries and garden centers in spring and is best planted at that time.

WHERE TO PLANT
Plant ajuga in sun or shade. It will grow very well where it is too dark for grass, under trees, and on the north side of the house. It will tolerate moist areas if the soil drains well.

HOW TO PLANT
Ajugas are sold like bedding plants in flats or pots. Prepare the soil by spading or tilling. Set the plants at the depth they grew in the container, spacing them 6 to 12 inches apart, depending upon how quickly you need cover. If the plants in the containers were grown in a light artificial soil mix, shake as much of it as you can off the

roots before planting. If the mix is left on the roots, the plant may be unable to grow out of it into the surrounding soil. Plants in this condition will wilt easily, and they will never become established.

CARE AND MAINTENANCE
Keep weeds out of the planting until the ajuga has become established. Crown rot is the major problem with this plant; if the planting becomes too dense or too wet, plants will die from this fungal disease. Prevent reinfection by working PCNB fungicide into the top 3 inches of soil before replanting. Water well during extended droughty periods. A balanced fertilizer in spring will aid in recovery from winter damage, and will hasten filling-in before weeds have the chance to become problematic.

ADDITIONAL INFORMATION
Ajuga comes from the Greek word *a* meaning "not" or "without" plus the word for yoke from which we get the word "conjugate." It refers to the structure of the flower, which has no upper lip on the corolla—hence no "yoke." *A. reptans* and the similar *A genevensis* are European in origin.

ADDITIONAL SPECIES, CULTIVARS, OR VARIETIES
There are several named cultivars of *A. reptans*. 'Braunherz' has deep bronze foliage. 'Jungle Beauty' has multi-colored leaves, but it reverts back to purple. The more aggressive 'Rainbow' has tricolored leaves. 'Silver Beauty' is cream and white.

Barren Strawberry

Waldsteinia ternata

Zones: All
Size: 4 to 6 inches tall, spreading by rhizomes
Blooms: Late spring
Flower Color: Yellow
Type: Evergreen

Light Requirement:

*B*arren strawberry plants look just like strawberry-producing plants. These evergreen plants have strawberry plant-like foliage in mats, but the flowers are yellow rather than white, and no fruits are produced. The attractive leaves are glossy green, giving the plants a pleasing, clean look and flowers are produced in profusion. The plant spreads by short rhizomes, so it is not aggressive. It makes an excellent edging plant that stays where it belongs without much care. Barren strawberry does best in full sun, but it tolerates light shade. It is tolerant of a variety of soils as long as it doesn't stand in water. It probably does best in the cooler parts of the state, as it sometimes stalls in hot, dry weather.

WHEN TO PLANT

As with most groundcovers, barren strawberry is best planted in spring. This allows it to become established before it must face the rigors of winter.

WHERE TO PLANT

Barren strawberries will grow in shade or full sun, and they tolerate most garden soils. Use them under trees, in front of shrub borders, as edging, or in beds to hide the ripening foliage of spring bulbs.

HOW TO PLANT

Barren strawberries are sold the same way as bedding plants, in flats or pots. Work the soil by tilling or cultivating, adding organic matter to hard, clay soils. Set the plants at the same depth they were grown in their containers, spacing them about a foot apart. If the plants in the containers were grown in a light artificial soil mix, shake as much of it off the roots as you can before planting. If it is left on the roots, the plant may be unable to grow out of the mix into the surrounding soil. Plants in such a condition will wilt easily, and they will never become established.

CARE AND MAINTENANCE
Barren strawberries benefit from watering in hot, dry weather. A balanced fertilizer in spring will help them recover from winter damage, as well as hasten filling-in before weeds can become problematic. Other than that, these plants need very little attention. Weeds can start before this plant becomes established. Clean-cultivate and apply a preemergent herbicide or a light mulch to prevent germination of weed seed.

ADDITIONAL INFORMATION
Barren strawberry, *W. ternata*, is native to the old Yugoslavia, Austria, Siberia, and northern Japan. Its botanical name, *Waldsteinia*, was given in honor of the Austrian botanist Count Franz Waldstein-Wartenburg.

ADDITIONAL SPECIES, CULTIVARS, OR VARIETIES
A slightly larger, related species is *W. fragarioides*. *W. ternata* is more compact and better suited as a groundcover plant than *W. fragarioides*.

Common Periwinkle

Vinca minor

Other Name: Vinca
Zones: All
Size: 3 to 6 inches, creeping
Blooms: Spring
Flower Colors: Lavender, lilac, blue, burgundy
Type: Evergreen

Light Requirement:

*V*inca is one of the most popular groundcovers for planting in Illinois. It makes an attractive cover and has blooms in the spring. Since it is slow to develop, weeds can become a problem before it is dense enough to keep them out. My experience has been that weeds, particularly grasses, will be a continuing problem, and vigilance is necessary to keep the planting from becoming a weed patch. Weeds are less troublesome when vinca is grown in the shade. The advent of the selective grass herbicides has made it much easier to keep the vinca clean. Fusilade applied according to label directions will kill the grass without damage to the vinca. Once established, vinca will spread, its long shoots rooting where they touch the ground.

WHEN TO PLANT

Vinca is available in pots from garden centers. Plant in spring so the plants can become well established before they face the rigors of an Illinois winter.

WHERE TO PLANT

Full sun or partial shade is satisfactory for this plant. Well-drained but moist soil is important to avoid stem rot.

HOW TO PLANT

Prepare the planting area by tilling or cultivating, incorporating organic matter if the soil is heavy. Consider raised beds or drain tiles if drainage is poor. Set plants at the same depth they grew in their containers. Space them 6 to 12 inches apart, depending upon how quickly you need cover. Plants on 12-inch centers will take 2 years to fill in. If the plants in the containers were grown in a light artificial soil mix, shake as much of it off the roots as you can before planting.

If it is left on the roots, the plant may be unable to grow out of the mix into the surrounding soil. Plants in this condition will wilt easily, and they will never become established.

CARE AND MAINTENANCE
Vinca requires very little care once it is established. Inspect it periodically for any weed invasion, and pull or hoe weeds immediately. During hot, dry weather, water carefully. Apply an inch of water, and don't water again until the soil is dry and plants begin to wilt. Water early in the day so the plants will dry off before nightfall. Keeping the plants wet is an invitation to stem rot. Winter sun may damage exposed plants. Before the plants begin to grow in spring, mow the bed with the power mower set at 3 inches. Remove the clippings and new green shoots will quickly fill in. Root and stem rot is vinca's major problem. If this disease appears, cut out the diseased plants and drench the planting with a copper fungicide such as Phyton 27 or Bordeaux mixture.

ADDITIONAL INFORMATION
Vinca is an effective cover for the ripening leaves of spring-flowering bulbs. Plant daffodils, tulips, squills, or other bulbs through the vinca in fall. There is no need to cut back the old leaves in spring, as they will disappear under the developing vinca foliage. *Vinca* is the Latin name that was used by Pliny for this plant. It probably derived from *vincio*, which means "to bind" and could refer to the long runners produced by this plant. Vinca has been grown since ancient times in Europe and western Asia. It is naturalized, having escaped from cultivation.

ADDITIONAL SPECIES, CULTIVARS, OR VARIETIES
There are many selections of vinca available in the trade, some with blue, pink, or white flowers or variegated leaves. Unfortunately, there is very little to choose from at garden centers: they stock whatever their contract growers produce. A garden center may carry a green with purple flowers, a variegated with white flowers, or another named cultivar. Take whatever you can get. Most will do just fine. If you want a specific cultivar, you may be able to get it through a mail-order catalog.

Common Wintercreeper

Euonymus fortunei cultivars

Other Names: 'Vegetus', 'Coloratus',
 'Euonymus'
Zones: All
Size: 6 to 12 inches high as groundcover
Blooms: June, July, insignificant
Flower Color: Green
Type: Semi-evergreen; foliage pale green,
 dark green with pale veins, variegated,
 or deep green turning purple in fall

Light Requirement:

*T*he wintercreepers are semi-evergreen plants with varying habits
from low and spreading to climbing vines. The most common are
E. f. 'Vegetus', and *E. f.* 'Coloratus', which are planted as ornamental
groundcovers where some refinement is needed. Some selections of
euonymus are too vigorous for such use. 'Coloratus' is one of the
more commonly used groundcover plants in Illinois. It is low-growing
and easy to keep under control. The color is deep green in summer;
in fall it turns plum-colored for the winter. In spring, new growth
develops a good green color, but quite often the overwintering foliage
never turns green again; it is best removed. 'Vegetus' is a larger, more
aggressive plant. The color is medium green, and the leaves are larger.
Unless there is sufficient room, this plant may be too much to handle.

WHEN TO PLANT
Wintercreeper transplants easily, but it is best transplanted in spring.
This allows it to become established before contending with a tough
Illinois winter.

WHERE TO PLANT
Wintercreeper tolerates full sun, and is also perfectly at home in the
shade. It isn't particular about soils as long as it doesn't stand in
water.

HOW TO PLANT
Euonymus plants are grown in quart-sized to 5-gallon-sized containers, and as balled-and-burlapped plants. The hole for planting
should be no deeper than the depth of the ball of the plant, and at

least twice as wide. Remove the plants from containers, and slice any circling roots. Set the plant in the planting hole and replace half the soil. Fill the hole with water. (Remove the burlap from a balled-and-burlapped plant and stuff it down in the hole.) Replace the remaining soil and fill the hole with water again. Make a saucer around the plant with any remaining soil. Space the plants at $1^{1}/_{2}$ to 2 feet.

CARE AND MAINTENANCE

These plants are susceptible to several insects and diseases. Crown gall, which causes large growths on the stems and roots, can kill the plants. Mildew and anthracnose disfigure leaves. Water early in the day and keep moisture off the leaves. Black vine weevils eat notches out of the margins of leaves and feed on the roots. Euonymus scale is the most damaging: spray with acephate about the time catalpas are in bloom to control it. Repeat 2 or 3 times during the season. To renew the planting, mow it in spring before the start of new growth with the lawn mower set at 3 to 6 inches. As the leaves begin to develop in spring, a balanced fertilizer will aid in recovery from winter damage. During dry spells, water early in the day so the foliage dries before nightfall. This will reduce foliar diseases.

ADDITIONAL INFORMATION

Wintercreeper is a native of China. It was introduced into the nursery trade in this country in 1906.

ADDITIONAL SPECIES, CULTIVARS, OR VARIETIES

This species mutates continuously and easily. There are so many cultivars that no one can keep track of them all. Find one that looks good to you, and use it. 'Coloratus' is probably the most reliably true to type, and you can't go too far wrong with it. In spite of its troubles, it is an attractive and serviceable groundcover.

Creeping Cotoneaster

Cotoneaster adpressus

Zones: All
Size: 1¹/₂ feet tall, spreading 4 to 6 feet.
Blooms: Spring
Flower Color: Pink
Type: Deciduous

Light Requirement:

With its glossy foliage and red fruits, creeping cotoneaster is one of the more attractive woody groundcovers. Its branches, spreading herringbone-like, pile themselves on top of one another, creating a layered effect. Cotoneasters are large plants that need their room. If planted too close together, they will require excessive pruning. With judicious pruning they can be kept in bounds and present a nice appearance. They are especially effective in rock gardens and cascading over walls.

WHEN TO PLANT

Cotoneasters can be planted in either spring or fall.

WHERE TO PLANT

Though tolerant of some shade, these plants are at their best in full sun. They do well in almost any soil, heavy or light, acid or alkaline, but they don't like wet feet. They do well in hot, dry situations as long as they are watered during extended dry periods.

HOW TO PLANT

Cotoneaster plants come in quart- to 5-gallon-sized containers, or balled and burlapped. The hole for planting should be no deeper than the depth of the ball of the plant, and at least twice as wide. Remove the plants from their containers, and slice any circling roots. Set the plant in the planting hole, and replace half the soil. Fill the hole with water. (Remove the burlap from a balled-and-burlapped plant and stuff it down in the hole.) Replace the remaining soil, and fill the hole with water again. Make a saucer around the plant with any remaining soil. Space the plants 2 to 3 feet apart.

CARE AND MAINTENANCE

Other than a little pruning and watering, these plants require very little care. Don't shear them; head them back. Cut overly long branches to a side branch that is growing in the same direction, but shorter. Prune in spring before growth starts or as needed during the season. Cotoneasters are low and twiggy, and they tend to collect trash that blows into them. Rake them out, or have a landscape contractor vacuum them out in spring. The shade produced by these somewhat open plants is not dense enough to keep out weeds. Pull or hoe the weeds; preemergent herbicides and grass preventers are also helpful. Cotoneasters are susceptible to attack by leaf roller caterpillars, webworms, and mites, as well as by fire blight disease. Control the caterpillars and webworms with *Bacillus thuringiensis*, the mites with insecticidal soap, and fire blight with Phyton 27 copper sulfate. Always follow label directions.

ADDITIONAL INFORMATION

Cotoneaster adpressus was introduced from western China in about 1896. These plants will spread by rooting where they touch the ground. The fruit—bright red berries (pomes)— are attractive in fall.

ADDITIONAL SPECIES, CULTIVARS, OR VARIETIES

Two cultivars known as 'Tom Thumb', and 'Little Gem' are available in the nursery trade. They make dense mounds of shiny green foliage and bear no fruit. These plants achieve a height of about half a foot in 10 years. Several other cotoneaster species and selections are listed in nursery catalogs. Some are taller, a few shorter.

English Ivy

Hedera helix

Other Name: Ivy
Zones: All
Size: 6 to 10 inches tall, trailing
Blooms: Fall, insignificant
Flower Color: Green
Type: Evergreen

Light Requirement:

nglish ivy is a beautiful plant with bright green leaves, the plant most people envision when they think of ivy. It spreads easily as a groundcover, quickly providing cover. As it spreads, it roots at nodes, providing good stability to the soils. It does an excellent job of holding banks. If supported, this plant can climb. It will go as high as the support allows, reportedly 90 feet in some cases. English ivy mutates freely. Many selections are made on the basis of hardiness in certain climates as well as for foliage form. In Illinois, these selections are made for both cold tolerance and summer heat tolerance.

WHEN TO PLANT

English ivy is available from garden centers in pots. It is best planted in spring so the plants can become well established before they must stand the rigors of an Illinois winter.

WHERE TO PLANT

Growing best in shade, English ivy especially needs protection from winter sun. It prefers a cool, rich, well-drained soil but will tolerate almost any situation. It tolerates dry sites and slopes when well established. It tends to be shallowly rooted.

HOW TO PLANT

Plants are sold in pots or flats. Prepare the planting area by tilling or cultivating, incorporating organic matter if the soil is heavy. Set plants at the same depth they grew in their containers. Space them 12 inches or more apart, depending upon how quickly you need cover. Plants on 12-inch centers will take 2 years to fill in. If the plants were grown in a light artificial soil mix, shake as much of it as you can off the roots before planting. If it is left on the roots, the plant may be unable to grow out of the mix into the surrounding soil. Plants in this condition will wilt easily and never become established.

CARE AND MAINTENANCE

English ivy needs annual pruning; heavily prune it in spring before growth begins. To keep the planting dense, mow every 2 years, using a rotary mower set as high as it will go. Rake out the clippings. Tips can be cut back at any time during the season to keep the plant in bounds. Aphids and mites can be troublesome. Insecticidal soap will control both. Leaf spot diseases develop in wet seasons. Use triforine or maneb fungicides where needed. Root rots will develop in wet sites. Provide adequate drainage, and water thoroughly but infrequently. Significant plant losses can occur when ivy plantings next to lawns are watered continuously by the lawn sprinkler system.

ADDITIONAL INFORMATION

Ivy roots easily from cuttings taken any time. Rooted sections can be taken up and used to fill in voids or to start new plantings. English ivy is a native of the Caucasian mountains, the Canary Islands, and North Africa. It has been cultivated since ancient times.

ADDITIONAL SPECIES, CULTIVARS, OR VARIETIES

Many selections of ivy have been made for Illinois conditions. 'Bulgaria' was selected by the Missouri Botanic Garden for cold tolerance and for its ability to stand droughty conditions. 'Thorndale' has larger leaves and will tolerate severe winters such as those of 1976-77. Some small-leaved selections of English ivy make excellent houseplants, pointing up the diversity of this species.

European Ginger

Asarum europaeum

Other Names: Shiny Ginger, Wild Ginger, Ginger
Zones: All
Size: 6- to 10-inch-tall clumps
Blooms: Late spring; insignificant
Flower Color: Green
Type: Semi-evergreen

Light Requirement:

European ginger is one of the most attractive groundcovers. It is slow-growing, spreading by short rhizomes, and thus is quite expensive. The glossy, kidney-shaped leaves are bright green and grow in neat mounds. This ginger does best in the shade, but it will tolerate filtered light and even some direct sun for part of the day. If planted in full shade or well covered by snow or straw, it will stay green all winter. Exposed leaves will dry up. This is not attractive, but the normal spring-cleanup will remove them. The plants quickly develop new, green leaves in spring and seem none the worse for the winter experience. The inconspicuous ginger flowers are borne under the leaves. They produce lots of seeds which germinate in the planting, helping to fill in.

WHEN TO PLANT
Plant ginger in spring so the plants can become well established before they must face the rigors of an Illinois winter.

WHERE TO PLANT
European ginger grows best in partial shade beneath overhanging trees or shrubs, or on the north side of a house. The soil must be moist and well supplied with organic matter. It is reported that this plant requires an acidic soil with a pH of 5.5 to 6.5. In our plantings, the pH is above 7.0 and the plants do very well.

HOW TO PLANT
European ginger is usually sold in 4-inch pots. Work the soil by tilling or cultivating. Set the plants only as deep as they grew in their containers, spacing them at 12 inches or closer. At 12 inches, they will take about 2 years to fill in. If the plants in the containers were

grown in a light artificial soil mix, shake as much of it off the roots as you can before planting. If it is left on the roots, the plants will not grow out of the mix into the surrounding soil. Plants in such a condition wilt easily and will never become established. We experienced this problem, losing many plants.

CARE AND MAINTENANCE
Little care is required once the plants have filled in. The cover is dense enough to keep weeds out. Pull or hoe weeds that start before the plants fill in. Protect the evergreen foliage with a 4-inch layer of straw applied in late November. Rake out damaged foliage in spring. Be careful to avoid damaging the rhizomes, which are very shallow. European ginger needs a lot of water. It wilts readily when too dry, so do not let it dry out. Water early in the day to allow foliage to dry off before nightfall. If it seems impossible to keep the plants wet enough, check to make sure the soil mix is not interfering with the rooting of the plants.

ADDITIONAL INFORMATION
The name ginger seems to refer to the pungent odor of the leaves and rhizomes. This species is native to Europe. The glossy leaves of this ginger make it especially useful in shaded areas because they reflect the little light that is available, brightening up the area.

ADDITIONAL SPECIES, CULTIVARS, OR VARIETIES
There are other gingers available as groundcovers, but none is as refined as European ginger. Canadian wild ginger, *A. canadense*, is coarser and taller. Its stems can be dried and used as a substitute for true ginger, *Zingiber officinale*. Canadian wild ginger is somewhat more heat-tolerant than European ginger. Sierra wild ginger, *A. hartwegii*, has evergreen leaves marked with silver. It is native to northern California and southern Oregon, and is hardy to Zone 5. It will grow in the southern part of Illinois. Mottled wild ginger, *A. shuttleworthii*, has mottled evergreen foliage. A native plant from the central Appalachians, it is marginally hardy in Illinois. Try it in sheltered locations in the far southern part of the state.

Gro-Low Sumac

Rhus aromatica 'Gro-Low'

Zones: All
Size: 1 to 2 feet tall, spreading as much
    as 10 feet
Blooms: Spring
Flower Color: Yellow
Type: Deciduous

Light Requirement:

Gro-Low sumac is a selection of the larger fragrant sumac made by the Burr Oak Nursery in Round Lake, Illinois. It is a dwarf, suitable for groundcover plantings in tough places. It is salt tolerant and grows best in dry, poor soils. It is adapted to either full sun or shade. These characteristics make Gro-Low sumac well suited to urban plantings where it actually likes the conditions instead of simply tolerating them as do most other plants. The plant develops a low mass of tangled stems, rooting where they touch the ground. It is excellent for stabilizing soils. Gro-Low has glossy bluish green leaves. Bright, yellow flowers in April are followed by red, showy fruit in late summer. Fall color is a good orange-red.

WHEN TO PLANT

Gro-Low sumac can be planted any time from containers. Balled-and-burlapped plants are available in spring and fall.

WHERE TO PLANT

This plant will be tolerant of just about any situation. Use it as a groundcover on banks, terraces, and fills, and next to walks and drives where it will get salted. Use it in newly developed, compact soils where other plants have difficulty.

HOW TO PLANT

Gro-Low sumac plants are grown in 1- to 5-gallon containers, and as balled-and-burlapped plants. The hole for planting should be no deeper than the depth of the ball of the plant and at least twice as wide. Remove the plants from their containers, and slice any circling roots. Set the plant in the planting hole, and replace half the soil. Fill the hole with water. (Remove the burlap from a balled-and-burlapped plant and stuff it down in the hole.) Replace the remaining soil, and fill the hole with water again. Make a saucer around the plant with any remaining soil. Space the plants 2 to 3 feet apart.

CARE AND MAINTENANCE

Gro-Low sumac is relatively trouble-free. There are a few leaf spot diseases that will affect it, and occasionally insects may take up residence. None is worth treating. If it gets too tall, Gro-Low can be sheared to 6 inches in spring. It will take about 2 seasons to get back to full height. Cut out any dead branches that may have been broken by snow load. A twiggy plant, Gro-Low will accumulate tree leaves and trash over the winter. Rake them out, or have a landscape contractor vacuum them out in spring.

ADDITIONAL INFORMATION

Leaves and stems of all the selections of fragrant sumac are pungently aromatic when crushed. Fall color is best on plants in full sun on dry sites. Withholding water late in the season may intensify the color.

ADDITIONAL SPECIES, CULTIVARS, OR VARIETIES

Gro-Low is the lowest-growing of the fragrant sumac selections. Other selections are larger, 6 feet tall and wide. They can be sheared to any height, but since they are naturally tall, it will be a continuous chore to keep them in bounds.

Japanese Spurge

Pachysandra terminalis

Other Name: Pachysandra
Zones: All
Size: 6 to 12 inches high, spreading 12 inches
Blooms: Early spring
Flowers: Greenish or pinkish white, fragrant
Type: Evergreen

Light Requirement:

any home gardeners finally give up trying to grow grass in difficult places such as a shaded garden or the north side of a house. When they ask for an alternative to grass, pachysandra is the one I usually recommend. Only hosta and lily of the valley seem as tolerant as this adaptable groundcover. Pachysandra will grow satisfactorily beneath trees and shrubs, but where it is exposed to too much sun or wind, it will develop an unattractive yellowish color. Under dense trees such as Norway maples or beech, these plants seem to compete easily with the shallow tree roots, and they thrive in the cool darkness.

WHEN TO PLANT

Pachysandra is available in pots or flats at garden centers. Though it seems to establish readily at any time during the season, it is probably best planted in spring so the plants can become well established before they must face the rigors of an Illinois winter.

WHERE TO PLANT

Dense to light shade is best. There are too many other kinds of groundcovers that do well in the sun to waste this one in sunny spots. It is one of the few that will stand dense shade. Soils should be well drained, but moist and cool.

HOW TO PLANT

Prepare the planting area by tilling or cultivating. Be careful not to disturb roots if you are planting beneath shallow-rooted trees, and incorporate organic matter into the soil if it is heavy. Set plants at the same depth they grew in the containers. Space them 6 to 12 inches apart, depending on how quickly you need cover. Plants on 12-inch centers will take more than 2 years to fill in. If the plants were grown in a light artificial soil mix, shake as much of it as you can off the roots before planting. If it is left on the roots, the plant will not grow out of the mix into the surrounding soil. Plants in this condition wilt easily and will never become established.

CARE AND MAINTENANCE

Pachysandra will have to be mowed down each spring before new growth begins, using a rotary mower set as high as possible. Collect the clippings. During the season, the plants may be clipped back to keep them in bounds if necessary. Pachysandra is a rather tidy plant and requires little tending. Stem rot, a fungus disease caused by *Volutella*, can be serious. If the disease is brought into a planting, a fungicide drench will be necessary to rescue it. Mancozeb, Daconil 2787, or Zyban drenched into the soil every 2 weeks throughout the season, starting in spring, is effective. Be very selective about where you acquire plants for your garden. Sometimes a gift plant will bring you more than you bargained for.

ADDITIONAL INFORMATION

White flowers appear in early spring just as new leaves begin. These flowers are otherwise not conspicuous, but because there is little else in bloom at the time, they are of interest. They are fragrant and seem to attract honeybees. Pachysandra lends itself well to inter-planting with small spring-flowering bulbs. Crocuses, squills, dwarf irises, trout lilies, or Chionodoxas are suitable. The pachysandra will hide ripening foliage.

ADDITIONAL SPECIES, CULTIVARS, OR VARIETIES

'Green Carpet' is a selection of pachysandra that has foliage that is deeper green and waxy. The cultivar is more upright than the species. Allegheny pachysandra *P. procumbens* is a native of the southeast, and grows as far north as Kentucky. It is not as hardy as *P. terminalis*, but it is suitable for the southern part of Illinois. It is otherwise very similar to *P. t.*, and is reported to be resistant to stem rot.

Juniper

Juniperus sp.

Zones: All
Size: 6 to 18 inches tall, spreading to 6 feet
   or more
Blooms: None
Type: Evergreen

Light Requirement:

*J*unipers are among the toughest of all evergreen plants. It has been said, "If you can't grow junipers, don't bother growing anything at all!" Juniper groundcovers are especially tough, and there are several species and cultivars. All have some similarities. They spread with long, horizontal stems that do not root where they touch the ground. Colors vary from bright green to blue. Junipers tolerate almost any well-drained soil. Some will grow in sand and endure droughty soils. They seem unaffected by soil pH; we have seen them growing nicely where the soil pH is near 8.0. Some can stand the salt from snow removal. All junipers prefer full sun. They grow in shade, but become sparse and leggy; there are other plants better suited for shade.

WHEN TO PLANT

Junipers can be planted anytime from containers. Balled-and-burlapped plants are available in spring and fall.

WHERE TO PLANT

Plant junipers in full sun on a well-drained site.

HOW TO PLANT

Junipers are grown in 1- to 5-gallon containers, and as balled-and-burlapped plants. The hole for planting should be no deeper than the depth of the ball of the plant, and at least twice as wide. Remove the plant from its container and slice any circling roots. Set the plant in the planting hole, and replace half the soil. Fill the hole with water. Be sure to remove the burlap from a balled-and-burlapped plant, and stuff it down in the hole. Replace the remaining soil, and fill the hole with water again. Make a saucer around the plant with any remaining soil. Space the plants at 2^1/$_2$ to 5 feet, depending on the cultivar.

CARE AND MAINTENANCE

Junipers require pruning. Winter-killed branches need to be cut out in spring, and overly long branches encroaching on walks or other plantings need to be headed back. Cut out entire branches to a vigorous side shoot growing in the same direction. If the cut in made beneath an overhanging branch, it will not be exposed. When cutting back severely, be sure to leave at least some green growth on the remaining branch or the plant will cease growing. Do not cut into the dead area in the center of the plant. Once established, junipers are usually dense enough to keep weeds out. Hoe or pull weeds that do get started. Some chemicals will help rescue weedy plantings, but preventing weeds is better than trying to correct a problem. Junipers are susceptible to mites, which can be controlled by insecticidal soap. Tip blight (Phomopsis) can be severe in wet weather; spray affected plants with benomyl or triforine according to label directions.

ADDITIONAL INFORMATION

Junipers have been overused in unsuitable situations and have received an undeserved bad reputation. When planted in the right conditions, they do very well.

ADDITIONAL SPECIES, CULTIVARS, OR VARIETIES

Dwarf Japanese garden juniper, *J. procumbens* 'Nana', is 1 foot tall and spreads 5 feet. Color is blue-green in summer, purplish in winter. Space the plants 1 to 2 feet apart. Sargent's juniper, *J. chinensis* var. 'Sargentii', is 1^1/$_2$ feet high, spreading 10 feet. Its color is green. Plant at a spacing of 3 to 6 feet. Salt tolerant and resistant to twig blight, it is one of the most commonly used junipers. Waukegan juniper, *J. horizontalis* 'Douglasii', is 6 inches tall spreading to 10 feet. Its color is gray-green, turning purple in fall. Waukegan juniper is susceptible to tip blight. Andorra juniper, *J. h.* 'Plumosa', grows to 15 inches tall and spreads 8 feet. Its blue-green color turns plum in fall. It has a soft texture, and is susceptible to tip blight. Blue rug juniper, *J. h.* 'Wiltonii', is the lowest growing at 6 inches. It spreads to 6 feet, but slowly. Its color is silvery-blue. It is somewhat susceptible to tip blight.

Lily of the Valley

Convallaria majalis

Zones: All
Size: 6 to 8 inches tall
Blooms: Spring
Flowers: White, pink, fragrant
Type: Deciduous; leaves die down in
   midsummer

Light Requirement:

*T*he fragrance! The fragrance alone makes this different kind of
flowering groundcover valuable. How many children have pulled
a handful of lily of the valley and rushed home to Mom with their
treasures? Just a few in a jelly glass on the kitchen table perfume the
whole room. Lily of the valley has attractive green foliage that comes
up early. The flowers are tiny, bell-shaped, and borne between pairs
of upright leaves along short stalks (forming racemes) in May. They
make good cut flowers and have been grown in greenhouses for
centuries. These plants spread aggressively and will cover an area in
a short time. Don't plant them where they can get away and invade
the lawn or flower border.

WHEN TO PLANT

Starts of these plants are called "pips." These are short pieces of
rhizome that have two or three buds. They are available from seed
catalogs or at some garden centers. Occasionally a garden center will
stock started pips in pots. Divisions may be made of existing plants.
Plant in spring.

WHERE TO PLANT

Lily of the valley is a shade plant; it is an excellent plant for a spot
where nothing else will grow. It tolerates terrible soils and will grow
in an alley if it has a chance. For best growth and flowering, however, a rich organic soil is preferred.

HOW TO PLANT

Prepare the soil by tilling or cultivating. Plant single pips 3 to 4
inches apart, setting them so that the buds on the pips are just at

the soil surface. Divisions can be spaced at 6 to 8 inches. Properly spaced and well fertilized, these plants will fill in the second year.

CARE AND MAINTENANCE

Lily of the valley dies down each fall, and the leaves should be raked out of the bed. If you are growing this plant for its flowers, apply fertilizer and organic mulch. In hot dry weather, plants may be damaged by spider mites. Insecticidal soap will help. In wet weather, slugs may be a problem. Baits are effective.

ADDITIONAL INFORMATION

The name *Convallaria* is derived from the Latin word *convallis*, "the valley." The plants are widely distributed throughout Europe. They have been grown in the Netherlands for centuries as cut flowers and for their pips; pips were formerly shipped in great numbers to greenhouses in this country to be forced for the florist trade. The berries are showy, but poisonous. Remove them!

ADDITIONAL SPECIES, CULTIVARS, OR VARIETIES

'Flora Pleno' is a double with flowers larger than those of the species. 'Rosea' has blooms that are pale pink instead of the normal white.

Sweet Woodruff

Galium odoratum

Zones: All
Size: 6 to 8 inches tall and wide
Blooms: May or June
Flowers: White, fragrant
Type: Deciduous; leaves die down in
   late summer.

Light Requirement:

*T*his is an old-fashioned garden plant that has been used for groundcovers, in naturalized areas, and in rock gardens for generations. Fragrant white flowers appear in late spring above whorls of 6 to 8 leaves spaced along upright stems. The fragrance is familiar to many of us who spent time in the country as children, though we may never have really known where the aroma came from. The dried and crushed leaves are used for potpourris and have the fragrance of newly cut hay. As a groundcover, sweet woodruff is perfectly happy in the shade of overhanging trees. It tolerates the deep shade of Norway maple and competes well with the tree's shallow roots. This is a plant that can be put in that spot under the maple in the front yard where nothing else will grow. Sweet woodruff combines well in less demanding situations with spring-flowering bulbs or with English ivy. If conditions are good, the plants will fill in rapidly, and they may invade lawn or other border plantings.

WHEN TO PLANT
Sweet woodruff is best planted in spring so the plants can become well established before they must face the rigors of an Illinois winter.

WHERE TO PLANT
Plant in medium to deep shade. It grows best in a cool, moist, but well-drained soil.

HOW TO PLANT
Sweet woodruff plants are sold like bedding plants in flats or pots. Prepare the soil by spading or tilling. Set the plants at the depth they grew in the container and space them 6 to 12 inches apart, depending upon how quickly you need cover. If the plants in the

containers were grown in a light artificial soil mix, shake as much of it as you can off the roots before planting. If it is left on the roots, the plant will not grow out of the mix into the surrounding soil. Plants in this condition wilt easily and may fail to become established.

CARE AND MAINTENANCE

Sweet woodruff dies down to the ground in fall, later than lily of the valley. The dead tops should be raked out in fall or in spring. Fertilize lightly in spring for best flower production. Shear during the season to keep in bounds. If the plants invade nearby plantings, hoe or pull them out. Sweet woodruff is free of serious diseases and insect pests.

ADDITIONAL INFORMATION

Sweet woodruff is native to Europe and western Asia. *Galium* is from the Greek word *galion*; according to Dioscorides, this was a plant used to curdle milk.

Ornamental Grasses

*I*LLINOIS IS THE PRAIRIE STATE—the prairies that now produce corn were once covered by tall grasses. The most important tall grass was big bluestem, reaching ten feet high and extending as far as the horizon. There isn't much native tall prairie grass left, but interest in these plants has increased, and more and more people are planting prairies. The Illinois Department of Conservation has restored prairies in various places throughout the state, and some conservation districts are doing the same thing. The plantings include the bluestems and other native grasses.

Big bluestem is only one of many ornamental grasses—in fact, there are hundreds. They have been gracing the natural landscapes throughout history, and now they are being planted to bring color and movement into the garden. They also bring sound and mass. The volume of grasses is one of their more interesting features. The plants grow from nothing in the spring to large masses of foliage and blooms by summer's end. Many stay through the winter, providing something to look at that is more interesting than snow-covered bare ground.

Ornamental grasses vary in height from a few inches to more than ten feet tall. They can be used as edging, as border plants, in the perennial garden, for hedges, and for screens. They can be planted in containers, next to water features, or as specimens. Many are excellent for cutting and for dried flower arrangements.

These grasses require so little care that they can be planted and forgotten until they enliven the landscape with their presence. They require no staking, pruning, or pest control. The native kinds will stand any weather that Illinois has to offer; they evolved with it.

Unheard of a decade ago, there are grass gardens being planted in which form, size, color, and texture create the interest. The grasses mix well with other flowers, too. The prairie was more than grass: sunflowers, Joe-Pye weed, rattlesnake master, and other taller kinds of plants shared the land with grasses. Today they fit together well in the garden.

Chapter Four

Ornamental grasses vary in hardiness. Those native to Illinois are hardy, most of them in all parts of the state. Exotic grasses may be partially hardy, or they may need to be handled like annuals and replanted each year. Some are worth trying even though they may be lost every few years. Some gardeners go to extremes to grow varieties that aren't recommended for Illinois—and make liars of us who say it can't be done! Tall pampas grass is not hardy in northern Illinois, but there are people who protect it and get it through winter so that it will later grace their gardens with magic plumes on 15-foot stems.

If you have never grown ornamental grasses in your garden, try one or two. Some of the smaller ones will fit in any garden. Some of these are described in the following pages. Most will grow in any good garden soil. If you are starting an ornamental grass garden, plant several of the kinds that interest you in a trial garden. Make note of the dates they begin to grow in spring, how tall the leaves become, and their color. Indicate when the flower arises, how tall it grows, and what color it is. Record how much the plant spreads and whether it stays presentable in winter or whether leaves and stalks needs to be removed in fall.

Once you have the profile for each grass, seeing where it fits in the garden plan is easy. Be sure to draw your plan, to scale if possible, and try to follow it as best as you can. Even after you have the garden planted, you will find yourself looking at other kinds of grasses that show up in neighbors' gardens, at the conservatory, and in demonstration plantings at garden centers. Take a few home and try them. If they fit, buy more.

Ornamental grasses, especially grass gardens, are new and there is a lot to be learned. If you begin to grow them, your garden will be different from anyone else's. No matter what anyone says, unless you try a grass in your garden, you won't know how it will grow there. That is part of the fun of gardening; every garden is different.

Here are some ornamental grasses worth trying in your garden. Plant some and enjoy them.

Dwarf Pampas Grass

Cortaderia selloana 'Pumila'

Zones: 7, treat as an annual elsewhere
Size: 3 to 5 or 6 feet tall
Blooms: Late summer
Flower Color: Ivory cream

Light Requirement:

*P*ampas grass is the only ornamental grass familiar to most people. The tall pampas grass reaches up to 12 feet with swaying, puffy white plumes. It is not hardy in Illinois, although some gardeners do try to winter it over by digging it up, putting it in a bushel basket, and bringing it indoors where it won't freeze. An alternative is to grow it in a tub that can be moved into a cold but frost-free place. Some gardeners say they save the clumps by covering them like hybrid tea roses. I seriously doubt that this is a practical system. Dwarf pampas grass is so vigorous that started plants can be set out after all danger of a freeze has passed, and they will flower before frost. This is the system used throughout Illinois. The plants are not overly expensive, so it is a practical means of growing them. Dwarf pampas grass is quite floriferous. The plumes are excellent for cutting for either fresh or dried flower arrangements. The leaves are attractive, gray-green, and about 3 feet tall. The plumes are carried well above the foliage.

WHEN TO PLANT

Don't be too hasty to get these plants into the ground, as they are warm-weather plants. Buy them as started plants. Set them in the garden in mid-May in the southern part of the state, about Memorial Day in northern Illinois.

WHERE TO PLANT

Plant dwarf pampas grass in full sun in a moist, well-prepared garden soil. Drainage must be good and fertility fairly high. These plants will have to do a lot of growing in a short time. Use them as specimen plants, temporary hedges, or accents in the perennial border, or use them in the cutting garden.

How to Plant

Prepare the soil as you would for a perennial garden. Turn the soil at least 2 spades deep, adding organic matter to each layer. If drainage is poor, consider forming raised beds. Dig the planting holes the same depth and twice as wide as the rootballs on the plants. Set started plants at the same depth they were growing in their containers. If the soil in the container is an artificial mix or much different from that in your garden, shake some of it off the roots and mix it with the soil that will go back in the planting holes. Water the plants thoroughly to settle the soil around the roots.

Care and Maintenance

Dwarf pampas grass will need watering if the weather is dry. Fertilize monthly with a balanced soluble fertilizer such as 20-20-20 (Peters, Miracle-Gro, etc.). Follow the directions on the label. In the southern part of the state, there is a good chance that the plants will overwinter. In the North, heavy snow cover or a mild winter may help the plants survive. Heavily mulching the crowns to prevent extreme temperature changes and heaving may provide enough protection to save them, but don't count on it.

Additional Information

If there is a greenhouse available, clumps may be divided in late fall, potted, and held over the winter for an early start indoors in spring.

Additional Species, Cultivars, or Varieties

Dwarf pampas grass is a cultivar of the tall species that comes from the pampas of Argentina. In California, the tall pampas grass is grown commercially for its plumes.

Feather Reed Grass

Calamagrostis acutiflora

Zones: All
Size: 4 to 5 feet tall
Blooms: Midsummer into fall
Flower Colors: Cream tinged with pink,
  turning gold in fall

Light Requirement:

Feather reed grass is one of the best of the medium-height ornamental grasses. It grows easily in full sun or light shade, in any good garden soil. It is not particular about alkalinity. While it is a grass of moist soils, it will grow in any soil as long as the drainage is adequate. It will tolerate heavier soils more than most ornamental grasses. Feather reed grass is a strongly upright plant, forming tight clumps. It is an orderly plant. The stems are stiffly vertical, and foliage, flowers, and seedheads stand upright, with flowers and seedheads held well above the foliage. The leaves are about 3 feet long with pointed tips, dull green, and rough. Feather grass is a cool-season grass, but it will tolerate the hottest summer days without looking tired. It stays attractive well into winter. It is one of the first grasses to begin growing in spring, about the time spring-flowering bulbs are in bloom. Although feather reed grass will grow in light shade, it tends to become weak and may not stand upright.

When to Plant

Divide plants in spring before or as growth begins. Potted plants are available during the season from ornamental grass specialists.

Where to Plant

Plant in full sun. Use feather reed grass as a specimen planting, as an accent at the end or back of the perennial border, around water features, by streams, or in masses. Soil should be moist but well drained.

How to Plant

Plants are available in containers, or they may be planted as divisions. Dig the planting holes as deep and twice as wide as the plant balls and set the plants in at the same depth they were growing in the nursery. Water them thoroughly to make sure the soil is settled around the roots. Space the plants about 2 feet apart; larger clumps may be planted slightly farther apart. These plants do not spread aggressively. They grow mostly within the clump.

CARE AND MAINTENANCE

As is true of most ornamental grasses, feather reed grass requires little maintenance. Remove the old leaves in spring.

ADDITIONAL INFORMATION

Feather reed grass is one of the easiest ornamental grasses to grow. If you are considering growing some grasses, this is a good one to try first. Its habits are neat, it has no pests, it is attractive all year, and its plumes can be cut for dried arrangements.

ADDITIONAL SPECIES, CULTIVARS, OR VARIETIES

Another cultivar, *C. acutiflora* 'Karl Foerster', is shorter, and it blooms earlier. Some place this cultivar in another species, *C. arundinacea*, but that hardly matters, because nurseries sell it by the cultivar name alone. Korean feather grass (growing upright to 4 feet) and bush grass (a tall weedy grass) are both *Calamagrostis* species. Make sure you know what kind you are getting when you buy these plants. Although their names may be similar, the plants are not.

ORNAMENTAL GRASSES

Fountain Grass

Pennisetum alopecuroides

Zones: All
Size: 1 to 2 feet tall, spreading the same
Blooms: Midsummer
Flower Colors: Green, turning reddish
or maroon

Light Requirement:

Slow-growing fountain grass grows into a fountain-shaped plant about 2 feet high. When planted in masses its characteristic shape is lost but its foliage and seedheads remain attractive. Its soft arching stems bear bottlebrush-like clusters of flowers at the ends. Fountain grass should be grown in a sunny, well-drained place. It will deteriorate in dry soils unless watered as needed; in shade, it will flower poorly or not at all. Its fresh flowers may be used in floral arrangements. Once they begin to dry, the flowers shatter and are no longer useful. The flowers eventually shatter outdoors as well, with seeds dropping into the clump. These flowers add nothing to the winter effect of the plants, but the foliage form persists all winter, offering something of interest in the garden. As the foliage ripens in fall, it turns briefly to shades of rose and gold before turning its winter almond-tan.

WHEN TO PLANT

Divide plants in spring. Seed may be sown in spring or fall.

WHERE TO PLANT

Plant in full sun in a moist and well-drained soil. Fountain grass is one of the best all-around grasses for the small home garden. Use it in the border, as an accent in the perennial garden, along walks, or next to water features. It tolerates moist soil and can be used near streams or ponds.

HOW TO PLANT

Sow seed in a small nursery bed. Set the seedlings in the garden when large enough to handle. Dig planting holes for plants and divisions the same depth and twice as wide as the plant ball. Set container-grown plants and divisions at the same depth they were growing at the nursery. Each clump should have several old stems and some well-developed roots. Set individual plants at least 3 to 4 feet apart; they will spread. For masses, set the plants at $2^1/2$ to 3 feet apart; the plants will grow into a meadow-like carpet.

CARE AND MAINTENANCE
Fountain grass requires no special care. These ornamental grasses are usually free of insect and disease pests. Water the plants in dry weather; these are plants of wet areas, and they will suffer in dry soils. In spring before growth begins, remove the overwintering foliage. Fountain grass is a warm-weather species. It will begin growth in May, later than the cool-weather kinds. If you are growing a cultivar, remove all seedlings that develop—sometimes they do not come true from seed.

ADDITIONAL INFORMATION
Fountain grass makes an excellent addition to plantings of 'Autumn Joy' sedum, Russian sage, or coneflowers.

ADDITIONAL SPECIES, CULTIVARS, OR VARIETIES
There are several species and cultivars of fountain grass. Black-seeded fountain grass is shorter with black flower heads and dark-green leaves. It is hardy to Zone 7, and it may winterkill north of that. Red fountain grass, *P. setaceum* 'Atrosanguineum', is an annual grass. It is spectacular, with dark-red leaves and flowers. Plant it as an accent, in masses, or in containers after danger of a freeze has passed.

Moor Grass

Molinia caerulea

Zones: All
Size: 4 to (sometimes) 7 feet tall, spreading
    to 2 feet
Blooms: Summer
Flower Colors: Green, turning brown in fall

Light Requirement:

*M*oor grasses are interesting specimens in the garden. Each one seems to have a special feature that makes it fun, even exciting. These are not plants to set at the back of the border where they will blend in. They won't blend in, and if they did, it would spoil their effect. Moor grasses are warm-season plants that are slow to start in the spring. They have erect, arching leaves to about 2 feet tall. The delicate flower clusters appear in early to midsummer; the flowers are held above the foliage, sometimes well above. Moor grasses do best in fertile, moist soils that have good drainage. They prefer full sun. In partial shade, their color is not as good, the plants may not be as strong, and the flower stalks tend to fall over. The soil should ideally be acidic, but the plants will grow in more alkaline soils too. High-pH soils are decidedly detrimental.

WHEN TO PLANT

Divisions are best planted in early spring. Container-grown plants may be planted any time during the season.

WHERE TO PLANT

Moor grasses may be planted as accents in the perennial border, though they are better as specimen plants or in beds or masses by themselves. These plants are too striking to be hidden among other plants. The soil must be moist and well drained; the pH should be at neutral or lower. If the soil is too alkaline, acidify it or import a more acidic soil. Acid peat will be helpful if there is good drainage. Aluminum sulfate or sulfur can be added to the soil to lower the pH.

How to Plant

Dig planting holes the same depth and twice as wide as the plant balls. Set divisions or containerized plants at the same depth they were growing in the nursery.

Care and Maintenance

No insects or diseases affect moor grasses. In fall the flower stalks and leaves break off just above the crowns of the plants. These must be removed, or they will blow around. This is one of just a few grasses that develop abscission layers and lose their leaves in fall.

Additional Information

Moor grasses are warm-season grasses that grow and develop slowly.

Additional Species, Cultivars, or Varieties

Cultivars of moor grass *M. c. arundinacea* may be short, as are 'Dauerstrahl' and 'Heather Bride'. They have compact foliage and 2- to 3-foot flower stems. Tall moor grass is a small, 3-foot tall plant, but it sends up a 6-foot-tall flower stem. The stems are slender and the flower heads airy. The slightest breeze sets them swaying, giving rise to a common name, "dancing moor grass." Listed in several catalogs is 'Karl Foerster', an older cultivar reaching 7 feet. Variegated moor grass, *M. c.* 'Variegata', is shorter, with upright arching leaves and purplish flower heads. The leaves are striped with white, from the bases to the tips.

Northern Sea Oats

Chasmanthium latifolium

Other Names: Spike Grass, *Uniola latifolia*
Zones: All
Size: 2 to 5 feet
Blooms: Late summer
Flower Colors: Pale green, turning brown

Light Requirement:

*N*orthern sea oats is a plant that is naturalized in some parts of Illinois. You might find it classified as *Uniola latifolia* by some authorities. The sea oats of the Eastern seaboard, *Uniola paniculata*, is closely related; it has extremely vigorous rhizomes that make the plants valuable for stabilizing seashores, but they are too aggressive for gardens. Northern sea oats plants are warm-season clump grasses that grow very slowly from rhizomes and are not aggressive. With their stiff stems and horizontal leaves, they resemble small bamboos. The flowers and seedheads are similar to those of eastern sea oats or to agronomic oats. They are borne on slender stems (culms), which droop under the weight of the flowers. Northern sea oats is excellent for cutting and for use in dry arrangements. The flowers do not shatter even if picked when the seeds are mature; they will last all winter in the garden as well. The darker brown color is a good contrast to the other grasses and perennials and to the snowcover in winter. The dried flowerheads are collected and sold at wholesale florist outlets and craft shops, sometimes dyed bright colors.

WHEN TO PLANT

Northern sea oats are planted in spring. Seed may be sown in late fall or in spring.

WHERE TO PLANT

These plants are natives of flood plains and they do best in a deep, fertile, moist soil. They are suited for use in shade gardens, borders, and sunny naturalized areas and around water features. They make good transition plants from the wooded areas to the lawn areas of a garden. They are interesting specimen plants which will be taller and may be weaker when growing in shaded locations. When planted densely, northern sea oats makes tall but satisfactory groundcovers.

How to Plant

Dig planting holes for divisions or container-grown plants the same depth and twice the width of the rootballs. Set the plants at the same depth they were growing at the nursery, spacing them 1 to 2 feet apart. The seeds may be sown in a small nursery bed. Set the seedlings in the garden when large enough to handle, or seed may be sown in naturalized plantings. Prepare the soil by tilling or disking. Broadcast the seed and drag to cover it lightly, or sow the seed with a conservation drill.

Care and Maintenance

This grass requires little care once it is established. Water it during dry weather the first season after planting. Remove the old leaves and stems in spring before growth begins. There are no diseases or insect pests that affect these grasses.

Additional Information

Northern sea oats will reseed itself within the planting. Seed may be collected for seeding elsewhere, but germination percentages may be low because many of the flowers are sterile. These warm-season plants may be late to start if spring is cool.

Additional Species, Cultivars, or Varieties

There are no cultivars of northern sea oats. There are several other *Uniola* species in addition to the eastern sea oats described above.

Plume Grass

Erianthus ravennae

Other Name: Ravenna Grass
Zones: All
Size: To 12 feet
Blooms: Late summer
Flower Color: Silver-gray

Light Requirement:

*P*lume grass is often called northern pampas grass because it looks very much like *Cortaderia selloana*. It is completely hardy throughout Illinois, while the pampas grass is not. Plume grass is coarser than pampas grass, but the color of the leaves, gray-green, is about the same. The foliage grows to about 4 feet tall. Later in the season the flower stalks rise to amazing heights, with many stalks per plant. An established clump will send up 2 dozen or more stems. In my estimation the plumes are not as clean-white as those of dwarf pampas; nevertheless, they are quite spectacular in the garden and are excellent as cut flowers for fresh and dried arrangements. Plume grass grows in moist soils, but in at least some areas it has been found growing wild in sandy soils. It may invade ditch banks if allowed to get away. Keeping it hungry may keep it under control.

WHEN TO PLANT
Plant in spring from divisions.

WHERE TO PLANT
These are large plants; give them plenty of room. They can be used as accent plants, for screening, or as specimens. They are effective next to large buildings, but they should be used with caution near smaller residences. Clumps near water features are effective if set high enough that the soil does not stay wet. Any well-drained garden soil is satisfactory for plume grass. The soil may be moist as long as it doesn't stay soggy.

HOW TO PLANT
Divisions and clumps are available in containers in spring. Dig the planting holes as deep and twice as wide as the clumps of roots. Set

the clumps at the same depth they grew at the nursery. Water them thoroughly to settle the soil around the roots. Set the plants on 5-foot centers.

CARE AND MAINTENANCE

No insect or disease problems are encountered in growing this sturdy grass. Clumps of plume grass will increase in size; they may be lifted and divided if they outgrow their situation. Remove the plumes and foliage in fall before the wind and snow knock them down. In the far northwestern part of the state, some winter protection may be helpful. Cover the clumps with straw to moderate the temperature fluctuations—freezing and thawing do more harm than steady cold temperatures.

ADDITIONAL INFORMATION

The plumes of this grass are not as wide or fluffy as those of pampas grass. Without the two to compare side by side, however, plume grass is a very handsome plant. Unless you are intent on taking the trouble to grow pampas grass, plume grass will serve in the same manner with a lot less work.

ADDITIONAL SPECIES, CULTIVARS, OR VARIETIES

There are a dozen or so cultivars and related species of plume grass.

Silver Grass

Miscanthus sp.

Other Names: Chinese Silver Grass
Zones: All
Size: Up to 6 feet tall, sometimes 12,
    spreading about half the height
Blooms: Late summer, fall
Flower Colors: Pale pink to reddish

Light Requirement:

*T*here are many cultivars of *Miscanthus*. Most are *M. sinensis* sold under a number of names. All are handsome plants, each with a distinctive character of its own. In general, all are 5 to 6 feet tall and half as wide. Giant silver grass is about twice as tall as the others. These are warm-season plants that do best in full sun. They do poorly in shade, failing to flower and eventually deteriorating in the reduced light. The soil type is not critical as long as it is well-drained; any good garden soil will do.

WHEN TO PLANT
Warm-weather grasses are best planted in spring.

WHERE TO PLANT
Silver grasses are used as specimens, in groups or masses, as screens or hedges, as backgrounds, and for cutting. The plumes are excellent for fresh or dried flower arrangements.

HOW TO PLANT
Nearly all the silver grasses are cultivars and must be propagated vegetatively. Divisions are sold in containers in spring. They may be available later in the season as well, sometimes in bloom. The planting holes should be as deep, and twice as wide as the division. Set the plants at the same depth they were growing at the nursery. Water thoroughly to settle the soil around the roots.

CARE AND MAINTENANCE
The silver grasses require little care once they are established. Water during dry weather the first season after planting and in extended droughts. These are warm-weather plants and can stand the heat if

they have adequate water. Remove the old leaves and flowers in the spring. The flowers are attractive all winter unless knocked down by unusually severe weather.

ADDITIONAL INFORMATION
One species of silver grass, *M. sacchariflorus*, is very aggressive; where it has escaped from cultivation, it may become a weed.

ADDITIONAL SPECIES, CULTIVARS, OR VARIETIES
Variegated silver grass is one of the most popular cultivars—*M. sinensis* 'Variegatus' has alternating green and creamy-white stripes running the length of its leaves. It has pink flowers late in the season but is grown primarily for its interesting foliage. *M. s.* 'Strictus', porcupine grass, makes stiff upright clumps 4 feet tall that are suitable for hedges. Most silver grasses are floppy, but this one is not. Its large plumed flowers are useful in fresh or dried flower arrangements. *M. s.* 'Purpurascens', flame grass, flowers earlier than do the others of the species. Its leaves turn fiery burnt-orange in fall. This cultivar is not as hardy as some of the others, and it may need winter protection. Giant silver grass, *M. floridulus*, grows to 12 or 14 feet. It is good for screening, but it requires a lot of room. With adequate water and fertilizer it will reach 12 feet by midsummer. Its stems are very strong and will support the plumes even in the wildest winter storms. Cut them down in spring. Not all of the *Miscanthus* cultivars are called silver grasses. Maiden grass is one of the oldest cultivars, but still one of the better ones. *M. s.* 'Gracillimus' flowers to 8 feet tall. It has narrow leaves with silver midribs and its flowers are white. Use them as cut flowers. 'Autumn Light' has golden fall color and grows to 6 feet tall. Eulalia has been an old favorite since Victorian times. *M. s. condensatus* grows to 7 feet tall and makes a magnificent specimen. The leaves bleach to a pleasing light tan with the first frost; the plumes are golden, turning purple, and excellent for cutting. Eulalia is hardy to Zone 4.

Tufted Hair Grass

Deschampsia caespitosa

Zones: All
Size: 1 to 4 feet tall and wide
Blooms: Summer
Flower Colors: Light green, silver, purple

Light Requirement:

*T*ufted hair grass is a cool-season grass that will stay green most winters. It is a plant that does well in moist places and partial shade, and it seems to prefer places where water seeps into the ground, keeping it soft. The grass will grow in shaded locations, so it is well suited to gardens beneath deciduous trees where most ornamental grasses find conditions too dark. Since the soil can be kept moist, the hair grasses will grow well and will even self-seed. These plants are grown mostly for the flower effects. The bloom period lasts all summer, and the flowers are borne in large dainty inflorescences. The clump of foliage is a mound, not much over a foot tall, but the flower stalk grows 2 feet or more above the leaves. It is ephemeral; unless planted against a darker background, its effect may be lost. Plant tufted hair grass in front of a dense yew planting or in front of dark-colored stones in a rock garden. A water feature with a waterfall or stream, especially with a dark-colored liner, will set these plants off very nicely. The flowerheads produce a delicate haze over the plants, and are excellent for cutting. The flowers, though they are delicate, are held up on thin stems that last all summer and well into winter. They will eventually be shredded by winter storms.

When to Plant

These cool-season plants may be divided in spring or fall. Container-grown plants may be set out anytime during the season.

Where to Plant

Plant these interesting grasses in full sun or shade in a moist, humusy, well-drained soil. Hair grasses should be used in the border, in naturalized areas, in shade gardens, as accents, or around water features.

How to Plant

Plants are available in containers, sometimes in bloom. Divisions may be purchased, or they may be acquired from other gardeners when they divide their plants. Prepare the soil by digging or tilling, adding organic matter. The soil should drain well; if it does not, consider raising the planting areas. Dig planting holes the same depth and twice as wide as the rootball on the plants. Set the plants at the same depth they were growing at the nursery. Water after planting to settle the soil around the roots. Space the plants about 3 feet apart, or plug individual plants into nooks and crannies in the garden. These plants will grow in soil-filled pockets or cracks in a rock garden. Tufted hair grasses can be started from seeds. Sow them in a nursery bed in fall, and move the seedlings when they are large enough to handle.

Care and Maintenance

No insect or disease problems affect tufted hair grasses. The plants must have water; soak them well in dry weather. Divide the plants if they become crowded.

Additional Information

Tufted hair grasses are naturalized throughout Illinois—there are lots of them where the conditions are right.

Additional Species, Cultivars, or Varieties

Tufted hair grass has some interesting cultivars. 'Bronzeschleier', which means bronze veil, produces huge numbers of arching golden-bronze flower stalks that cover the plant, hiding the mound of green leaves. 'Schottland' produces a more vigorous plant, usually 2 feet high with flower stalks about 4 feet tall. 'Goldstaub', "gold dust," is a good name for the tiny golden-yellow flowers of this plant. A different effect is created by 'Fairy's Joke', which has little plantlets among the flowers on top of the plant.

Perennials

*G*ROWING PERENNIALS IS A CHALLENGE to any gardener's skill and ingenuity. After several years of planting annuals and replanting them each year, many beginning gardeners decide that they will spend some money on perennials and save themselves a lot of work. The idea is that you simply plant the perennials, and every year they come up and burst into bloom.

Then reality sets in. After asking a few questions, the gardener will learn that perennial gardening is a whole new world, requiring special soil preparation and sometimes elaborate planning. But after the initial surprise, those who are serious will discover that this new world can provide a lifetime of pleasure, opening a door to a fascinating new group of plants with specific needs and challenges. The payoff is being able to grow a tremendous variety of plants with delightful flowers and surprising habits. There will be continuous change in the garden, day after day. Perennial flower growers can't wait to get out early in the morning to see what's new in the garden!

Getting started with perennials takes some thought and experimentation. The plant descriptions in this chapter will help you determine the perennials you would like to grow.

Because each garden is different, you will need to learn how your selections will grow in your garden. Soil, light, temperatures, water, and your attention will all affect how the plants behave. Plants that grow well in my garden (ten miles from Lake Michigan in a soil that has been tilled for a quarter of a century) may be utter failures in yours . . . and vice versa. The only way to find out is to plant some selections and see how they do. Start by setting out a dozen or so plants in a row. Label them so you can learn them by sight. Keep a record book, making observations such as where the plants were bought and when, planting date, flowering date, size, and any other information you think will be helpful. Some such as peonies that don't like to be moved will have to planted in their permanent spots, so take these qualities into consideration when you do your planning.

Chapter Five

Because perennials stay put for several years, soil preparation is especially important. The soil will need to be turned, and organic matter should be incorporated into it. When preparing a perennial bed, the rototiller just won't do. Annuals have shallow root systems, and tilling their soil 3 or 4 inches deep is enough to get them through the season, but preparing a perennial garden requires a lot more. We usually recommend that the garden be double-dug. That means to dig to at least two spade depths: 12 to 15 inches. This is not as daunting a task as it sounds, because you don't need to do it all at once. Dig a little now and more next week, and eventually the job will be done. Begin collecting organic matter: leaves, grass clippings, plant tops, kitchen scraps—whatever you can get. Compost the material on the garden or in a compost pile, or just dig it directly into the garden.

The third step is planning your garden. Study the descriptions of the perennials that interest you. Note size, color, when the plants flower, and whether there is a dead time when the plants will disappear from the garden. Draw the garden to scale on graph paper and mark the plants in areas on the plan. Changing them on a paper plan is easier than digging them up and starting over in your real garden.

After these preliminaries are completed, it is time to start planting. It is not necessary to plant perennials everywhere in the garden all at once. Where there are voids, fill in with annuals. A perennial garden is a dynamic thing and will change from day to day. Some plants you thought you wanted will not work out. Some plants you are thinking about discarding will later become interesting to you. When growing perennials, you will never stop learning new things. Visit the gardens in your area. Take notes. Talk to other gardeners. You will find we are all on a journey. Some have been on it longer, but all will happily share their experiences. Plant people are some of the greatest people in the world, and we're glad you are part of the family.

Aster

Aster novae-angliae, Aster novi-belgii

Zones: All
Size: 1 to 4 feet
Blooms: August to October
Flower Colors: Purple, pink, white, blue

Light Requirement:

 sters are reliable flowers for late summer and fall gardens. They bloom in profusion at a time when there are few perennial flowers left in the garden. Wild asters are in bloom at that time, but the hybrids have a wider range of colors, and larger and more prolific blooms. New England and New York asters are the kinds most often grown in Illinois gardens. Many are tall, about 4 feet, and they should be relegated to the back of the garden where they will have room to spread out. They usually need staking to keep them from falling over. Dwarf cultivars are suitable for the border and edging.

WHEN TO PLANT

Asters are planted in spring from started plants available from garden centers or mail-order houses. Some larger discount houses with garden departments are beginning to stock perennials.

WHERE TO PLANT

Plant asters in the sun or partial shade. Often these adaptable plants can be found growing naturalized along the edges of woodlands or old pastures. They will grow in any soil as long as it has sufficient drainage. Plant in the border, cutting garden, or naturalized areas; dwarf kinds may also be planted in rock gardens.

HOW TO PLANT

Work the soil by spading or tilling to a depth of 12 inches. Set the plants at the same depth they grew in their containers; space larger types 2 to 3 feet apart, smaller ones at 12 inches.

CARE AND MAINTENANCE

Asters require very little care, though you will probably have to stake the tall kinds. Pinching in July will reduce their height somewhat and increase the number of flowers. Clumps should be divided every 2 to 3 years in early spring. Few insects or diseases affect these plants.

ADDITIONAL INFORMATION

Asters are wonderful long-lasting cut flowers. Entire beds of asters can be developed by dividing large clumps and planting the pieces on 12-inch centers over a large area. Remember to pinch the plants when they are 12 inches tall. The result will be a mass of color in fall.

ADDITIONAL SPECIES, CULTIVARS, OR VARIETIES

'Alma Potschke', 36 inches tall, is bright pink. 'Harrington Pink' is 4 feet tall and light pink. New York aster, 'Marie Ballard', is powder blue and 3 feet tall. 'Professor Kippenburg' is 15 inches tall and sky blue. 'Snow Cushion' is short, 12 inches, with large white blooms. There are many other cultivars, and other species as well. Try a few of each of different kinds in your garden to see how they do. If you like them, divide them and plant more.

Astilbe

Astilbe × arendsii

Zones: All
Size: 1 to 4 feet tall
Blooms: June, July
Flower Colors: Pink, red, magenta, cream, white

Light Requirement:

*T*hough they are really from a different plant family, astilbes are often listed as florist's spirea in old books and garden catalogs. This misnomer doesn't affect their desirability in the garden, however. There is no shade garden that should be without at least a few astilbe plumes. Both the flowers and the foliage of these plants are delicate and feathery. Astilbes bloom about the time bleeding heart finishes, providing something new to look at in the garden. One of the most charming things about perennial gardens is the constant change; there is always something new just about to happen. Astilbes resent dry, hot weather. They can stand the heat, but they must have moist soil. If allowed to dry out, they will quickly deteriorate and will be finished for the year. Once established, astilbes would rather be left alone. The number of blooms and clumps will increase each year. Eventually, dividing will be necessary; postpone it as long as you can.

WHEN TO PLANT

Astilbe can be planted in spring or fall.

WHERE TO PLANT

These are shade plants. Put them in filtered light beneath somewhat open trees. They can stand full sun in the morning before temperatures rise; most important is a moist, well-drained soil.

HOW TO PLANT

Plants are available as divisions or potted seedlings from garden centers, nurseries, or wherever plants are sold. Mail-order catalogs list many cultivars. Prepare the soil by spading or tilling to at least a foot deep. These plants will stay put for several years, so good preparation is needed. Incorporate organic matter for improved structure and moisture retention. Set the plants at the depth they were growing in their containers. Water in thoroughly and mulch if the weather is hot.

CARE AND MAINTENANCE
Once established, astilbes require little care, though watering in hot, dry weather is essential. Fertilizer will often stimulate soft, floppy growth and fewer flowers. Slugs may be troublesome, as they are abundant in most damp locations. Baits are effective controls. These plants are affected by few other pests or diseases.

ADDITIONAL INFORMATION
Divide when plants become crowded. Lift entire clumps in early spring, cut into smaller clumps, and replant. Extra divisions are welcome gifts for other gardeners or neighbors. Try to keep track of the cultivar or at least the color when dividing the plants. Labels placed in fall are helpful. On darker-colored cultivars, the foliage is tinted red. It will stay attractive all season in protected, cooler sites. If growing in a hot location, it may deteriorate and need to be kept hidden behind other plants. Some cultivars make excellent long-lasting cut flowers.

ADDITIONAL SPECIES, CULTIVARS, OR VARIETIES
Astilbe × arendsii is the most commonly grown astilbe. Try 'Amethyst', with brilliant violet spikes that grow to 3 feet; or 'Deutschland', which is white, and 'Fanal', red (both are about 18 inches tall). Another astilbe is *A. chinensis* 'Pumila'. It is mauve, grows less than a foot tall, will stand dry spots, and may spread. It blooms later than the others, in August and September. The 4-foot 'Professor van der Wielen', white with arching plumes, and the coral-pink 'Ostrich Plume' are distinctive enough to be classified as specimen plants.

Bee Balm

Monarda didyma

Other Names: Monarda, Oswego Tea, Wild Bergamot
Zones: All
Size: 2 to 3¹/₂ feet tall and wide
Blooms: July, August
Flower Colors: Purple, red, pink, white

Light Requirement:

*B*ee balm is a popular plant for attracting hummingbirds, butterflies, and bees. If you can figure out where the bees are going, you may find the honey is good. (If you are allergic to bees, plant these flowers where you can see them but won't be getting too close.) Bee balm is attractive when in flower, covered with fluffy clusters of blooms, and after the small flowers fall, the seedheads remain attractive. This is a native plant, so it is perfectly at home in our Illinois conditions. It is a well-adapted, rather rambunctious plant; it will need room, and it may decide to spread. Plant it where you can control it. We find that taller cultivars need staking to keep them from being knocked down by storms. The center of the clump tends to die out after a few years, but the plants around the edge will continue to grow. This makes it unwieldy, and it takes up a lot of room. Dig it up and divide the live parts. In shade, it will grow taller and more floppy. Try the shorter kinds for the parts of the garden that receive less than full sun.

WHEN TO PLANT

Monarda can be planted in fall or early spring. Potted plants can be planted anytime during the season.

WHERE TO PLANT

These are large plants. Plant them at the back of the border, in naturalized areas, or in the cutting garden.

HOW TO PLANT

Divisions or plants are available at garden centers, nurseries, and at discount stores in spring. Other gardeners usually have more than enough divisions to spare. Prepare the soil by spading or tilling to at least a foot deep. These plants will stay put for 2 or 3 years, so some preparation is needed. Even though they will grow in wet places, they prefer the soil a little on the dry side. Make sure drainage is good; if the soil is wet, the plants will be taller and weaker. Set the plants at the depth they were growing in their containers. Space them at least 4 feet apart; they will spread. If tall cultivars can be planted closer together without looking too crowded, they will tend to hold each other up.

CARE AND MAINTENANCE
Bee balm requires only a little care. Tie up plants knocked down by storms and cut back tops after blooming. Most plants will make a new mound of leaves that stays attractive for the rest of the summer. Divide every 2 to 3 years.

ADDITIONAL INFORMATION
The leaves of bee balm make a pleasant herbal tea. The name *Monarda* was given in honor of Nicolas Monardes, a Spanish botanist. Few diseases or insects affect bee balm. Mildew will cover the foliage with white dust in fall when the nights are cool and dew is heavy. There is little that needs to be done, since the leaves have just about completed their work for the season by then.

ADDITIONAL SPECIES, CULTIVARS, OR VARIETIES
The species is red in color. Popular cultivars are 'Cambridge Scarlet', 'Croftway Pink', and 'Snow Queen'. 'Mahogany' is a little shorter and it blooms earlier. It is advertised as being mildew-resistant. Lemon mint, *M. pectinata*, flowers rose-pink on 2-foot stems. Shorter cultivars are reportedly available from some growers. Whether these are actually shorter is undetermined. All cultivars will be shorter in the wild where they receive less care and have competition from other plants.

Bellflower

Campanula sp.

Zones: All
Size: 1 to 3¹/₂ feet
Blooms: June to August
Flower Colors: Blue, violet, white

Light Requirement:

*B*ellflowers are a diverse group of plants, and include some biennials. They are suitable for the border, rock gardens, and the cutting garden. Some more aggressive kinds are useful in the wild garden or woodlands. The flowers are characteristically bell-shaped. The botanical name. *Campanula* means "little bell" in Latin. The most commonly grown campanula is probably Carpathian bellflower, *C. carpatica*. It is an excellent edging plant, generally a foot or less tall. Excellent for edging, it bears blue or white flowers all summer. The flowers are cup-shaped and face upward. *C. persicifolia*, peach-leaved bellflower, is 2 to 3 feet tall. Blue, lavender, or white flowers are cup-shaped and are borne on branched stems above the basal leaves. Excellent for cutting, the flowers will last as long as 2 weeks. This species will naturalize in woodlands; in the border it will spread, but it is not a nuisance. English harebell, *C. rotundifolia*, with dainty blue flowers, will naturalize and at times may be too aggressive. Some gardeners have labeled it a weed. If you can contain it, it will reward you with tiny blue bells throughout the season. Try a few before you commit your garden to it, and watch for signs that it wants to take over.

WHEN TO PLANT

Plant in spring or fall. Seeds of species may be sown in place in mid-summer. Named cultivars are available only as divisions or plants.

WHERE TO PLANT

Plant bellflowers in sun or light shade. The taller types prefer full sun, the shorter kinds partial shade. They prefer moist, well-drained soil. Carpathian bellflower will stand drier soil than most.

HOW TO PLANT

Prepare the soil by spading to a depth of 6 inches. Provide drainage if the area is wet. Plants are available from mail-order catalogs, garden centers, and nurseries in spring. Divisions and potted plants are available all season. Plant them in their permanent places in the garden in spring, summer, or fall. Set plants at the depth they were grown, spacing them 9 to 12 inches apart. Divide plants in early spring.

CARE AND MAINTENANCE

Campanulas require little care once they are established. Slugs can be troublesome in shaded, wet gardens, but baits will discourage them. English harebell may need to be restrained if it decides to take off on its own. Deadheading will keep the bellflowers blooming; flowering will cease if seeds are allowed to develop. Plan to divide the clumps every 3 to 4 years.

ADDITIONAL INFORMATION

Many other campanulas are used in the garden and in natural areas. Canterbury bells is a biennial member that is grown widely as cup-and-saucer bluebell. English harebell is listed under other common names such as bluebells of Scotland or Scottish bluebell, and also as a cultivar, 'Olympica'.

ADDITIONAL SPECIES, CULTIVARS, OR VARIETIES

Other campanula species listed in nursery catalogs are *C. garganica*, Adriatic bellflower; *C. portenschlugiana*, Dalmatian bellflower; and *C. poscharskyana*, Serbian bellflower. These may all be seen at botanical gardens and at many garden center displays. They are low-growing plants suitable for rock gardens or edging. They all require light shade. *C. glomerata*, the clustered bellflower, will grow to 18 inches. Two of its cultivars are noteworthy: 'Joan Elliott', 18 inches with deep violet-blue flowers in May and June, and 'Superba', which has purple blooms in early summer.

Bleeding Heart

Dicentra spectabilis

Zones: All
Size: 12 to 36 inches tall and wide
Blooms: May, June
Flower Colors: Pink and white, or white

Light Requirement:

*B*leeding heart is a favorite garden flower, identifiable to even the youngest child because of its distinctive flowers. The blooms are heart-shaped and have teardrop-like petals dripping from them, making them appear as if they are bleeding. These flowers are borne drooping along arching stems above deeply cut foliage. The large plants are attractive until summer when they suddenly disappear, leaving a large gap in the garden. Be prepared to replace them with large annuals or later-developing perennials—or plant them in natural-ized settings where their absence won't be noticed. Other species of *Dicentra spectabilis*, less familiar to most gardeners, are Eastern and Pacific bleeding hearts, Dutchman's breeches, and squirrel corn. These are native to the United States; *D. spectabilis*, bleeding heart, is an Asian species.

WHEN TO PLANT

Bleeding hearts can be planted in spring or fall. Potted plants can be planted all season.

WHERE TO PLANT

Partial to full shade is best. Direct sun early in the day before tem-peratures rise is acceptable. Full sun at midday will cause premature die-down of the foliage. A cool moist soil with good drainage is best.

HOW TO PLANT

Plants are available, potted and in bloom in spring, at garden cen-ters and nurseries. Divisions are available in fall or spring. Spade or till the soil to a depth of 12 inches. Set the plants at the same depth they were growing in their containers. Water thoroughly to settle the soil around the roots; a mulch to preserve moisture and keep the soil cool is helpful.

CARE AND MAINTENANCE

Bleeding hearts require very little care. When the foliage dies down, remove it; plants can be divided at that time.

ADDITIONAL INFORMATION

Bleeding heart plants increase in size and should be divided every 3 to 4 years. They produce seed in abundance as well, which means there are always extra plants to give away. These plants are always greatly prized by those who receive them. They require so little care that they are no burden, even for the most casual gardener.

ADDITIONAL SPECIES, CULTIVARS, OR VARIETIES

Two North American bleeding hearts are suitable for rock gardens. *D. eximia*, Eastern bleeding heart, is smaller and will bloom all summer in shaded gardens. It is pink, and there is a white form as well. *D. formosa*, Pacific bleeding heart, is best in cool damp locations. A hybrid of the two, 'Luxuriant', is superior in form, 2 feet tall, and blooms all summer; its foliage is finely cut. This cultivar stands heat without stalling if there is adequate moisture. *D. cucullaria* is the cream-over-white-flowered Dutchman's breeches. Tiny inflated breeches are borne over fern-like leaves. Squirrel corn is *D. canadensis*.

Columbine

Aquilegia hybrids

Zones: All
Size: 12 to 36 inches tall
Blooms: May to July
Flower Colors: Red, white, yellow, blue,
   violet, and bicolors

Light Requirement:

Whether they are a few tiny flowers blooming in an abandoned pasture or big hybrid flowers blooming in a garden, columbines are immediately recognizable. The unique flowers with their trailing spurs are favorites among gardeners and make excellent cut flowers for arrangements. The parents of present-day long-spurred columbines are native wildflowers of the Rocky Mountains. We have happened upon them while hiking in the mountains of Colorado, where they can be found blooming happily in May and June. Other species from Europe and Asia have contributed additional colors to the spectrum, which includes reds and yellows as well as the more common blue. The blooms of some hybrids are 3 inches across. Columbines will tolerate various soils as long as they are well drained and not allowed to become too dry. Full sun is fine, but flowering will be prolonged in light shade. These are mountain plants. They do grow in the open, but they are more commonly seen in the thin forests at high elevations. There are both tall-growing and dwarf kinds, suitable for the border or edging.

WHEN TO PLANT
Columbines may be grown from seed sown under lights in December. Sow the seeds and chill them in the refrigerator for 3 weeks. Then germinate at 75 degrees Fahrenheit. Started plants and divisions are available from seed catalogs or garden centers in spring. Set plants out when the soil is dry enough to till. Divisions may be made in fall.

WHERE TO PLANT
Plant columbines in full sun or partial shade in a well-drained, moist soil. Plant tall kinds at the back of the border; shorter kinds may be planted as edging. Columbines will lose their leaves in

midsummer, creating a hole where there once was a plant. Either tuck them in among other plants that will cover such bare spots, or plant annuals in place of them.

How to Plant
Prepare the soil by tilling or spading to a 6-inch depth. Plants are available as potted seedlings or divisions from garden centers. Set the plants at the same depth they were growing in their containers. Space tall cultivars at 12 inches, dwarf cultivars at 6.

Care and Maintenance
Columbines do require some care. The taller cultivars may need staking to keep them from being blown over in storms. Most cultivars are prolific seed producers and will reseed themselves very well. Some hybrids revert to their wild forms in the process. Deadhead to prevent seeding of hybrid cultivars which do not come true from seed. Leaf miners can disfigure the plants. Cut damaged foliage to the ground and destroy it. The plants will respond with a fresh mound of leaves.

Additional Information
The name *Aquilegia* may come from the word *aquila*, "like an eagle," perhaps referring to the similarity of the spurs on the flowers to the beak of an eagle. It is more likely that the name comes from *aqua*, "water," and *legere*, "to collect," in reference to the fluid that accumulates at the bases of the plant's hollow spurs.

Additional Species, Cultivars, or Varieties
The tall, large-flowered hybrids provide a good range of colors. 'Crimson Star' is crimson and white; 'Maxistar' is primrose yellow. 'Blue Shades' provides many tints of blue. 'Biedermeier Strain' is short, 12 inches, with white, purple, or pink flowers. 'Nora Barlow' is double-flowered, pink and red, and tinged with green. Species columbines are available as well. *A. caerulea* is blue and white, *A. canadensis* is red and yellow, and *A. chrysantha* is yellow. Shorter varieties for rock gardens include the white-flowered 'Nana Alba' (less than a foot tall) and the blue-and-white *A. flabellata* 'Mini-Star' (6 inches tall).

Coneflower

Rudbeckia nitida

Other Name: Rudbeckia
Zones: All
Size: 2 to 4 feet tall, sometimes 7 feet
Blooms: August to October
Flower Color: Yellow

Light Requirement:

*C*oneflower is a native North American plant. It is hardy and reliable, easy to establish, and rewarding in bloom. Most of the newer selections of hybrid coneflowers are short enough for the border garden. The species, *R. nitida*, is quite tall. It needs to be at the back of the garden and staked. All of the perennial rudbeckias make excellent cut flowers with long, sturdy stems. The flowers last a long time in floral arrangements, making them popular for use in late-summer bouquets. Coneflowers are at home in the middle to back of the garden, and in open naturalized areas as well. They will spread and persist without care as long as there is a little water.

WHEN TO PLANT

Coneflowers are best planted in the spring. Containerized plants may be planted any time during the season.

WHERE TO PLANT

Plant coneflowers in the border, in the middle of large beds, or in natural areas. They prefer full sun, but they will tolerate light shade. Stems may become floppy if grown in shaded spots. A moderately moist soil with good drainage is best.

HOW TO PLANT

Prepare the soil by tilling to a 12-inch depth. Any garden soil is satisfactory and there is no need to add organic matter. Plants in overly fertile soil will be weak and will need dividing sooner than necessary. Plants are usually sold in 1-, 2-, or 5-gallon cans. Set the plants at the depth they were growing in their containers, spacing them 2 to 4 feet apart.

CARE AND MAINTENANCE

Coneflowers need no care once they are established. Weeds are either choked out or shaded out. After the coneflower tops die down in fall, they can be cut down and composted; or they may be left for the birds who will try to get the last of the seeds in the flowerheads. When the plants become overcrowded, they can be divided. Dividing either in fall, after blooming has ceased, or early spring is satisfactory. The earlier the plants are divided, the better will be their flowering the next summer.

ADDITIONAL INFORMATION

The name *Rudbeckia* was given to the plant in honor of Olaf Rudbeck, a Scandinavian professor of botany, and his son Olaf. These lovely plants are especially attractive to butterflies.

ADDITIONAL SPECIES, CULTIVARS, OR VARIETIES

The species, *R. nitida*, is 2 to 4 feet tall. 'Herbstsonne' is a larger plant, growing to 7 feet in some sites, but usually nearer to 5 feet. It is one of the finest coneflowers, with sulfur-yellow flowers in late summer. 'Goldsturm' is a compact form of *R. fulgida*, growing to 2 or 3 feet. There are other kinds offered by various nurseries. Check with your local grower to see what grows best there. If it looks good in the nursery, try it. If it looks good in your garden, divide it or buy more.

Coreopsis

Coreopsis grandiflora

Other Name: Tickseed
Zones: All
Size: 2 to 3 feet tall, half as wide
Blooms: Early to late summer
Flower Colors: Yellow ray flowers with
yellow or coffee-colored disk centers;
sometimes rose-tinted flowers with
yellow centers

Light Requirement:

 odern coreopsis cultivars deliver masses of yellow blooms from the end of June until Labor Day! These are long-stemmed flowers that are long-lasting in the garden and excellent for cut flowers. Coreopsis is just about the easiest garden perennial to grow. It grows in full sun and is not particular about the soil it grows in, doing its best with a slightly dry soil and low fertility. In moist, fertile soils the plants will be overly vigorous, with reduced flowering, and will not support themselves. It is nice to have plants that do not want to be babied. A related coreopsis has found widespread acceptance in the landscape trade. Thread-leaf coreopsis, *C. verticillata*, makes an airy mound of foliage sprinkled with bright yellow, star-like flowers. It is a good border plant that does well in full sun, tending to fade out in shade.

WHEN TO PLANT
Plant in spring from started plants. Divide plants in spring or fall.

WHERE TO PLANT
Plant in dry soil and full sun. Coreopsis is best suited to the middle or front of the border, and is also well suited to naturalized areas.

HOW TO PLANT
Plants are available potted as started seedlings or divisions in spring. Prepare the soil by tilling or spading to a 6-inch depth. Do not improve the soil with added compost or fertilizer. Set the plants no deeper than they were grown in their containers.

CARE AND MAINTENANCE

These plants thrive on neglect. Water only in extended droughts. If plants are overly tall and begin to tumble, tie them to a stake. Deadhead the plants to keep them blooming; if you cut enough flowers for arrangements, there will be little need to deadhead. Several insects can find their ways into a coreopsis planting, but they seldom do any damage. The bright flowers attract butterflies.

ADDITIONAL INFORMATION

Coreopsis is a native prairie wildflower. It can be planted and left unattended in natural areas. It will grow happily and spread if conditions are favorable. Wildflower mixes that are used to establish natural areas usually contain coreopsis seeds. The name *Coreopsis* is derived from *koris*, "a bug," and *opsis*, which means "like." "Like a bug" refers to the appearance of the seeds.

ADDITIONAL SPECIES, CULTIVARS, OR VARIETIES

Most hybrids are *C. grandiflora* × *C. lanceolata* crosses. 'Early Sunrise' is an AAS winner (1989) and comes true from seed. *C. verticillata* 'Moonbeam' has light-yellow flowers on 15-inch mounds of lacy foliage. It blooms all season and has unusual heat tolerance. It is very popular in the landscape trade and was named the 1992 Perennial of the Year. 'Golden Showers' is 3 feet tall and not quite as lacy. *C. rosea* is about 2 feet tall and has rosy-pink flowers, unusual for coreopsis. It is native to the Eastern part of the U. S. and can become a weed if not contained. It is being listed as a "new" perennial in some catalogs.

Daylily

Hemerocallis sp.

Zones: All **Size:** 1 to 4 feet tall, half as wide **Blooms:** May to October **Flower Colors:** All except white and blue	**Light Requirement:**

*T*here is no perfect perennial flowering plant, but daylilies come close. They bloom faithfully with little care. They grow in any soil, sometimes doing better in poor soil. They grow in full sun or rather dense shade. They have no insect pests or diseases. Is it any wonder that these are the most popular and widely used of the perennials? Daylilies have been garden favorites for generations. I can recall rolling around in lush beds of "tiger lilies" as a child. These weren't really tiger lilies, which are true lilies, but the old tawny daylilies or roadside daylilies. These flowers are naturalized throughout the country, along roads, in long-forgotten gardens, in alleys . . . anywhere they can take root. They are rambunctious in the garden and will take over if not constrained. We have them growing in the alley behind our garden. There they get little light and are driven on regularly, but they flower every year. They do try to crawl under the fence once in a while. Common lemon lily is bright yellow and fragrant. It isn't quite as aggressive as the orange, tawny kind. Modern daylilies are hybrids of these two species. They have less of the wild nature and vastly improved flower color and form. These flowers last only one day, thus the name. But there are as many as 30 flowers on a stem, each opening for a full day, so the blooming period can be extended for weeks. The repeating cultivars produce multiple-flower stems during the season and may flower for months.

WHEN TO PLANT

Daylilies can be planted in spring or late summer. Containerized plants can be planted anytime during the season.

WHERE TO PLANT

Plant in full sun or light shade for best bloom. Avoid wet or overly fertile soils. Use in masses, as borders, naturalized, to stabilize banks, around water features, or along roadsides.

How to Plant

Potted plants are available all summer long. New divisions are made in August. Prepare the soil by tilling or spading to a depth of 6 inches. Set the plants or divisions at the depth they were growing in the containers. Space standard cultivars 24 inches apart, dwarf cultivars at 12 inches.

Care and Maintenance

Deadhead the plants to improve their appearance. When all the flowers on a stem have faded, remove it. The foliage of some cultivars may decline in late summer; mow it down. It may regrow before freeze-up. Divide the hybrid cultivars every 3 to 5 years. Species may never need dividing unless you want to obtain plants for another location.

Additional Information

The name *Hemerocallis* means "beautiful for a day" in Greek. These are some of the most useful plants in the landscape; they are increasingly being used as groundcovers rather than just flowering plants. They are in use at Chicago's O'Hare Field to stabilize banks where, for some unexplainable reason, cars have a propensity to drive off the road. Uprooted daylilies can be pushed back into the ground and they will resume growing.

Additional Species, Cultivars, or Varieties

Northern daylilies generally lose their leaves for the winter; there are evergreen cultivars, but they are usually not completely hardy in the north. Select cultivars that will grow in your area—these are the ones available from stores where you live. Colorful pictures in garden catalogs are tempting, but make sure that what you buy will survive in your climate. Thousands of new daylilies are named each year, and it is impossible to keep up with them. Some of the better ones are the "repeaters." 'Stella de Oro' was the first of these to find wide acceptance. 'Happy Returns', 'Baja', 'Frosty Beauty', 'Prairie Moonlight', and 'Yellow Lollipop' are others repeaters. If you want huge flowers, the tetraploids being developed by the Klehm nurseries in Barrington, Illinois, offer some blooms 6 inches in diameter.

Delphinium

Delphinium elatum

Zones: All
Size: 2 to 6 feet tall, 12 inches wide
Blooms: June to September
Flower Colors: Blue, white-and-violet, red,
    pink, yellow

Light Requirement:

 hen I was working my way through college in a California seed store, I was amazed by the California Giant delphiniums that grew there. Some were nearly 10 feet tall. They don't get that large here in Illinois, but they are still the most majestic of the border flowers. Averaging close to 4 to 5 feet tall, they produce magnificent flower-covered spikes in gentle, pastel colors. Considering their size and their gorgeous blooms, garden hybrid delphiniums aren't grown as much as you would expect. But they take work: a deep soil, disease control, and pest control. There are other species that are branched and not as tall. These are generally less demanding in the garden.

WHEN TO PLANT

Delphiniums can be grown from seed sown directly in the garden in August. Transplant seedlings when they are big enough to handle in the fall or the following spring. Started plants are available from garden centers in spring or fall. Spring planting is best so the plants have sufficient time to become established before confronting an Illinois winter.

WHERE TO PLANT

Plant delphiniums in full sun, or partial shade in the hotter parts of the state. Soil must be moist, deep, and well drained. Plant the tall kinds at the back of the border or in the cutting garden. Shorter kinds will fit in the middle of the border.

HOW TO PLANT

Planting is the key to successfully growing delphiniums. Prepare the soil deeply by spading to a depth of at least 12 inches or, even better,

2 feet. This will require double-digging. Incorporate organic matter into the prepared soil. Provide drainage if needed. Plants are available from garden centers and seed catalogs in spring; divisions are available in fall or early spring. Set the plants at the same depth they grew in their containers—deep planting would increase the likelihood of root or crown rotting. Space at 12 inches, which is close enough to allow these tall plants to support one another. Blend PCNB granules (Terraclor) into the soil or drench PCNB into the soil following planting. Be sure to follow the directions on the label every time you use this material. Water the plants to prevent wilting.

CARE AND MAINTENANCE

As plants start growth in spring, remove winter mulch. Drench the soil with PCNB to prevent root rot and set stakes for plants that will need support. Be careful not to injure the crowns of the plants. Fertilize with a complete balanced fertilizer such as a soluble 20-20-20 (Peters, Miracle-Gro, or similar). Follow directions on the package for mixing. Delphiniums need water; don't let them dry out, but don't keep the ground saturated either. Apply snail bait every 7 to 10 days. Cut the flowers to use in arrangements. Remove faded blooms, but leave as much foliage on the plants as you can. The plants will rebloom with shorter stems until frost. After frost has killed back the tops in fall, remove them. Lightly mulch the plants to prevent heaving. You can compost the spent tops, but do not put them back around the delphiniums.

ADDITIONAL INFORMATION

The most damaging problem affecting delphiniums is the disease *Sclerotium rolfsii*. Every effort must be made to keep it out of the planting, and to treat the soil to prevent infection. Purchase only disease-free plants and don't trade plants with other gardeners. Delphiniums are short-lived in this part of the country, particularly in the southern part of the state. Be prepared to set some new plants each spring to keep the planting renewed. Do not attempt to divide plants; the result is usually disappointing.

ADDITIONAL SPECIES, CULTIVARS, OR VARIETIES

The biggest delphiniums are the Pacific Giants hybrids with double flowers in purple, blue, pink, and white. The "bee" in the center of the flower is a contrasting color. Shorter hybrids include the 'Dwarf Pacifics', blue and 2 feet tall, and the *D. belladonna* and *D. bellamosa* hybrids. The latter are branched, 2 to 4 feet tall, and blue or white. Connecticut Yankees are short (to $2^1/2$ feet), bushy, blue, lavender, and white.

Ferns

Adiantum pedatum et al.

Zones: All
Size: 6 inches to 4 feet

Light Requirement:

*F*erns are plants for the cool, moist shade garden, grown not for flowers but for their magnificent foliage. Their soft texture brings another dimension to the garden. These are not flowering plants, and they don't produce seeds. They grow from spores that drop, usually from the lower sides of the leaves, to grow on the ground. There they grow into structures that look like tiny leaves (prothallia), where fertilization takes place and from which new plants will grow. Moisture is needed for this process; ferns are plants that belong to wet areas. The heavily shaded, moist areas in established neighborhoods with large trees and shrubs or on the north side of a home where the sun rarely shines are often thought of as liabilities. Most plants won't grow in such places, but these are exactly the conditions in which ferns do best. Once ferns are established and growing, little needs to be done to keep them going. Weeds don't grow well around them, and there are few insect or disease problems in heavy shade.

WHEN TO PLANT

Ferns are best planted in spring so they can become established before the onset of winter.

WHERE TO PLANT

Light to dense shade and a moist but well-drained soil are essential requirements. The soil type is immaterial; a pH near neutral is best, but the plants will tolerate quite a variation in acidity. Ours grow at a pH near 7.5.

HOW TO PLANT

Ferns are available in 1- to-5-gallon cans from garden centers and nurseries, or from catalogs in spring. Prepare the soil by tilling or spading to a depth of 6 to 12 inches. Incorporate organic matter to assure good soil structure and provide drainage if necessary. If the area is low, construct berms or raised beds. Set the plants no deeper than they were growing in their containers. Space larger kinds such as ostrich fern at 3 to 4 feet, smaller kinds such as maidenhair at 1 to 1^1/$_2$ feet.

CARE AND MAINTENANCE
Ferns must have water. When the weather is dry, they should be thoroughly watered to prevent wilting and scorching of the fronds. Remove dead foliage in the fall. These are essentially trouble-free plants.

ADDITIONAL INFORMATION
Ferns can be interplanted with spring-flowering bulbs beneath deciduous trees. The bulbs will finish flowering about the time the ferns begin to grow, and the ripening leaves of the bulbs will be hidden by the ferns. Smaller ferns mix well with hosta and tuberous begonias, which can be planted between or in front of the ferns for a pleasing contrast in texture and color. The new fronds that emerge in spring from some local species are called fiddleheads, and these are relished as a delicacy, especially on the Pacific coast and in the Canadian Maritimes. But use caution; some are poisonous. Don't pick any unless you know which ones are safe.

ADDITIONAL SPECIES, CULTIVARS, OR VARIETIES
Northern maidenhair fern, *Adiantum pedatum*, grows to about 18 inches tall and wide. The pinnules (leaflets) on the fronds are triangular in shape. It is native to dark moist woodlands from Canada to Oklahoma. *Dennstaedtia punctilobula*, hay-scented fern, grows to 3 feet and tolerates a wide range of conditions in moisture and light. Best, however, is partial shade and a moist, well-drained site. Its crushed fronds smell of fresh-mown hay. Ostrich fern, *Matteuccia struthiopteris*, is a tall plant. It will grow to 6 feet in the wild but rarely exceeds 4 feet in the garden. The soft, lacy fronds are shaped like an ostrich tail. It tolerates light shade as long as there is adequate water. If allowed to wilt, the fronds will scorch, ruining the appearance of this lovely plant.

Gay Feather

Liatris scariosa

Other Names: Blazing star, Liatris
Zones: All
Size: 3 to 4 feet tall, half as wide
Blooms: Midsummer to late fall
Flower Colors: Lavender, white, rose

Light Requirement:

*G*ay feather is a North American native plant, often included in prairie restoration plantings. It has not been used to its full potential in the garden. The flowers are borne, 50 or more, along a tall vertical stalk. The blooms are soft and pastel pink or lavender, and they open from the top of the stem rather than the bottom. The blooms are excellent as cut flowers. They are produced commercially for the florist trade and are in high demand for late-summer floral arrangements.

WHEN TO PLANT

Liatris is best planted in the spring before growth begins. Containerized plants may be planted in the garden anytime during the season.

WHERE TO PLANT

Plant in full sun or very light shade. Soil should be well drained, drier rather than wet; these prairie plants will decline in wet soils.

HOW TO PLANT

Containerized plants are available at garden centers and nurseries, and at discount stores in spring. Prepare the soil by spading or tilling to at least a foot deep. These plants will be there for 2 or 3 years, so some preparation is needed. Set the plants at the depth they were growing in their containers. Space them about 2 feet apart, which is close enough to allow them to hold each other up.

CARE AND MAINTENANCE

Liatris requires little care once established. Plants may need to be staked in windy locations. The plants will be stronger and better resist being blown over if fertility is low, and flowers will be larger and more abundant with a moderate level of fertility. These plants are not deeply rooted and can be shoved out of the ground; winter mulch will help prevent frost heaving.

ADDITIONAL INFORMATION

Liatris looks best planted in clumps of 6 to 12 plants. Don't plant them like rows of wooden soldiers unless you are planting a cutting garden. As well as being good as fresh flowers, liatris can be dried for permanent floral arrangements.

ADDITIONAL SPECIES, CULTIVARS, OR VARIETIES

Cultivars 'September Glory' (deep purple) and 'White Spire' bloom in late summer. They have a tendency to fall over if not staked. *L. pycnostachya* is Kansas gay feather; about 4 feet, it may be too tall for most gardens and needs staking. *L. spicata* 'Kobold', listed in the trade as spike gay feather, is short (24 inches) and blooms in an intense rose-lavender from July to September. 'Floristan White' produces white flowers in August and September.

Hardy Chrysanthemum

Dendranthema × morifolium

Other Name: Hardy Mum
Zones: All
Size: 1 to 2 feet tall and wide
Blooms: August to November
Flower Colors: White, yellow, pink, orange, bronze, red

Light Requirement:

Hardy mums take over where the annuals leave off in fall. The sturdy plants are covered with blooms of many colors and forms, including formal, ball-shaped pompons; daisy-like singles; spoons; and showy "football" types. These are the most colorful garden plants for flowering in late summer and fall. Mums are best planted in masses or in groups of 3 to 5 plants. Dwarf cushion types are suitable for edging; the tall kinds are best for the back of the border or for cutting garden. They are all excellent, long-lasting cut flowers.

WHEN TO PLANT

Spring is the best time to plant chrysanthemums. They are available in fall as potted plants in bloom to be planted as replacements for spent annuals.

WHERE TO PLANT

Full sun and a well-drained soil are the keys to success with mums. Poor drainage will lead to winter-kill.

HOW TO PLANT

Plants may be started from cuttings ordered from seed catalogs or from potted plants in spring. Overwintered plants may be lifted and divided. Prepare the soil by tilling or spading to a depth of 6 inches, adding organic matter. Provide drainage if necessary with tiles or raised beds. Set plants from containers at the same depth they were growing in their containers. Plant rooted cuttings so the roots are just covered with soil. Space plants 18 inches apart. For fall planting, plants are sold in 1- or-2-gallon cans. Prepare the soil as above and dig a hole for each plant as deep and twice as wide as the ball of soil on the plant.

CARE AND MAINTENANCE

Fertilize the plants when they are actively growing with a complete soluble fertilizer such as 20-20-20 (Peters, Miracle-Gro, or similar), following label directions. Water to prevent wilting. To develop bushy plants, pinch to remove the growing tips. Make the first pinch when the plants are 6 inches tall, the second when the shoots have grown another 6 inches. Simply roll out the growing tip of each shoot. Do not pinch early cultivars after June 15; don't pinch later cultivars after mid-July. Control aphids and mites with insecticidal soap, earwigs with Sevin, and foliar diseases with acephate or Orthene. Follow label directions carefully. When tops are frozen off, remove them and mulch the plants with 6 inches of straw. Plants set in the place of annuals may be removed and discarded, or line them out in the garden to be regrown for the following fall.

ADDITIONAL INFORMATION

Mums are traditional flowers from Japan and China, where they have been cultivated for nearly 3000 years. Our modern hardy mums are closely related to florist mums; the major difference is the normal flowering dates. Hardy mums flower in 4 to 8 weeks after nights begin to lengthen, while florist mums are 10- to 13-week cultivars. They flower much too late to bloom before being frozen.

ADDITIONAL SPECIES, CULTIVARS, OR VARIETIES

There are so many colors and forms that trying to buy mums by cultivar name is impossible. Try to buy plants already in bloom so you can see their color and form. Many growers force potted hardy mums into bloom in spring just for this purpose. Cuttings ordered from catalogs do have names, but pay closer attention to the plant descriptions and select plants based on them.

Heuchera

Heuchera americana

Other Names: American Alumroot,
Coral Bells
Zones: All
Size: Low, 6-to-12-inch clump of foliage,
flower stem to 18 inches
Blooms: Late spring, early summer
Flower Colors: Greenish-pink, red

Light Requirement:

*H*euchera is grown for its attractive foliage that may be marked with coppery or silver veins, or may be mahogany-colored in some hybrids. The form of the plant, a neat mound, makes it especially suitable for edging in front of shrubs or along the perennial border. (Coral bells is larger, and its flowers are showy.) Heuchera and coral bells have been hybridized extensively to improve their flowering. Flowers of the species are tiny and ephemeral. They are attractive, but not readily noticed. *Heucherella* hybrids are crosses between *Heuchera* and *Tiarella*.

WHEN TO PLANT

Potted plants are available in spring from nurseries and garden centers. Plants may be divided in early spring or fall. Seed may be sown in the garden in midsummer.

WHERE TO PLANT

Plant heucheras in full sun or light shade. They prefer a moist, well-drained soil. Plant as facers for shrub plantings, or as edging for the perennial garden. Some of the showy kinds are suitable for the cutting garden.

HOW TO PLANT

Prepare the soil by tilling or spading to a 6-inch depth. Add organic matter if possible, and make sure drainage is good (poor drainage will result in crown rot). Set the plants so that their crowns are buried up to the depth of the leaves. Space plants 12 to 15 inches apart.

CARE AND MAINTENANCE

These plants develop a bare, woody crown after a few years. Dig them up and remove and replant the shoots from around the woody part. Discard the old woody crown. Division will be necessary approximately every 3 years. Mulching or hilling up soil mix over the crowns will delay the need for division for a year or so. Be sure the plants are in a well-drained situation and that the soil used to hill them up is quite light. Otherwise crown rot may develop. Watering during droughty periods will enhance flowering and will prevent scorching of the leaves. Removal of the stalks will prolong flowering of the showy cultivars.

ADDITIONAL INFORMATION

The name *Heuchera* was given in honor of German botanist J. H. von Heucher. The plants are native to the eastern United States and the Rocky Mountains.

ADDITIONAL SPECIES, CULTIVARS, OR VARIETIES

Cultivars include 'Dales Strain', with silver-blue leaves; 'Garnet', with bright garnet-colored leaves in spring; and 'Pewter Veil', with purplish, metallic-silver leaves. Several cultivars of *H. micrantha* have been introduced into the trade. Notable is 'Purple Palace'; it has foliage that is purple-bronze on the upper surface and purplish-pink on the underside, and blooms white in July and August. It was selected the Perennial Plant of the Year in 1994. Many cultivars of coral bells, *H. sanguinea* , have excellent flowers and a long season of bloom. Varied foliage patterns and colors are being developed as well. The 'Bressingham Hybrids' strain is being offered as a mix of different colored flowers by some nurseries. *Heucherella* hybrid 'Bridget Bloom' has pink blooms edged with white. Its leaves are hairy in neat mounds.

Hosta

Hosta plantaginea, H. undulata

Other Name: Plantain Lily
Zones: All
Size: 1- to 2-foot-high mound, flower
  stalks to 3 feet
Blooms: Summer
Flower Colors: White or lavender (plant
  actually grown for foliage effects)

Light Requirement:

*H*osta is a dependable perennial plant that requires little care. Its foliage has a regal character and is so distinctive that it can be mistaken for nothing else. Flowers are borne above the leaves in summer, but they are not the main reason for growing these plants; this is a shade plant grown for its foliage. In fact, many gardeners remove the flower stalks so as not to clutter the formal look of the plantings. Hosta comes in many forms, sizes, and colors. These plants can be various shades of green from yellowish green to bright green, dark green, grayish green, or purple-green. Variegated cultivars can have white, gold, yellow, or cream-colored margins or other markings, or they may have various shades of green within each leaf. The leaves can be small or large. Some have wavy margins and others are smooth. One large-leaved variety has dusty-green leaves with large ribs running the full length of each leaf. These plants are spectacular when solidly planted beneath overhanging trees in a woodland setting. Hostas can be planted in waving masses of the same color or interplanted with other flowers. They are excellent companions to spring-flowering bulbs, filling in just as the bulb foliage dies down.

WHEN TO PLANT

Hosta divisions can be planted in spring or fall. Container-grown plants can be planted at any time during the season.

WHERE TO PLANT

Partial to full shade is best. Wavy-leaved hostas can stand sun better than most kinds, but excess sun will cause wilting and scorching of the leaves, destroying their usefulness. Soil must be well drained but moist. Use hostas in mass plantings under the shade of trees, around pools, in rock gardens, and in the border. They can be used in front of shrub plantings or interplanted around azaleas or rhododendrons in woodland settings.

How to Plant

Hostas are sold in 1-, 2-, and 6-gallon cans, or as divisions from mail-order suppliers. Plants can be divided in spring or fall. Prepared the soil by tilling or spading to a 6-inch depth. Add organic matter to improve water-holding and drainage. Holes will need to be dug for the larger, container-grown plants, as deep and twice as wide as the plant ball. Set the plants at the same depth they were growing in their containers. Space them about 18 inches apart; large-leaved cultivars can be set 2 feet apart. Soak the plants thoroughly following planting.

Care and Maintenance

Hostas need water. Soak them well during extended dry weather. There are several pests that can damage hosta plantings. Slugs are the most damaging; control them with slug bait spread around the plants, keeping the bait away from the plants to draw out the slugs. Begin applications early in the season—the small slugs are much easier to kill than the adults. Slug bait must be moistened to be effective. Wet it if there is no rain or dew. An application lasts only a week or so. Re-treat every week as long as evidence of new feeding appears. Divide plants every 5 years or when overcrowded.

Additional Information

Hostas are native to Japan and China. They are named after Dr. Nicholaus T. Host, an Austrian physician. The dense cover provided by hostas will keep out weeds.

Additional Species, Cultivars, or Varieties

There are many cultivars of hosta, and new ones are introduced every year. *H. plantaginea* hybrids are sometimes called fragrant hostas. *H. undulata* cultivars are wavy-leaved. Most are hybrids of undetermined parentage. One grower lists about 100 cultivars in several categories: green, white-margined, blue-leaved, yellow-margined, gold-leaved, and variegated. One highly advertised cultivar worthy of mention is 'Great Expectations', which has spectacular leaves with chartreuse, cream, blue, and green markings. Visit a nursery or grower and pick out a few plants that appeal to you. Try them in your garden. If they behave the way you want them to, buy more, or divide them and replant.

Oriental Poppy

Papaver orientale

Zones: All
Size: 2 to 4 feet tall in bloom
Blooms: June, July
Flower Colors: Orange, pink, white, orange-red

Light Requirement:

*A*s a child I was read the adventures of Dorothy and Toto in *The Wizard of Oz*. Enticed into a field of poppies by the beautiful blooms, Dorothy and Toto are overcome by the vapors and lulled to sleep. They are rescued by their friends, but the story left me with a vague feeling that some members of this floral family have a sinister nature. Of course the story was about the opium poppy, but the gorgeous blooms of all poppies are to be appreciated and enjoyed rather than feared. These brightly colored flowers are outstanding in the early-summer garden at a time when few things are blooming. They are striking in borders, but must be used with care to avoid over-doing them. Following bloom the leaves will dry up, leaving a hole in the garden. Poppies are crepe-like and delicate, easily injured by storms. With their varied, brilliant colors, they are excellent for flower arrangements. They need to be divided and replanted every 5 years or so.

WHEN TO PLANT

Poppies are planted in spring, or divided in midsummer after leaves die down. Fall planting is more likely than spring planting to result in flowers the first season.

WHERE TO PLANT

Plant these flowers in a sunny, well-drained spot in the garden. Place them so that their dying foliage will be hidden, or plan to plant annuals over their dormant roots.

HOW TO PLANT

Poppies are sold as divisions, in pots, in 1- and 2-gallon cans, and in 6-gallon cans with plants in bloom. Prepare the soil by tilling or spading to a depth of 12 inches. Add organic matter to improve moisture-holding and aeration and be sure the area drains well. Set the plants at the same depth they were growing in their containers, spacing them about 2 feet apart. The fleshy roots are easily damaged, so handle the plants gently. Dig holes the depth of the plant ball and twice as wide. Set root divisions on their sides, and cover with soil. Water thoroughly to settle the soil. Water to keep the soil from drying, but do not keep dormant plants wet; they will tolerate relatively dry soil.

CARE AND MAINTENANCE

Once planted, the thick, fleshy roots do not like to be disturbed. Leave them alone until it is time to divide them. Short root sections make new plants. Any sections left when clumps are lifted will grow; if they are unwanted, hoe them out. No diseases or insects are common to poppies. Judicious watering while the plants are growing and flowering is important—do not overwater.

ADDITIONAL INFORMATION

Poppies can be started from seed sown under lights at 55 degrees Fahrenheit in March. If planted in the garden when large enough to handle, they will flower the second year. Most gardeners end up with more poppy divisions than they can use. These make welcome gifts for neighbors. *Papaver* is the Latin name for poppy. Poppy is from the Old English *papig*, which apparently meant "sleepy," probably referring to the effect of extracts of the opium poppy.

ADDITIONAL SPECIES, CULTIVARS, OR VARIETIES

Many poppy cultivars are listed in catalogs. Many of these are seed strains; unless propagated vegetatively, the trueness of type can't be assured. 'Allegro' is 16 inches tall and brilliant scarlet; 'Prince of Orange' is 24 inches, orange; 'Princess Victoria Louise' is 24 inches, deep pink; and 'Pinnacle' is white edged with scarlet. All are worth trying. Most poppies are offered by color, not cultivar name. If you are fortunate enough to find a supplier growing poppies by cultivar name, buy your plants there. If not, just buy a color that appeals to you, plant it, and enjoy it.

Peony

Paeonia hybrids

Zones: All
Size: 24 to 36 inches tall and wide
Blooms: May, June
Flower Colors: White, pink, rose, red, some
  bicolors, some with yellow centers

Light Requirement:

I remember the peonies in Grandma's garden. They put forth their beautiful fragrant blooms just in time for Memorial Day. Pink and white, they were so special that one or two would be cut to bring indoors so the fragrance would fill the house. We still do that at our home today. Peonies are magnificent flowers reserved for those of us who reside in the cold parts of the country. They are strictly for northern gardens, requiring extended cold weather during their dormancy period. The plants emerge as pink sprouts from massive underground root systems in early spring. By May, large bush-like plants have developed, with flower buds topping every stem. The flowers, in warm colors, are 6 inches or more in diameter, in single, anemone, or double cultivars. The plants remain attractive following blooming, but they do take up room in the garden. Place them where they will be specimens instead of part of the perennial border. They are more like herbaceous bushes than flowers.

WHEN TO PLANT
Peonies are best planted in fall. Containerized plants are available throughout the season and may be planted at any time. Divisions are made only in fall, following die-down of the plant tops.

WHERE TO PLANT
Plant peonies in full sun or light shade. Soil must be deeply prepared and well drained. Allow enough room for the plants. Don't crowd them in with other perennials, and do not plant them where the roots of trees or shrubs will interfere with them.

HOW TO PLANT
Prepare the soil by spading to a 12-inch depth. To improve its condition, incorporate organic matter and a low-nitrogen fertilizer such as

5-20-20 or similar into the soil. Use a handful for each plant (10 square feet). Take your time when preparing the ground. Peonies will stay in the same place, undisturbed, for as long as 50 years. They do not need dividing. Root divisions must be planted so that the tips of the buds are exactly 1 inch below the soil surface. The buds are small, pink, and pointed; make sure the pointed ends are up. Set containerized plants at the same depth as they were growing in the containers and dig the planting hole the same depth and twice as wide as the plant ball. Allow at least 3 feet between plants, more if you have room. After planting, soak the soil to firm it around the roots.

CARE AND MAINTENANCE
Peonies require very little care once they are established, but controlling weeds, especially grasses, is important. If they get a start, they are difficult to remove. Pull or hoe the weeds as they appear. Peony flowers are heavy, and if it rains while they are in full bloom, they will fall over. To support them, you can install cages around the plants as they begin to grow in spring. After the petals have dropped, remove the flowers, but leave as much of the foliage as you can. A few diseases can damage peonies. Removal of the old stems and care in keeping the plant tops dry will help avoid disease. Spraying may be necessary in wet seasons; use benomyl, maneb, or mancozeb, carefully following label directions.

ADDITIONAL INFORMATION
Peonies originated in China, Europe, Japan, Mongolia, and Siberia, and have been cultivated for centuries. Excellent for cutting, they are grown commercially in Illinois; growers cut them when the buds just begin to loosen.

ADDITIONAL SPECIES, CULTIVARS, OR VARIETIES
Hundreds of peony cultivars are available. A major hybridizer is Roy Klehm of Barrington, Illinois; the Klehm family has grown and bred peonies for more than 100 years in Illinois, and has nurseries in all three climatic zones. Cultivars suitable for your part of the state are available as divisions from local garden centers in fall, or as blooming containerized plants throughout the season. Instead of trying to buy them by cultivar name, select those that look good to you. Usually a description and picture of the flower accompany the displays.

Phlox

Phlox paniculata

Zones: All
Size: 24 to 36 inches tall
Blooms: June to August
Flower Colors: White, pink, red, blue, purple

Light Requirement:

illsides covered with waves of lavender, pink, and white . . . that is perennial phlox at its best. These lovely flowers are produced in clusters as much as a foot across on 2-foot stems. Planted in masses, they produce a solid blanket of color from midsummer until frost. We had phloxes in our garden when I was a child and they still bloom in that garden every year. They are the perennial flowers of summer and no garden should be without at least a few of them. Unfortunately, phloxes in the garden are not trouble-free, making them less desirable for the casual gardener. If allowed to go to seed, the hybrid cultivars revert to the species. (This gardening difficulty is actually what make these plants so prolific along the roadsides.) Mildew and mites may disfigure the leaves so that by late in the season they are quite unattractive. The plants need to be divided regularly.

WHEN TO PLANT
Phloxes should be planted in spring or fall, though containerized plants can be planted all season.

WHERE TO PLANT
Plant in masses in the back of the border. They need full sun and a moist, well-drained soil.

HOW TO PLANT
Plants are available in 1-, 2-, and 6-gallon cans, and root cuttings are available from mail-order catalogs. Prepare the soil by tilling or spading to a 6-inch depth. Add organic matter to improve soil condition and moisture-holding. Set the plants at the same depth they were growing in their containers, setting them 12 to 15 inches apart.

Dig the holes for containerized plants the same depth and twice as wide as the plant balls. Plant root cuttings 2 inches deep on their sides.

CARE AND MAINTENANCE
Phloxes need water and fertilizer for best flowering. Apply a complete fertilizer such as 20-20-20 liquid (Peters, Miracle-Gro, or similar) as plants begin growth in spring, and every month during the season. Follow the mixing directions on the label. Control mites with insecticidal soap. Control mildew with triforine or sulfur and keep water off the leaves. Deadhead the plants without fail after blooms fade. If allowed to go to seed, the hybrid cultivars will be taken over by inferior seed types with fewer blooms and poor form. Deadheading stimulates continued flowering. Stake plants that have a tendency to fall over and divide the plants when they become crowded.

ADDITIONAL INFORMATION
Phlox is a native American wildflower. The name *Phlox* is Greek for "flame," and refers to the bright colors of the blooms of some phlox species. Phloxes are excellent for cutting; they last well, and some have a sweet fragrance.

ADDITIONAL SPECIES, CULTIVARS, OR VARIETIES
Nurseries and garden centers offer many cultivars of phlox. An even greater number is offered in seed catalogs. Worthy of mention are 'Blue Boy', true blue and 24 inches tall; 'Bright Eyes', pink with a red eye; and 'The King', deep purple. A related species with better mildew resistance, *P. maculata*, is wild sweet William. 'Miss Lingard' is pure white. Plants in the Greek series ('Alpha', lilac pink; 'Delta', white and pink; and 'Omega', white with a lilac eye) are listed by some growers for Illinois conditions.

Purple Coneflower

Echinacea purpurea

Zones: All
Size: 2 to 4 feet tall and wide
Blooms: Summer
Flower Colors: Purple or pink, with an
iridescent rust center

Light Requirement:

*P*urple coneflowers are native American wildflowers. They have been used in naturalized areas for many years, and are gaining popularity for the perennial garden, partly because of their long season of bloom and improved cultivars. Many people are just now discovering this adaptable plant. Purple coneflower tolerates all the conditions that make gardening difficult in Illinois. It is fully hardy; it tolerates heavy soils and the alkalinity; and it suffers through the summer dry periods and heat, continuing to bloom. After the ray flowers (outer petals) fall and the plants dry up, the seeds in the fruiting heads (cones) will attract little birds that hang on to the swaying stems to find a seed. Chickadees and finches are good at this—don't be in a rush to remove the dry tops! The flowers are excellent for cutting. The cones are good for dry arrangements after the ray flowers fall.

WHEN TO PLANT
Purple coneflowers may be planted in spring or fall. Containerized plants can be planted at any time during the season.

WHERE TO PLANT
Purple coneflowers prefer full sun and a well-drained soil. They will tolerate partial shade, though they may become tall and weak. In the southern part of the state, partial shade during the middle of the day will prevent fading of the flowers. Use these plants in the back, middle, or at the ends of the border, or plant them in naturalized areas or the cutting garden.

HOW TO PLANT
Purple coneflower plants are available in pots, in 1- and 6-gallon cans, and as divisions in spring or fall. Prepare the soil by tilling or spading to a 6-inch depth. Make sure the area is well drained, but

there is no need to enrich the soil. Coneflowers tolerate heavy soils. Dig the planting hole the same depth and twice as wide as the plant ball and set divisions at the same depth they were growing in their containers. Space the plants 2 feet apart. If the containerized plants were growing in a light soil mix, shake some of it off the ball, and mix it with the soil going back into the planting hole. After planting, water to settle the soil around the roots.

CARE AND MAINTENANCE

Purple coneflower requires no special treatment. It the plants start to fall over, stake them up. Deadheading will prolong flowering, but it also removes the interesting cones. These plants will reseed themselves. If you are growing a hybrid selection, cut off the cones before they drop seeds; these plants do not come true from seed, and the seedlings will revert back to the species.

ADDITIONAL INFORMATION

The name *Echinacea* is from the Greek *echinos* or "hedgehog." This may refer to the spiny scales on the receptacle beneath the flowers, or to the appearance of the fruiting head. The flowers are attractive to butterflies, and the seeds attract small birds.

ADDITIONAL SPECIES, CULTIVARS, OR VARIETIES

Several cultivars offer some unusual colors: 'Alba' is creamy white; 'Crimson Star' deep crimson red; 'Magnus' deep rose; and 'White Swan' has creamy-white flowers and a copper cone. Nurseries and garden centers offer the best selections. Since there aren't too many, your chances of getting what you want are good.

Russian Sage

Perovskia atriplicifolia

Zones: All
Size: 3 to 4 feet
Blooms: July, August, persisting into winter
Flower Color: Lavender-blue

Light Requirement:

ussian sage is a relative newcomer on the perennial plant scene. It is not one of the usual herbaceous perennials, but a semi-woody plant. Its advantages are its attractive all-season value and its ability to grow where nothing else will. This is a perennial that will grow in hot, dry parking lot islands, that strip between the south side of the house and the driveway, or a hot, dry parkway with cracked soil. The only condition Russian sage will not tolerate is soggy soil; without proper drainage, it will decline and winter-kill. The plant is attractive in leaf with aromatic gray-white leaves and stems. The flowers are borne in lavender-blue spikes that appear above the leaves in July. The flowers are tiny and delicate, excellent for cutting, and they contrast nicely with the yellows and oranges of the daylilies that bloom at the same time. The spikes persist and stay attractive through winter.

WHEN TO PLANT

Russian sage is planted from divisions or containerized plants. Divisions may be planted in either spring or fall. Containerized plants are often sold in bloom in 2- and 6-gallon cans, and can be planted at any time during the season.

WHERE TO PLANT

Plant in full sun in a well-drained soil. If planted in shade or with poor drainage, this plant will decline and die out. Russian sage is suitable as a filler plant in the border, as an accent plant, as a landscape plant, or in beds in difficult places.

HOW TO PLANT

Prepare the soil by spading or tilling to a depth of 6 inches. If drainage is less than adequate, incorporate organic matter and sand to a 12-inch depth. Set the plants at the depth they were growing in their containers. Dig the hole for container-grown plants the same depth and twice the width of the plant ball. Soak the plants thoroughly to settle the soil. Do not water again unless the plants wilt.

CARE AND MAINTENANCE

These plants require very little care. They are affected by no bugs or diseases. Their woody stems should be cut down to about 6 inches in spring before growth begins. This will keep the plants from becoming straggly and untidy.

ADDITIONAL INFORMATION

Russian sage has become such a valuable landscaping plant that it was selected as the 1995 Perennial Plant of the Year. This award is made annually by the Perennial Plant Association for perennials that perform well in all parts of the country. Russian sage is native to the central Asian highlands from Afghanistan to Tibet.

ADDITIONAL SPECIES, CULTIVARS, OR VARIETIES

A few selections have been made of Russian sage. Two of them are pale-blue 'Blue Haze', with leaves that have few notches, and 'Blue Spire', which has finely cut leaves and lavender flowers. 'Longin' is narrower with violet flowers. Chances are good that your local garden center will have one cultivar, and that it will not have a cultivar name on the tag. Buy it, plant it, and enjoy it.

Shasta Daisy

Leucanthemum × superbum

Zones: 5 with care, 6, and 7 **Size:** 1 to 3 feet tall and half as wide **Blooms:** June to September **Flower Colors:** White with yellow centers	**Light Requirement:**

Shasta daisy is what most people envision when they think of a daisy: neat white petals (ray flowers) and a bright-yellow center. Kids pick them to take home to mother. Schoolgirls may receive daisies as their first bouquet. They are favorite subjects for the artist's brush, finding their way into laces and onto summer prints and dishware. Daisies fit well in the garden. They are best in the middle to back of the border, or at the ends due to their height, but they should not be placed so far back that you can't get to them to cut a few blooms for the table. Daisies are excellent cut flowers. The Shastas are the daisies of the florist trade, the ones that appear in the shops for summer enjoyment. The cultivar 'Thomas Killen' is most popular for growing in gardens. Shasta daisies are available as single or double flowers on plants from 1 foot to about 3 feet tall. They can fit almost anywhere.

WHEN TO PLANT

Shasta daisy is best planted in spring. Containerized plants can be planted at any time.

WHERE TO PLANT

Plant in full sun, though midday shade may be helpful in the southern part of the state. A fertile, moist, well-drained soil is best. Do not plant where water will stand in winter; if necessary, consider raised beds. Shasta daisies can be naturalized in prairie plantings.

HOW TO PLANT

Plants are available as divisions, or in pots and 1-, 2-, and 6-gallon cans, sometimes in bloom. Prepare the soil by tilling or spading to a 12-inch depth. Incorporate organic matter and sand to improve structure, and provide drainage if necessary. Dig the holes for containerized plants the same depth and twice as wide as the plant ball.

Set divisions at the depth they were growing, spacing the plants 2 feet apart. Water to settle the soil around the roots.

CARE AND MAINTENANCE

Shasta daisies do not have many pest problems. Pinch taller cultivars as they grow to improve their branching. They need to be watered in dry weather to continue flowering. Cut the flowers or deadhead to stimulate continuing bloom. In fall, cut down the plants; in Zone 5, mulch with straw to prevent heaving and cold injury. Divide the clumps every 2 or 3 years. Discard the woody center of the clump and replant the perimeter pieces.

ADDITIONAL INFORMATION

If growing for cut flowers, do not pinch the stems as they grow; if they are too long to stand up, tie them to stakes. Keep them growing straight up for nice, straight stems. Disbud (remove all side buds) to develop large central flowers. Certain varieties are better suited for cut flowers.

ADDITIONAL SPECIES, CULTIVARS, OR VARIETIES

Not all cultivars of Shasta daisies are fully hardy throughout Illinois. Some cultivars listed for Illinois conditions are 'Alaska' (with large single flowers) and 'Snowcap' for profuse blooming. 'Thomas Killen' has the long, thick stems which make it good for cutting. 'Esther Read' has fully double flowers, and 'Polaris' has flowers more than 6 inches across.

Speedwell

Veronica sp.

Other Name: Veronica
Zones: All
Size: 1 to 3 feet with equal spread
Blooms: Summer
Flower Colors: Blue, white, rosy-pink

Light Requirement:

Speedwells, often called Veronicas, are some of the most hardy of garden perennials. They are semi-woody plants that produce spikes of blue flowers most of the summer. The foliage is rich green or, in the case of woolly speedwell, woolly-white. The plants are generally orderly and upright, though Hungarian speedwell tends to fall over. Veronicas are easy to work into the garden because they flower almost all season, and the plants are attractive even when not in bloom. This means they can be planted anywhere in the garden and without having to be hidden behind another plant. So many perennials deteriorate after blooming that one that maintains its appearance is welcome.

WHEN TO PLANT

Speedwells can be planted in spring or fall.

WHERE TO PLANT

Full sun is best, but these plants will tolerate some light shade. Shaded plants may grow more loosely and tend to flop. Soils should be moderately fertile and well drained. Standing water in winter will kill the crowns. Plant in the front to middle of the border, in masses, in beds, or in the cutting garden.

HOW TO PLANT

Speedwells are available in pots or 1- to 6-gallon cans, often in bloom. Divisions can be made in spring or fall. Prepare the soil by tilling or spading to a 6-inch depth. Incorporate organic matter for improved condition. If drainage is poor, consider tiles or raised beds. Set the plants at the same depth they were growing in their containers. Dig the holes for containerized plants the same depth and twice as wide as the plant balls.

CARE AND MAINTENANCE
Veronicas have very few pests. Leaf spot diseases may turn lower leaves brown in wet weather. Care consists of watering in dry weather, and deadheading the plants to keep them blooming. Cut the plants down after frost has killed the leaves in fall. Divide the plants in early spring or fall when they become crowded, which will be every 3 to 4 years.

ADDITIONAL SPECIES, CULTIVARS, OR VARIETIES
V. spicata, spike speedwell, has a good, upright habit and shiny green leaves. Some cultivars are 'Blue Spires', with glossy green leaves and blue flowers; 'Heidekind', 10 inches tall with rose-pink flowers; and 'Icicle', a true white. Woolly speedwell, *V. spicata incana*, has woolly leaves and lavender-blue blooms. Crosses between long-leaved speedwell, *V. longifolia*, and spike speedwell have resulted in some excellent cultivars, such as 'Sunny Border Blue', the 1993 Perennial Plant of the Year. This one has done well in our garden the last 3 years, even with floods, drought, and one terrible winter. *V. prostrata*, the harebell speedwell, is low-growing to 6 inches. It is well suited for the front of borders, for edging, or for rock gardens. 'Heavenly Blue' has deep blue flowers and is 4 inches tall and excellent for edging.

Stonecrop

Sedum sp.

Other Name: Sedum
Zones: All
Size: 6 to 24 inches high, 24 inches wide
Blooms: Summer
Flower Colors: Pink, yellow, red

Light Requirement:

*S*edums are among the easiest garden plants to grow: plant them and forget them. There are many kinds of sedums, all succulents with fleshy leaves. The flowers are tiny and star-shaped, but they usually grow in masses of showy heads. Many of the sedums are rock garden plants, low-growing and perfectly satisfied with a hard, infertile soil. The name stonecrop comes from the habit these plants have of growing among stones or on stony ledges. The botanical name *Sedum* means "to sit," referring to the way these plants "sit" among the rocks. The sedums suitable for perennial gardens are taller growing, and they may not look like the typical stonecrop. But they are succulents, and they have sedum's tiny star-shaped flowers. Some sedums are invasive, but the upright-growing ones are not. They are just about indestructible; the only thing that kills them is too much water.

WHEN TO PLANT

Sedums may be planted in spring or fall. Cuttings can be taken and will root easily in summer. Containerized plants are available all season, often in bloom.

WHERE TO PLANT

Plant sedums in full sun in a well-drained, well-prepared soil. They are suitable in borders, as edging, in masses, over rocks, or as groupings of 3 to 5 plants.

HOW TO PLANT

These plants are available potted or in 1-gallon cans. Divisions are available in spring and fall. Prepare the soil by spading or tilling to a depth of 6 inches. Set the plants at the same depth they were growing in their containers. Dig the holes for the containerized plants the same depth and twice as wide as the plant ball. After planting, water the plants to settle the soil. Do not water again until the soil is dry. Remember, these plants can be killed by overwatering.

CARE AND MAINTENANCE

Once established, a stonecrop requires almost no attention, and it has no serious insects or diseases. The plants will grow unattended, requiring no watering, fertilizing, pinching, or staking. If weeds invade before the stonecrop has filled in, remove them. Before new growth begins in spring, remove the dead, overwintering plant tops.

ADDITIONAL SPECIES, CULTIVARS, OR VARIETIES

Sedum kamtschaticum grows about 9 inches tall, essentially covered with yellow flowers. It is used for edging and borders, and can be planted in pockets in stones, on walls, or on banks. It does not develop a dense mat so is not used as a groundcover. Two-row stonecrop, *Sedum spurium*, has scalloped leaves and grows to about 6 inches tall. It is a groundcover type, used for edging. Flowers of pink to deep red are borne above the clump of leaves. 'Dragon's Blood' is another popular cultivar. The most spectacular of the sedums is *Sedum spectabile*, a plant 2 feet tall and wide. It emerges in spring to develop a mound of foliage. The flowers developing well above the leaves resemble broccoli. As they open they turn pale pink, rosy-red, and then bronze. Finally they dry and turn brown, remaining attractive all winter. These plants truly have all-season appeal. The cultivar 'Autumn Joy' is considered by many to be one of the ten best perennials grown in the United States today.

Yarrow

Achillea millefolium

Other Name: Common yarrow **Zones:** All **Size:** 1 to 3 feet tall **Blooms:** June to September **Flower Colors:** Yellow, pink, lavender	**Light Requirement:**

*Y*arrow is a plant that is often overlooked for the perennial garden. Actually it is a very useful plant, with larger kinds that are suited to the middle of the border, and shorter ones that can be used as edging. The flowers are excellent for cutting, lasting well and keeping their color after drying. Yarrow is a plant that flourishes in poor soil as long as drainage is good. It does best in full sun, but it can be grown in light shade. Yarrow quickly becomes adapted in natural areas and will grow in such areas indefinitely without further care. No pests bother it.

WHEN TO PLANT

Yarrow may be planted in spring or fall.

WHERE TO PLANT

Plant in full sun in a soil with good drainage. These plants can thrive in tough situations. Use them in the border, in naturalized masses, or in the cutting garden.

HOW TO PLANT

Plants can be divided in spring or fall. Yarrow is available in pots or 1- and 6-gallon cans, often in bloom. Prepare the soil by tilling or spading to a 6-inch depth. Any decent garden soil is satisfactory. Dig the holes for containerized plants the same depth and twice the width of the plant ball. Set the plants or divisions at the same depth they were growing in their containers. Water thoroughly to firm the soil. Do not water again until the soil dries out. These plants do not tolerate soggy soils.

CARE AND MAINTENANCE

Yarrow does not require a lot of care. Taller cultivars or plants growing in partial shade may need to be staked and tied to keep them from falling over. Plants in fertile or moist soils will be larger and weaker. Remove spent blooms to keep the plants flowering. In fall, cut the plants to the ground.

ADDITIONAL INFORMATION

The name *Achillea* is for Achilles, who is said to have used the plant to heal wounds after the Siege of Troy. According to Greek mythology, he was taught the uses of the plant by Chiron the Centaur. This is called "herb of carpenters" by the French, in reference to its use in healing the cuts carpenters regularly endure. *Millefolium* means "of a thousand leaves"—its finely cut foliage looks like thousands of leaves. Yarrows are good for cutting. The fresh flowers keep well, lasting for many days. Flowers cut before the pollen ripens can be dried and they will keep their color. They may be used in dried arrangements and will last indefinitely.

ADDITIONAL SPECIES, CULTIVARS, OR VARIETIES

Several species of yarrow are grown in gardens. Common yarrow is a floppy plant, but the hybrids stand up well. The species is better as a naturalized plant, in poor, infertile soils. It can be found in the wild along railroad embankments and in other open areas. In fertile soils the plants spread very quickly. Crosses of common yarrow and *A. taygetea* have produced some excellent cultivars. 'Appleblossom' has rosy-pink blooms and an open habit. It regrows from cutting quite well in our garden. Even though it is less than 3 feet tall, it does need staking. 'Summer Pastels' is a mixture of red, white, pink, cream, orange, and mauve blooms. It was named an AAS winner in 1990. Fernleaf yarrow, *A. filipendulina*, is a taller plant, growing to 4 feet or more. It requires staking. Its flowers are yellow and will keep their color for years after drying; they are often seen in large dried arrangements.

The idea is that you simply plant the perennials, and every year they come up and burst into bloom.

The

Gardener

who plans

reaps

the

Greatest

Reward

COOL
SPRINGS
PRESS

The Illinois Gardener's Guide
Photographic gallery of featured plants

ANNUALS

Ageratum
Ageratum houstonianum

Alyssum
Alyssum maritimum

Begonia
Begonia semperflorens-cultorum

Browallia
Browallia speciosa

Celosia
Celosia cristata

Cleome
Cleome hassleriana

Coleus
Coleus x *hybridus*

Cosmos
Cosmos sp.

Dusty Miller
Senecio cineraria

Flowering Tobacco
Nicotiana alata

Four-O-Clock
Mirabilis jalapa

Gaillardia
Gaillardia pulchella

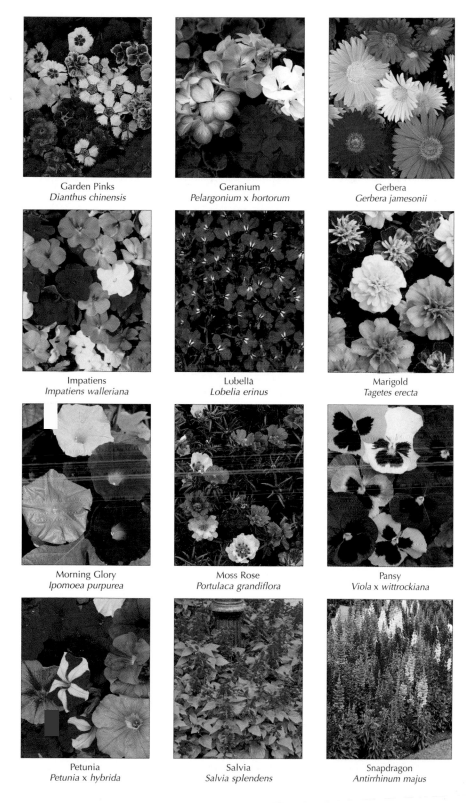

Garden Pinks
Dianthus chinensis

Geranium
Pelargonium x *hortorum*

Gerbera
Gerbera jamesonii

Impatiens
Impatiens walleriana

Lobella
Lobelia erinus

Marigold
Tagetes erecta

Morning Glory
Ipomoea purpurea

Moss Rose
Portulaca grandiflora

Pansy
Viola x *wittrockiana*

Petunia
Petunia x *hybrida*

Salvia
Salvia splendens

Snapdragon
Antirrhinum majus

Sunflower
Helianthus annuus

Verbena
Verbena x *hybrida*

Zinnia
Zinnia elegans

Bearded Iris
Iris hybrids

Caladium
Caladium x *hortulanum*

Canna
Canna generalis

Daffodil
Narcissus hybrids

Flowering Onion
Allium sp.

Gladiolus
Gladiolus x hortulanus

Lily
Lilium sp.

Spring Flowering Bulbs
*Crocus vernus, Chionodoxa luciliae,
Scilla sibirica*

Tuberous Begonia
Begonia x tuberhybrida

Tulip
Tulipa hybrids

Ajuga
Ajuga reptans

Barren Strawberry
Waldsteinia ternata

Common Periwinkle
Vinca minor

Common Wintercreeper
Euonymus fortunei cultivars

Creeping Cotoneaster
Cotoneaster adpressus

English Ivy
Hedera helix

European Ginger
Asarum europaeum

Gro-Low Sumac
Rhus aromatica 'Gro-Low'

Japanese Spurge
Pachysandra terminalis

Juniper
Juniperus sp.

Lily of the Valley
Convallaria majalis

Sweet Woodruff
Galium odoratum

Dwarf Pampas Grass
Cortaderia selloana

Feather Reed Grass
Calamagrostis acutiflora

Fountain Grass
Pennisetum alopecuroides

Moor Grass
Molinia caerulea

Northern Sea Oats
Chasmanthium latifolium

Plume Grass
Erianthus ravennae

Silver Grass
Miscanthus sp.

Tufted Hair Grass
Deschampsia caespitosa

Aster
Aster novae-angliae

Astilbe
Astilbe x arendsii

Bee Balm
Monarda didyma

Bellflower
Campanula sp.

Bleeding Heart
Dicentra spectabilis

Columbine
Aquilegia hybrids

Coneflower
Rudbeckia nitida

Coreopsis
Coreopsis grandiflora

Daylily
Hemerocallis sp.

Delphinium
Delphinium elatum

Ferns
Adiantum pedatum et al.

Gay feather
Liatris scariosa

Hardy Chrysanthemum
Dendranthema x *morifolium*

Heuchera
Heuchera americana

Hosta
Hosta plantaginea

Oriental Poppy
Papaver orientale

Peony
Paeonia hybrids

Phlox
Phlox paniculata

Purple Coneflower
Echinacea purpurea

Russian Sage
Perovskia atriplicifolia

Shasta Daisy
Leucanthemum x *superbum*

Speedwell
Veronica sp.

Stonecrop
Sedum sp.

Yarrow
Achillea millefolium

Floribunda Rose
Rosa x *hybrida*

Grandiflora Rose
Rosa x *hybrida*

Groundcover Rose
Rosa x *hybrida*

Hybrid Tea Rose
Rosa x *hybrida*

Miniature Rose
Rosa x *hybrida*

Shrub Rose
Rosa x *hybrida*

Alpine Currant
Ribes alpinum

Arbor Vitae
Thuja occidentalis

Barberry
Berberis sp.

Boxwood
Buxus microphylla

Cotoneaster
Cotoneaster sp.

Dogwood
Cornus sp.

Forsythia
Forsythia sp.

Fragrant Sumac
Rhus aromatica

Holly
Ilex sp.

Honeysuckle
Lonicera sp.

Hydrangea
Hydrangea sp.

Juneberry
Amelanchier arborea

Juniper
Juniperus sp.

Lilac
Syringa sp.

Mock Orange
Philadelphus coronarius

Mugo Pine
Pinus mugo

Potentilla
Potentilla fruticosa

Privet
Ligustrum sp.

Redbud
Cercis canadensis

Rhododendron
Rhododendron sp.

Rose of Sharon
Hibiscus syriacus

Saint John's Wort
Hypericum prolificum

Smoketree
Cotinus coggygria

Snowberry
Symphoricarpos albus

Spicebush
Lindera benzoin

Spirea
Spiraea sp.

Viburnum
Viburnum sp.

Witchhazel
Hamamelis sp.

Yew
Taxus sp.

Ash
Fraxinus sp.

Bald Cypress
Taxodium distichum

Beech
Fagus sp.

Birch
Betula sp.

Black Tupelo
Nyssa sylvatica

Callery Pear
Pyrus calleryana

Catalpa
Catalpa speciosa

Crab Apple
Malus sp.

Flowering Dogwood
Cornus florida

Ginkgo
Ginkgo biloba

Hackberry
Celtis occidentalis

Hawthorn
Crataegus sp.

Honeylocust
Gleditsia tricanthos inermis

Hornbeam
Carpinus caroliniana

Horsechestnut
Aesculus hippocastanum

Japanese Tree Lilac
Syringa reticulata

Katsuratree
Cercidiphyllum japonicum

Kentucky Coffeetree
Gymnocladus dioicus

Larch
Larix decidua

Linden
Tilia sp.

Magnolia
Magnolia sp.

Maple
Acer sp.

Oak
Quercus sp.

Pine
Pinus sp.

Redbud
Cercis canadensis

Spruce
Picea sp.

Sweet Gum
Liquidambar styraciflua

Tuliptree
Liriodendron tulipifera

American Bittersweet
Celastrus scandens

Boston Ivy
Parthenocissus tricuspidata

Clematis
Clematis x jackmanii

Climbing Hydrangea
Hydrangea anomala petiolaris

Dropmore Honeysuckle
Lonicera sempervirens x *hirsuta*

English Ivy
Hedera helix

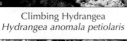

Japanese Wisteria
Wisteria floribunda

Trumpet Vine
Campsis radicans

Wintercreeper
Euonymus fortunei

Black-eyed Susan
Rudbeckia hirta

Blue Boneset
Eupatorium coelestinum

Bluestem
Andropogon sp.

Butterfly Weed
Asclepias tuberosa

Goldenrod
Solidago sp.

Jack-in-the-Pulpit
Arisaema triphyllum

Joe-Pye Weed
Eupatorium purpureum

May Apple
Podophyllum peltatum

Milkweed
Asclepias sp.

Prairie Phlox
Phlox pilosa fulgida

Purple Coneflower
Echinacea purpurea

Trillium
Trillium sp.

Virginia Bluebells
Mertensia virginica

Wild Columbine
Aquilegia canadensis

Wild Geranium
Geranium maculatum

Plant people are some of the greatest people in the world, and we're glad you are part of the family.

CHAPTER SIX

Roses

*T*RECEIVED AND PLANTED A ROSEBUSH when I was still a teenager in Pasadena, California, working for Campbell's Seed Company. It was a 'Chrysler Imperial' and, I think, an AARS (All-America Rose Selection) that year. It was about 1952 or 1953.

I had no intention of becoming a rosarian. (I had no intention of becoming a horticulturist then either.) I had the plant, and had a place to plant it. When that plant began to bloom it piqued my interest, because the only flowers I had ever grown were things like zinnias and nasturtiums. This thing actually made a gorgeous, big red flower, and people came to smell and admire it.

Eventually my gardening space expanded to include a dozen or so different roses, including 'Peace'. Not long after that I headed off to college, not as an aspiring musician as I had once planned, but to learn as much as I could about the fascinating world of horticulture. Other factors were involved in this decision, but roses started it all. I still grow roses, and for a good part of my career, grew them commercially.

Roses are the most popular flower with gardeners across America, and we are no different in Illinois. We had roses in our garden when I was a child, and there were roses in Grandma's garden, too. Ours were not hybrid tea roses, but shrub roses with deliciously fragrant double pink flowers that bloomed every June. They were moss roses, I suppose, because the stems were covered with moss-like thorns. I can still remember the aroma.

Since the end of World War II, rose gardeners have embraced the hybrid teas as the ultimate roses. In our part of the country the flowers are beautiful, but getting them through the winter is a hit-or-miss adventure. I have to admit that I made lots of misses. Caring for them requires spraying, fertilizing, watering, pruning, and worrying.

There had to be a better way. The shrub roses are an answer. The current popularity of things Victorian means a resurgence of interest in the old-fashioned roses, which are, of course, shrub roses. They are nearly maintenance free, and most will survive Illinois winters without protection. The newer landscape-type bush roses, many of which are from the House of Meilland, are smaller, hardy, and just about trouble free. Simply plant these roses like any other shrub, get out of the way, and let them grow!

The bush roses flower in spring, and some flower throughout the summer. The flowers can be singles or doubles, sometimes cabbage-like. They have a singular beauty. Many are scrumptiously fragrant. I hope there are enough rose lovers who would be perfectly happy each spring with a cluster of single roses, or roses the size and shape of cabbages. Maybe shrub roses will become respectable, and every-one can grow at least one rosebush.

For many rose fanciers, the bush roses, in spite of their admirable qualities, just can't compete with the classical roses such as hybrid teas, floribundas, and grandifloras. Most rose gardeners persist in growing these admittedly beautiful, but cantankerous, plants. So . . . how do you grow roses in Illinois?

PLANTING

Hybrid tea roses—and the closely related floribundas, grandifloras, and miniatures—must have full sun and a well-drained soil. Throughout this book we talk about the necessity of good drainage, but for no plant is it more important than for roses. Without good drainage they simply will not survive the winter. If the soil does not drain, construct raised beds or install drain tiles.

If the soil is a good loam with plenty of organic matter (a good black soil), the roses can be planted directly in it. If the soil is poor, prepare it by turning it over to at least one spade depth. If you are planning to plant just one or two roses, spade just the couple of square feet where each plant will be set. Incorporate into the soil organic matter such as compost, peat moss, or whatever you can get your hands on. Shredded leaves, manure, shredded bark, or even corn cobs will work.

Hybrid tea types are all grafted plants. The flowering part (the scion) is grafted to a root that is a different kind of rose. The roots are vigorous plants that do not flower. When planting, the scion must be placed so that it is just at the soil's surface, so that the graft and part of the scion can be covered for winter. An unprotected scion exposed to the rigors of an Illinois winter will not survive, and the rootstock, ultimately more hardy, will grow instead. Roses of the hybrid tea type require continuous care throughout the season.

WATERING AND MULCHING ROSES

Water to provide a measured inch a week if nature does not cooperate. Keeping water off the leaves cuts down on diseases. Drip irrigation or leaky pipe systems will put the water on the ground instead of on the plants.

Mulching reduces the chances of rainstorms splashing water and soil-borne diseases onto the leaves. Mulches keep the soil from compacting and reduce surface evaporation. Use leafmold, shredded bark, wood chips, or compost. When I started growing roses, cracked corncobs were the only mulch, according to most rosarians. Nothing else would work. Of course, there are really many things that will work. Use whatever you can find that stays put and looks attractive. I wouldn't use any of the landscape stones, however.

FERTILIZING ROSES

Roses must be fertilized throughout the spring and early summer. Use a complete, balanced fertilizer (such as 10-10-10) three times per season . . . early spring, after the first flush of blooms, and about mid-July. An alternative is a soluble fertilizer such as Peters or Miracle-Gro. Follow label directions. Do not fertilize after August 1, or the plants might not harden off for winter.

CONTROLLING ROSE PESTS

Black spot and mildew, the most serious diseases, can be quite troublesome in rainy weather. Spray with triforine (Funginex) every week as long as the weather is wet.

Insect pests include aphids and mites; insecticidal soap will control both of them. Orthene will control most other insects. Be sure to read and follow the directions on the label.

PRUNING ROSES

Roses are pruned in early spring, to remove weak and dead stems and to shape the plant. Select two or three strong canes. Cut them

Chapter Six

back to side buds facing away from the center of the plant, leaving the canes about a foot long. Remove all other canes.

When cutting flowers or deadheading, cut to a "five" (a leaf with five leaflets) near the middle of the stem. Try to leave two "fives" on the remaining stem. The cut should be made $1/4$ inch above the leaf. If you have had trouble with cane borers in your area, dab the cut with a little yellow shellac to protect it.

WINTER PROTECTION FOR ROSES

Rose plants will lose their leaves in fall when temperatures begin to go below freezing. Cut the canes back to 15 or 18 inches high. When the ground begins to freeze in late fall, cover the bases of the plants with foot-high piles of topsoil from elsewhere in your garden. After the soil freezes, cover the piles of topsoil with another foot of mulch.

A few of the many kinds of roses are discussed in this chapter, and some cultivars are listed as well. These may have received AARS recognition, or they may have rated very high on the ARS evaluation scales. Since this chapter is only an introduction to the wonderful world of roses, lots of good roses are left out. For more information on roses, contact your local Rose Society chapter, or the American Rose Society, P. O. Box 30,000, Shreveport, LA 71130-0030.

Floribunda Rose

Rosa × hybrida

Zones: All (semi-hardy)
Size: To 3 feet
Blooms: Summer, depending on kind
Flower Colors: White, pink, red, orange,
    yellow, bicolors (all colors except blue)
Type: Deciduous

Light Requirement:

Floribundas are small-flowered roses that bear clusters of blooms at the ends of their stems. The flower forms are varied, but most are button-like with 25 to 40 petals and typical rose form. There are some cultivars that have few petals and even a few singles. The plants produce a good display with all the flowers in the clusters blooming about the same time; a plant covered with these clusters is spectacular indeed.

WHEN TO PLANT

Floribunda roses are planted in the spring in Illinois—they are too susceptible to winter injury to risk losing them by planting them in fall. Plants are available in containers and in bloom all season long. If these are bought at fire sale prices, they may be worth the risk. March is usually a good time to plant dormant bareroot roses throughout Illinois. The plants can stand a freeze even if they have started to grow. Started plants may lose their first shoots if planted out too early and exposed to low temperatures. Even if the shoots are killed back, the plants will grow new ones in a short time and be no worse for the experience.

WHERE TO PLANT

Plant floribunda roses in masses, in the border, or as specimens in the perennial garden. They are most often planted in the rose garden where they can easily be given the necessary care. Any good garden soil will suffice, but it must be well drained. Roses are at their best in full sun.

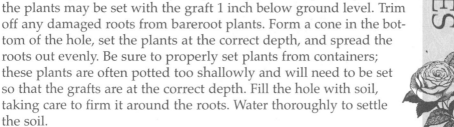

HOW TO PLANT

Prepare the soil by spading to a 12-inch depth. Incorporate organic matter. Drainage is essential. If the garden does not drain, consider constructing raised beds. Dig the planting holes deep enough so that the plants may be set with the graft 1 inch below ground level. Trim off any damaged roots from bareroot plants. Form a cone in the bottom of the hole, set the plants at the correct depth, and spread the roots out evenly. Be sure to properly set plants from containers; these plants are often potted too shallowly and will need to be set so that the grafts are at the correct depth. Fill the hole with soil, taking care to firm it around the roots. Water thoroughly to settle the soil.

CARE AND MAINTENANCE

Floribunda roses require a lot of care. Water them when the soil is dry—do not let them wilt. Water early in the day and keep water off the foliage. The major diseases of roses are severe if the leaves are allowed to be wet overnight. Deadhead the plants to keep them blooming. Dusting or spraying will be necessary to control black spot disease in wet weather. Use Funginex (triforine) according to label directions. Mites and aphids may be troublesome; control them with insecticidal soap.

ADDITIONAL INFORMATION

Floribundas are part of the parentage of the grandiflora roses. The sweetheart roses used for corsages are floribundas. Garnette was one of the earliest ones and is still grown in some greenhouses.

ADDITIONAL SPECIES, CULTIVARS, OR VARIETIES

There are literally dozens of hybrid floribundas. 'Iceberg' is a highly rated white and 'Europeana' is a top-rated velvet red. An excellent yellow is 'Sunsprite'. These have all performed well; the 'Europeana', however, does sunburn in the hottest weather, even though it is better than most reds.

ROSES

Grandiflora Rose

Rosa × hybrida

Zones: All (semi-hardy)
Size: To 3 feet tall
Blooms: Summer
Flower Colors: All except blue
Type: Deciduous

Light Requirement:

*G*randiflora roses include some of the best hybrids, and they have received many ARS awards. These plants were originally crosses between hybrid teas and floribundas, but they now constitute a class of their own. The flower size approaches that of many hybrid teas, but the flowers are borne in clusters that all open at about the same time. Some of the grandifloras have inherited the troubles of their large-flowered parents: those cultivars are very susceptible to black spot and mildew. Grandifloras are better specimens than floribundas, but they do not put on the mass floral display typical of beds of floribundas.

WHEN TO PLANT

It's best to plant grandiflora roses in the spring in Illinois. If you plant them in fall, you risk losing them to winter injury before they have begun to bloom. Potted plants are available in bloom all season. If these are bought cheaply, they may be worth the risk. March is usually a good time to plant dormant bareroot roses throughout Illinois. The plants can stand a freeze even if they have started to grow. Started plants may lose their first shoots if planted out too early and exposed to low temperatures, but even if the shoots are killed back, the plants will grow new ones in a short time.

WHERE TO PLANT

Plant grandiflora roses in full sun in a well-drained garden soil. Grandifloras may be planted as specimens in the perennial garden, but most often they are planted in the rose garden where the necessary care can be easily given.

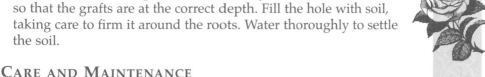

How to Plant

Prepare the soil by spading to a 12-inch depth, incorporating organic matter. Drainage is essential. If the garden does not drain, consider constructing raised beds. Dig the planting holes deep enough so that the plants may be set with the graft 1 inch below ground level. Trim off any damaged roots from bareroot plants. Form a cone in the bottom of the hole, set the plants at the correct depth, and spread the roots out evenly. Be sure to properly set plants from containers; these plants are often potted too shallowly and will need to be set so that the grafts are at the correct depth. Fill the hole with soil, taking care to firm it around the roots. Water thoroughly to settle the soil.

Care and Maintenance

Grandifloras roses require a lot of care. Water them when the soil is dry—do not let them wilt. Water early in the day and keep water off the foliage. The major diseases of roses are severe if the leaves are allowed to be wet overnight. Control black spot disease in wet weather. Dust or spray with Funginex (triforine) according to label directions. Mites and aphids may be troublesome; control them with insecticidal soap.

Additional Information

Deadhead the plants to keep them blooming. Each spring, prune out dead wood and small weak canes. Leave 2 or 3 good sturdy canes, and trim them to an outside bud so they will spread instead of growing to the center of the plants.

Additional Species, Cultivars, or Varieties

Grandifloras are the result of crossing hybrid tea roses and floribundas. The first grandiflora was 'Queen Elizabeth' in 1955; it received the AARS in 1956. It is a tall plant, growing very strongly upright with well-shaped pink blooms. It is a one-of-a-kind—there is nothing else quite like it. 'Gold Medal', a medium yellow, is the only other grandiflora rated higher than 8.5 by the American Rose Society. Other AARS winners have been 'Scarlet Knight' in 1968, 'Arizona' in 1975, and 'Sundowner' in 1979.

Groundcover Rose

Rosa × hybrida

Zones: All
Size: To 1 foot, sometimes more
Blooms: Summer
Flower Colors: Pink, white, red, yellow
Type: Deciduous

Light Requirement:

Groundcover roses are hardy, low-growing ramblers. They cover the ground with a thicket of canes dense enough to keep weeds out. These plants can be described as procumbent (they have stems that trail along the ground without rooting). They are much wider than they are high, a trait that makes them very useful in the landscape. They can be used as groundcovers in beds, in parking lot islands, in office sites, or on banks and slopes in the landscape where mowing is difficult. These roses are just now becoming popular in this country, but they have been used in Europe for many years. Some European cultivars are being used here now.

WHEN TO PLANT

Groundcover roses should be planted in spring so they become established before the onset of winter. Containerized plants are available throughout the summer and can be planted until the ground freezes up. While these plants are hardy, there is still the risk of damage to plants that are not well rooted.

WHERE TO PLANT

Plant groundcover roses wherever groundcovers are needed; they should be in full sun in a well-drained soil.

HOW TO PLANT

Groundcover roses are grown in 5-gallon-sized containers. The hole for planting should be no deeper than the depth of the ball of the plant, and at least twice as wide. Remove the plants from their containers and slice any circling roots. Set the plant in the planting hole and replace half the soil. Fill the hole with water. Replace the remaining soil, and fill the hole with water again. Make a saucer around the plant with any remaining soil. Space the plants at 2 to 4 feet apart.

CARE AND MAINTENANCE

Other than some pruning and watering, these plants require very little care. Don't shear them; head them back. Cut overly long branches to a side branch growing in the same direction, but shorter. Prune in spring before growth starts, or as needed during the season. Groundcover roses are low and twiggy and tend to collect trash that blows into them. Rake them out, or have a landscape contractor vacuum them out in spring.

ADDITIONAL INFORMATION

Until they are established, the shade produced by these somewhat open plants is not dense enough to keep out weeds. Pull or hoe the weeds. Preemergent herbicides and grass preventers are also helpful.

ADDITIONAL SPECIES, CULTIVARS, OR VARIETIES

Some older groundcover cultivars are 'Max Graf', a *Rosa rugosa* × *wichuraiana* hybrid from 1919, and 'Raubritter', a low-mounded plant with pink single flowers in early summer (1936). More recent is 'Ferdy' a taller pink (3 feet tall), spreading at least 6 feet. 'Max Graf' spreads by sending out long canes that take root. It will take over a bank if allowed to do so, and produces fragrant pink flowers in June. The most exciting groundcover rose is 'Flower Carpet' Pink. It is one-of-a-kind for now, but more are certainly on the way. It blooms from spring to fall with pink-and-white flushed flowers in clusters. The plants are about 2 feet tall and spread 6 feet or more; deadhead to keep them tidy.

Hybrid Tea Rose

Rosa × hybrida

Zones: All (semi-hardy)
Size: To 4 feet
Blooms: Summer
Flower Colors: Red, white, yellow, pink,
   orange, bicolors (all except blue)
Type: Deciduous

Light Requirement:

*H*ybrid tea roses created a sensation when the first of them was introduced in 1867 by Jean-Baptiste Guillot. 'La France' was produced by crossing a tea rose with a hybrid perpetual. These were the first large roses that would bloom all summer on fairly long stems. Prior to that, most roses bloomed in early summer and sporadically after that. The hybrid perpetuals did bloom all summer, but they had shorter stems and their blooming was erratic, not at all predictable. Hybrid tea roses are difficult to work into the landscape. They can be situated as specimens in a border, but it may be difficult to give them the care they require. More often they are planted in a rose garden.

WHEN TO PLANT

Hybrid tea roses are planted in the spring. Plants are available potted, or bareroot in packages. Later in the spring potted plants can be bought in bloom so you can see what you are getting. Potted plants may be planted all summer, but late planting may not allow them to become established before the onset of bad weather. Hybrid teas are marginally hardy in Illinois. If winter is unusually severe or very changeable, alternating hot and cold, the plants may be killed. If you can get plants at bargain prices late in the season, it may be worth trying them. If they winterkill, there is little lost—though you may not have gotten many flowers from them either!

WHERE TO PLANT

Plant hybrid tea roses in full sun in a well-drained soil. These roses may fit into the flower border as specimen plants. They can be tall, so set them to the back. Be sure to leave room to get to them for tending. You may choose instead to plant them in a rose garden.

HOW TO PLANT

Prepare the soil by spading to a 12-inch depth, incorporating organic matter. Drainage is essential. If the garden does not drain well, consider constructing raised beds. Dig the planting holes deep enough so that the plants may be set with the graft 1 inch below ground level. Trim off any damaged roots from bareroot plants. Form a cone in the bottom of the hole, set the plants at the correct depth, and spread the roots out evenly. Be sure to properly set plants from containers; these plants are often potted too shallowly and will need to be set so that the grafts are at the correct depth. Fill the hole with soil, taking care to firm it around the roots. Water thoroughly to settle the soil. Space the plants 3 to 4 feet apart so there is room to get between them for spraying and pruning.

CARE AND MAINTENANCE

Hybrid tea roses require a lot of care. Do not let them wilt, but do not keep the soil continuously soaked either. Water them early in the day, and keep water off the foliage. The major diseases of roses are severe if the leaves are allowed to be wet overnight. To increase the numbers of blooms, pinch out the center bud when it is the size of a grain of rice. For large blooms, disbud (remove the side buds) as soon as the buds are big enough to handle. Deadhead the plants to keep them blooming. Cut the stem to a leaf that has 5 leaflets, usually about halfway down the stem. Dusting or spraying will be necessary to control black spot disease in wet weather. Use Funginex (triforine) according to label directions. Mites and aphids may be troublesome; control them with insecticidal soap.

ADDITIONAL SPECIES, CULTIVARS, OR VARIETIES

There are hundreds of hybrid tea roses. The 'Chrysler Imperial' was my favorite as a new gardener; it was an AARS in the 1950s, and still is a good one. The list of highly rated hybrid teas includes some other familiar names. 'Peace' is a blend, pale yellow petals touched with pink, and an AARS in 1946. 'Touch of Class' is orange-pink. 'Olympiad' and 'Mister Lincoln' are red. My current favorite is 'Fragrant Memories', a delicate pink with a wonderful fragrance and long stems. It will last a week as a cut flower.

Miniature Rose

Rosa × hybrida

Zones: All
Size: 1 to (sometimes) 2 feet tall
Blooms: Summer
Flower Colors: Red, white, yellow, pink,
    orange, bicolors (all except blue)
Type: Deciduous

Light Requirement:

*M*iniature roses are not new, but they are enjoying a resurgence in popularity. The origin of the miniatures is clouded in mystery. Many authorities accept the theory that they were the result of a dwarf clone of *Rosa chinensis* which they have named *R. c. minima*. These little roses were popular as pot plants in Europe in the early 1800s, but there was a greater interest in large flowers at the time. Shortly after World War I, a Swiss army medical officer named Roulet spotted a plant growing in a pot on a windowsill in Geneva. He propagated it under the name of 'Rouletii'. The modern miniatures are the result of the hybridizer Ralph Moore, of Sequoia Nurseries in Visalia, California. He, more than anyone, is responsible for the multitude of miniatures available today. For show purposes, miniatures must be scale models of the larger roses: the flowers, leaves, stems, and even the thorns are to be in the exact proportions.

WHEN TO PLANT
Most miniatures are potted for sale. They are best planted in spring when the worst of the cold weather is over.

WHERE TO PLANT
Plant these little roses in full sun in a well-drained soil. Raised beds work well, allowing the plants to be a little higher and more visible. Miniature roses can be planted in borders, as edging, as accents, in masses, or in planters or containers.

HOW TO PLANT
Prepare the soil by tilling or spading. If the drainage is not good, consider constructing raised beds. Miniature roses are sold as potted plants in bloom, in 4- or 6-inch pots. When planting in beds, set

them about 1 to $1^1/2$ feet apart, and only as deep as they were grow-ing in their containers. When planted in planters, flowerboxes, urns, or hanging baskets, they are usually spaced plant-to-plant.

CARE AND MAINTENANCE

Miniatures are beset with the same problems as their larger counter-parts. Water them as needed, early in the day so the foliage dries before nightfall. Dusting or spraying will be necessary to control black spot disease in wet weather. Use Funginex (triforine) accord-ing to label directions. Mites and aphids may be troublesome; control them with insecticidal soap. Prune out dead twigs and remove spent blooms as the flowers fade.

ADDITIONAL INFORMATION

Miniature roses are excellent for flower arrangements. Try to cut long stems, but leave at least two 5-leaflet leaves on the plant.

ADDITIONAL SPECIES, CULTIVARS, OR VARIETIES

Many miniatures have rated above 8.5 on the ARS scale. 'Peggy T' is a medium red. 'Pacesetter' and 'Snowbride' are white. 'Pink Meillandina' and the yellow 'Rise 'n' Shine' are excellent choices, but 'Jean Kenneally', an apricot blend, rates an ARS 9.7, one of the all-time highest scores. It has classic-form flowers and blooms from June until frost.

Shrub Rose

Rosa × hybrida

Zones: All
Size: To 4 feet tall
Blooms: Summer
Flower Colors: Pink, red, white, yellow,
    orange, bicolor
Type: Deciduous

Light Requirement:

The shrub roses are a catchall classification for plants that don't seem to fit anywhere else. They may be large bushes, as are some of the species, or they may be tame and easily controlled as are landscape roses. Shrub rose seems to mean different things to people from various parts of the country. Here we tend to classify them as winter-hardy plants that are for all practical purposes disease resistant as well. The landscape roses are hybrids that have been bred for use as hedges, borders, or accents. Species roses and hybrid shrub roses are of any form, and may be either spring-blooming or may repeat.

WHEN TO PLANT

Shrub roses are planted in spring, or from containers anytime during the season. They are hardy, but they do need to be established before the onset of severe weather.

WHERE TO PLANT

Plant shrub roses as accents, as specimens, in masses, for screens, as hedges, or in the shrub border. These plants need full sun. They will grow in partial shade, but the flowering will suffer. The soil should be fertile, moist, and well drained.

HOW TO PLANT

Shrub roses are generally sold in containers; sometimes small plants are sold bareroot. The hole for planting should be shallower than the depth of the ball, and at least twice as wide. Soak bareroot plants for several hours before planting. Space plants of landscape cultivars 3 to 6 feet apart in masses. Larger plants should be spaced 10 to 15 feet apart or farther, and specimen plants should be at least the same distances from any structure. Set each plant in the hole, keeping it slightly higher than it grew in the nursery. Remove the burlap from balled-and-burlapped plants, stuffing it in the hole. Soak the plants thoroughly after planting to settle the soil around the roots.

CARE AND MAINTENANCE

Pruning to keep the plants tidy and in bounds is the major maintenance chore with bush roses. Remove old or damaged canes in spring. Disease control should not be required; insects that may stumble into the planting can be dealt with if necessary.

ADDITIONAL INFORMATION

One of the most famous roses of all time was the hybrid perpetual 'American Beauty'. According to legend, the rose was a European cultivar named 'Mme. Ferdinand Jamin', not a popular name. It was renamed 'American Beauty' by Ulysses S. Grant's White House gardener, James Brady. It became the most popular rose of all time, and huge greenhouse complexes were built just to grow it for the florist trade. The rose-growing center of Pana, Illinois, the Pullman greenhouses in Chicago, and the huge Premier Roses in Des Plaines were built in the early part of this century to grow 'American Beauty' roses. It is no longer grown commercially, but plants are available from nurseries specializing in old-rose cultivars.

ADDITIONAL SPECIES, CULTIVARS, OR VARIETIES

Landscape roses are short and well behaved. The first of these to receive wide notice was 'Bonica'. 'The Fairy' and the 'Meidiland' series that includes pink-, white-, and scarlet-flowering types are being planted enthusiastically by landscape contractors happy to have roses that don't require a full-time maintenance person to care for them. The species and hybrid shrub roses have been separated into 15 categories. The first of them is Species Roses. It includes, among others, *R. rugosa*, *R. hugonis*, *R. setigera*, and *R. foetida*. One of the most stunning roses is *Rosa × harisonii*, 'Harison's Yellow'. This large plant is covered with fragrant yellow double blooms around Memorial Day—a real show-stopper. Other categories are moss roses, damasks, teas, various hybrid categories, and the hybrid perpetuals.

CHAPTER SEVEN

Shrubs

*S*HRUBS CREATE A TRANSITION from the lawn to the home. If the landscape is well designed, shrub plantings point the way to the house's entrance. They identify the boundaries of spaces, the public and the private areas of your property. They break the winds in winter and direct cooling breezes in summer. They can hide undesirable views while accenting desirable ones.

Shrubs provide flowers, attractive summer foliage, and fall color, and some display colorful fruit. The structure and texture of leafless stems provide contrast and interest in the winter landscape. Shrubs attract wildlife. They are refuges for birds, providing secure nesting sites and shelter from storms.

Shrubs are the most used (and misused) plants in the home landscape. There are many, many kinds of shrubs, but if you drive down a typical street you are likely to see the same ones used over and over again in the same way: a line of evergreens in front of the house and a Christmas tree at the corner. (At the turn of the century the overused shrub arrangement was a line of VanHoutte spireas on either side of the entrance walk in front of a porch.)

In this chapter are descriptions of more than two dozen shrub species and many more cultivars. Each of these has a place in a landscape. Some are familiar to almost everyone, while others are less well known. This is just a partial selection of the shrubs that are available.

When designing your plantings, try to think of new things to do with your plants. There's no need to do the same things your neighbors are doing. Similar adjacent landscapes may be pleasing, but variety is more interesting. And it is not necessary to use evergreens in front of your house. It is true that evergreens stay green all year, but other plants have interesting things to offer during all four seasons. The bare stems of winter will give way to emerging leaves in spring, flowers in summer, and colors in fall . . . these changes can be a lot more interesting than the same old green stuff!

Chapter Seven

Visit the botanical gardens or arboretums in your area. Each university maintains plantings, often labeled with plant names. When you try something new in your garden, the worst thing that can happen is that you will change your mind after you plant it. If this happens, pull it out and start again. Gardening is not a goal; it is an adventure. The fun is in the doing.

Before buying shrubs, draw a plan of your yard, showing the garden and the various areas that are for public viewing, for privacy, or for utility. Mark the things needing to be hidden such as a telephone pole, the neighbor's compost heap, or a church's parking lot.

Plantings in the front of the house should emphasize the entrance. Draw a picture of the front of your house, marking the main entrance. Then draw lines from the bottom of the entrance, angling to a point 2/3 of the way up to the corners of the house, extend these lines to the property lines. All the plants in front of the house should fit under those lines, smallest at the entrance, largest at the ends. Be sure your plants will not hide windows.

Decide the sizes of the plants needed in each location in your yard. Then select suitable proper-sized plants that you would enjoy seeing in your yard. Mix textures, shapes, and colors. Have some fun making selections. Do a little bit at a time so it doesn't become a chore.

The plants in this chapter are shrubs we have used and enjoyed. We hope this information will get you started on a fascinating adventure with shrubs that will brighten your Illinois garden.

Alpine Currant

Ribes alpinum

Zones: All	**Light Requirement:**
Size: 3 to 6 feet tall and wide	
Blooms: April	
Flower Colors: Green, not showy	
Type: Deciduous	

*A*lpine currant is a dense, twiggy shrub with light green foliage. Adapted to shaded areas, it makes good hedges and borders. It is particularly useful for formal hedges, as it takes shearing exceptionally well. At the University of Illinois campus with its large buildings and trees, there are many shaded walkways lined with alpine currant. It thrives in these spots, surviving the perils of high-traffic areas. Alpine currant does well in full sun, too. In the sun, its foliage is more dense and leaf spot problems are lessened.

WHEN TO PLANT

Balled-and-burlapped alpine currant can be planted in spring or fall. Containerized plants can be planted at any time.

WHERE TO PLANT

Plant in sun or in semi-shaded locations. It does well in any good garden soil; acidity does not seem to matter to this adaptable plant. Use it in mass plantings or as a hedge.

HOW TO PLANT

Alpine currant plants are available balled and burlapped or in containers, and sometimes small plants are sold bareroot. The hole for planting should be shallower than the depth of the ball and at least twice as wide. Soak bareroot plants for several hours before planting. Remove plants from containers, and slice any circling roots. Space plants 1½ to 2 feet apart in hedges, 5 feet apart in masses. Set each plant in its hole, keeping it slightly higher than it grew in the nursery. Remove the burlap from balled-and-burlapped plants, stuffing it in the hole. Replace the soil and fill the hole with water. Currants will need regular watering their first year after planting.

CARE AND MAINTENANCE

Alpine currant can be sheared to fit nearly any location. Shearing is best done in spring after the first flush of new growth. Be sure to trim hedges wider at the bottom than at the top; vase-shaped hedges soon lose their lower leaves, ending up with leaves only at the tops of the plants. Should this happen, currant can be renovated by cutting it down to 6 inches and letting it regrow. Leaf spot disease can be troublesome during wet weather. It is controlled with maneb or mancozeb, applied as leaves emerge in spring. Carefully follow the directions on the label.

ADDITIONAL INFORMATION

Almost all *Ribes* species are alternate hosts of white pine blister rust. This is a serious disease of white pines, often killing them one branch at a time. If there are large plantings of white pine in your county, check with the state forester to see if alpine currant is safe to plant. Male plants of alpine currant are thought to be resistant to the rust. These plants are used extensively as dwarf hedges in formal gardens. The dwarf selections require less trimming.

ADDITIONAL SPECIES, CULTIVARS, OR VARIETIES

Quite a bit of selection has been done for shorter and more dense plants. Illinois growers have been leaders in this endeavor. *Ribes alpinum* 'Pumilum' grows to 3 feet (slightly taller in Zones 6 and 7). It spreads twice as wide, and produces tiny scarlet berries in early summer. 'Green Mound' is a little smaller, with good, bright-green color. It was introduced by Burr Oak Nurseries in Round Lake. It is used extensively in the landscape industry, particularly in the small courtyards and commons areas of many condos and townhouses being built lately. Nursery catalogs list selections as 'Compactum', 'Nanum', or 'Pumilum'. These are all described as shorter than the species; only by trying them will you know for sure. It is best to buy these plants from a local grower or supplier who knows how they will grow in your area.

Arbor Vitae

Thuja occidentalis

Zones: All **Size:** 20 feet or more if allowed **Type:** Evergreen	**Light Requirement:**

*A*rbor vitae is a native woodland evergreen tree that grows among deciduous trees such as ash and white pine in Illinois, and oaks in Michigan. It grows as an understory tree in fairly dense shade, often in wet areas. At the forest edge it grows in sun at least part of the day. In the landscape it can be grown as a specimen or accent, foundation plant, windbreak, living fence, or screen. Arbor vitae is an excellent hedge plant, and will take shearing without trouble. These plants are used extensively for screening; as they are evergreen, they work well during all seasons. Properly located, they are effective for many years, and with judicious trimming can be kept attractive and within bounds indefinitely. There are many cultivars of arbor vitae, with differing forms, sizes, and colors; they differ in winter hardiness as well. In selecting plants, it is wise to consider where they were grown and where the stock was selected. Some cultivars were selected in climatic zones quite different from those in Illinois.

WHEN TO PLANT

Plant arbor vitae in spring or fall. Containerized plants may be planted any time during the season.

WHERE TO PLANT

Plant in full sun or light shade. In heavy shade, a plant will lose its needles, and its crown will be quite thin and open. Soil should be deep, moist, and well drained. In the wild, these plants can tolerate soils that are either too wet or too dry, but the quality of the plant suffers.

HOW TO PLANT

Arbor vitaes are grown as balled-and-burlapped plants, and in containers. The hole for planting should be no greater than the depth of the ball of the plant, and at least twice as wide. Remove the burlap from a balled-and-burlapped plant, and stuff it down in the hole. Replace the soil, and fill the hole with water.

CARE AND MAINTENANCE

It is essential that these plants receive adequate water. If they dry out, their needles will drop. Trim the plants after the first flush of new growth has hardened off in late spring. Pruning can be severe if necessary, but do not cut into the "dead" zone in the middle of the plant. Twigs with no needles will not grow again. Keep the plants wider at the bottom than at the top. Mites can be troublesome in hot weather. Treat them with insecticidal soap. Bagworms can strip trees in a short time. Control them with *Bacillus thuringiensis kurstaki*, following the directions on the label.

ADDITIONAL INFORMATION

There are several "yellow" cultivars of arbor vitae. These should be used sparingly, as they will overwhelm the rest of the landscape. Individual plants of the green cultivars can be severely formal, and they must be used with care as well. In masses they blend together and don't stick out as much. If you plant of arbor vitae in full sun and windy sites, you will risk winter desiccation damage. Protected plants fare better. There is a significant difference between cultivars selected for northern areas and those selected for other regions. Most of the dissatisfaction with arbor vitae comes from buying plants of unknown origin, only to discover that the cultivar is not hardy, or from buying plants grown in a soil different from that into which they are planted. Buy plants selected for local conditions, and grown in local soils. Beware of discount plants from itinerant peddlers.

ADDITIONAL SPECIES, CULTIVARS, OR VARIETIES

The best upright cultivar for density, for use as screens, and with the best winter-hardiness is 'Techny'. Sometimes sold as 'Mission', it was selected by Brother Charles at the Techny Seminary in Northbrook for Illinois conditions. 'Emerald', a Danish cultivar, and 'Nigra' have good winter color retention. There are many dwarf cultivars. 'Canadian Green', 3 feet; 'Hetz's Midget', 3 to 4 feet; and 'Woodwardii' deserve mention. These cultivars are being grown by Illinois nurseries. If the people at your garden center cannot locate one of them for you, have them contact the Illinois Nursery Growers Association at Springfield for a list of nurseries that grow what you are looking for.

Barberry

Berberis sp.

Zones: All
Size: 1¹/₂ to 6 feet tall, sometimes twice
   as wide
Blooms: Spring
Flower Color: Yellow, beneath the leaves,
   not showy
Type: Deciduous

Light Requirement:

*B*arberries comprise a large group of landscape plants that are all thorny and make good barriers. These plants have been used since Colonial times when the common barberry was introduced by early immigrants and became naturalized in many parts of the United States. Unfortunately, it is the alternate host of wheat stem rust, a devastating disease of grain crops. Tremendous effort has been expended to eliminate common barberry and the other species that can harbor the disease. The ornamental cultivars, however, are resistant to the disease and constitute no hazard to grain production. Barberries are tough plants. Growing best in full sun, they can stand drought better than most ornamental plants. They are not affected by the pollution and grime of the city or the dust of the country roadside. All take shearing without difficulty. Barberries will not tolerate wet sites.

WHEN TO PLANT

Barberries are grown mostly in containers. Larger sizes are balled and burlapped. They can be planted any time the soil can be worked.

WHERE TO PLANT

Plant as specimens, in masses, in groupings, or as barriers or hedges.

HOW TO PLANT

Any garden soil will suffice for barberries. Dig the planting hole the same depth and twice as wide as the plant ball. Space the standard cultivars 4 feet apart, dwarf cultivars 1¹/₂ feet apart. In hedges, set them plant to plant. Hedges can be planted by opening a trench, setting the plants at the right spacing, and backfilling all of them at the same time.

CARE AND MAINTENANCE

Barberry does not require a lot of care. Shearing of hedges is best done after early growth has hardened off in late spring. Few insects or diseases affect it, though verticillium wilt, a soil-borne disease, can kill these plants. If the disease is introduced into the planting on soil or other plants, it will often kill one plant and then work its way down a hedge, killing a plant at a time on either side. There is no cure for this disease. Remove the plants, and replant the hedge with a resistant species.

ADDITIONAL INFORMATION

Barberries have attractive red berries that may persist well into the fall. Some cultivars have green foliage, but the red kinds seem to be the most popular. (I have never figured out why.) The green foliage is bright and fresh; I think the red becomes tiresome after a while.

ADDITIONAL SPECIES, CULTIVARS, OR VARIETIES

The most commonly grown selections are those of Japanese barberry, *Berberis thunbergii*. Many are varieties of *B. t.* 'Atropurpurea', the red barberry, and they come in all sizes. 'Crimson Pygmy' is one of the best, 2 feet tall and wide. 'Rose Glow' grows to 5 feet and is mottled purple-red. 'Sparkle' is dark green with red berries, growing to 4 feet. It is a Synnestvedt (Round Lake, Illinois) introduction. 'Thornless' is just that: no thorns! Mentor barberry, *Berberis × mentorensis*, is one of the best barberries for hedges. It will make a dense 5-foot mound if left on its own. Korean barberry, *B. koreana*, is upright to 4 feet and very thorny, making it the best barrier plant of the group. Leaves are larger than others, and the red berries last well into winter.

217

Boxwood

Buxus microphylla koreana × B. sempervirens

Other Name: Korean Box
Zones: All
Size: 4 feet
Blooms: March
Flower Color: Not showy
Type: Evergreen

Light Requirement:

oxwoods have been part of gardening in America since Colonial times. Most are common box, which will reach a height of 20 feet. Huge old specimens can be seen at Mount Vernon and other historic locations. The edging box, *B. suffruticosa*, has been used in plantings on the Eastern seaboard for nearly 200 years. This is a true dwarf type, and ancient plants are still only about 3 feet tall. Boxwoods have evergreen foliage and a neat form. Even when allowed to grow without trimming, these plants maintain good form. They are usually severely trimmed into hedges in formal gardens, knot gardens, and foundation plantings. Common box is not hardy in Illinois. In fact, many old plantings in the East have suffered because of the severe winters of the last few years. The Korean box, *B. microphylla koreana*, has been crossed with common box, and the result is a series of hardy evergreen boxwoods that can stand the Northern winters. These cultivars have been accepted widely in the landscape industry, performing well where used correctly. They are delightful little plants. They stay small without shearing, but they take shearing very well. The color is bright green, and some of them hold their color into winter.

WHEN TO PLANT

Boxwood may be planted in spring or fall. In either case, some protection will be needed from sun and wind until the plants are established.

WHERE TO PLANT

Plant in a well-prepared soil. The plants are tolerant of soil type, but a cool, moist soil is best. Good drainage is important; they cannot stand in water. Use for foundation plantings, edging, specimen plants, or hedges.

HOW TO PLANT

Boxwoods are nearly always sold as balled-and-burlapped plants. Prepare the soil by tilling or spading to a 6-inch depth, and incorporate organic matter. Dig the planting hole the same depth and twice as wide as the plant ball. If the soil in the ball is much different from that in the hole, mix some soil from the ball with that going back into the hole to avoid an interface problem. It is best to buy plants grown on a soil as nearly like that in your yard as you can find. Locally grown plants are best. Soak the plants well after planting. A couple of inches of mulch will help maintain soil moisture and coolness.

CARE AND MAINTENANCE

During the first season, boxwood needs to be watered during dry spells. Boxwood will need protection from midday sun and from drying winds in summer and especially in winter. During winter, a temporary burlap screen will work fine. Drive stakes around the south and west sides, and tack the burlap to them. Several insects and diseases can damage boxwood, though most of these are minor problems. Poorly drained soil will result in root rot and affected plants will die. If the plants are growing in a hedge, the plants nearest a downspout will be the first to turn yellow; redirect the downspout.

ADDITIONAL SPECIES, CULTIVARS, OR VARIETIES

Four selections of the *koreana* x *sempervirens* hybrids are prominent in Northern landscapes. 'Green Gem' is 2 by 2 feet and can be described as a round ball. 'Green Mountain' is upright, 5 feet tall and 3 feet wide. 'Green Mound' and 'Green Velvet' are 3 by 3 feet and dark green. 'Wintergreen' is light green and has been used extensively at the Chicago Botanic Gardens in Glencoe. It suffered during the nearly snowless, cold winter of 1995-96, but it recovered.

Cotoneaster

Cotoneaster sp.

Zones: All
Size: 6 to 12 feet tall and wide, sometimes more
Blooms: Spring
Flower Colors: Pink, white, rose; tiny in size
Type: Deciduous

Light Requirement:

otoneasters are among the more attractive shrubs, with their glossy foliage and red fruits. They are large plants and need plenty of room. Some types are quite upright and suited for hedging or screening. Others are spreading; if planted too close together, they will need excessive pruning. Cotoneasters tolerate pruning well. With judicious pruning, spreading types can be kept in bounds and present a nice appearance. Hedge cotoneaster and Peking cotoneaster, both high-quality hedges, can be sheared. Few shrubs are easier to grow than cotoneasters. They have vigorous fibrous root systems, transplant easily, and will grow in almost any kind of soil.

WHEN TO PLANT
Cotoneasters are planted in either spring or fall.

WHERE TO PLANT
Tolerant of some shade, these plants are at their best in full sun. They do well in almost any soil, heavy or light, acid or alkaline, but they don't like wet feet. They do well in hot, dry situations as long as they are watered during extended dry periods. Use in shrub beds or foundation plantings, or as screening or hedges.

HOW TO PLANT
Cotoneaster plants are grown in quart- to 5-gallon-sized containers, or as balled-and-burlapped plants. The hole for planting should be no deeper than the depth of the ball of the plant, and at least twice as wide. Remove the plants from their containers and slice any circling roots. Prepare the soil by spading or tilling to a 12-inch depth, incorporating organic matter if possible. Space the plants 5 to 6 feet apart in beds or screening, 2 feet apart in hedges.

CARE AND MAINTENANCE

Other than some pruning and watering, these plants require very little care. Don't shear the spreading types; head them back. Cut overly long branches to a side branch growing in the same direction, but shorter. Prune in spring before growth starts or as needed during the season. Hedge types may be sheared after the new growth has hardened off in late spring. Spreading cotoneasters are twiggy. The branches, spreading herringbone-like, pile themselves on top of one another, creating a layered effect. They tend to collect trash that blows into them. Rake them out, or have a landscape contractor vacuum them out in spring. The shade produced by these somewhat-open plants is not dense enough to keep out weeds. Pull or hoe when necessary. Preemergent herbicides and grass preventers are helpful. Cotoneasters are susceptible to attack by leaf-roller caterpillars, webworms, mites, and fire blight disease. Control the insects with *Bacillus thuringensis*, control mites with insecticidal soap, and control fire blight with Phyton 27 copper sulfate. Follow label directions carefully.

ADDITIONAL INFORMATION

The name *Cotoneaster* comes from the Greek *ketoneon*, "quince," and *aster*, which means "similar."

ADDITIONAL SPECIES, CULTIVARS, OR VARIETIES

Cotoneaster divaricatus, the spreading cotoneaster, is an arching shrub reaching about 6 feet tall and wide. It has tiny leaves and its flowers are rose-colored in spring, partially hidden by the leaves. Bright-red fruit in fall persists until the leaves turn red and yellow before dropping. This is one of my favorite shrubs and is used, where there is room, in many of the plantings we design. Hedge cotoneaster, *C. lucidus*, and Peking cotoneaster, *C. acutifolius*, are often sold interchangeably, usually as Peking cotoneaster. The ones with the nice, glossy leaves are actually hedge cotoneaster. This is an excellent hedge, attractive and easily maintained. Many-flowered cotoneaster, *C. multiflorus*, is a large plant growing to 8 feet or more. It produces showy, white flowers along arching stems in May on a fountain-like plant. The effect is not unlike a large Vanhoutte spirea. Red fruit is produced in abundance in late summer. This is an excellent plant for a shrub border or massing where there is room.

Dogwood

Cornus

Zones: All
Size: 6 to 20 feet tall and wide
Blooms: Spring
Flower Colors: White or yellow
Type: Deciduous

Light Requirement:

ogwoods are among our best woody ornamentals. They are four-season plants with something of interest to see at any time of the year. Their flowers are usually tiny but are often present in such numbers as to be highly effective. Cornelian cherry is covered net-like with yellow flowers before the leaves appear in spring. Foliage in this genus is usually bright green, but some types have variegated foliage. Fruits are berry-like—red, white, or black. The fruit is readily eaten by birds, but pink fruit stalks of some species persist all winter. Fall color is brilliant red on most kinds; twigs of some are bright yellow or red all winter. Dogwoods are tolerant of many conditions. Soils should be well drained, but moist; either full sun or filtered shade is satisfactory. The smaller cultivars are suitable for foundation plantings, the larger ones for shrub borders or naturalized plantings. Red-twig and yellow-twig dogwoods are adapted to moist soils and will naturalize in wetland settings.

WHEN TO PLANT

Dogwoods may be planted in spring or fall. Containerized plants may be planted at any time.

WHERE TO PLANT

Plant these shrubs in full to filtered sun in the shrub border, for screening, as hedges, in foundation plantings, in naturalized areas, or in masses and around water features.

HOW TO PLANT

Dogwoods are available balled and burlapped or in containers; sometimes small plants are sold bareroot. The hole for planting should be shallower than the depth of the ball, and at least twice as wide. Soak bareroot plants for several hours before planting. Space plants of the smaller cultivars 2 feet apart in hedges, 5 feet apart in masses. Space larger plants such as Cornelian cherry 10 to 15 feet apart. Set each plant in its hole, keeping it slightly higher than it grew in the nursery. Remove the burlap from balled-and-burlapped plants, stuffing it in the hole. Hedges can be planted by opening a trench, setting the plants at a 2-foot spacing, and backfilling them all at the same time.

CARE AND MAINTENANCE

Dogwoods will need to be watered during dry spells their first season after planting. Shrubby types with colored stems should be renewed annually by cutting $1/3$ of the stems to the ground; the new shoots will exhibit brighter color for the next 2 or 3 winters. If the plants become overgrown without proper pruning, cut them down completely. They will regrow in 2 seasons.

ADDITIONAL INFORMATION

The shrubby dogwoods are susceptible to cankering, which kills a branch at a time from the bottom. Scale can be serious as well. Cankering affects only older branches and can be reduced by systematically renewing the plants annually. The removal of the branches eliminates scale at the same time.

ADDITIONAL SPECIES, CULTIVARS, OR VARIETIES

Red-twig and yellow-twig dogwoods are strictly upright-growing plants, with most stems unbranched. At least 3 species are listed in nursery catalogs as "red twig": *Cornus alba* 'Sibirica', *Cornus buileyi*, and *Cornus sericea*. *C. sericea* 'Flaviramea' is yellow-twig dogwood. Several dwarf red-twig cultivars are sold, 'Kelseyi' being the more common; 'Alleman's Dwarf' is another. The nomenclature of these plants is so confusing that no one knows for sure what is what. Buy whatever your supplier has to offer. If it was locally grown, it will probably do fine. Cornelian cherry, *C. mas*, a large plant to 20 feet, is one of the best large landscape shrubs. Several types with varying flower colors and plant sizes are available. Other shrubby dogwoods, and some with tree-like form, can be found at various nurseries and garden centers.

Forsythia

Forsythia sp.

Zones: All
Size: 3 to 9 feet, spreading the same or more
Blooms: Early spring
Flower Color: Yellow
Type: Deciduous

Light Requirement:

orsythias are gracefully arching or upright plants covered with masses of bright-yellow blooms along their stems in early spring. This is the reason we grow these delightful plants. When forsythias are at their best, there is nothing in the garden to compare with them. Only a few crocuses popping up in sunny places might be in bloom at the same time. Forsythia blooms are our first reminder that spring is on the way after the long, dreary Illinois winter. Standard forsythias are large plants. Dwarf types are shorter, but they do spread and need room. Unfortunately, many forsythias are planted in such cramped quarters that they must be pruned yearly to fit, resulting in mutilated plants and poor flowering. Flowers are produced on 1-year-old stems; buds for the next year are set soon after flowering. If you prune after the buds are set, you will remove the flowers for the next spring. Some of forsythia's popularity is due to the ease with which it can be grown. It tolerates almost any soil, and is unaffected by urban conditions. If properly selected for the conditions and placed where it has room enough to grow, it can be planted and with minimal care, forgotten, blooming happily year after year.

WHEN TO PLANT

Forsythias may be planted in spring or fall. Containerized plants may be planted anytime during the season.

WHERE TO PLANT

Plant in full sun for best blooming, allowing plenty of room for the plants to spread out. Any well-drained garden soil will suffice. Forsythias are best used in the shrub border, groupings, or masses. They have no business in foundation plantings unless the home is huge and they can be planted at least 10 feet from the foundation.

A single specimen in the middle of a front yard will be beautiful in bloom but unattractive the other 50 weeks of the year.

HOW TO PLANT

Forsythias are available balled and burlapped or in containers, and sometimes small plants are sold bareroot. In spring, garden centers are full of them in bloom. The hole for planting should be shallower than the depth of the ball and at least twice as wide. Soak bareroot plants for several hours before planting. Space plants of smaller cultivars 6 feet apart in masses, and larger plants such as border forsythia or weeping forsythia 10 to 15 feet apart. Set each plant slightly higher than it grew in the nursery. Soak the plants thoroughly after planting to settle the soil around the roots.

CARE AND MAINTENANCE

Forsythias are essentially pest-free, but yearly pruning to renew the plants is important. Immediately following flowering, remove $1/4$ to $1/3$ of the oldest branches all the way to the ground. This will stimulate new stems from the bases of the plants. If the plants get out of hand, they may be cut to 6 inches above the ground and will regrow in about 3 years. In either case, flowering will not be interrupted.

ADDITIONAL INFORMATION

Although forsythias are hardy throughout Illinois, the flower buds of some cultivars are not. They may be killed at temperatures of minus 5 degrees Fahrenheit. Most Illinois winters have temperatures colder than this. That is why plants often bloom only on branches that were below the snow line in the coldest weather. Plant only cultivars with known flower bud hardiness. There are quite a few available, and the better garden centers and nurseries will have them. Plants brought in from other parts of the country and offered in bloom during spring may be disappointing.

ADDITIONAL SPECIES, CULTIVARS, OR VARIETIES

Don't bother with cultivars of limited flower bud hardiness. The following are cultivars developed in the cold parts of North America: 'Happy Centennial', a dwarf shrub 2 feet tall and 5 feet wide, developed at the Central Experimental Gardens, Ottawa, Ontario, and reported hardy to minus 20 degrees. 'Meadowlark', 6 to 9 feet high from North and South Dakota State Universities and Arnold Arboretum; flower buds hardy to minus 35 degrees. 'Sunrise' from Iowa State University, hardy to -20 degrees, a compact plant about 5 feet high and wide.

Fragrant Sumac

Rhus aromatica

Zones: All
Size: To 6 feet tall, spread 6 to 10 feet
Blooms: Spring
Flower Color: Yellow
Type: Deciduous

Light Requirement:

Fragrant sumac is an excellent plant for naturalized or wooded areas, shrub borders, screens, or roadsides. The tiny-but-lovely yellow flowers produced before the leaves emerge on many plants are certainly welcome after the dark, dreary Illinois winter. The foliage appears in mid-spring. The three-lobed leaves are bright green. The foliage turns crimson in fall. Sumac is a tough plant that tolerates salt and difficult soils. In fact, it grows best in dry, poor soils. This makes it well suited for use in the damaged soils common in new developments. It thrives in urban conditions with the grime and pollution, so it is useful in inner-city locations. On some sites, the fragrant sumac is the only shrub doing well. Fragrant sumac is a spreading shrub with the tips of its bottom branches turning up. Where they touch the ground, the branches take root. This characteristic makes it unusually good at stabilizing damaged banks and slopes. The name fragrant sumac is appropriate; an aroma is emitted when leaves or stems are crushed.

WHEN TO PLANT

Fragrant sumac can be planted either in spring or fall. Containerized plants can be planted at any time.

WHERE TO PLANT

Sumac is tolerant of soils and locations. Plant it in sun or shade; it is one of the few plants that will grow in full shade. Use it for masses, shrub borders, or screening.

HOW TO PLANT

Fragrant sumac plants are sold balled and burlapped or in containers, and sometimes small plants are sold bareroot. The hole for planting should be the same depth as the plant ball, and at least twice as wide. Soak bareroot plants for several hours before plant-

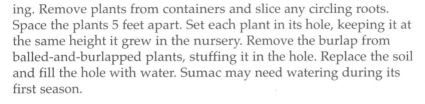

ing. Remove plants from containers and slice any circling roots. Space the plants 5 feet apart. Set each plant in its hole, keeping it at the same height it grew in the nursery. Remove the burlap from balled-and-burlapped plants, stuffing it in the hole. Replace the soil and fill the hole with water. Sumac may need watering during its first season.

CARE AND MAINTENANCE

Sumac is relatively trouble-free, though leaf spot diseases may be troublesome in wet seasons. Hot dry seasons may result in mite infestations. Generally these problems do not require treatment. Fragrant sumac is a loosely branched plant and may become overgrown and straggly. If so, it can be cut down to the ground and will regrow.

ADDITIONAL INFORMATION

Fragrant sumac is closely related to such unwelcome plants as poison ivy, poison oak, and poison sumac, all *Rhus* species. Varnish tree of China is a *Rhus* as well. It and the poison types contain an oil that causes the characteristic rash. The varnish tree also produces the lacquer used on Oriental furniture.

ADDITIONAL SPECIES, CULTIVARS, OR VARIETIES

A few selections have been made of fragrant sumac. 'Green Globe' is a rounded, dense plant growing to about 6 feet tall and wide. 'Gro-Low' is a low, spreading plant used as a groundcover. (See the description on page 114 in the Groundcovers chapter.)

Holly

Ilex sp.

Zones: All
Size: 9 to 18 feet tall, spreading to
  half of height
Blooms: Late spring
Flower Color: White
Type: Some evergreen, most deciduous

Light Requirement:

ollies will grow in Illinois; they won't all look like Christmas holly, but they all have bright, red berries (drupes) and are interesting garden plants. The sexes are borne on separate plants and only female plants have drupes, so there must be a male pollen-plant in your planting. This means you must have at least two plants of a cultivar if you want berries. Better nurseries will sell winterberry designated as male or female plants (*I. verticillata* × *I. serrata*). Hollies are plants of the lowlands. Especially in the winter, they prefer to be in partial shade protected from sun and wind. Evergreen American holly in particular needs to be in a protected location for the winter. Soils for hollies need to be moist and well drained. Hollies tolerate alkalinity, but they will be chlorotic (yellow) in soils that have a high pH. An organic soil is best; it holds moisture without excluding air.

WHERE TO PLANT

Plant in a protected, semi-shaded area that is safe from the wind. Use in masses or as understory plants in woodland settings. Winterberry can be used in a shrub border or around water features or ponds. It will withstand wet soils, while American holly will not.

HOW TO PLANT

Transplant balled-and-burlapped or containerized plants in the spring. Try to buy plants grown in a soil as much like that in your garden as you can find. The soil should be a good garden loam and it must have adequate drainage. Dig the planting hole the same depth and twice as wide as the plant ball, and set the plant at the same depth it was grown at the nursery. If planting a container-grown plant, mix some of the soil in the container with the soil that goes back into the planting hole. This will create a gradual change from one soil to another, preventing a soil interface problem.

CARE AND MAINTENANCE

Hollies resent pruning until they have been established for several years, then they will stand some shearing. It is most important to give them adequate water during dry periods and winter protection. American holly cannot stand winter wind. If necessary, install some kind of protection such as a burlap screen to stop the wind. Better yet is to plant the holly in a sheltered location. Except for requiring this kind of care, hollies thrive on neglect. Once it is established, American holly can be cut or sheared to keep it adequately small. Cutting branches for holiday decorations will help to keep the plant within bounds.

ADDITIONAL INFORMATION

Prune in the fall to collect berry-laden stems. This will help keep the plants in shape and at a manageable size.

ADDITIONAL SPECIES, CULTIVARS, OR VARIETIES

Winterberry is *Ilex verticillata*. This is a deciduous holly that keeps its leaves well into the fall. The fruit is a red drupe, developing in late summer while the leaves are still green. After leafdrop, the fruit is very showy until it is eaten by birds. Male cultivars are listed separately from the female, drupe-producing cultivars. Two male cultivars are 'Southern Gentleman' and 'Jim Dandy Dwarf'. Among the female plants are 'Red Sprite', Harvest Red', and 'Winter Red'. American holly, *Ilex opaca*, will grow throughout Illinois in protected spots and will even grow into a large tree if allowed to do so. It is usually grown as a conversation piece in northern Illinois and it does require some extra work. Some selections of American holly will withstand temperatures of minus 25 degrees Fahrenheit as long as they are out of the wind. Some gardeners go to great extremes to protect these plants, even constructing tents over them.

Honeysuckle

Lonicera sp.

Zones: All
Size: 3 to 10 feet
Blooms: Spring
Flower Colors: White, pink, yellow
Type: Deciduous

Light Requirement:

*H*oneysuckles are the workhorses of the landscape industry. There are hundreds of cultivars listed in the reference works, each good for some imagined purpose. The main advantages of these plants are that they have fragrant flowers in early summer and they can take mistreatment and keep right on growing. Honeysuckle never looks really good. It is stemmy, and its foliage is dull. Its flowers last only a short time. But these plants can be stuck in the ground and forgotten. They never look great, but they don't die. They can be sheared to death, but they come back with new shoots every time. They can be made into hedges or planted in masses. It doesn't matter. When they get overgrown and straggly, cut them to the ground. They'll come back better than ever. In the 1980s, something came along that nearly put an end to the use of honeysuckles: honeysuckle aphid. This pest seems to have hopped off a plane from Europe at O'Hare Field and settled on the first honeysuckle it found. A native of Eastern Europe, it is an endemic pest there. The first few seasons here, it spread throughout the northern part of the state, and along Interstate 80 into Iowa. It caused a witches'-broom on the plants, disfiguring and finally killing them. Gardeners began looking for resistant cultivars, but as time has passed, natural controls have arrived and the situation is somewhat in hand. Honeysuckles are still being planted; they still leave a lot to be desired, but they are cheap and they work. They are rounded spreading shrubs with fragrant flowers and red berries in late summer.

WHEN TO PLANT

Honeysuckle can be planted any time plants are available, spring, summer, or fall.

WHERE TO PLANT

Plant in sun or partial shade in any soil that drains well. Use in shrub borders, masses, or screens. Dwarf types are suitable for hedging.

HOW TO PLANT

Honeysuckle plants are available in containers, balled and burlapped, or bareroot. Dig the planting holes the same depth and twice as wide as the plant balls and set the plants the same depth they were growing in their containers. Soak bareroot plants for 12 hours before planting them. Hedges may be planted by digging a trench, setting the plants at the right spacing, and backfilling the trench. This is a great labor-saving system. Space large plants 10 feet apart. Dwarf plants can be set 3 to 4 feet apart, or 2 feet apart in hedges.

CARE AND MAINTENANCE

Honeysuckles should be renewed after flowering to remove $1/4$ to $1/3$ of the branches to the ground. Head back overly long branches to a shorter side shoot growing the same direction. Hedges may be sheared after new growth hardens off in spring, about the end of June. Overgrown plants should be renovated by cutting them all the way to the ground in midwinter. They will regrow in 2 to 3 years, full to the ground.

ADDITIONAL INFORMATION

These plants were named for Adam Lonitzer, a 16th-century German naturalist.

ADDITIONAL SPECIES, CULTIVARS, OR VARIETIES

A few cultivars of honeysuckle are worth mentioning. 'Arnold Red', a selection of *Lonicera tatarica*, Tartarian honeysuckle, is a standard-sized plant with resistance to the honeysuckle aphid. Several dwarf cultivars are suitable for hedges and low plantings; a few are selections of European fly honeysuckle, *L. xylosteum*. 'Clavey's Dwarf' and 'Hedge King' were developed by the Clavey Nurseries in Northern Illinois. 'Emerald Mound' and 'Miniglobe' are sold as *L. × xylosteoides*, but that is academic. They are all small, 3 feet or so, and have good green color and no aphids! Honeysuckles are still extremely popular and useful plants, especially in newly developed sites and other tough situations. There are far too many kinds; a few good ones will be sufficient. When used intelligently they fulfill an important function in the landscape.

Hydrangea

Hydrangea sp.

Zones: All
Size: 6 to more than 15 feet tall and wide
Blooms: Summer, persisting into fall
Flower Color: White
Type: Deciduous

Light Requirement:

ydrangeas are grown for their massive clusters of flowers produced in summer when few other shrubs are in bloom. Smooth hydrangea is the snowball bush of early summer. It grows to a height of about 5 feet, spreads, and will sucker if allowed to do so. These are specialty plants. Often they are killed to the ground by winter cold, but their flowers are borne on current-season wood; even if not winter-killed, these plants are best cut to the ground in spring. This will keep them tidy and symmetrical, and flowering is enhanced if all of the stems are fresh each spring. Panicle hydrangea is a large plant. It produces pyramids of white blooms that change to pink, rose, and brown and persist all winter. Working it into the landscape is difficult because of its size and coarseness. It blooms on new wood too, and can be pruned heavily, which vastly improves its form and character. The flowers make this plant worthwhile, but it must be planted where it has room to grow, and it must be kept under control.

WHEN TO PLANT

Hydrangeas may be planted in spring or fall. Spring planting will allow a full season of growth before freeze-up, and may be advantageous where the plants are killed to the ground in winter.

WHERE TO PLANT

These plants prefer a well-drained, loamy, moist soil and are partial to full sun. They are best located in the shrub border or in masses away from the house. It can be difficult to place them in the landscape because they are so unruly and overwhelming.

HOW TO PLANT

Hydrangeas are available balled and burlapped or in containers. Dig the hole for planting the same depth and twice as wide as the plant ball. Roots are fibrous and transplant well. If the soil in the container is one of the soilless mixes or is much different from the soil from the planting hole, shave some from the ball and mix it with the soil going back into the hole. This will prevent any interface problems. (See the section on soils in the introductory chapter for futher explanation.)

CARE AND MAINTENANCE

Hydrangeas are messy plants—remove the spent blooms when they have faded. The plants need severe pruning in winter or early spring. Cut smooth hydrangea to the ground; panicled hydrangea should be pruned hard to remove weak stems and reduce the number to about a dozen or so main stems. These stems will produce uniformly large clusters of blooms. Remove the blooms before they turn brown and ugly. The plants will need watering during dry spells the first season after planting. For best flower production, plan to water the plants thoroughly any summer when the weather is dry.

ADDITIONAL INFORMATION

Smooth hydrangea blooms can be dried and used for permanent arrangements. They hold their petals well, not shattering. They are often used in big dry arrangements in hotel lobbies and historic mansions.

ADDITIONAL SPECIES, CULTIVARS, OR VARIETIES

There are two cultivars of hydrangea worthy of growing in Illinois gardens. A selection of smooth hydrangea, *Hydrangea arborescens*, by J. C. McDaniel of the University of Illinois is called 'Annabelle'. It has extra-large heads, sometimes a foot in diameter. They are especially good for drying. Cut them as they begin to fade, and hang them upside down in a warm, dry place. A second flush of blooms may develop, usually in late summer. 'PeeGee' hydrangea, *Hydrangea paniculata* 'Grandiflora', has huge clusters of flowers, white turning pink in midsummer. If blooms are removed as they fade and the plants are severely pruned every year, they can be kept respectable. These are large plants, so plant them away from the house where they can be seen and have room to grow.

Juneberry

Amelanchier arborea

Other Names: Amelanchier, Shadblow **Zones:** All **Size:** 15 to 20 feet tall, half as wide **Blooms:** Spring **Flower Color:** White **Type:** Deciduous	**Light Requirement:**

*J*uneberries are native woodland plants. In spring the woods are brightened by the tiny white star-like flowers on the branches of these shrubs. They appear about the time the leaves emerge, while there is still sunlight reaching the forest floor. Other plants in bloom at that time are wildflowers such as trillium, spring beauty, and trout lily. Whether large shrubs or small trees, juneberries are excellent in the shrub border, especially in front of evergreens. Well suited to naturalized plantings, they can be used along stream banks, next to water features, or at the edges of woodlands. With the trend to larger houses, juneberry is being used in foundation plantings. It is a little large for the average ranch house, but away from the corner of a two-story house it can be allowed to grow to its full size without pruning. The plant is delicate in spring, has pleasant gray-green foliage, orange to rusty-red fall color, and smooth red-gray bark in winter. Juneberry is an attractive plant at all seasons. It can be trimmed into tree form, but it is generally grown as a multi-stemmed shrub, as it much more interesting and easier to handle in that form. It doesn't need pruning if it is allowed to assume its normal branched shape. Once established, these plants need very little care. Some diseases will occur in unusually wet weather; the plants are related to crab apples. Insects are seldom troublesome. These are relatively clean plants.

WHEN TO PLANT

Juneberries may be planted in spring or fall. Containerized plants may be planted at any time.

WHERE TO PLANT

Amelanchiers can be planted in slight shade or full sun. They prefer a rich, woodland soil, but any good garden soil with adequate drainage and organic matter will suffice. Use in naturalized plantings, shrub borders, or foundation plantings, or near water features.

How to Plant

Transplant plants that are balled and burlapped or from containers in spring. Try to buy plants grown in a soil as much like that in your garden as you can find. The soil should be a good forest soil or garden loam and it must have adequate drainage. Dig the planting hole the same depth and twice as wide as the plant ball. Set the plant at the same depth it was grown at the nursery. If planting a container-grown plant, mix some of the soil in the container with the soil that will back into the planting hole. This will create a gradual change from one soil to another and will prevent an interface problem. (See the soils section in the introductory chapter for futher explanation.)

Care and Maintenance

Juneberries are nearly maintenance-free. Water during extended dry weather.

Additional Information

All amelanchiers are grown for their flowers and year-round attractiveness; few gardeners know about their delicious fruit. The fruit does attract birds—in fact if you are late in getting to them, the birds will harvest them for you. The fruits are typically purple, berry-like, and sweet. In Europe, they are available packed in jars at markets. Some plant experts have said that pies of juneberries surpass those from the highbush blueberries.

Additional Species, Cultivars, or Varieties

Many selections and crosses of amelanchiers have been made for improved flowering and winter hardiness. The taxonomy of these plants is quite confused. Usually the cultivar names are correct, but the species may not actually be as labeled. Juneberry is *Amelanchier arborea*, but it is often listed as *A. laevis*. Many of the amelanchier cultivars sold in Illinois are actually *A. × grandiflora* selections. These are collectively called Apple Serviceberries and are hybrids of *A. arborea* and *A. laevis*. 'Autumn Brilliance', 'Cole's Select', and 'Forest Prince' are three cultivars worth trying. They were selected for Illinois conditions and should do well throughout the state.

Juniper

Juniperus sp.

Zones: All
Size: 5 to 20 feet tall, spreading.
Type: Evergreen

Light Requirement:

*J*unipers are members of a large family of evergreen plants that come in all growth types: trees, groundcovers, and shrubs. The low-growing junipers are discussed in the chapter on groundcovers. The shrub types are widely planted as foundation plantings and in shrub borders. These are some of the toughest evergreen landscape plants as long as they are growing in enough light. In shade they become thin and eventually decline to a point at which they are no longer attractive. Shrub-type junipers vary in size and texture. They tolerate almost any well-drained soil; some will grow in sand and endure droughty soils. They seem unaffected by soil pH. We have seen them growing nicely where the soil pH is near 8.0. Some will even stand the salt from snow removal.

WHEN TO PLANT

Junipers can be planted at any time from containers. Balled-and-burlapped plants are available in spring and fall.

WHERE TO PLANT

Plant junipers in full sun on a well-drained site.

HOW TO PLANT

Junipers are grown in 1- to 5-gallon-sized containers, and as balled-and-burlapped plants. The hole for planting should be no deeper than the depth of the ball of the plant, and at least twice as wide. Remove the plants from their containers, and slice any circling roots. Set the plant in the planting hole and replace half the soil. Fill the hole with water. Be sure to remove the burlap from a balled-and-burlapped plant, and stuff it down in the hole. Replace the remaining soil and fill the hole with water again. Make a saucer around the plant with any more remaining soil. Space the plants 5 feet or more apart, depending on the variety.

CARE AND MAINTENANCE

Junipers require pruning. Winter-killed branches need to be cut out in spring and overly long branches encroaching on walks or other plantings need to be headed back. Cut out entire branches to a vigorous side shoot growing in the same direction. If the cut is made beneath an overhanging branch, it will not be exposed. When cutting back severely, be sure to leave at least some green growth on the remaining branch or it will cease growing. Do not cut into the dead area in the center of the plant. Junipers are susceptible to mites, which can be controlled by insecticidal soap. Tip blight (Phomopsis) can be severe in wet weather. Spray affected plants with benomyl or triforine, following label directions.

ADDITIONAL INFORMATION

Junipers have been overused in unsuitable situations (shade or tight spaces), and have received bad reputations. When planted in the right conditions, they do well.

ADDITIONAL SPECIES, CULTIVARS, OR VARIETIES

Pfitzer juniper, *Juniperus chinensis* 'Pfitzeriana', is the most familiar shrub juniper, having been used in foundation and mass plantings for generations. Though planted as tiny seedlings from gallon-sized cans, these plants soon achieve an overwhelming size. They may be 10 feet high and at least as wide, hiding part of a house. They can be trimmed to keep them in bounds but trimming needs to be started early, not after the plants are out of control. Pfitzers are bright green, but there are some with yellow-colored tips. Try 'Pfitzeriana Aurea', which is not as obtrusive as some other yellow kinds. Compact pfitzer, 'Pfitzeriana Compacta', stays low, under 4 feet, and is gray-green in color. 'Hetzii' is a gray-green hybrid with the same size and form as pfitzer. Meyer juniper, *J. squamata* 'Meyeri', is blue and stays lower than the pfitzer. The selection 'Blue Star' has the best color and form. Old brown needles tend to stay on the plant, so it will become ratty in time.

Lilac

Syringa sp.

Zones: All	**Light Requirement:**
Size: 4 to 10 feet tall and wide	
Blooms: May	
Flower Colors: White, pink, lilac, violet	
Type: Deciduous	

*W*ho doesn't like lilacs? The blooms in spring aren't just beautiful, the fragrance (as Jane, my wife and best friend says) is "Heavenly!" For a short time in May, these wonderful plants burst forth with their wonderful blossoms, becoming the center of attention in the shrub border. The flowers are good for cutting. I recall that when we were children, every spring we set out for the "lilac jungle," an abandoned planting along the railroad tracks, to pick flowers. Loaded with armfuls, we headed home enjoying the fragrance and knowing they would be appreciated by the rest of the family. Lilac plants are untidy and difficult to fit into the landscape. The larger types are upright and woody, best used in the shrub border or in masses. Often they are planted next to the house where they either demand severe pruning to stay in bounds, or simply overwhelm everything else. Dwarf cultivars are easier to use; they stay smaller and they fit into foundation plantings. Their flowers, however, are not as spectacular.

WHEN TO PLANT

Lilacs may be planted in spring or fall. Containerized plants may be planted any time during the season.

WHERE TO PLANT

Plant in full sun for best blooming and allow plenty of room for the plants to spread out. Any well-drained garden soil will suffice. Plant them in masses or in the shrub border. They have no business in foundation plantings unless the home is huge and they can be planted at least 10 feet from the foundation. A single specimen in the middle of a front yard will be beautiful when in bloom, but unattractive the other 50 weeks of the year.

How to Plant

Lilacs are available balled and burlapped or in containers, and sometimes small plants are sold bareroot. The hole for planting should be shallower than the depth of the ball, and at least twice as wide. Space smaller varieties 6 feet apart in masses. Larger plants should be spaced 10 to 15 feet apart. Set each plant slightly higher than it grew in the nursery. Remove the burlap from balled-and-burlapped plants, stuffing it in the hole. Soak the plants thoroughly after planting to settle the soil around the roots.

Care and Maintenance

Lilacs must be pruned to keep them blooming and in bounds. Remove blooms when they have faded, and renew the plants by cutting out $1/4$ to $1/3$ of the oldest stems all the way to the ground. Head back overly long stems to shorter side shoots growing in the same direction. All pruning should be completed as soon as possible after blooms fade to allow the plants to develop flower buds for the next season. Lilacs are subject to insect troubles: scales may be controlled with summer oil or acephate, borers with clorpyrofos in June. Mildew will damage leaves in August, but while it is unsightly, it does no harm. Applying triforine will help. Be sure to read and follow the instructions on the labels.

Additional Information

Sometimes lilacs are stubborn and refuse to bloom. This may happen after transplanting, and it can happen to plants growing in the shade. The transplant problem will solve itself with time; the shade problem will need to be corrected, or the plants will never bloom. A yellows disease caused by a mycoplasma-like-organism has affected some lilacs in Northern Illinois. Whether this disease will become serious has not been determined yet. No one knows how it is spread, but leaf hoppers are suspected.

Additional Species, Cultivars, or Varieties

Common lilac, *Syringa vulgaris*, has been hybridized for centuries. Most of the hundreds of named cultivars are from this species. Nurseries usually list a few cultivars, but the plants are most often simply offered by color. Persian lilac, *S. × persica*, is a smaller (to 6 feet) and better-behaved plant. Its flowers are pale lilac and fragrant. The dwarf, Miss Kim lilac, is a hybrid of Manchurian lilac (*S. patula*). It grows to 4 feet high and wide and has blue blooms.

Mock Orange

Philadelphus coronarius

Other Name: Sweet Mock Orange
Zones: All
Size: 3 to 10 feet tall and wide
Blooms: June
Flower Color: White
Type: Deciduous

Light Requirement:

ock oranges are grown for their fragrant white blooms in June. The plants are woody and unwieldy, difficult to place in the landscape; it may seem they are tolerated for 50 weeks of the year only so their flowers can be enjoyed for two. But in truth these plants are no bother to grow, they flower easily, are completely hardy, have no serious pests, can be pruned and shaped without flinching, and make a beautiful, usually fragrant, display every year—just about the time we begin to spend a lot of time outdoors. There are different forms and sizes of mock oranges, and some of them will fit into the landscape. The more difficult ones need to be relegated to the shrub border, or to mass plantings where they can be enjoyed when blooming but ignored the rest of the season. Dwarf cultivars are suitable for foundation plantings if they are used carefully.

WHEN TO PLANT

Mock orange can be planted balled and burlapped in spring or fall, or from containers any time during the season.

WHERE TO PLANT

Plant in full sun or light shade. Any fertile garden soil is satisfactory as long as it is well drained. The taller kinds are suited to shrub borders or mass plantings. Lower-growing cultivars are suitable in borders, or they may be worked into foundation plantings. A single specimen in the middle of a front yard will be beautiful when in bloom but unattractive the other 50 weeks of the year.

HOW TO PLANT

Mock oranges are available balled and burlapped, and in containers. The hole for planting should be shallower than the depth of the ball and at least twice as wide. Space plants of smaller varieties 6 feet apart in masses, larger plants 10 to 15 feet apart. Set each plant in its hole, keeping it slightly higher than it grew in the nursery. Remove the burlap from balled-and-burlapped plants, stuffing it in the hole. Soak the plants thoroughly after planting to settle the soil around the roots.

CARE AND MAINTENANCE

Mock oranges are essentially pest-free, but yearly pruning to renew the plants is important. Immediately following flowering, remove $1/4$ to $1/3$ of the oldest branches all the way to the ground. This will stimulate new stems from the bases of the plants. If the plants get out of hand, they may be cut to 6 inches above the ground; they will regrow in about three years. In either case, flowering will not be interrupted.

ADDITIONAL INFORMATION

These plants are sometimes called syringas. This practice is unfortunate because *Syringa* is the botanical name for the lilacs.

ADDITIONAL SPECIES, CULTIVARS, OR VARIETIES

The *P. coronarius* cultivars are of dubious value; most are no better than the species. *Philadelphus* × *lemoinei* has a mounded habit to 6 feet or so tall. Some cultivars are smaller. 'Avalanche' grows to 3 or 4 feet and has arching branches and flowers more than 2 inches across. The upright *Philadelphus* × *virginalis* 'Minnesota Snowflake' grows to 8 feet tall and half as wide. Its flowers are double and 2 inches in diameter. Two useful mock oranges of unknown origin are 'Frosty Morn', 4 to 5 feet tall and mounded in form, and 'Miniature Snowflake', a compact plant 3 feet tall. 'Silver Showers' grows to $2^{1}/2$ feet tall and spreads 3 feet.

Mugo Pine

Pinus mugo

Other Name: Swiss Mountain Pine
Zones: All
Size: 4 to 10 feet tall, sometimes more,
 spreading twice as wide.
Type: Evergreen

Light Requirement:

*M*ugo pine is a confusing plant. It is a bush pine, but how big the bush will become can be anyone's guess. This is unfortunate, because the true dwarf form is an excellent plant for use in both small and larger landscapes. The rank, large-growing kinds quickly outgrow their situations and become liabilities. The difficulty seems to be due to tremendous variation in selections and in plants grown from seed. The location from which the seed was collected may help determine what kind of plant will develop. Seed collected from low, dwarf plants at a cool 6000 feet in the mountains may grow much larger in fertile, warm soils at 600 feet in central Illinois. Since most mugos are seed-produced, it is difficult to predict just how they will develop. Some nurseries are careful about the collection of seed, roguing out the plants that are obviously too vigorous. The truly dwarf mugo is an excellent plant for foundation plantings, masses, and specimens.

WHEN TO PLANT
Mugo pines can be planted either in spring or fall. Containerized small plants may be planted any time during the season.

WHERE TO PLANT
Shrub pines are suitable for massing, and for foundation plantings. Plant in a well-drained soil in full sun or light shade.

HOW TO PLANT
Mugo pines are grown as balled-and-burlapped plants, and in 1-gallon to 5-gallon-sized containers. The hole for planting should be no deeper than the depth of the ball of the plant, and at least twice as wide. Set the plant in the planting hole, and replace half the soil. Fill the hole with water. Be sure to remove the burlap from a

balled-and-burlapped plant, and stuff it down in the hole. Replace the remaining soil and fill the hole with water again. Make a saucer around the plant with any remaining soil. Dwarf selections are preferred for most landscape plantings. Space the plants 5 to 10 or more feet apart, depending on the cultivar.

CARE AND MAINTENANCE

Mugo pines are subject to attack by pine sawflies; their larvae appear magically in mid-spring as masses on individual branches. When disturbed, they all jump at once, startling predators (or unsuspecting people). You can solve the problem by wiping them off by hand or spraying with Malathion. Follow directions on the label carefully. These pines can be kept within bounds indefinitely by shearing or by removing half the new growth every summer. Christmas-tree growers use machetes to shear pines. Hedge trimmers work as well. Be sure to leave some green needles on each branch or it will cease growing.

ADDITIONAL INFORMATION

Mugo pine is sometimes listed as *Pinus montana*. Mugo is a dwarf cultivar.

ADDITIONAL SPECIES, CULTIVARS, OR VARIETIES

Various named cultivars are listed by nurseries. If these have been grown by a reliable grower, and if you buy locally, the chances are better that you will get what you expect. Buying from discount suppliers is risky. 'Compacta' is very dense and round in form, reaching a height of 4 feet and a width of 8. The variety 'Pumilio' is a plant from the mountains of eastern Europe; it grows a couple of feet tall and spreads 10 feet. 'Mops' is 3 feet high and wide, and probably one of the better selections.

Potentilla

Potentilla fruticosa

Zones: All
Size: 1 to 4 feet tall, spreading 4 feet
Blooms: June to frost
Flower Colors: Yellow, some white or red
Type: Deciduous

Light Requirement:

*T*hese little plants are welcome in the landscape because of their profusion of bright-yellow flowers that last all summer. They are neat little plants if properly maintained; they have dark bluish green or gray-green foliage and few pest problems. These are stemmy shrubs that form low mounds. They are low enough to use as facer plants, in the foundation planting, as low hedges, in the perennial border, and in masses. If used in masses, it is particularly important to renew them regularly or they will deteriorate into a twiggy mess. They can be used in raised beds and planters, or may be potted as specimens. Potentillas are completely hardy throughout Illinois. Winter damage may occur to plants standing in water or those exposed to wind and sun in extremely cold weather. These plants can be cut back and will recover when growth starts in spring.

WHEN TO PLANT

Properly handled bareroot potentillas may be planted in either spring or in fall. Container-grown plants may be planted at any time during the season.

WHERE TO PLANT

Potentilla can be planted in full sun in any moist well-drained soil. It does best in fertile soils, however, which allow it to produce more vigorous growth and correspondingly more flowers. These plants will tolerate some light shade and will withstand dry soils; the droughts of 1988 and 1991, however, killed many plants. Potentilla will also deteriorate in wet soils.

HOW TO PLANT

Potentillas are sold as balled-and-burlapped plants, or in 2- or 5-gallon containers.

If the plants are to be set in beds or masses, prepare the area to be planted by tiling or spading to a 6-inch depth. Incorporate organic matter and set the plants at the depth they were growing. Dig the holes the depth of the plant ball and twice as wide. Space the plants 2$^{1}/_{2}$ feet apart. If they will be hedges, set them 1$^{1}/_{2}$ feet apart or plant-to-plant. Hedges can be planted by opening a trench, setting the plants at the 1$^{1}/_{2}$ foot-or-closer spacing, and backfilling them all at the same time. Be sure to water thoroughly after planting to settle the soil around the plant roots. If the soil on the roots of the plant is much different from that in the hole, mix some with that going back into the hole to avoid a soil interface problem. It is best to buy plants grown on a soil as nearly like that in your yard as you can find.

CARE AND MAINTENANCE

Potentillas need watering in dry weather. If they are allowed to wilt, flowering is disrupted. These plants require regular pruning. In late winter or early spring, cut out any dead or overly long branches. Reduce the overall height of the plants by $^{1}/_{2}$, and remove a few of the remaining branches to the ground. Pruning must be done before the start of growth in spring. This will delay flowering, but will allow the plants to be more floriferous throughout the summer.

ADDITIONAL INFORMATION

Potentilla is from the Latin *potens* ("powerful").

ADDITIONAL SPECIES, CULTIVARS, OR VARIETIES

Hundreds of cultivars of potentilla are listed in various plant identification manuals. These lists are meaningless to most gardeners; local producers will grow only a few, usually the ones that do best in their area. If you are interested in seeing various types to compare growth characteristics and flowers, botanic gardens and arboreta often grow several different kinds, including some unusual ones. 'Gold Drop' has smallish blooms on a 2-foot plant, but this seems to have become a common name for many different yellow-flowered potentillas. 'Goldfinger' with 1$^{3}/_{4}$-inch flowers and dark green foliage, is superior in the Midwest. The clone 'Mount Everest' is white—not my favorite color, as it lacks the crispness of the bright yellow. 'Abbotswood' and 'McKay's White' are better. 'McKay's White' has excellent dark-green foliage and is rust resistant. 'Primrose Beauty' has excellent primrose-colored flowers, silver-gray foliage, and a good rounded form.

Privet

Ligustrum sp.

Zones: All
Size: 5 to 15 feet tall, nearly as wide
Blooms: May, June
Flower Color: White
Type: Deciduous

Light Requirement:

*I*n Illinois, there are more privet hedges than any other kind of hedge, and it is unusual to see a privet in any planting other than a hedge. There are only three or four kinds that need to be discussed. They differ in size, color, or disease resistance. If left unsheared, privets are dense, upright, stemmy plants. The flowers are slightly fragrant and people either like or strongly dislike the smell. Privets are valuable because they will tolerate severe conditions and mistreatment as well as any plant we know, even growing in poor, dry, high-pH soils. If privets will not grow in a particular soil, you will know that it is useless to try any other woody plant in that spot. They can stand the pollution and grime of the city, and they withstand pruning like no other plant.

WHEN TO PLANT

Privets can be planted in spring or fall from balled-and-burlapped or bareroot plants. Bundles of 2-year-old seedlings are sold in spring as economical starts for hedges. Containerized plants can be planted at any time during the season.

WHERE TO PLANT

Privets are useful only as hedges. They have no features that would foster them for any other purpose. (The exception is golden privet, which is sometimes used as a specimen.)

HOW TO PLANT

Any garden soil will suffice for privet. Dig the planting holes the same depth and twice as wide as the plant balls. Space the standard cultivars 3 feet apart, dwarf cultivars 1^1/$_2$ feet apart. Soak bareroot plants for 12 hours before planting them. Hedges may also be planted by digging a trench, setting the plants 1¹/₂ to 3 feet apart, and backfilling the trench. This is a great labor-saving system.

CARE AND MAINTENANCE

Privets require little care, only shearing to maintain the hedge. Try not to keep these plants at the same size all season. Every time you shear, cut a little farther out to leave at least some new leaves. In late winter, cut the plants below the desired size, and let them grow out again. Keep the bottom of the hedge wider than the top so that all branches will receive some light and the plants won't become bare at the bottom.

ADDITIONAL INFORMATION

These plants are very easy to propagate. Simply take a 6-inch-long twig and stick it in the soil! If there is any moisture at all, the twig will root and grow into a new plant.

ADDITIONAL SPECIES, CULTIVARS, OR VARIETIES

European privet, *Ligustrum vulgare*, is the privet most commonly planted in our state. It makes a hedge 8 feet tall or more, but is not dense. It is a large, rank plant if left unpruned. Two selections of this species are more suitable, 'Densiflorum' and 'Lodense'. 'Densiflorum' is upright and will maintain good foliage cover even if left unpruned. 'Lodense' is a dwarf, compact form that will stay under 5 feet indefinitely. It is susceptible to a canker disease that makes it less desirable than it otherwise would be. Amur privet, *L. amurense*, is resistant to the canker disease that is fatal to European privet types, but aside from that, there is little difference. The flowers of this species are showy if pruning is delayed until after they drop. The fragrance is strangely sweet—I like it, but many people do not.

Redbud

Cercis canadensis

Zones: All
Size: 20 feet, sometimes to 30, spreading 25
Blooms: April
Flower Colors: Rose-pink, white
Type: Deciduous

Light Requirement:

edbud is my favorite flowering shrub. It provides all-season interest with its interesting branching, its delicate blossoms that tightly cover all the branches (even the four-inch-diameter limbs), and its clean heart-shaped leaves. We decorate the plants in front of our house with tiny Christmas lights for the holidays, and the redbud becomes a sparkling umbrella over the lower-growing shrubs. In spring it is a welcome sight as it blooms after the tough Illinois winter. Redbud is a woodland plant, native to Illinois. It grows as an understory plant in the woods or at the forest's edge. It blooms at the same time as the dogwoods in the southern part of the state, and between the two of them, the woods come alive, welcoming spring just before leaves emerge. Redbud is sometimes considered a small tree (see page 320), but I prefer to grow it as a multi-stemmed shrub. It is very tolerant of the soils of Illinois, heavy or light, acid or alkaline, as long as they aren't continuously wet.

WHEN TO PLANT

Redbud should be planted in spring in a well-prepared moist soil.

WHERE TO PLANT

Plant in full sun or light shade. Redbud can be used as a specimen, in groupings, as an accent in the shrub border, or in the foundation planting. Be sure to give it enough room in a foundation planting, placing it at least 15 feet from the house. The soil should be deep and well drained.

HOW TO PLANT

Redbuds are available balled and burlapped, or in containers. The planting hole should be shallower than the depth of the ball and at least twice as wide. Remove the plant from its container and slice any circling roots. Set the plant in the hole, keeping it slightly higher than it grew in the nursery. The result of deep planting or poor drainage is root rot and plant loss. Remove the burlap from balled-and-burlapped plants, stuffing it in the hole. Replace the soil, and fill the hole with water. Make a saucer around the plant with any remaining soil. Redbuds will need regular watering their first year after planting.

CARE AND MAINTENANCE

Once established, redbud requires little care. Pruning will be necessary as the tree grows, to thin out weak branches from inside the plant and to select the main limbs for the frame of the plant. Pruning should be done immediately after flowering. Provide water in dry weather.

ADDITIONAL INFORMATION

Redbuds grow from Minnesota to Florida, but the plants that grow in Florida are not the same as the ones that grow up north. We hear many reports of people in our area buying a redbud that dies to the ground each winter; it is obviously a Southern selection or another species. Most nurseries simply list redbuds without mentioning sources or cultivar names. Choose plants grown from seed that was collected locally. There is tremendous variation in hardiness if regional types are grown outside their normal range.

ADDITIONAL SPECIES, CULTIVARS, OR VARIETIES

A white-flowered selection is listed as alba in nursery catalogs. This is a wild native plant. If the emerging leaves of a redbud lack the plant's normal purplish color, this is an indication that the plant is actually alba. Cultivars of *Cercis canadensis* have been selected for flower color, and some have been selected for hardiness. Unfortunately for those of us in the North, much of the selection has been done at North Carolina State University! Although this does not automatically eliminate these kinds from use in the North, more testing will need to be done to see which ones will survive here. The University of Minnesota Landscape Arboretum is growing seedlings from trees that have survived winters there. Use care in buying plants. If they were grown locally, they are likely to survive in your garden.

Rhododendron

Rhododendron sp.

Zones: All
Size: 3 to 6 feet high and wide
Blooms: Spring
Flower Colors: Lavender, pink, white,
    yellow, orange, red
Type: Deciduous/evergreen

Light Requirement:

hododendrons are plants that we Illinois gardeners wish we could grow as well as gardeners in other parts of the country. But while the list of kinds that will grow in our state is short, we can and do grow them. Rhododendrons may be either evergreen or deciduous. Their flowers are typically bell- or funnel-shaped and are borne in clusters at the tips of the stems in early to mid-spring. There used to be confusion about whether particular plants are azaleas or rhododendrons, but the controversy has been settled: now they all are classified as *Rhododendron*.

WHEN TO PLANT

Rhododendrons are planted in spring to allow sufficient time for roots to develop before the onset of the tough Illinois winter. Containerized plants may be planted until midsummer or later.

WHERE TO PLANT

Rhododendrons are extremely particular about their situation. The soil must be deep and well drained; hard and wet soils are not tolerated. Soil pH should be neutral or lower, though some kinds grow in soils with a higher pH. These are shade plants—they need protection from the midday sun in summer and winter. Winter sun and wind are especially damaging. The northeast side of the house is fine, or plant them so there are trees or other shrubs to the southwest.

HOW TO PLANT

Prepare the soil by spading to a 24-inch depth if possible. Incorporate organic matter, preferably acidic peat moss. If drainage is not adequate, install tiles or construct raised beds at least 5 feet wide (any smaller and they may freeze-in from the sides in winter, killing the roots). Rhododendrons are available balled and burlapped, or in containers. The hole for planting should be shallower than the depth of the ball, and at least twice as wide. Space the plants to allow for their mature size. Set the plant in the hole, keeping it higher than it grew in the nursery. The result of deep planting or poor drainage is root or crown rot and plant loss. Remove the burlap from balled-and-burlapped plants, stuffing it in the hole. Backfill the hole, adding 25 percent peat to the soil. Soak thoroughly. Mulch the plants with 2 to 3 inches of shredded bark or compost.

CARE AND MAINTENANCE

Watering will be needed in dry weather, as the beds of modified soil will not re-wet from the still-moist soil beneath the planting. Reapply mulch in spring and fall and provide winter protection if necessary. Rhodies do not take kindly to pruning.

ADDITIONAL INFORMATION

Root and crown rot, *Phytophthora cinnamomi*, is a devastating disease of rhodies. It is usually unnoticed until a plant begins to turn gray-green and dries up. This disease is a slime mold and occurs where soils are too wet or poorly drained. If the wetness is due to something other than poor soil conditions or unusually wet weather, try drenching the planting with Banrot, Truban, or Banol fungicide. Read and follow the directions on the label.

ADDITIONAL SPECIES, CULTIVARS, OR VARIETIES

These are some of the rhododendrons that can be grown in Illinois: Molle hybrids are *R. × kosterianum*. Three to 6 feet high and wide, they have orange, pink, yellow, or white flowers. Zone 5A. Korean rhododendrons are *R. mucronulatum*, growing up to 8 feet tall and sporting wide, pink blooms. Zone 4B. Royal azalea, *R. schlippenbachii*, 6 feet high and wide with fragrant pink or white flowers spotted with reddish blotches. Zone 5B. Exbury and Knap Hill Hybrids are colorful "azaleas" with red, orange, yellow, pink, and white flowers. They grow to 5 feet high. Zone 5B. Ghent hybrids, to 10 feet tall, red, yellow, orange, or white; selections vary in hardiness. Zone 5B. Northern Lights azaleas are from the University of Minnesota breeding program and are hardy to minus 40 degrees Fahrenheit. Zone 2. The *Rhododendron* P. J. M. hybrids are large-flowered pinks and lavenders. They are the "top of the line" flowering rhodies in our state. Zone 5.

Rose of Sharon

Hibiscus syriacus

Other Name: Shrubby Althaea
Zones: All
Size: 10 feet tall and wide
Blooms: July through September
Flower Colors: Purple, pink, red, white
Type: Deciduous

Light Requirement:

*I*n my opinion, rose of Sharon has only one thing going for it, as far as beauty goes: it has beautiful flowers late in the season when there isn't much else going on. But this appears to be a minority opinion, because many people plant them and thoroughly enjoy them. Let me temper my harsh criticism by agreeing that these plants are hardy, stand the dirt and grime of the city, will grow in almost any soil with drainage and some water, and flower faithfully year after year. They are indeed tolerant of difficult sites. They are used in parks, industrial sites, and roadside and municipal plantings. They are planted in front yards where kids can run around them, trampling the soil. They are planted along driveways where they get little water, and in winter the salt drips off parked cars onto their roots. I have seen rose of Sharon in all of these situations, growing, not looking too good, but blooming with abandon. I guess that is sufficient reason to include them in this listing. Rose of Sharon can be used in shrub borders and masses, and as screening. It tolerates shearing, but flowering will be sacrificed unless the shearing is done in early spring. The flowers are large, like hollyhocks. Flower size can be increased by cutting back the previous year's growth to half a dozen buds on each shoot. This looks terrible until the plants start growing, but the flowers will be larger (if fewer in number).

WHEN TO PLANT

Plant rose of Sharon in spring or fall. Containerized plants can be planted any time during the season.

WHERE TO PLANT

Plant in full sun or light shade. Any decent garden soil should suffice, but a well-drained soil with added organic matter is better.

How to Plant

Rose of Sharon is available balled and burlapped or in containers. Dig the hole for planting the same depth and twice as wide as the plant ball. Roots are fibrous and transplant well. If the soil in the container is one of the soilless mixes or much different from the soil from that of the planting hole, shave some from the ball and mix it with the soil going back into the hole. This will prevent interface problems (see the section on soils in the introductory chapter). The plants need watering during dry spells their first season after planting.

Care and Maintenance

Pruning is the most important maintenance practice for rose of Sharon plantings. If they are allowed to grow wild, they will become upright, stemmy, and thinly branched, with all of their flowers at the top. Prune severely in spring. Rose of Sharon is thought by many to be drought-tolerant, but it does better when given adequate water during dry spells.

Additional Information

These plants are normally hardy throughout Illinois, although the tough winter of 1977-78 caused some injury. Where leaves or weeds are allowed to accumulate around the plants in fall, mice will take up residence and will girdle the plants at the soil line.

Additional Species, Cultivars, or Varieties

Many cultivars are listed by nurseries, and keeping track of them all is impossible. Buy plants by the color of the flowers, choosing either singles or doubles, whichever suits your needs. Local nurseries grow and sell cultivars that do the best in their area.

Saint John's Wort

Hypericum prolificum

Other Name: Shrubby Saint John's Wort
Zones: All
Size: 1 to 4 feet tall and wide
Blooms: Late July
Flower Color: Yellow
Type: Deciduous

Light Requirement:

*S*aint John's wort is a low woody shrub forming a dense, twiggy mound that is covered with bright yellow flowers for much of the summer. Its attractive foliage is blue-green and has a medium-fine texture. This small plant is tidy enough to be used in the perennial border, as a facer plant, in the foundation planting, or in masses. The bright-yellow flowers are borne at a time when few other shrubs are flowering. Saint John's wort in bloom is so noticeable that people often ask what it is. Most have never heard the name and are surprised by the colorful plant often found growing in tough, dry places. It is not unusual to find one tucked into the corner of a parking lot or island planting where it seems unlikely such a bright little plant would thrive. Sometimes these are the sole survivors of a planting long since forgotten. Saint John's wort does very well in dry, rocky, or limy soils. It is often found in newly developed sites where the topsoil has been stripped away and the subsoil compacted by construction. Why Saint John's wort hasn't found more acceptance as a plant for these kinds of plantings is a mystery.

WHERE TO PLANT

Saint John's wort should be planted in light shade, but it will grow in full sun. Although these plants will grow in poor soils, they do as well or better in a moist soil that has good drainage. Sandy soils are ideal.

How to Plant

These plants should be planted from containers. If the soil is quite heavy, prepare it by adding organic matter and sand. Dig the planting holes the same depth and twice as wide as the containers. Set the plants at the depth they grew in their containers. Soak the soil to settle it around the roots. Space the plants 1½ to 2 feet apart.

Care and Maintenance

Saint John's wort must be pruned to keep it tidy and blooming well. Prune it in early spring to stimulate new growth. It flowers on current-season's wood. Faded flowers are messy; deadhead the plants by cutting off the old flowers.

Additional Information

Saint John's wort has been used in landscapes since the middle 1700s. The dried fruit capsules are used in dry flower arrangements.

Additional Species, Cultivars, or Varieties

Several other species of *Hypericum* are grown in Illinois. The Kalm's Saint John's wort, *H. kalmianum*, is a plant native to cliffs and lakeshores in Illinois, Michigan, Quebec, and Ontario. Its form is more rank than that of shrubby Saint John's wort, but its bright-yellow flowers are larger. It is listed in some nursery catalogs. The other species seem not to be adapted to Illinois conditions. No hybrids or improved cultivars of shrubby Saint John's wort appear to have gained entrance into the nursery trade. Only the species is listed.

Smoketree

Cotinus coggygria

Other Name: Common Smoketree
Zones: All
Size: 15 feet tall and wide
Blooms: June
Flower Color: Yellow, tiny, and
inconspicuous
Type: Deciduous

Light Requirement:

Smoketree is grown for the airy inflorescences, or clusters of fruits, that develop after its flowers drop. This display is produced by the pubescence (hairs) on the fruit stalks that persist in the cluster. These "hairs" turn smoky-pink and last through summer into fall. The effect is a haze of color surrounding the plant . . . like smoke. This is a large plant and is best used in masses or in the shrub border, though it is used most often as a specimen, typically in the middle of the front yard. I do not recommend planting this way, but people who dedicate their front yards to these plants so the rest of us can enjoy them are to be thanked, not disparaged. Smoketrees transplant easily and they prefer any well-drained garden soil. They tolerate high pH's and will grow in dry, rocky soils.

WHEN TO PLANT

Plant smoketrees in spring or fall. Container-grown plants can be planted any time during the season.

WHERE TO PLANT

Plant in full sun, in masses or in the shrub border.

HOW TO PLANT

Smoketrees are available balled and burlapped, or in containers. The hole for planting should be shallower than the depth of the ball and at least twice as wide. Space plants 10 to 15 feet apart. Set each plant in its hole, keeping it slightly higher than it grew in the nursery. Remove the burlap from balled-and-burlapped plants, and stuff it in the hole. Soak the plants thoroughly after planting to settle the soil around the roots.

CARE AND MAINTENANCE

Smoketrees can be pruned to stimulate better flowering. The plants can be cut to the ground in late winter to stimulate vigorous shoot growth, larger leaves, and fewer but larger flower clusters. Scale insects, rodents, and *Verticillium* wilt are the main pest problems encountered by smoketrees. Severe pruning will eliminate the scales, or use dormant oil in late winter. Keep debris or weeds from accumulating around the trunks of the plants so that mice don't take up residence there before winter. If mice spend the winter there, they will girdle the plants. *Verticillium* is a soil-borne disease. Make every effort to avoid bringing this disease into the planting in soil or on other plants.

ADDITIONAL SPECIES, CULTIVARS, OR VARIETIES

The cultivar 'Purpureus' has purple leaves and flowers. Several selections of this cultivar are available, but they tend to be less cold hardy than the species. 'Nordine', a selection made at Morton Arboretum in Lisle, Illinois, is the hardiest of the group.

Snowberry

Symphoricarpos albus

Zones: All
Size: 3 to 6 feet tall and wide
Blooms: June
Flower Color: Pink, inconspicuous
Type: Deciduous

Light Requirement:

Snowberry is grown not for its flowers, but for its pure white berries (drupes) that appear in late summer and may persist into winter. The plants are bushy and twiggy with a broad rounded form. The stems are ascending until loaded with berries; then they are pulled down by the berries, arching over and exposing the silvery undersides of the leaves. These plants are rather difficult to use in the landscape, but do add another dimension: that of white fruit. Snowberry is best used as a facer plant in shrub borders. It is particularly useful in semi-shaded areas and at the edges of naturalized plantings. If allowed to do so, it will sucker and spread. The suckering habit is beneficial where the plant is used on slopes, stabilizing and preventing erosion. Snowberry is very tolerant of soil conditions, and it will grow in places that generally provide difficulty for establishing plants, such as slopes, berms for sight and sound barriers, and banks for detention and retention ponds.

When to Plant

Snowberry can be planted at any time during the season. Plants are available balled and burlapped, and in 2- and 5-gallon cans.

Where to Plant

Plant in full sun to partial shade. These plants are probably more useful in shade, where other plants grow with difficulty. Any garden soil is satisfactory, but good drainage is important. The plants will deteriorate in soggy soils.

How to Plant

The hole for planting should be the same depth as the plant ball and at least twice as wide. Remove plants from their containers, and slice any circling roots. Space the plants 3 to 4 feet apart. Set each plant in its hole, keeping it at the same height it grew in the nursery. Remove the burlap from balled-and-burlapped plants, stuffing it in the hole. Replace the soil and fill the hole with water. Snowberry may need watering during the first season.

CARE AND MAINTENANCE

Once established, snowberry needs little attention. Pruning early in the season will increase its flowering and fruiting. The plants flower on current season's wood. If suckering and spreading are to be controlled, hoe out the sprouts or kill them with glufosinate-ammonium (Finale) herbicide. Follow directions carefully and keep the material off desirable green plants.

ADDITIONAL INFORMATION

These plants are native to limestone and clay outcroppings. They will tolerate the worst of limy soils.

ADDITIONAL SPECIES, CULTIVARS, OR VARIETIES

Some improved selections develop more and larger fruit, and are more vigorous growers. The species tends to be twiggy and open. The variety *S. a. laevigatus* is one of the better ones. Some related species produce pink fruit. Coralberry, *S. orbiculatus*, grows about 4 feet high and wide. The drupes are coral-colored. *Symphoricarpos × chenaultii* is a 3-foot arching shrub with showy pink flowers and pink, white, or pink-tinged drupes. The shady side of the plant produces white drupes. Drupes in the sun have a blush.

Spicebush

Lindera benzoin

Zones: All
Size: 6 to 10 feet tall and wide
Blooms: April
Flower Color: Yellow, fragrant
Type: Deciduous

Light Requirement:

Spicebush is a native shrub that will grow in deep shade to full sun, in any kind of soil at just about any pH. It prefers moist soil and filtered sun, but it is so adaptable that it can be grown in just about any situation. The plant is a rounded shrub, quite open and loose when grown in a shaded site. In the open and in full sun, it will be dense and compact. Spicebush blooms in early spring with tiny yellow flowers in clusters along the stems. It is attractive because there is little else blooming at that time, and the leaves are not yet starting to develop. Male and female flowers are produced on separate plants. The flowers are fragrant, as are the stems and leaves when broken.

The fruit is a bright red berry (drupe) that develops in late summer, but only on the female plants. It is colorful but somewhat hidden until after the leaves fall. The leaves turn clear yellow in fall. As they drop, the fruit is gradually revealed, and the combination of yellow leaves and red fruit is quite attractive. The fruit persists until taken by birds; it is especially attractive to migrating species looking for places to feed on their way south.

WHEN TO PLANT

Spicebush may be planted in spring or fall. Large plants do not transplant easily; the coarse, fibrous root system is slow to redevelop.

WHERE TO PLANT

Plant in light to full shade in a well-drained soil. Spicebush can be used in the shrub border, in some foundation plantings (especially in the shade), in masses, and in naturalized areas around water features or stream banks. It is a woodland plant and can be planted at the edge of wooded areas where its color can be appreciated and the birds it attracts can be seen. I have seen spicebushes in naturalized areas on the North Shore, especially along the ravines leading to Lake Michigan. Large trees create almost continuous shade in summer. In the filtered sunlight of spring, the flowers of these plants are welcome after the dreary winter.

How to Plant

Spicebushes are available balled and burlapped, sometimes in containers. Make sure the soil has adequate drainage. These plants do better in dry soil than in wet situations. Dig the planting hole the same depth and twice as wide as the plant ball. Set the plant at the same depth it was grown in the nursery. If planting a container-grown plant, mix some of the soil in the container with the soil that will go back into the planting hole. This will create a gradual change from one soil to another and will prevent an interface problem.

Care and Maintenance

There is little that needs to be done to care for spicebushes once they are established. Water them their first season during extended dry weather. No insect or disease pests that affect these plants.

Additional Information

Lindera is named for Johann Linder, an 18th-century Swedish botanist. The species is native to the eastern half of the United States.

Additional Species, Cultivars, or Varieties

Only two selections of spicebush are listed in the literature: 'Xanthocarpa' has yellow fruit; 'Rubra' is a male plant with brick-red flowers. A related species, *L. obtusiloba*, Japanese spicebush, is an attractive large shrub that is hardy to Zone 7. It has good fall color and may be a good choice for the far southern part of the state.

Spirea

Spiraea sp.

Zones: All
Size: 2 to 10 feet tall and wide
Blooms: Spring, summer
Flower Colors: White, pink
Type: Deciduous

Light Requirement:

Spireas are diverse and useful landscape plants. They range in size from the small, upright bumalda types with pink flowers, to the arching 7-foot Vanhoutte with white flowers. These plants are grown mostly for their flowers, which are small and borne in flat clusters. The Vanhoutte spirea used to be a fixture in landscapes, having found its niche as a foundation plant in front of the high front porches of turn-of-the-century homes. Its high arching form and fountain-like display of bright white blooms fit the styles and times. With the advent of the single-story ranch houses of the 1950s, these large plants no longer fit (although they do continue to be planted, and butchered to fit). The lower types are now fixtures in landscapes. They are colorful in bloom, and their flowers are produced all summer rather than just in spring. Another attractive feature of spireas is their ability to grow almost anywhere. They tolerate almost any soil and will grow in sun or shade. They do flower better in full sun. Spireas can become ragged, but they tolerate pruning so well that reshaping them is not difficult.

WHEN TO PLANT

Spireas can be planted in spring or fall. Container-grown plants can be planted all season.

WHERE TO PLANT

Spireas are suited to shrub borders, mass plantings, and foundation plantings, or may be used as hedges or screens. They are sometimes planted as specimens, one plant in the middle of the front yard, but this is not the best use. Plant in full sun or partial shade. A moist, well-drained soil is best.

How to Plant

Spireas are available in containers or balled and burlapped. Set the plants at the same depth they were growing in their containers. Hedges may be planted by digging a trench, setting the plants at the right spacing, and backfilling the trench. This is a great labor-saving system. Space large plants at least 10 feet apart and 10 feet from walls, fences, or other structures. Dwarf plants can be set 3 to 4 feet apart, or 2 feet apart in hedges.

Care and Maintenance

Intelligent pruning is the key to success with spireas. They should be allowed to develop their natural form, not sheared into artificial shapes. Renewal pruning to remove $1/4$ to $1/3$ of the stems to the ground will keep the plants in good shape. Sometimes it is a good idea to rejuvenate the plants by cutting them to the ground and allowing them to regrow.

Additional Species, Cultivars, or Varieties

Vanhoutte spirea is a tough plant; even weed-killer won't kill it. Too often it is sheared to an ice cream cone shape, narrow at the bottom with a ball on top. In this condition it will not flower, and it looks atrocious. It is a graceful, vase-shaped plant with arching branches. It grows to 6 feet tall and may be 10 feet wide. If there isn't room to let it grow, replace it with something else. The dwarf spireas are much easier to use and maintain. Snowmound spirea, *S. nipponica* 'Snowmound', is a good replacement for Vanhoutte in smaller spaces. It grows to about 4 feet high and wide, sometimes more. Flowers are white, borne in clusters in May. The *Spiraea × bumalda* cultivars are the most commonly used today. Short, about 2 feet high, with pink or deep-rose flowers, they bloom in late spring and summer. Plant in beds, masses, hedges, and foundation plantings. Prune severely in early spring to improve form and flowering. There are dozens of selections of these plants, too many to list. 'Anthony Waterer' is one of the most common. There are many others, including some yellow cultivars which I find to be quite unattractive. They look as if they are suffering from iron chlorosis . . . but to each his own!

Viburnum

Viburnum sp.

Zones: All
Size: 3 to 10 feet tall and wide
Blooms: Spring, summer
Flower Colors: White, pink
Type: Deciduous

Light Requirement:

The viburnums are suitable for nearly all landscape uses. They are valued for their flowers, some of which are wonderfully fragrant; for their luxurious foliage; and for their various forms. They grow in most garden soils, tolerating alkalinity fairly well. They need decent drainage, and some will grow in relatively dry soils. Viburnums are high-quality plants that come in many forms and textures. The taller kinds are suitable for massing, screens, and shrub borders. Some are narrow and upright, good for narrow screens. Lower types are excellent for foundation plantings, massing, or borders. The smallest kinds are used for low masses in public areas, island planters, or low hedges. All viburnums flower, many with large and sometimes fragrant blooms. The flowers are borne in clusters, either flat, mounded, or snowball-like. One of the most fragrant is the Koreanspice viburnum, outstanding for a couple of weeks in May. When it is in bloom, the fragrance fills the air, especially in the evening. Open the windows and let it in! Isn't there some way to bottle it?

WHEN TO PLANT

Viburnums transplant easily; move them in spring or fall. Containerized plants can be planted all season long.

WHERE TO PLANT

Plant in full sun or light filtered shade. A well-drained soil is important.

HOW TO PLANT

Viburnums are available balled and burlapped, and in containers. The hole for planting should be shallower than the depth of the ball and at least twice as wide. Space smaller cultivars 6 feet apart in masses. Larger plants should be spaced 10 to 15 feet apart. Set each plant slightly higher than it grew in the nursery. Remove the burlap from balled-and-burlapped plants, stuffing it in the hole. Soak the plants thoroughly after planting to settle the soil around the roots.

CARE AND MAINTENANCE
Viburnums must be pruned to keep them blooming and in bounds. Remove blooms when they have faded. Renew the plants by cutting out $1/4$ to $1/3$ of the oldest stems all the way to the ground. Head back overly long stems to a shorter side-shoot growing in the same direction. All pruning should be completed as soon as possible after blooms fade to allow the plants to develop flower buds for the next season. Viburnums are subject to insect troubles: scales are controlled with summer oil or acephate, borers with clorpyrofos in June. Leaf spot may damage leaves in August; spray with triforine. Be sure to read and follow the instructions on the labels. Crown borers can be serious on plants under stress. One viburnum, European cranberrybush, is one of the most susceptible; American cranberrybush seems less so. Drench the crown with Dursban in spring to protect the plants. Read label directions.

ADDITIONAL INFORMATION
The fruit of some viburnums is spectacular (cranberrybushes in particular).

ADDITIONAL SPECIES, CULTIVARS, OR VARIETIES
There are many cultivars of viburnum. A few have wide acceptance and are available nearly everywhere in the state. Koreanspice is my favorite. The flowers alone are enough to make this plant worthwhile, but it also offers attractive foliage on a dense plant. It is easily maintained in foundation plantings and grows to about 6 feet. Judd viburnum, a *V. carlesii* cross, is coarser and larger. *V. lantana* 'Mohican' is large, to 20 feet, and used for masses and screening. Its fruit persists until November and attracts birds. American cranberrybush viburnum, *V. trilobum*, is large with maple-like leaves and bright fruit that lasts all winter if not gathered by birds. The edible fruit makes interesting jam. A dwarf cultivar is listed in nursery catalogs as 'Compactum'. European cranberrybush viburnum, *V. opulus*, is quite similar, and offers several dwarf cultivars that are more adaptable to smaller landscapes. 'Nanum' is very dwarf, supposedly 2 feet tall, but there is variation in the selection. Arrowwood viburnum, *V. dentatum*, is strongly upright and can be sheared to make a narrow screen, which is especially useful in tight places. It grows to 8 to 10 feet. Two arrowwoods introduced by the Chicagoland Grows program are 'Autumn Jazz' and 'Chicago Lustre'.

Witchhazel

Hamamelis sp.

Zones: All
Size: 15 feet high and wide
Blooms: Spring, fall
Flower Color: Yellow
Type: Deciduous

Light Requirement:

There are two witchhazels used in landscape plantings: vernal witchhazel blooms in late winter, often January and February, and common witchhazel blooms from October to December. These plants are quite unusual because they will bloom in winter-like weather, often when temperatures are below freezing. The flowers are fragrant and open on sunny days and close when temperatures drop. They stay in bloom for several weeks. These plants are well adapted to Illinois conditions. They seem to grow equally well in heavy or light soils as long as the soils are moist but well drained. In some landscape situations these plants can be found growing quite well in poorly drained, damaged soils, though these are not the conditions in which to plant if it can be helped. Witchhazels do best if allowed to grow to their full size. Use them in masses, shrub borders, screens, groupings, or naturalized areas, or as specimen plants.

WHEN TO PLANT

Witchhazels do not like to be moved. They are best transplanted in spring.

WHERE TO PLANT

Plant in full sun or partial shade. Soils should be well drained. Provide enough room so that they can grow without needing to be trimmed to fit the space.

HOW TO PLANT

Plants are available balled and burlapped from local nurseries and garden centers. Dig the planting hole the same depth and twice the diameter of the plant ball. Make sure the hole drains—if there is doubt, check by filling the hole with water and allowing it to drain. Set the plant slightly higher than it grew in the nursery. If the soil on the plant is different from that of the planting hole, shave some from the ball and mix the two together for backfilling the hole. Water thoroughly to settle the soil around the roots.

CARE AND MAINTENANCE
Witchhazels require very little care once they are established. Remove any dead stems in spring and head back overly long branches to a shorter side shoot growing in the same direction.

ADDITIONAL INFORMATION
Witchhazel grows in the wild on wooded banks and high dunes, and also on stream banks where the soils are inundated with water each spring. As long as the soil drains, this causes no lasting damage. The witchhazel astringent sold in drug stores is extracted from the roots, leaves, and bark of these plants.

ADDITIONAL SPECIES, CULTIVARS, OR VARIETIES
Common witchhazels, *H. virginiana*, are large plants growing up to 15 feet tall. In the wild they are ragged, but in a sunny landscape they may be kept dense and nicely shaped. Vernal witchhazel, *H. vernalis*, is a smaller plant, and more dense. It has many named cultivars, most selected for better flowers. The interesting 'Christmas Cheer', selected by J. C. McDaniel at the University of Illinois, blooms at Christmas. *H. mollis*, Chinese witchhazel, is listed as a plant for Zones 6 and 7. Apparently it can be injured by temperatures of minus 15 degrees Fahrenheit. Plants at Morton Arboretum in Lisle, Illinois, have survived for 45 years, and a cultivar of it has been growing there for 58 years. It is the most fragrant of the witchhazels and blooms prolifically in March.

Yew

Taxus sp.

Zones: All
Size: 4 to 20 feet tall and wide
Type: Evergreen

Light Requirement:

Yews are the top-of-the-line evergreens for landscape use. They are attractive, bright-green, soft-needled plants that come in a wide variety of sizes and growth forms. They tolerate the soils of Illinois and will grow in either full sun or shade. They are the best shade-tolerant evergreens after hemlock, which because of its size, form, and intolerance of wind, is less usable in the home landscape. Yews can be pruned severely and they will keep growing. They can be systematically reduced in size so they can be used in places that might seem far too small. They make excellent hedges that can be kept at a predetermined size for as long as someone is interested in maintaining them. Some plants in the East and in Europe have been kept at their present sizes for hundreds of years. Yews produce colorful fruit, but the sexes are on separate plants. The red "berries" are not really fruits at all but fleshy arils, each surrounding a naked seed. For them to develop, you must have female plants, but there must be at least one male plant as well.

WHEN TO PLANT

Yews transplant easily. If balled and burlapped, they may be moved in spring or fall. Containerized plants may be planted whenever the soil is workable. Exposed plants or those in difficult situations are best planted in spring so they can develop roots before the onset of the tough Illinois winter. The winter of 1995-96 was disastrous for newly planted yews, particularly those in raised beds or planters.

WHERE TO PLANT

Plant yews in full sun or shade. They are best protected from winter sun and wind. Use them for foundation plantings, masses, and groupings, and as facer plants and hedges. Any good garden soil is satisfactory, but good drainage is essential. Poor drainage will result in loss of the plants.

How to Plant

Plants are available balled and burlapped, and in various containers. Dig the planting hole slightly less deep and twice as wide as the plant ball. If the soil in the ball is much different from that in the hole, mix some soil from the ball with that going back into the hole to avoid an interface problem. It is to your advantage to buy plants grown in a soil as nearly like that in your yard as you can find. Locally grown plants are definitely best. The importance of good drainage cannot be overemphasized. If the soil is not well drained, set the plants with the balls half out of the ground and hill soil up to them; or construct raised beds. Hedges may be planted by digging a trench, setting the plants at the right spacing, and backfilling the trench. Set the plants high. This is a great labor-saving system. Space large plants 5 to 10 feet apart. Spreading yews should be no closer than 10 feet from a structure. Space dwarf plants at their advertised spread. Hicks yews in hedges should be spaced 2 to 4 feet apart. Soak the plants well after planting. A couple of inches of mulch will help maintain soil moisture and coolness.

Care and Maintenance

During their first season, yews will need to be watered during dry spells. In winter they will need protection from the midday sun and from drying winds. A temporary burlap screen will work fine; drive stakes around the south and west sides and tack the burlap to them.

Additional Species, Cultivars, or Varieties

The nomenclature of the yews is hopelessly confused. Most of the cultivars are listed as *T. cuspidata* or *T. × media*, with the cultivar name following. Most cuspidata types are spreading plants of various sizes. The 'Nana' cultivar is a dwarf, but the degree of dwarfing varies. Ask your nurseryman how big it will get. *T. cuspidata* 'Capitata' is an upright, Christmas tree-like form. The *Taxus × media* types are of various forms: 'Brownii' and 'Brownii Globe' are densely rounded in form. 'Hicks' is a narrow, upright form, excellent for hedges. 'Densiformis' and 'Tauntonii' are small spreading types, usually to about 4 feet tall and twice as wide. 'Tauntonii' seems to resist winter burn.

Trees

ONE OF THE MOST STRIKING DIFFERENCES between the new communities emerging on the Illinois prairie lands and the established older neighborhoods is the presence of beautiful big trees. Such trees provide a charm and coziness that cannot be created by anything else.

Because I grew up in an older community, I took trees for granted; they had always been there and would always be there. They provided shade in summer and broke the wind in winter. Children on the way home from school would take momentary shelter from wintry blasts behind the trunk of a big friendly elm. Birds nested in the trees in summer, and children climbed them so they would have a platform from which to view the neighborhood from an elevated perspective. Something about the trees provided a sense of security that was missing in the part of town where the new postwar bungalows were being built. The advent of Dutch elm disease changed all that. Entire communities were suddenly denuded, and the true value of trees became apparent. Today, mature oaks are in jeopardy, and wilt threatens pines.

Trees frame and shelter a house, making it appear more homey. Yet trees are not only aesthetically important. They are natural air conditioners—just drive from an open highway into a forest preserve on a hot day and notice the difference. They break the wind in winter, saving on heating bills. They screen out sights and sounds, and they filter dirt and grime from the air. Wooded building lots are premium properties. Homes with big trees properly located are worth more, and real estate prices always reflect this.

Trees are living creatures with finite lives. If our ancestors had not planted trees, we would not have them to enjoy now. We need to do the same for the generations who will follow us.

Selecting and placing trees in the landscape must be done with care. A poor decision now may be a headache for years or may be costly to correct.

Chapter Eight

Take your time. Select trees that will grow without too many problems in your location. If you have limey soil, don't plant a tree that needs acidic conditions. It's easy to modify the soil that will go back into a planting hole, but the tree will outgrow that in a short time. Continuous treatments will be costly over the years, and others may not be interested in keeping up the treatments.

Be sure the trees you select will fit their spaces when full-sized. Pruning-to-fit can destroy the natural form and beauty of the plants.

Select plants that will grow in your climatic zone. Some species are not hardy in all of Illinois. Even more important, subtypes of some native species may not be hardy in certain areas. A red maple grown from seed collected in Florida is unlikely to survive in Springfield. Redbuds bought from mail-order houses and planted in Waukegan may be killed to the ground every winter, but redbuds are growing normally in the nearby Botanic Gardens. These are obviously not the same trees. Check with your nurseryman to make sure you know where the plants come from.

Finally, avoid soil incompatibility problems by planting trees that were grown in a soil as nearly like that on your site as possible. Planting a sand-grown plant in a clay loam soil is a prescription for failure. Locally grown plants are always the best choice. They have grown in your kind of soil and have survived your climate for years.

Planting a tree is one of the nicest things you can do for yourself, for your kids, and for your community.

Ash

Fraxinus sp.

Zones: All
Size: 50 to 60 feet in urban and suburban
   locations, to 100 feet in woodlots
Blooms: Spring, before leaves emerge
Flower Colors: Green to purple, insignificant
Type: Deciduous

Light Requirement:

White ash and green ash have received most of the attention of the landscape industry. Both are native American trees. White ash is a huge plant, reaching as much as 60 to 80 feet in height in landscape plantings and spreading at the same rate. It is found throughout Illinois in woods, woodlots, forest preserves, and open areas, growing as tall as 100 feet. It is a lowland tree, tolerant of wet and alkaline soils. Green ash is smaller, growing 50 feet and spreading about 40 feet in landscape plantings. It, too, is a lowland tree found along rivers and streams. Both trees are well adapted to all parts of Illinois. They tolerate wet soils, but also grow well in drier locations. They have been vigorously selected for type, size, and lack of seeds. Ashes grow at a moderate rate, adding about two feet a year.

WHEN TO PLANT

Ashes are best planted while dormant, in spring or in fall after leaves have fallen. With the advent of anti-desiccants, tree spades, and other innovations, they can be moved whenever the ground is workable.

WHERE TO PLANT

Tolerant of most soils, these trees can be planted almost anywhere there is sufficient room. Ashes will grow in sun or shade.

HOW TO PLANT

Ashes are grown as balled-and-burlapped plants and in containers. The hole for planting should be no deeper than the depth of the ball of the plant, and at least twice as wide. Remove the plants from their containers, and slice any circling roots. Set the plant in the planting hole. Remove the burlap from a balled-and-burlapped plant, and place it in the hole. Replace the soil and fill the hole with water. Make a saucer around the plant with any remaining soil.

CARE AND MAINTENANCE
Ashes are messy trees. They are often damaged by storms, and repairs are usually too difficult for the average homeowner. Obtain a certified arborist to evaluate and correct any problems. Borers, scales, mites, ash plant bugs, anthracnose, cankers, and verticillium wilt are among the difficulties these trees may encounter. If the trees are otherwise healthy, they will be able to withstand these problems and continue to prosper. Young trees struggling to overcome transplanting shock may require treatment.

ADDITIONAL INFORMATION
In spite of difficulties, ash trees are widely planted in landscapes throughout Illinois. They are fast growing and are especially useful for planting in disturbed soils where little else will grow. Sometimes ash is planted as a temporary tree until conditions improve and another specimen is planted. Ash wood makes durable tools and handles, and is excellent firewood.

ADDITIONAL SPECIES, CULTIVARS, OR VARIETIES
Fraxinus americana 'Tures', Windy City ash, is a recent introduction in the Chicagoland Grows program which evaluates plant material for Illinois conditions. It is narrower and more upright than the species, and has good fall color. *F. a.* 'Autumn Purple' has excellent fall color and adapts to poor drainage. The widely planted *F. pennsylvanica* 'Patmore' and 'Summit' green ashes are reliable shrubs. They tolerate terrible soil conditions, but may be short lived.

Bald Cypress

Taxodium distichum

Zones: All
Size: 50 to 70 feet tall and spreading 25 feet
Blooms: March or April, insignificant
Flower Color: Yellow
Type: Deciduous conifer

Light Requirement:

ald cypress is one of three deciduous conifers grown through-out Illinois. It is the best of the three, with a fine texture, good form, and site tolerance. A stately, deciduous conifer, this is the cypress of the Florida swamps, and hardy as far north as Wisconsin—quite a feat for any plant! It prefers moist soils but will stand upland sites. A large 60-foot-tall specimen was located on the University of Illinois campus, pinched between a building and sidewalk; it had to put up with foot traffic, salt, and little care. It survived everything except the chain saw when it succumbed to the need for more buildings. Many municipalities are listing bald cypresses as recommended street trees. Bald cypress is a fast-growing, durable tree that does well unless the soil pH is above 7.5.

WHEN TO PLANT

Small container-grown specimens may be planted at any time, but spring is preferred.

WHERE TO PLANT

Full sun and moist, well-drained, acid to neutral soil are ideal condi-tions. These trees do not grow well in the shade. This is a narrow tree, requiring less room than most large trees.

HOW TO PLANT

Bald cypresses are grown as balled-and-burlapped plants and in containers. The hole for planting should be no greater than the depth of the ball of the plant and at least twice as wide. Remove the plants from their containers, and slice any circling roots. Set the plant in the planting hole. Remove the burlap from a balled-and-burlapped plant and place it in the hole. Replace the soil and fill the hole with water. Make a saucer around the plant with any remaining soil.

CARE AND MAINTENANCE
Acid soil is necessary for best results. Test the soil pH before deciding to plant a bald cypress. Maintaining soil acidity is an unnecessary maintenance chore. Instead of fighting high pH, plant something else. When planted, bald cypresses need watering the first year. Later, they require little care. They are intolerant of pruning, so let them grow.

ADDITIONAL INFORMATION
These trees are best suited for the southern parts of Illinois where soils are more likely to be acidic, although some are doing fairly well in northern municipalities. Older specimens develop the characteristic spreading, flat top. They are beautiful in full leaf, with a more dramatic character in winter.

ADDITIONAL SPECIES, CULTIVARS, OR VARIETIES
There are several named cultivars, but most of these trees are not sold by name. Catalogs list only bald cypress. There is diversity within the species: some trees are wide spreading, some columnar. It is possible to find strains that will tolerate the alkaline soils of the northeastern part of the state. 'Prairie Sentinel', 'Monarch of Illinois', and 'Shawnee Brave' are three cultivars suited to west-central Illinois conditions.

Beech

Fagus sp.

Zones: All
Size: 40, 50, to 90 feet tall, spreading 40 feet
  or more
Blooms: Unimportant
Type: Deciduous

Light Requirement:

Among the deciduous trees of Illinois, there is nothing quite as magnificent as a beech. These are large trees, slow growing and durable, but where there is room, there is no other tree that can compare with them. They are splendid in any season of the year with crisp dense foliage in summer, and sturdy with strong branches in winter. Beeches are so spectacular that certain specimens are memorable. A tremendous row of American beeches stood as sentinels along the shore of Lake Michigan south of Ludington, Michigan. Their silver bark glistened at sunset. These trees, some with 4-foot diameter trunks, were removed to make way for the pumped storage reservoir. I'll never forget them. There are three copper beeches in front of a modern high-rise along Chicago's Lake Shore Drive. It is worth an early-morning trip to see these trees as the rising sun illuminates them. Beeches aren't particularly fond of pollution, so they are better off away from the inner city. They do tolerate our limy soils, however, if they are kept moist and well drained.

WHEN TO PLANT
Plant beeches only in spring.

WHERE TO PLANT
Before investing in a beech, I recommend seeing the specimens at the Missouri Botanic Garden, Chicago Botanic Garden, Morton arboretum, or in a local planting. Give these large trees plenty of room. Plant in a sunny, well-drained site. They develop shallow root systems and dense shade where grass rarely grows.

HOW TO PLANT
Beech trees are grown as balled-and-burlapped plants. These trees have shallow roots and need well-aerated soil. Dig the hole for

planting a little less deep than they grew in the nursery, and at least twice as wide as the ball. Set the plant in the planting hole; remove the burlap and place it in the hole. Replace the soil and fill the hole with water. Make a saucer around the plant with any remaining soil.

CARE AND MAINTENANCE

Once established, these trees require little care. Beeches are susceptible to some diseases and several insects, including the two-lined chestnut borer. Healthy trees, however, are perfectly able to withstand these attacks without trouble. In dry weather, thoroughly soak the soil under the branch spread of the tree once a month.

ADDITIONAL INFORMATION

European beech takes shearing very well and can be kept as a hedge.

ADDITIONAL SPECIES, CULTIVARS, OR VARIETIES

The America beech, *Fagus grandifolia*, has smooth silver-gray bark, dark-green summer foliage, and golden fall color. Even in a forest planting it stands out. There are no named cultivars of this species, but there are regional differences. American beech is fully hardy throughout the state. European beech, *Fagus sylvatica*, is a smaller tree; the bark is darker in color, and fall color is bronze. There are many selections of this species. Two worthy of special mention are the copper beech, probably *F. s.* 'Purpurea Latifolia', and weeping beech, *F. s.* 'Pendula'. European beech is intolerant of heat and not recommended for the southern part of the state.

Birch

Betula sp.

Zones: All
Size: Heights to 40 or 50 feet, spread less
Blooms: Spring, unimportant
Type: Deciduous

Light Requirement:

hite birches are familiar, even to young children. The white, peeling bark creates interest at any time of the year. Stories explaining the use of the bark for canoes, shoes, and other items fill children's books, and visits to the north woods often include stops at souvenir shops where birch-bark items are displayed. Birches are also popular in landscapes because of their graceful form and striking bark. The weeping white birch is particularly popular. The stark white color may seem out of place in suburbia unless placed carefully.

WHEN TO PLANT

Some birches do not transplant well. Plant them in the spring only.

WHERE TO PLANT

These are plants of the lowlands and ravines. They prefer moist, well-drained soils.

HOW TO PLANT

Birch trees are grown as balled-and-burlapped plants and in containers. The hole for planting should be no deeper than the depth of the ball of the plant and at least twice as wide. Remove the plants from their containers and slice any circling roots. Set the plant in the planting hole. Remove the burlap from a balled-and-burlapped plant, and place it in the hole. Replace the soil and fill the hole with water. Make a saucer around the plant with any remaining soil.

CARE AND MAINTENANCE

Birches require regular watering the first year after planting. All birches should be watered in droughty periods. There is some indication that resistance to the bronze birch borer is improved if the plants are vigorous. River birch will be less likely to become chlorotic if kept well watered. To protect white birches from borers, spray the trees or apply a band of dimethoate concentrate to the trunks in early June. Chlorotic river birch can be treated with chelated iron injected into the soil to improve the color. All pruning should be done in the fall to reduce bleeding.

ADDITIONAL INFORMATION

Birches are fast-growing, short-lived trees, grown for their graceful form and ornamental white, cinnamon, or yellow bark.

ADDITIONAL SPECIES, CULTIVARS, OR VARIETIES

River birch and red birch, *Betula nigra*, are reported to be resistant to attack by bronze birch borer. Red birch has attractive cinnamon-colored bark that, when peeled, reveals a lighter-colored inner bark. 'Heritage' river birch has bark that peels open white to salmon-white. 'Little King' river birch has been tested at Morton Arboretum and the Chicago Botanic Garden and introduced through the Chicagoland Grows program. 'Whitespire', a selection of Asian white birch, *B. platyphylla*, has shown excellent resistance to borers due in part to its tolerance of warmer weather. Only plants vegetatively propagated from the original 'Whitespire' are resistant. Many clones of 'Whitespire' are from seed and do not exhibit the same characteristics. Be wary of possible 'Heritage' clones, also. 'Little King' is available only from selected nurseries. Buy plants of these cultivars from reputable nurseries only.

Black Tupelo

Nyssa sylvatica

Other Names: Black Gum, Sour Gum, Tupelo
Zones: 5B and 6
Size: 50 feet with spread of 30
Blooms: Insignificant
Type: Deciduous

Light Requirement:

*T*he black tupelo is a beautiful native tree with a distinctive pyramidal form, good branching, and excellent fall color. It is one of the most consistent of our native trees for its fall display of brilliant scarlet leaves. This tree prefers swampy places, but may be found in upland sites, woodlots, and abandoned farmlands. It does not tolerate alkaline soils or highly urbanized areas. This is an especially good tree to consider in the southern part of the state, where old soils tend to be acidic.

WHEN TO PLANT

Black tupelo reportedly transplants with difficulty. Plants in containers, and smaller-sized plants, however, seem to move and become established quite easily. Plant in spring only.

WHERE TO PLANT

Deep, well-drained, acidic soil in full sun or a semi-shaded location is ideal. This plant makes a good street tree or an excellent specimen. It is not overly large and will fit into most residential yards.

HOW TO PLANT

Black tupelos are grown as balled-and-burlapped plants. They are hard to transplant because they develop deep taproots. The hole for planting should be no deeper than the depth of the ball of the plant and at least twice as wide. Set the plant in the planting hole. Remove the burlap from the ball and place it in the hole. Replace the soil and fill the hole with water. Make a saucer around the plant with any remaining soil.

CARE AND MAINTENANCE

Black tupelo is a trouble-free plant. It prefers swampy soil, so water it thoroughly once a month during droughty periods. Tupelos require regular watering during the first year after planting.

ADDITIONAL INFORMATION

This tree is seldom seen growing in the Chicago area, although there are a few in Cook County. Alkaline soil and urban pollution relegate it to other, better-suited parts of the state. It is common in the Indiana Dunes. The fruits of black tupelo are dark blue, about the size of cherries, and are attractive to birds. The name *Nyssa* is the name of a mythical Greek water nymph, and refers to the affinity of these trees for wet sites.

ADDITIONAL SPECIES, CULTIVARS, OR VARIETIES

There are no named cultivars of black tupelo. Water tupelo, *Nyssa aquatica*, is found in wet locations in the southern tip of the state.

Callery Pear

Pyrus calleryana

Zones: All	**Light Requirement:**
Size: Height to 30 feet, equal spread	
Blooms: Spring	
Flower Color: White	
Type: Deciduous	

*C*allery pear was introduced from China in an attempt to introduce fire blight resistance into commercial pear production. The experiment was unsuccessful, but the result is an interesting landscape plant. In spring these little trees are covered with small white single flowers. Fall color can be spectacular, but it will fail to develop fully if there is an early frost.

WHEN TO PLANT

This plant is easily moved in either spring or fall if fully dormant. Do not move balled-and-burlapped specimens in leaf. Small containerized plants may be planted at any time.

WHERE TO PLANT

The Callery pear is a small, short-lived tree suited for planting in restricted places. It grows well under power lines, is tolerant of many soil types and urban pollution, and makes an attractive street tree. Although Callery pears are site tolerant, they require full sun.

HOW TO PLANT

Callery pears are grown as balled-and-burlapped plants and in containers. The hole for planting should be no deeper than the depth of the ball of the plant and at least twice as wide. Remove the plants from containers and slice any circling roots. Set the plant in the planting hole. Remove the burlap from a balled-and-burlapped plant and place it in the hole. Replace the soil and fill the hole with water. Make a saucer around the plant with any remaining soil.

CARE AND MAINTENANCE

These plants are somewhat messy. Prune in winter or early spring to
remove damaged, diseased, and crossing branches. Later pruning
may result in fire blight infection. Although Callery pear is drought
tolerant, the trees will benefit from watering during extended dry
periods. Pears require regular watering the first year after planting.

ADDITIONAL INFORMATION

Callery pears are extremely brittle as they age. They have a multitude of small branches with narrow crotches that tend to split the
tree open as it reaches maturity. Plan to replace these trees every
twenty years.

ADDITIONAL SPECIES, CULTIVARS, OR VARIETIES

'Bradford' Callery pear is the most common cultivar. It is the most
disease resistant and has the best flowering characteristics, but is
also the most likely to split open. It has a rounded form, nearly as
wide as tall. 'Chanticleer', which is more upright, is considered less
likely to disintegrate. 'Aristocrat' has better form with a central
leader and good vigor. Fire blight, however, has been serious on this
cultivar in the South.

Catalpa

Catalpa speciosa

Other Name: Northern Catalpa
Zones: All
Size: Height to 50, sometimes 60 feet,
    spread 30 feet
Blooms: June
Flower Colors: White "orchids" with
    purple fringes
Type: Deciduous

Light Requirement:

*C*atalpas aren't for everyone. These are old-fashioned trees, more closely associated with the South than the Midwest. The trees are contorted, with loose, coarse branches growing in no clear direction. The catalpa is a tree for all seasons, however. It leafs out late, after danger of frost has passed. (Some gardeners swear it is not safe to set out tender plants until the catalpa leaves are at least the size of a man's hand.) Leaves are a pale green, large and heart-shaped. The flowers, which suddenly appear in late June or early July, cover the tree with purple-fringed white "orchids." When they drop, they create a summer snow on the lawn (or a mess on the sidewalk after a rain). Long seedpods appear after the flowers and remain on the tree all winter. The long, crooked branches are fascinating in winter.

WHEN TO PLANT

Catalpas transplant most easily in spring. Plants growing in containers can be planted anytime.

WHERE TO PLANT

While catalpas probably do best in a well-drained, moist soil, they seem to tolerate wet, dry, or compact alkaline soils without difficulty. Allow growing room and plant in full sun. These trees seem unaffected by extremely hot, dry sites.

HOW TO PLANT

Catalpas are grown as balled-and-burlapped plants and in containers. The hole for planting should be no deeper than the depth of the ball of the plant and at least twice as wide. Remove the plants from their containers and slice any circling roots. Set the plant in the planting hole. Remove the burlap from the ball, and place it in the hole. Replace the soil and fill the hole with water. Make a saucer around the plant with any remaining soil.

CARE AND MAINTENANCE

Catalpas require very little care. Cut out dead or broken branches as they appear. Water during extended dry spells. Dormant catalpas are slow to leaf after transplanting. Be patient and do not overwater.

ADDITIONAL INFORMATION

Catalpa is an American Indian name. The wood is light in weight, strong, and resists rotting when in contact with the soil. It is used for railroad ties. Catalpas are susceptible to verticillium wilt. Every effort should be made to avoid bringing this disease into contact with a catalpa.

ADDITIONAL SPECIES, CULTIVARS, OR VARIETIES

There are some named varieties of catalpas, but they are never sold by name. *C. bignonioides*, southern catalpa, is more prevalent in the southern part of the state. It is almost impossible to tell it from the northern species. The two species probably hybridize, and any wild plants could be natural hybrids. *Catalpa bignonioides* 'Nana' is a French selection that was grafted on a five-foot-tall standard trunk to produce a weeping, umbrella-like plant. Common during the Victorian era, these plants are in favor again, in keeping with the current popularity of Victorian style.

Crab Apple

Malus sp. and cv.

Zones: All
Size: 6 to 25 feet tall, spreading as wide or wider
Blooms: Spring
Flower Colors: White, pink, rose, deep red, carmine
Type: Deciduous

Light Requirement:

Few trees suitable for the northern climate compare to the beauty of crab apples in full bloom. They are spectacular, with color ranging from white to pink, rose, and carmine. Fruits can be inconspicuous or sizable and provide fall color as well as food for wildlife. Crab apples have been hybridized indiscriminately for centuries. The primary objective for this effort was the profusion of flowers, flower size, and color. Unfortunately, little effort was expended for disease resistance, resulting in a tremendous number of cultivars that are useless in this part of the country. Within the last two decades, there has been emphasis on screening the current cultivars and hybridizing for disease resistance. New cultivars are increasingly disease resistant.

WHEN TO PLANT

Crab apples are easily transplanted. They are available in garden centers and wherever plants are sold in spring and fall. Containerized plants may be planted at any time.

WHERE TO PLANT

Crab apples are well adapted to the heavy soils of Illinois. If drainage is adequate, any soil will do. Plant in full sun and allow enough room for the plants to develop fully; otherwise plants will need a lot of pruning.

HOW TO PLANT

Crab apples are sold bareroot, balled-and-burlapped, and in containers. The hole for planting should be shallower than the depth of the ball and at least twice as wide. Soak bareroot plants for several hours before planting. Remove plants from containers and slice any circling roots. Set each plant in the hole, keeping it slightly higher than it grew in the nursery. The result of deep planting or poor drainage is root rot and plant loss. Remove the burlap from balled-and-burlapped plants and place it in the hole. Replace the soil and fill the hole with water. Make a saucer around the plant with any remaining soil.

CARE AND MAINTENANCE
Properly sited crab apples need little pruning. Prune immediately after bloom. Remove vertical shoots growing through the center of the tree. If the plant was grafted to a rootstock, there will be suckers to remove. Spray them with diquat as they begin to grow, keeping the diquat off the desirable foliage. Follow label directions. Crab apples will need regular watering the first year after planting.

ADDITIONAL INFORMATION
Crab apples have been around a long time. Pests have found and affected many plantings: flat-headed apple borers, scales, aphids, fire blight, other cankers, cedar-apple rust, and the ever-present apple scab. Selecting cultivars with resistance eliminates much of the difficulty in caring for them. Selecting own-root plants eliminates any suckering problem. If fruit-drop is a problem, select a cultivar with tiny fruit. There are plants to fit any landscape, small and large.

ADDITIONAL SPECIES, CULTIVARS, OR VARIETIES
The list of cultivars is quite long and confusing. Buy plants from a reliable grower who knows what was planted and can guarantee what you buy. These cultivars show resistance to scab: *M.* × *atrosanguinea*, 'Carmine crab'; *M.* 'Beverly'; *M.* 'Donald Wyman'; *M. floribunda*; *M. halliana* var *parkmanii*; *M. hupehensis*, 'Tea Crab'; *M.* 'Profusion'; *M. sargentii*, 'Sargent Crab'; *M.* 'Snowdrift'; and *M.* 'White Angel'. *M.* 'Spring Snow' is a sterile plant (no fruit). *M.* 'Joy Morton', Morning Sun crab apple, is a recent Chicagoland Grows introduction.

Flowering Dogwood

Cornus florida

Zones: All
Size: Height to 30 feet, spread equal
  or greater
Blooms: Early spring
Flower Colors: White or pink bracts
  surrounding small green flowers
Type: Deciduous

Light Requirement:

Flowering dogwood is one of the most beautiful and best known of the flowering trees. In April, the woods come alive with its flower clusters (actually showy bracts surrounding an inconspicuous flower). It has white or pink blooms in spring, bright, clear green leaves all summer, and finishes the fall in a blaze of red. Flowering dogwood is a small deciduous tree with horizontal branching that gives it a layered or stratified effect, especially when in bloom. While it is a woodland plant, it is well adapted to residential landscapes, particularly in wooded areas. The dogwood is popular in floral paintings, decorative china, jewelry, and lacework.

WHEN TO PLANT
Plant balled-and-burlapped plants in spring or fall. Container-grown plants can be planted all season.

WHERE TO PLANT
Flowering dogwood is an understory tree and adapted to shaded locations. It prefers a cool, moist, acidic soil, but can be found growing and doing well in hot, dry places.

HOW TO PLANT
Flowering dogwoods are available balled-and-burlapped and in containers. The hole for planting should be shallower than the depth of the ball, and at least twice as wide. Remove plants from their containers and slice any circling roots. Set the plant in the hole, keeping it slightly higher than it grew in the nursery. The result of deep planting or poor drainage will be root rot and plant loss. Remove

the burlap from balled-and-burlapped plants and place it in the hole. Replace the soil and fill the hole with water. Make a saucer around the plant with any remaining soil.

CARE AND MAINTENANCE

Flowering dogwood requires little care once established. Provide water in extended droughts. Water regularly the first year after planting. Pruning, if needed, should be done immediately after flowering.

ADDITIONAL INFORMATION

Dogwood anthracnose, a disease of flowering dogwoods, has been traced to the eastern states. Discovered about fifteen years ago, it causes the progressive death of stems and eventually the entire tree. The disease is prevalent in wet springs and more commonly affects plants under stress. Several fungicides are effective in preventing the disease. Apply just before flowers open and repeat as long as wet weather persists. Flowering dogwood blooms reliably in the southern half of the state. In the north, blooming has been variable. This could be attributed to differences in subtypes. Those grown from seed or cuttings of northern types tend to be hardier.

ADDITIONAL SPECIES, CULTIVARS, OR VARIETIES

There are many selections of flowering dogwood. The pink *Cornus florida rubra* is unusual. Others are largely regional selections. Most nurseries simply list flowering dogwood with no mention of varieties. Select plants grown from seed or cuttings collected locally. There is a wide variation in hardiness and flowering if regional types are grown outside their normal ranges. Kousa dogwood, *Cornus kousa*, blooms later and is probably better suited to the southern part of the state, although the flower buds are more hardy than those of flowering dogwood.

Ginkgo

Ginkgo biloba

Zones: All
Size: 40 to 50 feet tall, narrow in youth,
   spreading with age
Blooms: Spring
Flower Color: Green, insignificant
Type: Deciduous, broadleaf gymnosperm
   (conifer)

Light Requirement:

*G*inkgo is probably the most ancient tree now under cultivation. Fossil records show that it was a native plant in North America when the dinosaurs roamed. No one knows where the plants we grow today originated; there are none in the wild. They were brought to this country in 1784 from eastern China. Ginkgo is unusual in other ways. The leaves are shaped like a fan, yet the tree is more closely related to a pine than to any broadleaf tree. Female trees tend to be broad; male trees are more upright. Although the ginkgo is a wonderful tree, there are some drawbacks. The female trees produce a fruit that is messy and foul smelling. One of the most magnificent specimens I have ever seen, however, is a female tree in the back yard of a large home. It spreads over the house and yard like a huge umbrella and is glorious in fall. (Fortunately, it doesn't bear fruit every year.)

WHEN TO PLANT

Gingko transplants easily. Spring or fall planting is equally successful. Containerized plants can be planted anytime.

WHERE TO PLANT

Deep, moist soil is preferred, but these trees are very adaptable and will accept almost any situation. They tolerate alkaline or acidic soils, sand or clay, if there is adequate drainage. They thrive in full sun and are excellent for parkways or yards. Ginkgo is relatively salt-tolerant.

HOW TO PLANT

The ginkgo is grown as a balled-and-burlapped plant and in containers. The hole for planting should be no greater than the depth of the ball of the plant and at least twice as wide. Remove the plants from containers and slice any circling roots. Set the plant in the planting hole. Remove the burlap from a balled-and-burlapped plant and place it in the hole. Replace the soil and fill the hole with water. Make a saucer around the plant with any remaining soil.

CARE AND MAINTENANCE
There are no insects or diseases affecting these trees. Any pruning for shaping should be done in spring. Water regularly the first year after planting.

ADDITIONAL INFORMATION
Don't be disappointed by the looks of a young gingko tree. The branches are sparse, strongly upright, and open, but it will develop into a handsome tree with age. This is good tree as for city plantings. Ginkgo is equally suited for the open spaces where it can spread to its full potential.

ADDITIONAL SPECIES, CULTIVARS, OR VARIETIES
There is only one species of ginkgo, but there are many cultivars. Some of the best selections are 'Autumn Gold', with a rather broad form and exceptional fall color; 'Mayfield', very narrow; and 'Pendula'. The latter is undoubtedly the name given to quite a number of drooping selections, so be sure to check the origin. If the parent plant droops, the offspring should as well. There is some indication that the location on the plant from which budwood is taken for grafting will affect the kind of growth exhibited by the resulting plants.

Hackberry

Celtis occidentalis

Zones: All
Size: 50 to 60 feet tall and spreading 40 feet
Blooms: Spring as leaves open
Flower Color: Insignificant
Type: Deciduous

Light Requirement:

*T*he hackberry is a large deciduous tree, a tough native of the bottomlands from which our most adaptable tree species have been selected. It tolerates wet or dry, acid or alkaline, sunny or shaded, urbanized or rural situations equally well. These are the attributes that made the American elm so useful. With the loss of the elms, hackberry seems to be a logical replacement, but an unsightly condition called "witches' broom" affects many hackberries. This ailment is caused by a mite and mildew growing on the buds. It results in masses of twiggy growth at the tips of branches, but it doesn't seem to bother the tree at all. Elms presented problems, too, but they were graceful, vase-shaped trees. Hackberries are similar in form and will thrive in rough conditions, but aren't nearly as picturesque.

WHEN TO PLANT

Hackberries can be planted either spring or fall.

WHERE TO PLANT

These trees tolerate almost any situation. They are excellent street trees because they will stand salting and compaction. Sun or shade and plenty of room are all they need.

HOW TO PLANT

Hackberries are grown bareroot, as balled-and-burlapped plants, or in containers. The hole for planting should be no deeper than the depth of the ball of the plant and at least twice as wide. Soak roots of bareroot plants in a bucket of water for several hours before planting. Remove the plants from their containers and slice any circling roots. Set the plant in the planting hole at the same depth it grew in the nursery. Remove the burlap from a balled-and-burlapped plant and place it in the hole. Replace the soil and fill

the hole with water. Make a saucer around the plant with any
remaining soil.

CARE AND MAINTENANCE

Hackberries tend to be messy trees. They drop berries and sticks
from the witches' brooms that require raking. They are susceptible
to numerous insects, the nipplegall being the most troublesome.
Insects causing the galls leave the tree in fall and may migrate
indoors seeking winter quarters. They don't bite, eat, or reproduce
indoors. Swat them and vacuum them up. Although beset with
a myriad of problems, these trees simply shrug them off and
grow on.

ADDITIONAL INFORMATION

The name hackberry comes from hagberry, the Scottish name for
European bird cherry, which has similar small fruits. If you want to
find out what grows best in your part of the state, look at the wild
plants in out-of-the-way places. You will probably find seedlings of
elms, silver maples, box elders, and hackberries thriving.

ADDITIONAL SPECIES, CULTIVARS, OR VARIETIES

As well suited to Illinois conditions as hackberries are, it would
seem that some selection is in order to eliminate the undesirable
aspects of the plants. At least two Illinois nurseries have done just
that. Cultivars resistant to the witches' broom with superior habits
have been introduced. 'Prairie Pride', from the Wandell Nursery,
Urbana, has good green color, compact growth, and no witches'
broom. 'Chicagoland' from Klehm Nurseries, South Barrington,
develops a single leader; its resistance to witches' broom is presently
unknown. Sugarberry, *C. laevigata*, is native to southern Illinois and
is a more refined plant. Wandells have made a selection of this
species called 'All Seasons' sugarberry. A hybrid hackberry × sugarberry is 'Magnifica'. It is reportedly free from witches' broom.

Hawthorn

Crataegus sp.

Zones: All
Size: 20 to 30 feet tall and spreading about the same
Blooms: Spring
Flower Colors: White with variously colored anthers
Type: Deciduous

Light Requirement:

*W*hen plowed ground returns to nature, hawthorns are often the first trees to take root. They appear as solitary plants or in groves. These rugged little trees are dense, twiggy, and armed with thorns. They bear attractive flowers and fruits, tolerate heat and cold, wet and dry, excellent and poor soils, urban and rural situations . . . all of the conditions we find here in Illinois. In city parks, there are hawthorns that have survived adverse conditions for decades. They rarely look too good, but they flower faithfully every year and provide some green in places that would otherwise be barren. As landscape plants, hawthorns are durable and attractive when cared for adequately. They can make effective barriers because of their thorns.

WHEN TO PLANT

Hawthorns can be planted in spring or fall. Plants grown in containers can be planted any time the soil is workable.

WHERE TO PLANT

Hawthorns are not particular. They tolerate all kinds of conditions but appreciate a rich, deep soil. They can be planted in sun or shade.

HOW TO PLANT

Hawthorns are grown as balled-and-burlapped plants and in containers. The hole for planting should be about the depth of the ball of the plant and at least twice as wide. Remove the plants from their containers and slice any circling roots. Set the plant in the planting hole. Remove the burlap from a balled-and-burlapped plant, and place it in the hole. Replace the soil and fill the hole with water. Make a saucer around the plant with any remaining soil.

CARE AND MAINTENANCE

Hawthorns are self-sufficient plants and require little care, but they are susceptible to several insect pests and a disease that spots the leaves. The worst of the insects are leaf miners, which turn leaves brown with little tunnels running through them. Treat plants with acephate in May when the first brown spots appear. Control cedar-hawthorn rust with funginex as leaves open, and several more times if the weather is wet. Read and follow directions on the labels.

ADDITIONAL INFORMATION

Crataegus comes from the Greek *kratos*, meaning "strength." All hawthorns will stand shearing. They are easily kept in bounds but are better planted where they have room to grow.

ADDITIONAL SPECIES, CULTIVARS, OR VARIETIES

'Cockspur Thorn', *Crataegus crus-galli*, is a rounded plant with shiny, green foliage. It will reach 20 feet and spread even farther. If used as a corner plant in a foundation planting, give it enough room. These plants have strong, 3-inch thorns and should not be used where little children might encounter them. There is a thornless variety, *C. c. inermis*, which has the same growth characteristics and should be used wherever possible. Washington thorn, *C. phaenopyrum*, is a vase-shaped plant reaching 20 feet tall and wide. If growing in full sun, the form remains broadly oval; in the shade, lower branches are lost. Washington thorn has white flowers in June and may be covered with bright-red fruits from late summer well into winter. The fruit display may be so outstanding that people ask what kind of plant it is. This desirable plant does, unfortunately, bear thorns.

Honeylocust

Gleditsia tricanthos inermis

Zones: All
Size: To 70 feet tall, usually less. Spread
   to 30 feet
Blooms: May-June
Flower Color: Green, not showy but
   fragrant
Type: Deciduous

Light Requirement:

The loss of the elms initiated a quest for the perfect tree to replace them. One of the first candidates was honeylocust. This is a delightful large tree with finely cut foliage. It is broad and round-topped with a decidedly layered effect. Some newer selections develop a vase shape, reminiscent of elms. The fine foliage allows filtered light to reach the ground and grass grows easily in its shade. Honeylocust is native to the bottomlands, the situation from which our most adaptable tree species have been selected. Like the American elm, it tolerates wet or dry, acid or alkaline, sunny or shaded, urbanized or rural situations equally well. Honeylocust is salt-tolerant, which has endeared it to urban landscape architects. In fact, it is so widely used that should a disease as devastating as Dutch elm afflict these trees, the effects on the shade tree population would be detrimental indeed.

WHEN TO PLANT

Honeylocust is easily transplanted and can be moved either spring or fall.

WHERE TO PLANT

Adaptable honeylocust can be planted in any soil, sun or shade, in the parkway or as a lawn tree. Its filtered shade will not affect the lawn or flower plantings.

HOW TO PLANT

Honeylocust plants are sold bareroot, balled-and-burlapped, or in containers. Set the plant slightly higher than it grew in the nursery. Deep planting or poor drainage may result in Ganoderma root rot and plant loss.

CARE AND MAINTENANCE

Prune to a single stem while the tree is small. These trees tend to develop in a zigzag manner, often with no central leader, in open situations. (In a forest setting they grow straight up, seeking the light.) Once the trunk has developed to a satisfactory height, allow the plant to assume its normal growth pattern. Honeylocust is tolerant of pruning and can even be sheared.

ADDITIONAL INFORMATION

The species honeylocust is well armed with thorns on all branches and along the trunk. It also produces large pods that can cover the lawn in a heavy year. All of the cultivars are selected to be free of thorns, and most bear very few pods. The leaves of this tree are pinnately or bipinnately compound. They have tiny leaflets along a middle rachis (stem). Raking is unnecessary, as only the leaflets are shed, not the entire leaves. The rachises are easily shredded while mowing. Three insect pests and one disease seriously affect this tree. Honeylocust plant bug feeds on developing leaves in spring, distorting them and rendering the tree leafless for a few weeks. Carbaryl or acephate spray or patience will solve the problem. Mimosa webworm is serious in the southern part of the state. *Bacillis thuringensis* will control it. Honeylocust mite (not an insect) turns leaves bronze in late summer; use insecticidal soap when injury is first noticed. Read and follow directions on insecticide labels. Ganoderma root rot is a secondary invader that affects damaged plants; in the home lawn, the most common sources of this damage are wet soils and the lawn mower. There is no cure for the disease once it begins.

ADDITIONAL SPECIES, CULTIVARS, OR VARIETIES

The first named selection of thornless honeylocust was 'Moraine'. It is still one of the best cultivars. It has shown resistance to webworm. 'Skyline' is more upright than other selections. 'Shademaster' is considered by most to be the best selection for form, color, growth, and freedom from pods.

Hornbeam

Carpinus caroliniana

Other Names: Blue Beech, Ironwood, Musclewood
Zones: All
Size: 20 feet tall and wide, sometimes much larger
Blooms: Spring
Flower Color: Light green in catkins
Type: Deciduous

Light Requirement:

*A*n interesting smaller tree, hornbeam is a tough native of the bottomlands. It tolerates wet or dry, acid or alkaline, sunny or shaded situations equally well. These are the attributes that make many native plants so useful in our landscapes. This is a particularly useful plant in a shaded site where overhanging trees could create a challenge to landscape designers. Such sites are common in older neighborhoods throughout the state. Hornbeam will stand the shade and relish the moist soil normal in these sites. Hornbeam is interesting in all seasons. The catkins are light green as leaves begin to open. Foliage is somewhat small and allows the interesting structure of the plant to show through. Fall color is yellow to orange. In winter, the beautiful smooth, gray bark on multiple, muscular trunks lends contrast to the white snow.

WHEN TO PLANT

Balled-and-burlapped hornbeam transplants well when small. Plant in spring.

WHERE TO PLANT

Plant in sun to partial shade. Hornbeam prefers well-drained but moist soil. It tolerates alkalinity and other difficult situations. It is suitable as an understory plant at the edge of the yard or as a corner planting near the house. Hornbeam will spread 20 feet, so place it no closer than ten feet from a structure.

How to Plant

Hornbeams are grown as balled-and-burlapped plants. These trees are shallowly rooted, needing a well-aerated soil. Dig the hole for planting them a little more shallow than they grew in the nursery and at least twice as wide. Set the plant in the planting hole; remove the burlap and place it in the hole. Replace the soil and fill the hole with water. Make a saucer around the plant with any remaining soil.

Care and Maintenance

There are no serious pests that affect hornbeam. It is tolerant of pruning but seldom needs any. Water during extended dry periods.

Additional Information

The wood of both the native species and the related European hornbeam is hard and heavy. The name "hornbeam" probably came from the use of its wood as the beam placed across the horns of oxen in harness. Axles, wagon spokes, and other agricultural implements were sometimes made from the tough hornbeam wood.

Additional Species, Cultivars, or Varieties

The related species, European hornbeam, *C. betulus*, has received much more attention in the nursery trade than the American species. It may be somewhat less hardy than *C. caroliniana*, but it is hardy enough for all parts of Illinois. It is a more refined plant, but with similar bark and muscled trunk. There are many cultivars of this plant, which has been cultivated widely in Europe for centuries. An upright form is used for hedges and takes shearing well. *C. b.* 'Fastigiata' is the only one regularly listed in nursery catalogs here. There are pendulous selections and some selections of European hornbeam for fall color, though American hornbeam remains superior for fall color. There are few cultivars of American hornbeam; it has not been as widely used as the European variety. It is simply listed as hornbeam. Closely related is hophornbeam, or ironwood, *Ostrya virginiana*. It has a similar habit and interesting fruits resembling hops. It is used in the same manner and will tolerate some of the same conditions as the above varieties. Interestingly, where both American hornbeam and *Ostrya* grow in the same areas, hornbeam populates floodplains, but the hophornbeam does not, apparently due to its lower tolerance of wet soils. It is rarely available.

TREES

Horsechestnut

Aesculus hippocastanum

Other Name: Buckeye (more correctly
  A. glabra)
Zones: All
Size: Height to 40 feet with an equal
  spread
Blooms: June
Flower Colors: White, pink
Type: Deciduous

Light Requirement:

The horsechestnut is a popular tree in spite of some difficulties. It is a handsome, dense, deciduous tree, showy in flower. As its buds open in spring, there is a succession of developing flower clusters at the ends of the twigs, followed by the unfolding of hand-like leaves. It produces gorgeous, upright spikes (panicles) of blooms in late spring. The palmate leaves, compound and light green as they open, are favorites of schoolchildren making leaf collections. The fruits are spiny nuts that are attractive food for squirrels and other wildlife. Children are also attracted to the nuts, which, when peeled, reveal the familiar buckeye. Horsechestnuts are useful as street trees and for tree lawns where there is ample room.

WHEN TO PLANT

Horsechestnut is usually planted balled-and-burlapped in spring. Container plants can be planted at any time during the season.

WHERE TO PLANT

These plants prefer a moist situation in sun or shade. Some perfectly healthy examples, however, are found in heavy, dry locations.

HOW TO PLANT

Horsechestnut trees are grown as balled-and-burlapped plants. These trees have fibrous descending roots that need well-aerated soil. Dig the hole for planting them twice as wide and a little less deep than they grew in the nursery. Set the plant in the planting hole. Remove the burlap and place it in the hole. Replace the soil and fill the hole with water. Make a saucer around the plant with any remaining soil.

CARE AND MAINTENANCE

Horsechestnut is free from insect pests, but is often afflicted by the foliar disease blotch. The nuts can be troublesome if they litter the driveway. Leaves are large and fall all at once. Some pruning of young plants to train them may be necessary. Be certain to maintain a single leader.

ADDITIONAL INFORMATION

Horsechestnuts are native to the mountains of Greece, Bulgaria, and Albania.

ADDITIONAL SPECIES, CULTIVARS, OR VARIETIES

There are many selections of horsechestnut in Europe where the tree is widely grown. *A. c.* 'Baumannii', the Baumann horsechestnut, is listed by several nurseries in Illinois. It has double blooms and no fruit. A cross between red buckeye, *A. pavia*, and horsechestnut produced red horsechestnut with red blooms and good blotch resistance. It is listed as *Aesculus × carnea* 'Briotii' by nurseries in Illinois. Ohio buckeye, *A. glabra*, is native throughout most of Illinois, but is severely affected by blotch. There has been no hybridizing to overcome this problem. Red buckeye is susceptible to blotch, but not as severely as horsechestnut. It is native in the southern tip of the state.

Japanese Tree Lilac

Syringa reticulata

Zones: All
Size: 20 feet, sometimes more
Blooms: Late June
Flower Color: White
Type: Deciduous

Light Requirement:

The Japanese tree lilac differs from most other lilacs—it is more correctly a single stem or multi-stemmed tree than a bush. It flowers a full month later than most other lilacs with creamy-white blooms borne in foot-long, upright panicles literally covering the plants. The flowers are less fragrant than other lilacs with an aroma resembling privet. Leaves are typically heart-shaped and the bark is cherry-like, smooth and reddish, marked with horizontal white lenticels. It is striking in winter. The Japanese tree lilac is subject to many of the pests affecting others of the species but it seems to be more vigorous, having little difficulty with borers or scale.

WHEN TO PLANT

As is true of other lilacs, these trees move with ease in either spring or fall. Container-grown plants can be planted at any time.

WHERE TO PLANT

Japanese tree lilac tolerates almost any soil that has adequate drainage. It does not seem to be pH sensitive and grows well in the alkalinity of urban soils in northern Illinois. The tree lilac prefers full sun but tolerates some shade. Flowering, however, may be diminished.

HOW TO PLANT

Japanese tree lilacs are grown as balled-and-burlapped plants and in containers. The hole for planting should be no deeper than the depth of the ball of the plant and at least twice as wide. Roots of these plants are fibrous and shallow. Set the plant in the planting hole; remove the burlap and shove it down in the hole. Replace the soil and fill the hole with water. Make a saucer around the plant with any remaining soil. Japanese lilacs will need regular watering the first year after planting.

CARE AND MAINTENANCE
Japanese tree lilacs are relatively care-free. They can be pruned immediately after flowering to keep them in bounds. The faded flowers turn brown and tend to hang on the tree. They can be removed with a pole pruner. If planted in a tight location, heavy pruning can keep them in bounds indefinitely.

ADDITIONAL INFORMATION
These plants are shallowly rooted in heavy soils. They make a mat of roots which would seem to compete with groundcover plants. Grass has a difficult time beneath them, but the groundcover European ginger thrives as long as both are supplied with sufficient water. If flowers are allowed to remain on the plants, heavy seed loads will develop and drop. The result is a proliferation of seedlings although some propagators report difficulty with germinating seed. They can be hoed or pulled without difficulty.

ADDITIONAL SPECIES, CULTIVARS, OR VARIETIES
The cultivar 'Ivory Silk' is compact and flowers heavily. 'Ivory Silk' and the species are the only ones listed by most Illinois nurseries. *Syringa pekinensis*, Peking lilac, is a similar species. Little hybridizing has been done on it, although a tree form, 'Summer Charm', was introduced by Wandell Nurseries, Urbana.

Katsuratree

Cercidiphyllum japonicum

Zones: All
Size: 40 to 50 feet tall, spreading 30 to 50 feet
Blooms: Prior to leaving
Flower Color: Green; inconspicuous
Type: Deciduous

Light Requirement:

Katsura is a magnificent pyramidal tree with apricot fall color. It is rare to see a mature one, but most tree aficionados seem to know the location of at least one spectacular specimen. Two places in Illinois are the Morton Arboretum and the campus of the University of Illinois at Urbana-Champaign. Katsura starts out as a strongly upright tree, becoming broad with age. The tree has often been planted too close to buildings, requiring drastic pruning or removal.

WHEN TO PLANT

Katsura is difficult to transplant. Plant it only in early spring, balled-and-burlapped, or as a container plant.

WHERE TO PLANT

Plant in a rich, moist soil with good drainage. Tolerant of either acid or alkaline soils, these trees do best and color up more intensely in full sun. Be sure to provide enough room for this tree. It is often as wide as it is high. Katsura is an excellent street tree where there is enough room and is outstanding as a lawn tree. The rather open crown allows some light and air.

HOW TO PLANT

Katsura trees are grown as balled-and-burlapped plants. The trees have shallow roots, needing well-aerated soil. Roots form a mat at the soil surface. Dig the hole for planting twice as wide and a little less deep than the depth of the ball. Set the plant in the planting hole. Remove the burlap and place it in the hole. Replace the soil and fill the hole with water. Make a saucer around the plant with any remaining soil.

CARE AND MAINTENANCE

Katsura is relatively trouble-free. There are no insects or diseases that seriously affect the tree. Exposed bark may be subject to scalding. Be careful when pruning not to expose bark to the sun suddenly. Try to orient the tree so that the south side remains south in its new location. Getting the tree established is sometimes difficult. Supplemental watering is essential during the first few seasons until the tree develops a good root system.

ADDITIONAL INFORMATION

Katsura leaves are similar to those of redbud, *Cercis*, thus the generic nomen. *Cercidiphyllum*, roughly translated, is "leaf like a redbud." In its native Japan, these trees reach a height of well over 100 feet. The related *C. j.* var. *sinense* is reported to reach a height of 130 feet, easily the largest deciduous tree in that country. Where there is room and a suitable site, katsura ranks among the best trees for Illinois.

ADDITIONAL SPECIES, CULTIVARS, OR VARIETIES

There are several selections listed in various places, but the species is the only one grown by nurseries and the only one available to plant.

Kentucky Coffeetree

Gymnocladus dioicus

Zones: All
Size: 60 to 70 feet tall, sometimes to 90 feet;
   spread, 40 to 50 feet
Type: Deciduous

Light Requirement:

*K*entucky coffeetree is large with foliage that is doubly pinnately compound. The leaves are large, sometimes three feet long with leaflets about three inches long and half as wide. The effect is quite airy in summer. It is one of the last trees to leaf out in spring. In winter, the structure of the tree is evident, showing large spreading limbs rather bereft of branches, quite coarse but bold. The seedpods, a foot long, hang on female trees all winter to rustle in the wind. Kentucky coffeetree is suited for larger sites, parkways, large lawns, and parks. It is a somewhat messy tree at times, though the leaflets that drop from the leaves in fall are small and no problem. They can be shredded as the lawn is mowed and disappear. The rachises (stems) of the leaves persist and usually fall in late winter and the pods fall in spring. This can mean cleaning up several times. If that coincides with other cleanup times or with mowing the lawn, it need not be an overwhelming chore. Kentucky coffeetree is a native inhabitant of bottomlands, ravines, and moist slopes. It tolerates wet or dry, acid or chalky, sunny or shaded, urbanized or rural situations equally well.

When to Plant

This tree may be planted balled-and-burlapped in either spring or fall. Container plants may be planted at any time.

Where to Plant

Full sun and a well-drained, moist soil are preferred, but coffeetree is quite adaptable. Kentucky coffeetree is a large plant that needs room to develop to its full size.

How to Plant

Set balled-and-burlapped plants at the same depth they grew in the nursery. Be sure to remove the burlap and twine. Be sure to cut any girdling roots on container-grown plants and mix some of the container soil with that in the planting hole to avoid soil incompatibility problems. Roots are fleshy, with a few fibers growing downward.

CARE AND MAINTENANCE
Kentucky coffeetree is relatively maintenance-free. Few insects or diseases affect it. It requires regular watering the first season after planting.

ADDITIONAL INFORMATION

The seeds of Kentucky coffeetree are considered poisonous. The local natives taught settlers in Kentucky and Tennessee to make a coffee by roasting and grinding the seeds. Speculation is that roasting eliminated the toxic substance. The name *Gymnocladus* is from the Greek *gymnos*, "naked", and *klados*, "a branch". This refers to its stout, twig-free branches.

ADDITIONAL SPECIES, CULTIVARS, OR VARIETIES
Little has been done to improve this tree. There is interest in a good male clone that would not develop pods. Listed in catalogs is an improved cultivar, 'Expresso'. For all practical purposes, any plants available from your local nurseryman will perform quite well in your garden.

Larch

Larix decidua

Other Names: European Larch, American
Larch, Tamarack (*Larix laricina*)
Zones: *L. decidua*, all zones; *L. laricina*,
better suited for Zone 5
Size: Usually about 50 feet tall, sometimes
to 100; spread, 25 feet
Blooms: Early spring with opening leaves
Flower Colors: Pink or yellow
Type: Deciduous conifer

Light Requirement:

*L*arches are unusual conifers that lose their leaves in fall. (Most conifers are evergreen, but larches are deciduous.) In the spring, soft, light-green leaves join tiny pink-and-yellow "flowers." Later, the leaves are deeper green but retain their soft appearance. Fall color can be spectacular depending on the weather and site. Larches are graceful pyramidal trees with sweeping, pendulous branches. They provide light shade and do not interfere with the lawn beneath them. In the fall, the leaves that drop fall filter into the lawn and disappear without raking. Reportedly not for the urban residential lot, larches have been planted throughout our community as parkway and lawn trees. Many have been in place for over fifty years and remain healthy.

WHEN TO PLANT

Plant larches in spring when fully dormant. Fall planting can be successful if not followed by a particularly harsh winter. Container-grown plants can be planted anytime during the season.

WHERE TO PLANT

Larches require cool, moist soils and good drainage. They tolerate periodic inundation and perform well for pondside planting. Full sun and additional organic matter create ideal conditions.

HOW TO PLANT

Set balled-and-burlapped plants at the same depth they grew in the nursery. Be sure to remove the burlap and twine. Cut any girdling roots on container-grown plants. Mix some of the container soil with that in the planting hole to avoid soil incompatibility problems.

CARE AND MAINTENANCE

Larches require very little care once they are established. Water as needed to keep them from wilting. There are few pests that bother them.

ADDITIONAL INFORMATION

Deciduous conifers, those that lose their leaves in winter, are quite unusual. The form is that of an "evergreen," and the uninitiated may believe the tree has died when it drops its leaves. Many larches are being planted around the water features that have become common because of the need for retention ponds.

ADDITIONAL SPECIES, CULTIVARS, OR VARIETIES

'Fastigiata' is narrow with short ascending branches and is a good replacement for Lombardy poplars. *L. d.* 'Pendula' seems to be a classification rather than a cultivar and represents all larches with a weeping habit. Japanese larch, *L. kaempferi*, is listed in nursery catalogs. It is probably the most graceful of the larches and is resistant to some diseases that can affect others. Selections of Japanese larch, not generally available, are hardy in Zones 5 and 6.

Linden

Tilia sp.

Zones: All
Size: Height 50 feet, sometimes more,
     spread 2/3 of the height.
Blooms: Late June, July
Flower Colors: Cream-yellow,
     inconspicuous, very fragrant
Type: Deciduous

Light Requirement:

Lindens are some of our most valuable shade trees, and there has been extensive selection to improve them. Lindens are excellent for planting in the lawn, as street trees, in malls, in sidewalk tree pits, in parking lots, or wherever shade is desired or as relief from concrete and stone. The larger species are especially good in the industrial parks where trees of grand scale are needed. Lindens are attractive trees with a neat form and inconspicuous, beautifully scented flowers. An evening walk when the lindens are in bloom is a memorable experience. Lindens are attractive trees. They have good neat form for the most part and stay fairly clean. There is a long list of insects and diseases, but fortunately, lindens aren't often stricken. Wood rot which hollows out the center of the tree is fairly common. The condition usually does not affect the longevity or sturdiness of the tree. In the wild, bees will build hives in the hollows of lindens, explaining the common name for American linden, "bee tree."

WHEN TO PLANT

Lindens transplant easily. They may be planted in spring or fall. Container-grown plants may be planted any time during the season.

WHERE TO PLANT

Lindens prefer a deep, moist, well-drained soil, but will grow in most Illinois soil. They inhabit limy sites in the wild. Full sun or partial shade is satisfactory.

HOW TO PLANT

Set balled-and-burlapped plants at the same depth they grew in the nursery. Be sure to remove the burlap and twine, or untie it and place it in the planting hole. Cut any girdling roots on con-

tainer-grown plants. Make a saucer around the plant with any
remaining soil.

CARE AND MAINTENANCE
Lindens require very little care. Pruning to shape them while they
are young is helpful. These plants take pruning very gracefully and
can be sheared into hedges, a practice common in Europe. Water
plants regularly the first season after transplanting. Rarely do insects
or diseases strike the linden, but wood rot that hollows out the
center of the tree is fairly common. If cultivars are grafted on
seedling rootstock, the rootstock may sucker. Trim off, or apply a
burn-off herbicide such as diquat.

ADDITIONAL INFORMATION
Grafting can result in incompatibility problems—lodging or a sudden decline of the top can occur. Try to buy plants grown on their
own roots. The wood of lindens is light and used for boxes, drawers,
and other types of fabrication. Lindens are known as boxwood trees
in some parts of the country.

ADDITIONAL SPECIES, CULTIVARS, OR VARIETIES
Tilia americana, American linden, basswood, or bee tree, is a large
tree with large leaves. The species is excellent for park-like settings
or street trees. The cultivars 'Redmond' and 'Rosehill' are more suitable for street or lawns. 'Redmond' is pyramidal with large leaves. It
is used regularly in sidewalk cutouts. Littleleaf linden, *T. cordata*, a
smaller tree, is outstanding for a variety of landscape uses and is
tolerant of pollution. 'Greenspire' is pyramidal with a strong central
leader. Graft problems limit the longevity of these trees. Crimean
linden, *T. × euchlora*, is a more refined linden which easily survives
hot, dry, polluted locations. Silver linden, *T. tomentosa*, is also listed
by many nurseries. It withstands tough city conditions. Its leaves are
silvery on the undersides, dark green on the upper.

Magnolia

Magnolia sp.

Zones: All
Size: 15 to 30 feet, equal spread
Blooms: April, May, June
Flower Colors: White, often tinged with
   pink or maroon
Type: Evergreen

Light Requirement:

*M*agnolias are small to medium-sized trees, often grown for their large, spectacular, fragrant flowers. Several magnolia species are hardy enough for Illinois gardens. The star magnolia, *M. stellata*, blooms in early spring before the leaves emerge. The flowers are fragrant with strap-like white petals. The plant is a small, often multi-stemmed tree growing to about 20 feet. Since the flowers open so early, it is possible for them to be frozen. Planted out of the direct sun, this plant will flower later in the season, possibly avoiding the loss of the flowers. The saucer magnolia flowers later with large, saucer-shaped blooms, white on the inside, maroon on the reverse. The tree may grow to 20 or 30 feet with a spread as wide as it is tall. Often the lower branches are low and wide spreading, producing a pyramid-shaped mound. *Magnolia grandiflora*, the southern magnolia, is widely planted in the south and reportedly hardy in Zone 5. Trees that have survived Illinois winters have been in protected spots. It is recommended only in the southern part of the state (Zones 6 and 7).

WHEN TO PLANT

These plants do not move gracefully. Buy them in containers or balled and burlapped and plant them in spring.

WHERE TO PLANT

Plant in a sunny spot with good air circulation. Soil must be moist but well drained and with a pH that is neutral or lower. Star magnolia will turn yellow if planted in an alkaline soil.

HOW TO PLANT

Set balled-and-burlapped plants at the same depth they grew in the nursery. Be sure to remove the burlap and twine. Cut any girdling roots on container-grown plants. Mix some of the container soil with that in the planting hole to avoid any soil incompatibility problems. Magnolias have fleshy roots and care must be taken to minimize damage to them. Damaged roots will rot, and recovery from transplanting will be jeopardized.

CARE AND MAINTENANCE

Magnolias are clean plants that require very little care. Pruning should be minimal. Water in dry periods is essential. Soak thoroughly and let dry before watering again.

ADDITIONAL SPECIES, CULTIVARS, OR VARIETIES

M. acuminata, cucumbertree, produces large blooms held high in the tree and hidden by foliage. The fruit resembles a small cucumber. This is a large tree, growing to 50 feet with an equal spread at maturity. Several crosses of Loebner magnolia, *M. × loebneri*, are available. 'Ballerina' has a pure white flower with over 30 petals and reportedly escapes frost. Anise magnolia and Kobus magnolia and cultivars of that type can be used throughout the state. Check with your local nursery for recommendations of cultivars that do best in your locale. There are many cultivars, and new ones appear each year. A tremendous amount of work remains to be done to develop hybrids that truly tolerate and flower reliably in Illinois conditions.

Maple

Acer sp.

Zones: All
Size: 40 to 60 feet tall, sometimes more.
  Spread ⅔ or equal to height
Blooms: Early spring before or with
  developing leaves
Flower Colors: Yellow, red, green
Type: Deciduous

Light Requirement:

*S*pectacular fall color! That is reason enough to plant maples. Maples are some of the best trees for shade in the lawn or garden, for the street, or for specimens in larger spaces. They are tidy in form, easily transplanted, and undemanding. Some even produce colorful flowers in spring. The characteristic shape of a sugar maple or Norway maple leaf, palmately veined with three or five pointed lobes, is familiar to even the youngest school child.

WHEN TO PLANT

Maples transplant easily in spring or fall. If container grown or dug while dormant, they may be planted all season.

WHERE TO PLANT

Most maples will tolerate any decent garden soil. The pH may be acidic or alkaline, though red maples will lose color and become chlorotic in limy soil. They do best in full sun, but will grow in filtered or even quite dense shade. Maples require room. Some develop shallow roots and dense shade, preventing the growth of grass.

HOW TO PLANT

Set balled-and-burlapped plants a little higher than they grew in the nursery. These are shallowly rooted plants that suffer from collar rot at the soil line if planted too deeply.

CARE AND MAINTENANCE

Prune to develop single leaders. They are best pruned in winter to reduce bleeding. Many pests affect maples. Cottony maple scale on silver maple generally attracts enough natural predators that it disappears after a few years. Spray if needed with dormant oil in late winter or Malathion in early summer. Maples need water in prolonged dry periods because of their shallow roots. Norway and sugar maples allowed to wilt in high temperatures may suffer the loss of branches.

ADDITIONAL SPECIES, CULTIVARS, OR VARIETIES

Sugar maple, *A. saccharum*, lights up the land in fall, and is handsome in any season. The crown is somewhat open, allowing light to grass underneath. This upland tree can be grown in any well-drained soil. The hybrid sugar × black maple, 'Green Mountain', performs better and is more consistent than seed-grown species plants. Norway maple, *A. platanoides*, is dense and rounded. It has become the most widely planted maple lately, surpassing the silver maple. Norways have large, deep green leaves turning gold in fall. 'Crimson King', with maroon foliage all season, and 'Schwedleri', purple in spring turning to green, are selections of Norway maple. Norways are very susceptible to verticillium wilt; avoid introducing this disease into the soil. Silver maple, *A. saccharinum*, is still a satisfactory tree for disturbed soils and wet places. If allowed to develop multiple trunks, it will become brittle and may split in storms or under snow load. Red maple, *A. rubrum*, is another tree of the lowlands. It is native from Newfoundland and Minnesota to Texas and Florida. Selections made from eastern stands where soils are acidic do poorly in Illinois, turning light green instead of dark green. *A. freemani* 'Marmo', a silver × red maple cross, is a Chicagoland Grows introduction with better tolerance of our Illinois conditions. Flowers are red in spring. Fall color is blazing red.

Oak

Quercus sp.

Zones: All	**Light Requirement:**
Size: 40 to 80 feet or more, spread ²/₃ or equal to height	
Blooms: Inconspicuous catkins with opening leaves in spring	
Flower Color: Green	
Type: Deciduous	

Oaks are among our finest trees; the white oak is the state tree of Illinois. Big, beautiful trees, they are most prized by tree aficionados. Oaks are generally slow growing, although red oaks may grow up to 2 feet per year in optimum settings. They are excellent street, parkway, and lawn trees, suited to acidic soils, but seem to do very well in the chalky soils of Illinois when there is adequate drainage. This may be due to the symbiotic association with fungi called mycorrhizae that serve as the functioning roots of oaks in these soils. Old stands of oaks make inviting home sites, but construction often results in killing of the mycorrhizae, followed by decline and death of the old trees. New trees on these sites seem to grow well, as they adjust to the conditions when young.

WHEN TO PLANT

Oaks are best planted in spring. Dig when leaves are the size of a mouse's ear, and relocate promptly.

WHERE TO PLANT

Oaks will tolerate most well-drained soils. Full or partial sun is best. Plant in parkways, tree lawns, or other large areas for shade. Groves of oaks are appealing for large industrial park sites.

HOW TO PLANT

Set balled-and-burlapped plants a little higher than they grew in the nursery. These are shallowly rooted plants. If planted too deeply, some may suffer from collar rot that will girdle them at the soil line when they approach mature size. Transplant trees when young.

CARE AND MAINTENANCE

Oaks require very little care once established. Prune to a single leader. Many insects and diseases will live on oaks. If the trees are healthy, they will live in comfortable association with these parasites. If the trees are weakened, the pests may damage or kill the trees. Leaf miner and anthracnose will turn leaves blotchy-brown some seasons. Unless this happens every year, no treatment is needed. Consult a certified arborist for treatment.

ADDITIONAL SPECIES, CULTIVARS, OR VARIETIES

Quercus alba, white oak, is a large, handsome tree. It grows straight and tall without too much spread in a crowded urban setting. (It is normally crowded in the woods too.) Swamp white oak, *Q. bicolor*, is a closely related species that is better adapted to landscape plantings, and transplants more easily. As a lowland plant, it tolerates wetness and compaction. Coarser than white oak, it is still beautiful. Bur oak, *Q. macrocarpa*, is a huge coarse tree that withstands all kinds of abuse. When planted as a street tree, it seems to adjust to the space. Red oak, *Q. rubra*, is a faster growing species that tolerates city conditions better then either of the whites. It will develop chlorosis in alkaline soils. Pin oak, *Q. palustris*, is fast growing and widely planted. In alkaline soils, it becomes chlorotic after a few years and declines in spite of treatment. Other oaks: *Q. robur*, English oak, dense and compact with good color and form; *Q. muhlenbergii*, chinquapin oak, Zone 6 and a tree of alkaline bottomlands; *Q. imbricaria*, shingle oak, has laurel-like leaves without lobes, and becomes chlorotic at high pH's.

Pine

Pinus sp.

Zones: All
Size: 50 feet or so in landscape plantings,
   Spread ¹/₂ to ²/₃
Type: Evergreen

Light Requirement:

*P*ines are forest plants. They are upright in forest situations and tend to be conical in open spaces. At maturity some "top out," becoming broadly umbrella-like. In the landscape, they are often used as screens and seldom achieve mature size. With their persistent needles and good green color, pines are excellent evergreen landscape conifers. Unfortunately, pine wilt disease has decimated plantings of Scotch and Austrian pines. Occasionally, Christmas tree farms are besieged by the pine shoot borer. With careful selection and care, however, pines can still serve well.

WHEN TO PLANT

Balled-and-burlapped plants are best moved in spring but can be moved in the fall. Container plants can be planted any time during the season.

WHERE TO PLANT

Pines develop taproots and wide-spreading laterals. They need deep, well-drained soil, either heavy or light. Some will tolerate compact soils. Full sun to partial shade is satisfactory. Protect from winter sun and wind.

HOW TO PLANT

Pines move easily if root-pruned in the nursery. Many are container grown. Set balled-and-burlapped plants at the same depth they grew in the nursery. Be sure to remove the burlap and twine, or untie it and place it in the planting hole. If planting potted or canned plants, mix some container soil with that in the planting hole to avoid any soil incompatibility problems. Replace the soil and fill the hole with water. Make a saucer around the plant with any remaining soil.

CARE AND MAINTENANCE
Newly set pines need to be watered freely the first year. Prune out dead branches and maintain a single leader. Zimmerman pine moth will bore into the trunk at the branch whorls of Austrian and Scotch pines. Treat with Dursban or Cygon in April and August. Treat for Sphaeropsis tip blight with copper or thiophanate methyl in spring. Follow label directions.

ADDITIONAL INFORMATION
Holes in distinct geometric patterns with lines up and down or around the trunk are the work of sapsuckers. These are migratory birds that peck holes in trees and lap up the sap.

ADDITIONAL SPECIES, CULTIVARS, OR VARIETIES
Pinus strobus, white pine, has a soft texture and graceful form. It grows best on moist, well-drained sites and will even grow in sand if there is enough water. High pH and wet soils are not satisfactory. The white pine can be damaged by road salt leaching into the soil or salt spray on the foliage. Major losses of white pines in Illinois the last few years have corresponded with excessively wet weather and with poor drainage. Austrian pine, *P. nigra* is a stiff tree with long, stout branches and long, stiff needles. It is a good specimen tree, screen, or windbreak and tolerates urban conditions. Sphaeropsis tip blight can be severe. Water when dry. Scotch pine, *P. sylvestris*, is a smaller tree and very susceptible to both Zimmerman and Sphaeropsis. This pine is not suitable for screening because it soon loses its lower branches, topping out and becoming umbrella-shaped. It is a picturesque tree where it can be allowed to develop its mature form. Tolerant of poor soils and pH, it needs water during extended dry periods

Redbud

Cercis canadensis

Zones: All
Size: 15 to 20 feet tall, rarely 30 in landscapes;
  spread approximately the same
Blooms: April, before the leaves emerge
Flower Colors: Pink with a purple tinge;
  also white
Type: Deciduous

Light Requirement:

edbud is a native plant of the hardwood forests and will grow from Minnesota to Florida. Moist woods are full of redbud and dogwood in the spring. They are breathtaking after a dreary winter. The foliage of redbud is dark green and the individual leaves are heart-shaped. Fall color can be quite good on some cultivars. There is some variation. Redbuds for landscape use are almost always multi-stem. They adjust well in the landscape where a small tree is desired. A redbud can serve as an anchor for foundation plantings. The blossoms cover the stems in spring, and the leafy canopy provides welcome relief from the harshness of the city. Redbuds are especially attractive in woodland or naturalized settings.

WHEN TO PLANT

Redbuds are best planted in the spring so they can become established before the onset of winter.

WHERE TO PLANT

Redbuds tolerate all kinds of soils as long as they are moist and well drained. Full sun or partial or full shade is satisfactory. In shade, there may be losses of interior small twigs from insufficient light, and growth will be slower.

HOW TO PLANT

Set balled-and-burlapped plants at the same depth they grew in the nursery. Be sure to remove the burlap and twine. Cut any girdling roots on container-grown plants. If planting potted or canned plants, mix some container soil with that in the planting hole to avoid any soil incompatibility problems. Replace the soil and fill the hole with water. Make a saucer around the plant with any remaining soil.

CARE AND MAINTENANCE

Redbuds require watering the first season after transplanting. Otherwise, they need very little care. There are some diseases and insects that can become troublesome, but rarely do they require treatment. Pruning to shape and to keep the plants in bounds may be necessary. Verticillium wilt is a serious disease and can kill redbuds; avoid bringing the disease in on soil or on other plants. Redbuds can defend themselves from the disease if they are well watered and vigorously growing. It may be helpful to use organic mulch that stimulates antagonistic soil organisms that attack the fungus.

ADDITIONAL INFORMATION

The growing range for redbuds extends from Canada to the Caribbean. Be careful where you buy plants and ask where the seed was collected. The redbud from Florida will not grow here. When ordering from a catalog or buying from a discounter, there are no guarantees. Local growers grow local varieties and are more reliable.

ADDITIONAL SPECIES, CULTIVARS, OR VARIETIES

Some selection has been done for improved flowering and for additional colors. *Cercis canadensis alba* is white. 'Royal White' has pure white flowers larger than those of alba. Most nurseries list only the species and the white form, usually alba.

Spruce

Picea sp.

Zones: All
Size: 40 to 50 feet tall and half as wide, or with dwarf forms, to 15 feet
Type: Evergreen

Light Requirement:

*S*pruces are evergreen trees of considerable importance in landscaping. They are strongly conical with stiff or descending branches. Their form is lovely while young, but some do not grow old gracefully. Spruces are used as screens, in masses, and as individual specimens, sometimes not very wisely. These are large trees. A single blue spruce planted in the middle of a front yard on a 50-foot city lot will fill it when the tree reaches maturity. Often these lovely little plants in 5-gallon cans are set into the foundation planting, only to become huge monsters years later. Appropriately used, they are assets; poorly used, they are liabilities. There are dwarf varieties that fit small sites; larger kinds will not.

WHEN TO PLANT

Spruces are best planted in the spring. Container plants can be planted any time during the season.

WHERE TO PLANT

Spruces prefer rich, moist, well-drained soil. They are not particular about pH. Best in full sun, they will grow in partial shade but may become thin, losing leaves and lower branches.

HOW TO PLANT

Set balled-and-burlapped plants slightly less deeply than they grew in the nursery. Be sure to remove the burlap and twine. Cut any circling roots on container-grown plants.

CARE AND MAINTENANCE

Spruces tolerate pruning well. They can be sheared after new growth has hardened off in spring. Some can be hedged effectively. To retard plants so they don't rapidly outgrow their situations, clip off half of the new growth on selected branches each spring. Plants will become dense, and size will increase at half the normal rate. Watering is important in dry periods.

ADDITIONAL INFORMATION

Several diseases and insects are pests of the spruces. Cytospora canker attacks large trees under stress, killing individual branches throughout the plants. Ultimately the affected plant is of no aesthetic value and should be removed. Spruce gall adelgids cause distorted tips on branches. Control with Malathion, following label directions, in spring as new growth begins.

ADDITIONAL SPECIES, CULTIVARS, OR VARIETIES

Colorado blue spruce, *Picea pungens*, is a magnificent tree, variously green to silver-blue with a stiff, upright, conical form. These trees are beautiful in masses where they can develop to their full size. Often used as screens, they are rather formal and strikingly beautiful. Allow plenty of room since the spread will be as much as 40 feet at the base. There are many selections of Colorado blue spruce, vegetatively propagated on the basis of color. Plants of *P. p.* 'Glauca' are some of the bluer seedlings. Extremely blue are 'Hoopsii' and 'Thompsen'. There are dwarfs and contorted selections listed by some evergreen specialists. Norway spruce, *P. abies*, can be used as a windbreak and screen but is commonly planted as a specimen in the front yard. Norways are not specimen-type plants. With age they lose their looks and form. Use them as temporary plants, and expect to cut them out and replace them. A dwarf suitable for foundation plantings is Black Hills spruce, *P. glauca densata*. It grows very slowly to about 15 feet, and has a very soft texture and good conical form.

Sweet Gum

Liquidambar styraciflua

Zones: 5B and 6
Size: 40 to 50 feet, more in the open,
   spread to $2/3$ of the height
Blooms: Late spring with the leaves
Flower Color: Green, not showy
Type: Deciduous

Light Requirement:

$\mathscr{S}$weet gum has a neat, symmetrical outline and the potential for great size. It is pyramidal when young, becoming rounded at maturity. Sweet gum has glossy, green, star-shaped leaves in summer and fall color that rivals red and sugar maples. There is a lot of variability in color from one year to another, and between individual plants. Quite a bit of selection has been done for improving the color and hardiness. They are not reliably hardy north of Interstate 72. Sweet gum is native to bottomlands and swamps. It will tolerate different soil types as long as they are moist and well drained. A pH at neutral or lower is preferred. Chlorosis will develop in alkaline soils.

WHEN TO PLANT

Sweet gum should be planted in spring only. Container plants are slightly more tolerant and can be planted in spring or early summer.

WHERE TO PLANT

This tree performs best if planted in full sun and a moist, deep, slightly acid soil. The roots of sweet gum need a lot of room to develop. These are trees for suburbia and rural sites, not for areas of urban pollution. As street, lawn, or specimen trees in pristine areas, there are few trees that are more suitable.

HOW TO PLANT

Set balled-and-burlapped plants at the same depth they grew in the nursery. The roots are fleshy and take a long time to recover from transplanting injury. Container-grown plants may have been grown in an artificial soil. If so, shake some off the ball and mix it with the soil in the planting hole. Make sure the soil is well watered for it to settle around the roots.

CARE AND MAINTENANCE

Water the tree the first season after planting, but avoid inundation. Pruning may be needed as the tree develops to maintain a central leader. Slow recovery from transplanting may result in dead twigs that need to be removed. Once the tree is established and growing, there is little care required. Golfball-sized fruit that falls in lawns should be raked up.

ADDITIONAL INFORMATION

Sweet gum is widely planted in southern California as a street tree. It seems to tolerate the heat and smog there.

ADDITIONAL SPECIES, CULTIVARS, OR VARIETIES

One cultivar, 'Moraine', is an improvement over the species. The named cultivar has more reliable color in fall. Nursery catalogs list only the species, so finding anything else may be difficult.

Tuliptree

Liriodendron tulipifera

Other Names: Tulip Magnolia, Tulip Poplar
Zones: All
Size: 60 to 70 feet tall, maybe more;
    spread, 35 to 45 feet
Blooms: May, after leaves appear
Flower Colors: Greenish-yellow with
    orange centers.
Type: Deciduous

Light Requirement:

*T*he tuliptree is large with high branches that spread with age. It needs a lot of room to develop to its full potential. In the wild, it may reach 100 feet or more and be free of branches for half its height. Pyramidal in its youth, tuliptree eventually develops a framework of several large branches high in the tree. For all of its massive size, tuliptree can be brittle and may break up in storms or under snow load. The leaves of the tree are tulip-shaped in profile and the flowers resemble tulips as well. Fall color is clear bright yellow.

WHEN TO PLANT
Transplant balled-and-burlapped in spring. Container plants can be transplanted in spring or early summer.

WHERE TO PLANT
Deep, well-drained soil with a pH of neutral or lower is preferred. These plants need full sun and plenty of room for roots. Protection from wind or planting in groves will reduce storm damage.

HOW TO PLANT
Plant balled-and-burlapped or from containers. Set plants at the same depth they grew in the nursery. Be sure to remove the burlap and twine or untie it and place it in the planting hole. Cut any girdling roots on container-grown plants. This tree transplants with difficulty. Water as needed to prevent wilting. Do not overwater.

CARE AND MAINTENANCE

Tuliptrees are slow to recover from transplanting. They have fleshy, poorly branched root systems. Prune to maintain a single leader as high as possible. Trees with multiple trunks are more easily damaged in storms. A physiological condition, yellows, causes sudden yellowing and dropping of leaves and can be troublesome for newly planted trees or during droughts. Regular watering usually prevents this condition.

ADDITIONAL INFORMATION

Tuliptree is one of the tallest of our native trees, reaching nearly 200 feet and achieving an age of over 200 years in Eastern forest plantings. The name *Liriodendron* comes from the Greek *lirion*, "lily," and *dendron*, "tree." The wood of large trees is knot-free and used for furniture. Large numbers of board feet can be cut from one tree.

ADDITIONAL SPECIES, CULTIVARS, OR VARIETIES

A narrow, upright-growing cultivar, 'Fastigiatum', is known but is not being grown by nurseries. Only the species is listed in most catalogs. If you have room for this magnificent tree, it will provide unique bloom, foliage, and color for decades.

CHAPTER NINE

Turfgrasses

*N*EARLY EVERY HOME AND BUSINESS HAS A LAWN. In terms of the dollars spent on installation and care, turfgrasses are the number-one agricultural crop in Illinois. The lawn is one of the most important parts of the landscape. It ties the entire landscape together. It provides the setting for the home, business, or office building. It connects the grounds with surrounding features, walks, streets, or neighboring properties. The lawn can enhance the appeal of the entire property, making it friendly and inviting.

On a more practical level, lawns reduce the dust and dirt that get into the home or office. They absorb noise. Lawns reduce erosion and runoff in storms, reduce glare from the summer sun, and absorb heat. If you walk barefoot from a sandy beach or from a blacktop parking lot onto a well-kept lawn, the temperature difference is immediately noticeable.

A well-maintained lawn is an asset, while a poorly maintained, weedy lawn can be an eyesore, a detriment to any neighborhood. Maintaining a nice lawn requires some work, and it requires some skill as well. No longer is it simply a matter of cutting the grass if it gets too tall. When I was growing up, mowing was the only lawn-care chore. Watering was a luxury, and it was usually a by-product of a children's game of running under the sprinkler.

How Grass Grows

Turfgrasses are complex little plants, not just tufts of green poking out of the ground. A grass plant grows from a structure called a **crown** that is just below the soil surface. Leaves arise from the crown and roots grow from the bottom of the crown into the soil. If the grass is not mowed, it elongates into a stalk called a **culm**. At the top of the culm are flowers and, eventually, seeds.

Some grasses grow horizontal stems from their crowns. When underground, they are called **rhizomes**; if they lie along the top of the ground, they are called **stolons**. Sometimes more than one culm will grow from a crown, making a bunch grass. Other structures,

Chapter Nine

auricles and **ligules**, are helpful in identifying the various species. These structures are quite tiny, and those of us who spend a lot of time examining grasses develop green knees and elbows from crouching down to investigate. Different kinds of grasses grow in different ways, so it is important to know which one you are growing.

Most lawns in Illinois are cool-season grasses, though some warm-season grasses may be grown in the southern part of the state, in the transition zone. The basic care for all grasses is just about the same. Timing and mowing heights will differ.

Establishing a Lawn

Prepare the site by leveling it to the proper grade. Do a good job, because you will live with any imperfections. Kill the vegetation with glyphosate. Apply lime, sulfur, superphosphate, and potash according to soil test recommendations. Disk or till to prepare a finely pulverized seedbed. Up to this point, it makes no difference whether you chose to seed, hydroseed, or sod the lawn. The preparation is the same.

Sodding: Buy sod grown on a soil as nearly like that on your site as you can find. The sod should be thinly cut, fresh, dark green, and absolutely free of weeds. Moisten the soil and apply a starter fertilizer to provide 5 pounds of nitrogen per 1000 square feet of lawn. Roll out the sod, staggering the ends and making sure that the rolls are butted tightly against each other. Roll to firm the sod to the soil. Water daily to keep the sod wet for two weeks, or until it begins to knit. Then reduce the watering frequency. Do not let the sod wilt. Mow when the grass is 33 percent higher than the cutting height.

Seeding: Buy top-quality seed; do not look for bargains at this point in the process. Sow the seed with a drop spreader, half back and forth in one direction, and the other half at a right angle to this direction. Be sure to overlap the wheel tracks. Gently rake the seed into the soil. I use a wire grass rake, upside down, and just drag it back and forth over the seed. This covers the seed with about 1/4 inch of soil. Roll with a medium roller. If seeding in spring, cover with 2 inches of lightly laid straw to provide about 50 percent shade. Hydroseeding applies seed and mulch in one operation. Water frequently to keep the seed from drying, but do not soak it to the point of runoff.

Chapter Nine

Mowing: Mow the grass often enough to remove only $^1/_3$ to $^1/_2$ of the blades. Mowing will be necessary more often in cool, moist weather, sometimes more often than once a week. Set the mower at the correct height for the kind of grass. The cool-season grasses should be kept mowed at $2^1/_2$ inches high; that means mowing before they reach 4 inches. The warm-season grasses are cut at $^1/_2$ to 1 inch, mowed before they reach 1 to 2 inches.

Watering: Many lawns are watered more often than they need to be. The grass does not need to be watered until it wilts. Wilted grass turns a hazy purplish color, and footprints don't spring back after you walk across it. Apply a measured inch of water. Use a coffee can under the sprinkler to measure the amount. When there is an inch of water in the bottom of the can, move the sprinkler.

Automatic sprinkler systems must be set to apply an inch of water per cycle. After watering, turn the water off, and do not water again until the grass wilts. Running the sprinkler a few minutes every day does not sufficiently water the grass. Running the sprinkler hours every night will force the root system to the surface and eventually drown the grass.

Fertilizing: Fertilizer should be applied just before the maximum growth of the grass plant. For cool-season grasses, that is in late August; for warm-season grasses, it is late spring. Apply 1 pound of nitrogen per 1000 square feet of lawn. If applying a slow-release fertilizer, double the rate. If applying fertilizer to a cool-season grass before or during hot weather, apply it at half rate.

Cool-season grasses may benefit from a second application if fertilized in late fall, with another application in midspring.

Weed control: Apply crabgrass preventer when the honeysuckles are in bloom. Apply a broadleaf herbicide when the weeds are vigorously growing, either spring or fall.

Insect control: Control grubs (annual white grub, white grub, Japanese beetle, and billbug) with Merit applied in June or July. Control *Ataeneus* grubs with Merit applied in May. After application immediately apply $^1/_2$ inch of water to wash the Merit into the feeding zone before the material dries on the surface.

Chapter Nine

Control sod webworm with diazinon applied two weeks after the small adult moths are noticed flying over the lawn at dusk. Do not water the diazinon into the lawn.

Control greenbugs with insecticidal soap. Carefully read and follow the directions on the labels of all pesticides. Keep the materials out of the reach of children.

Disease control: Most turf diseases are due to cultural problems. Summer patch, necrotic ringspot, and other ring and spot diseases are the result of stresses. Stress often comes from compaction or layering of the soil due to accumulated thatch. To repair, core-aerify the lawn to produce a hole every two inches, 36 holes per square foot. Some lawn-care companies and landscapers are reluctant to do a proper job of this; make sure they do by checking the placement of the holes before you pay them.

Minor accumulations of thatch, $1/4$ to $1/2$ inch, can be controlled by power raking.

Mildew and leaf spot diseases are controlled by planting resistant cultivars. Dollar spot is a disease of hungry grass. Rust is controlled by mowing frequently enough so that the rust never matures.

Turfgrass Repair: In spring or fall, small damaged spots in the lawn can be scratched up with a garden rake or cultivator, then seeded. Larger areas can be cut out and the soil scratched up and sodded. Make sure the sod was grown on a soil like the one in your yard.

Thin lawns or lawns badly damaged by insects, diseases, drought, or winter desiccation can be slit-seeded. Have the seeder run at two directions, with a difference of 45 degrees, to avoid the appearance of rows.

Lawns infested with quackgrass or other perennial weedy grasses can be killed off with glysophate in mid-August and slit-seeded a week later. If perennial ryegrass is included in the seed mix, the new grass will be green and growing before the old grass turns brown.

If you are planting Kentucky bluegrass, always plant a blend of different cultivars, and incorporate 10 to 20 percent turf-type perennial ryegrass for increased site tolerance and disease resistance.

Bentgrass

Agrostis sp.

Zones: All (better in Zones 4B, 5, and 6A)
Cutting Height: $1/6$ to $3/4$ inch
Climate: Cool season, 80 degrees Fahrenheit best
Color: Light green
Texture: Fine
Wear Resistance: Low

Light Requirement:

*T*wo species of bentgrass are used for ornamental turf in Illinois: creeping bent, *A. palustris*, and colonial bentgrass, *A. tenuis*. These are temperate-zone plants and they perform best in 80-degree temperatures, though creeping bent is more tolerant of high temperatures than is colonial. The bentgrasses are high-maintenance plants, used for high-quality lawns and for sport turf.

WHEN TO PLANT

Bentgrasses are best planted in late summer or fall. Temperatures moderate by then, and there is more likely to be rain. Fewer weeds germinate in fall to compete with the grass. Spring seeding until June 1 is successful if crabgrass, which germinates at the same time, can be controlled.

WHERE TO PLANT

Plant bentgrasses in high-quality, high-maintenance areas. These grasses are generally not for typical lawns but are used primarily for golf courses, bowling greens, tennis courts, and other closely mowed sports turf. Where a high-quality turf is needed under unusual circumstances in a home lawn, and where the owner is willing to expend the energy, bentgrass is an option.

HOW TO PLANT

Bentgrasses are started from seed or sprigs, and occasionally from sod or hydroseeding. The soil must be pulverized, then graded to eliminate any high or low spots. Sow seed at the rate of 2 pounds per 1000 square feet of lawn. Sprigs are planted at a rate of 5 to 10 bushels per 1000 square feet. Gently rake the seed into the top $1/4$ inch of soil. Sprigs may be planted in furrows or worked into the soil mechanically. Install sod over well-prepared soil, butting the joints together well. Water every day until the grass has knitted to the ground.

CARE AND MAINTENANCE

Bentgrasses require a lot of care. Remove no more than $1/4$ to $1/3$ of the leaf area each time you mow. Apply water as needed to prevent wilting. Fertilize to maintain good color and a moderate rate of growth. Diseases will appear in inclement weather; be prepared to spray to keep them from destroying the turf.

ADDITIONAL INFORMATION

The name for the bentgrasses, *Agrostis*, is from an old Greek name for a forage grass, *agros*. Many related species are pasture grasses.

ADDITIONAL SPECIES, CULTIVARS, OR VARIETIES

Creeping bentgrass, *A. palustris*, is a stoloniferous, spreading grass and the more demanding of the two kinds of bentgrass. It is aggressive and will invade neighboring areas unless confined. It requires 5 to 6 pounds of nitrogen fertilizer per 1000 square feet of turf per season and must be mowed every other day. Water to provide $1^1/2$ inches per week and apply fungicides as needed to prevent diseases. Slice and topdress to prevent puffiness and core-aerify to eliminate layering. Colonial bentgrass, *A. tenuis*, has been combined with bluegrass and ryegrass in seed mixtures for shady lawns. This is because it tolerates shade, but it will overcome other grasses in the same population. It is a different color than the other grasses, and should be cut shorter; if cut at the $2^1/2$-inch height, it falls over, revealing brown stolons. It makes a patch of lighter-colored grass in the midst of the bluer bluegrass and rye, so it is really not compatible with them. Colonial bent can be grown as a lawn in the cooler areas of the state or in the shade. It can be cut at about an inch and needs less care than the creeping bents, though it is still a high-management grass.

Bermudagrass

Cynodon dactylon

Zone: 6B
Cutting Height: $1/2$ to $1^1/2$ inches
Climate: Warm season
Color: Bright or dull green, depending
  on variety
Texture: Medium to fine
Wear Resistance: Good

Light Requirement:

*B*ermudagrass is a highly variable warm-weather grass. It is aggressive and will establish very quickly. The common seed-grown types are weeds throughout the South. Hybrid Bermudagrass is the best-quality turfgrass for the Southern states, and it is also the kind that should be planted in Illinois. Hybrid Bermuda is hardy in southern Illinois, and its range is being extended by hybridization for increased cold tolerance. Bermuda has excellent heat tolerance; it survives cold by going dormant. It turns brown in early fall and greens up in mid-spring. A hybrid strain bred for Northern conditions was installed on the new St. Louis baseball stadium playing field. It does make an excellent playing surface, but its winter performance is still being evaluated.

WHEN TO PLANT
Bermuda is started in the spring.

WHERE TO PLANT
Plant it in full sun. It will not tolerate shade.

HOW TO PLANT
Start Bermudagrass from sod, plugs, or sprigs. Sod provides an instant lawn. Prepare the soil as for seeding, pulverizing it finely. Lay the strips of sod, being careful to butt the seams tightly together. Plugs are planted in holes punched in the soil surface. A bulb planter can be used to punch the holes. A plug is dropped in a hole and a little soil is pushed over it and stepped on to firm. Sprigs can be planted individually, by plowing a furrow and dropping a sprig

every couple of feet, or with a sprig planter. Thoroughly water the lawn after planting, and keep it moist until plants have rooted. Hybrid Bermuda cannot be grown from seed.

CARE AND MAINTENANCE
Mow Bermuda at a height of 1 to $1^1/2$ inches. Apply nitrogen fertilizer monthly. Bermuda produces thatch with a vengeance— thoroughly core-aerify monthly. Slicing and power raking may be necessary if a heavy thatch does develop. This is a drought-tolerant grass; water as needed to maintain the level of growth you want.

ADDITIONAL INFORMATION
Bermuda is a soft grass, not stiff like zoysia. It is a tough grass and must be mown with a sharp mower, preferably a reel type. Sharpen a rotary mower every few times the grass is mowed.

ADDITIONAL SPECIES, CULTIVARS, OR VARIETIES
Two Bermudagrasses with superior cold hardiness are Midway and Midiron. Many of the new selections are not named at this time. Suppliers at garden centers in the southern part of the state will normally handle cultivars that will stand conditions in that area. Check with them to see what is new.

Creeping Red Fescue

Festuca rubra

Zones: All
Cutting Height: 2¹/₂ inches
Climate: Cool season
Color: Dark green
Texture: Very fine
Wear Resistance: Poor

Light Requirement:

*C*reeping red fescue is a grass for infertile soils and shaded sites. It is not a particularly aggressive grass, and will not stand a lot of traffic. It will stand short periods of drought, but it does not like hot weather. Although it is a soft grass with very fine, needle-like leaves, its color and growth characteristics are very similar to those of Kentucky bluegrasses and perennial rye. These three kinds are often included in mixtures. In shade or on poor soils, the fescue will out-grow the Kentucky blue and rye, eventually predominating. It is suitable only for shade areas in the southern part of the state where summer temperatures will force it into dormancy. Creeping red fescue spreads by means of short rhizomes.

WHEN TO PLANT

Creeping red fescue is best planted in late summer or fall. The cooler weather and increased chances of moisture provide good conditions for germination and growth. Weeds are less likely to germinate and to compete with the developing grass.

WHERE TO PLANT

Plant creeping red fescue in areas where shade or infertile soil would make the growth of Kentucky bluegrass and perennial rye difficult.

HOW TO PLANT

Creeping red fescue is available as seed, not as sod; rhizome devel-opment is not sufficient to develop a sod that will stay together for harvesting. Some fescue sod has been grown on mesh to overcome that problem. Level and work the soil to produce a fine seedbed. Sow seed at 4 pounds per 1000 square feet of lawn. Cover lightly with soil.

CARE AND MAINTENANCE

Creeping red fescue is a low-fertility species. Avoid fertilizing it in the shade unless it is consistently off color and stops growing. Overfertilization will result in a reduced root volume and declining turf. Enough fertilizer to provide about $1/2$ pound of nitrogen per 1000 square feet of turf in early fall should suffice. Mow at $2^1/2$ inches and often enough to remove only $1/3$ to $1/4$ of the leaf area. Apply water as needed to prevent wilting. Red fescue kept constantly wet will be destroyed by fungal diseases.

ADDITIONAL INFORMATION

Extensive hybridizing of creeping red fescues has improved their heat tolerance and disease resistance. Selections with more aggressive rhizome growth are being sought.

ADDITIONAL SPECIES, CULTIVARS, OR VARIETIES

There are several related fescues that are used for special kinds of turf. Sheep fescue, *F. ovina*, and hard fescue, *F. ovina duriuscula*, are used in low-maintenance areas. Both are bunch-type grasses. Lower-growing selections are being used in some roadside and naturalized plantings, avoiding the necessity of mowing. Chewings fescue, *F. rubra commutata*, is a bunch grass closely related to creeping red fescue. It is naturalized in wooded areas where there is insufficient light for much competition from other plants. It has been included in lawn grass seed mixtures, but unless the plant population is quite high, the lawn becomes uneven with tufts of grass. Tall fescue, *F. elatior arundinacea*, is a tough wide-bladed grass, often recommended for play areas or athletic fields. It must be planted heavily to develop a turf instead of bunches. It does not develop rhizomes and will not fill bare areas. As an athletic turf, it does not repair damage. Tall fescue is also called Kentucky 31 fescue, and it must not be confused with Kentucky bluegrass. It is a weed in a bluegrass lawn.

Kentucky Bluegrass

Poa pratensis

Zones: All
Cutting Height: 2¹/₂ inches
Climate: Cool season
Color: Dark green
Texture: Medium to coarse
Wear Resistance: Moderate

Light Requirement:

Kentucky bluegrass is the most widely planted turfgrass in Illinois. It a medium-textured grass, attractive and well adapted to the climate. It is a native of central Europe, which has a climate much like ours, though the summers are not as hot as those in most of Illinois. The grass has become naturalized throughout the "bluegrass area" of central Kentucky and has resulted in the common name Kentucky bluegrass. The USDA yearbook of agriculture indicates that farmers 200 years ago considered the bluegrass turf more valuable than crops that could be grown on the land, and they were reluctant to break the sod.

WHEN TO PLANT

Kentucky bluegrass is best seeded in late summer to early fall. At that time, cooler weather and the prospect of sufficient rain make success likelier. Weed pressure at that time is much lower as well. Spring seeding until June 1 is successful if crabgrass, which germinates at the same time, can be controlled. Dormant-seeding after mid-November will result in germination early the next spring, before soils are dry enough to work and seed. Sodding may be done whenever the soils are not frozen and there is sufficient water available.

WHERE TO PLANT

Kentucky bluegrass does best in full sun or filtered shade. Some selections can tolerate shaded conditions better than others.

HOW TO PLANT

Kentucky bluegrass lawns may be started from seed or sod, or they may be hydro seeded. The soil should be finely pulverized and graded. Sow seed at the rate of 2 pounds per 1000 square feet of lawn and cover lightly. If seeding in spring, cover with straw to provide 50 percent shade. Hydro seeding provides shade as well. Water daily or more often if necessary to keep seed moist until germination has taken place. Reduce frequency of watering after the grass has come up. Lay sod over properly prepared soil, butting the joints together well. Water every day until the grass has knitted to the ground.

CARE AND MAINTENANCE

Mow at $2^1/2$ inches and often enough to remove no more than $^1/3$ to $^1/4$ of the leaf area. Fertilize in fall, also early and late spring to maintain a moderate green color. Water to apply 1 inch per week. Apply a measured inch, and do not water again until the grass wilts. Many diseases can affect Kentucky bluegrass. The severity of most of these can be reduced by proper maintenance practices and using resistant varieties. Sodded lawns may deteriorate if the soil on which the sod was grown is different from that on which the sod is installed. The resulting interface can prevent rooting of the sod into the underlying soil. The condition can be remedied by thorough core-aerification to produce a hole every 2 inches, 36 holes per square foot, repeated until rooting has occurred.

ADDITIONAL INFORMATION

High-quality bluegrass lawns require cultivation to control thatch. Low-maintenance bluegrass lawns can be grown without the benefit of added water and fertilizer. Use common Kentucky bluegrass rather than the improved varieties. There are many varieties of Kentucky bluegrass. Some are deeper green in color than others. For the deepest green lawn, be sure to buy seed of a green variety. It is important to use a blend of 3 to 5 Kentucky bluegrass varieties in a lawn. This provides a wider range of site tolerance and disease resistance.

ADDITIONAL SPECIES, CULTIVARS, OR VARIETIES

Disease-resistant Kentucky bluegrass varieties include Adelphi, America, Baron, Fylking, Glade, Nassau, and Parade. There are other bluegrasses used in lawns. *Poa trivialis*, rough bluegrass, is adapted to shade. Canada bluegrass, *P. compressa*, may be used in mixtures, but it produces a stemmy, low-quality turf. *Poa* 'supina' is a recent introduction from Europe said to be much more shade tolerant, and tougher under sports-turf conditions, and very expensive. There have been mixed results from its use. *Poa annua*, annual bluegrass, is a winter annual germinating in fall and growing through the winter. It may flower under the snow. It can be maintained as a turf under some conditions, but it usually dies out in midsummer, ruining the lawn. There is some indication that *P. supina* may be a persistent strain of *P. annua*.

Perennial Ryegrass

Lolium perenne

Zones: All
Cutting Height: 2¹/₂ inches
Climate: Cool season
Color: Dark green
Texture: Medium
Wear Resistance: Good

Light Requirement:

*P*erennial ryegrass is a native of central Europe, and like Kentucky bluegrass, is well adapted to the climate of Illinois. Common perennial ryegrass is a coarse, tough grass. Germination from seed is very rapid, sometimes 4 or 5 days. It has been used as a nurse grass to provide cover while slower-developing Kentucky blue-grasses or fescues germinate. The coarse common ryes persisted as weeds in the bluegrass lawns; they were hard to mow and never attractive. As a result of hybridization, turf-type ryegrasses fully com-patible with the finer bluegrasses are now available. These grasses can be permanent parts of the turfgrass population. To most gardeners, they are indistinguishable from bluegrass. The ryes can be employed for fast repairs of sports turf, and by season's end many athletic fields are mostly rye. The color is the same as bluegrass, and most fans and players never know the difference. These newer selections have much better high- and low-temperature tolerance as well. Many home lawns are mostly perennial rye even though the owner may not know it. The perennial rye provides a greater range of disease resistance, and often persists after something has killed the bluegrasses. The drought of 1991 killed much of the bluegrass, as did the terrible winter of 1995. Despite rye's reputation for being less hardy than bluegrasses under such circumstances, all that was left was rye. We have some clients who have acceptable, even beautiful, ryegrass lawns as a result of losses of other grasses species from these two weather extremes. (Our lawn is one of them.)

WHEN TO PLANT

Perennial rye is best planted in fall before October 1 or after November 15, or in early spring. Worn or damaged areas can be seeded any time during the season.

WHERE TO PLANT

Perennial rye can be sown in sun or shade. The soil should be well drained and not compacted.

HOW TO PLANT

Perennial ryegrass may be seeded or hydroseeded. The soil should be finely pulverized and graded. Sow the seed at the rate of 5 to 10 pounds per 1000 square feet of lawn and cover lightly with soil. If seeding in spring, cover with straw to provide 50 percent shade; hydroseeding will also provide shade. Water daily or more often if necessary to keep seed moist until germination has taken place. Reduce the frequency of watering after the grass is up.

CARE AND MAINTENANCE

Perennial rye should be mowed at $2^1/2$ inches, often enough to remove no more than $1/3$ to $1/4$ of the leaf area. To maintain a moderate green color, fertilize in fall, and also in early and late spring. Apply a measured inch of water per week, and do not water again until the grass wilts.

ADDITIONAL INFORMATION

Perennial ryegrass in a Kentucky bluegrass lawn will add another dimension of disease resistance, and it is thought to impart more resistance to the bluegrasses themselves in some way.

ADDITIONAL SPECIES, CULTIVARS, OR VARIETIES

The improved turf-type perennial ryegrasses have better growth characteristics and better disease resistance than the species. Look for Manhattan II, Yorktown II, or others. The University of Illinois publishes updated lists of varieties yearly. Annual ryegrass, *L. multiflorum*, is a related species used for quick germination and cover. It is an annual, but it may survive the winter if protected. It is light green in color and has wide blades. Because it does not blend well with the permanent turfgrasses, it really should be avoided. Cheap grass seed mixtures are sometimes advertised as having miraculous capabilities, but they often consist of mostly annual rye. Read the labels.

Tall Fescue

F. elatior arundinacea

Zones: All
Cutting Height: 3 to 3^1/$_2$ inches
Climate: Cool season/warm season transition
Color: Medium green
Texture: Coarse to medium
Wear Resistance: Good

Light Requirement:

*T*all fescue is a tough wide-bladed grass. It was originally introduced into this country as a range or forage grass and has adapted to a wide range of conditions. It flourishes with neglect. It tolerates drought or periodic inundation, will grow without supplemental fertilization, and is often used in forest preserve plantings. Its leaves have tough fibers and are resistant to abrasion, so it is often recommended for play areas or athletic fields. It must be planted heavily to develop a turf instead of bunches. It does not develop rhizomes and will not fill bare areas. As an athletic turf, it cannot repair damage because it can't spread. To successfully sustain a planting of tall fescue, plan to overseed constantly so that new plants will be growing into the population to replace damaged or missing plants. Tall fescue can make a satisfactory turf and is well adapted to the southern part of the state, Zone 6. It can stand high summer temperatures better than some other temperate-climate grasses. It was interesting that during the hot, dry summer of 1988, in some plantings tall fescue did not survive as well as perennial rye.

WHEN TO PLANT

Plant tall fescue in fall or spring. For increasing the plant population as an established turf, it may be sown all season long.

WHERE TO PLANT

Tall fescue can be planted in sun or filtered shade. Plant it where it will be allowed to grow naturally—it will crowd out other weedy plants. Heavily seeded tall fescue lawns make a satisfactory turf.

HOW TO PLANT

This grass does not develop a rhizome system and cannot be grown as sod. Some growers have resorted to growing it on mesh so that it can be handled without falling apart. It is usually seeded. The soil should be finely pulverized and graded. Sow the seed at the rate of 2 pounds per 1000 square feet of lawn and cover lightly with soil. Water as needed to keep the seed moist until germination takes place.

CARE AND MAINTENANCE
Mow at a height of 3 to $3^1/2$ inches, often enough to remove no more than $1/3$ to $1/4$ of the leaf area each time. Keep the mower sharpened; a dull mower will have a tough time cutting this grass. Fertilize to maintain a moderate to light-green color.

ADDITIONAL INFORMATION
Some tall fescue strains contain endophytes that provide some resistance to insect damage. Where these are available, it is suggested they be incorporated into the seed mixture.

ADDITIONAL SPECIES, CULTIVARS, OR VARIETIES
Two tall fescue varieties, Alta and Kentucky 31, have been used for many years, and they exhibit most of the characteristics of the species. Kentucky 31 fescue must not be confused with Kentucky bluegrass. It grows twice as fast, is much coarser, and is considered a weed in a bluegrass lawn. Some seed companies have invested a lot of time and money improving these fescues, resulting in varieties with finer leaves and less fiber. Adventure, Carefree, Legend, Monarch, Sundance, and Thoroughbred are some of these. If sown heavily, they will develop a respectable turf. If damaged, they will not repair themselves. Some athletic fields seeded to these varieties have reverted to the coarse types after several years.

Zoysiagrass

Zoysia japonica

Zones: All
Size: Cutting height: $1/2$ to 1 inch
Climate: Warm season
Color: Light green
Texture: Coarse
Wear Resistance: Good

Light Requirement:

oysiagrass is a turfgrass that grows all over the South, and will also grow throughout Illinois. There are those who would have nothing else. Once established, it does not take a lot of care, and it looks very nice all summer. Zoysiagrass is a tough, durable grass, even resisting salt damage. It does have some peculiarities. It is a warm-season turfgrass that survives our winters by going completely dormant, turning brown in mid-fall when temperatures are in the mid-50-degree range. It is very slow to green up in the spring and stays brown into May, a time when the cool-season turfgrasses look their best. Zoysia is rather expensive to install. It is usually started from plugs, which take several years to fill in. Sod is prohibitively expensive. While the grass is becoming established, it is necessary to keep weeds under control. Once well established, the zoysia will keep weeds out during the summer, but it will be invaded by cool-weather weeds when it is dormant. Zoysia is a coarse, light-green grass that spreads by means of above-ground stolons. The blades are stiff, not soft like bluegrass. It is more like a doormat to walk on than like our more familiar lawngrasses. But zoysia does require mowing like any other turfgrass—it is tough stuff, and it takes a good sharp mower. The grass is aggressive and will invade beds and borders. The stolons are attractive to sparrows and crows that will collect them for nest-building. Sprigs dropped in neighboring lawns will take root, becoming weeds. If you are willing to put up with the idiosyncrasies of this grass and need something tough, it may serve your purpose. It isn't really a grass for this area, but it will grow throughout the state and does serve some people well.

WHEN TO PLANT
Plant zoysia about the time it is greening up in spring.

WHERE TO PLANT

This is a grass that does best in full sun. It is tolerant of heat and drought. It will grow reasonably well in shade.

HOW TO PLANT

The soil should be finely pulverized and graded. An even surface is essential because this grass must be mowed quite short. If the ground is uneven, scalping will be a problem. Plant plugs in holes punched in the soil surface (a bulb planter can be used to punch the holes). The plug is dropped in the hole, a little soil is pushed over it, and it is stepped on to firm. You may space the plugs at about 12 inches; at that spacing, the grass will be established in 2 to 3 years. Closer planting will fill in more quickly.

CARE AND MAINTENANCE

Following installation, weed control will be needed to keep weeds from taking over the planting. If all vegetation was killed off prior to planting, preemergent herbicides can be used. Mow zoysia at 0.5 to 1.0 inch tall, mowing often enough to remove only $1/3$ to $1/4$ of the leaf area. Because of the density of the grass, a heavy reel-type mower is best. A rotary mower will ride up on the grass, giving a very uneven cut. Fertilize as necessary to maintain color, and water during extended droughts. Zoysia develops dense thatch, requiring core-aerification or power raking. A large volume of material for disposal will result from power raking.

ADDITIONAL INFORMATION

During the time zoysia is brown and dry, it will burn off if ignited by a discarded cigarette. Some gardeners have been known to burn off the lawn as a thatch control measure.

ADDITIONAL SPECIES, CULTIVARS, OR VARIETIES

The zoysia grown in Illinois is called Meyer. It is the only one hardy enough to survive our winters.

CHAPTER TEN

Vines

*V*INES ARE USEFUL IN ANY GARDEN. They can be used strictly as ornamentals, or they can be for utilitarian purposes. They may be grown on fences, trellises, pergolas, arbors, or gazebos. In these places, they are pleasing to look at and may give you some privacy as well. If they are flowering vines, the blooms alone may be sufficient reason to plant them.

Vines can be grown up the sides of buildings and may reach several stories high. It is not unusual to see Boston ivy or climbing hydrangea covering the side of a 6-story building. Some college campuses are noted for their ivy-covered buildings; almost every campus has at least a few. The modern glass-and-steel buildings aren't too well suited for this treatment, but there seems to be a trend toward traditional brick and mortar buildings. Many apartments and condominiums in our area are being built of masonry—and vines are being grown on them.

Some vines are better suited to the north sides of structures than almost any other woody plant. They do well in the shade, don't require a lot of ground space, and need protection from winter sun. These are perfect for such uses.

Vines grow in three different ways. Some, such as Boston ivy, climb by means of little root-like holdfasts that attach themselves to the support. Clematis and grape vines, on the other hand, climb by winding tendrils or petioles around the supports. The wisteria stems twine around their supports.

Before selecting a vine, it is important to know how it climbs so you can provide the right kind of support structure. If you intend to grow a twining bittersweet up a wall, for example, you will need to provide something for it to twine around.

The supports for the vines must be strong enough to hold them up—you will be surprised to find out how heavy some vines can be. And make sure the structure you want to grow a vine on won't be

Chapter Ten

damaged by it. A Boston ivy growing on one of the newer stucco-over-styrofoam buildings will quickly pull off the stucco.

Vines growing up trees are very attractive, and this is an excellent use of vines, but you must take a few precautions. If the vine encircles the tree, unwind it every year so it doesn't girdle it. It won't strangle the tree, but if it encircles a small tree, the expanding tree trunk will eventually grow too large for the vine. As it tries to grow around the vine, it will be girdled, unable to expand any further. If the vine is not removed, the tree will be strangled at that point. Wintercreeper growing on maple trees does this all too often. Don't let this discourage you from growing vines on trees—just be sure you do it right.

Each type of vine has particular needs, and some experimentation will be necessary to figure out how to handle your vines. An important requirement is regular pruning. The old wood needs to be removed, forcing new, vigorous stems to grow. Don't be afraid to do this cutting. Plants grow back; vines grow back fast.

We see plantings of vines that have been beautiful for many, many years. They may have some large, old stems, but often these plants are not the same ones that were set there at the beginning. To keep vines vigorous and young, interplant them with new plants every year or so, and remove the old ones. Seeds can be collected from some kinds of vines and seedlings started in styrofoam cups. The vines at Wrigley field are maintained this way. With proper care, some vines like wisteria can grow to an extremely old age.

Nine interesting vines are described in the following pages. These are just a few that can be grown in Illinois. Try at least one, and take a look at others. You will find them at botanical gardens and arboreta, labeled with their names. Take note of which ones are growing in your area, and how they grow.

American Bittersweet

Celastrus scandens

Zones: All
Size: Twining to 20 feet
Blooms: June
Flower Colors: Yellow, greenish, inconspicuous
Type: Deciduous

Light Requirement:

*B*ittersweet is a hardy vine that climbs by twining; it will grow to a height of 20 feet or more if provided with adequate support. It is a native plant, so it is perfectly able to contend with Illinois conditions. It will grow just about wherever it gets a start, and it can become a tangle of vines if allowed to grow wild. In nature, this is not a disadvantage; in the garden, it can cover whatever it decides to grow on in a very short time. Bittersweet will climb shrubs and trees, some with large trunks. The vines twine tightly and are very sturdy. If allowed to encircle a tree, a vine can eventually girdle it. As the tree increases in diameter, it will try to grow around the vine, but unable to do so, it will be killed from that point up—a girdling vine is no different from a girdling root or twine. Bittersweet can be pruned heavily to keep it contained; prune in fall as stems with the colorful berry-like fruits are collected, and if needed, in spring after the first flush of growth. Bittersweet vines have male and female flowers on separate plants, requiring at least one of each to produce fruit.

WHEN TO PLANT
Bittersweet is planted in either spring or fall. Containerized plants may be planted at any time during the season.

WHERE TO PLANT
Plant in naturalized areas where it can crawl over rocks and hills. In the woods it can be allowed to climb trees. Use it as a screen, along the side of the house, or to soften the effects of utility poles or rough fences. Grow bittersweet up a trellis for cutting. Its stems with their colorful fruits are excellent for flower arrangements. Bittersweet will grow in full or partial sun, but fruit production is better in full sun.

The soil can be any decent garden loam. Actually, these plants will grow in just about any soil, including that found in the alley.

HOW TO PLANT
Plants are available in containers in spring and fall. Many producers now plant a male and a female plant in each container. These are vegetatively propagated plants, so the sex is known. If plants are sold separately, make sure you buy a male plant and a female plant. Dig the planting holes the same depth and twice as wide as the containers in which the plants were grown. Plant a male and a female plant in the same hole to make sure there will be good pollination. One or two pairs of plants are usually sufficient for most homes. These are big plants!

CARE AND MAINTENANCE
Bittersweet needs heavy pruning to keep it civilized. Do not be afraid to cut! If you do it "wrong," the plant will grow back anyway, and you will have another chance to do it right. Try not to fertilize bittersweet plants or they will grow even more aggressively. Keeping the soil a little dry and withholding fertilizer will slow down the plant and improve fruit production.

ADDITIONAL INFORMATION
If the nursery doesn't know whether the plants are males or females, either buy somewhere else or buy in the fall when the plants have fruit on them. Bittersweet can be found in many locations throughout Illinois growing along roadsides, over fences, or wherever it has escaped from cultivation or where birds have distributed the seed. Bittersweet stems with colorful fruits are collected and sold to florists for flower arrangements.

ADDITIONAL SPECIES, CULTIVARS, OR VARIETIES
There are no cultivars of *C. scandens*. A related species, *C. orbiculatus* or Chinese bittersweet, is even more rambunctious than American bittersweet. The plant has escaped from cultivation and has become a terrible weed in some parts of the East.

Boston Ivy

Parthenocissus tricuspidata

Zones: All
Size: Vining to 50 feet or more
Blooms: Spring
Flower Color: Green; inconspicuous
Type: Deciduous

Light Requirement:

*B*oston ivy is the plant of ivy-covered walls, a sturdy vine with attractive foliage. The leaves have three-pointed lobes on the upper part of the plant; lower down are leaves with three leaflets. The vine climbs and attaches itself with tendrils, each with an adhesive "foot." Boston ivy will easily climb a five-story building in just a few years. It tolerates city conditions very well and will grow in any of the city soils. I have seen it in dry sand and in moist loamy soils, doing very well in both cases. The walls of the "Friendly Confines," Wrigley Field, are covered with Boston ivy. It is probably the most scrutinized and meticulously maintained Boston ivy anywhere.

WHEN TO PLANT

Boston ivy seeds need cold to break their dormancy. They may be planted in the fall in nursery beds—or plant them in a moist, artificial soil mix, keeping them in the refrigerator for about 3 months, and germinating them at 70 degrees Fahrenheit under lights indoors. Transplant to pots and then outdoors when the soil is dry enough to work. Containerized plants may be planted anytime during the season.

WHERE TO PLANT

Plant at the bases of walls, fences, or trellises, or around rock gardens. It can be used as a groundcover plant.

HOW TO PLANT

Set plants from small pots in holes the same as you do when planting annuals. Water them thoroughly after planting. Plants are available in 1- and 2-gallon cans from nurseries and garden centers. Dig planting holes as deep and twice as wide as the containers. Set the plants at the same depth they were growing at the nursery. Water thoroughly to settle the soil.

CARE AND MAINTENANCE
Boston ivy may need some help in getting started up a wall or other support. Fasteners are available from garden stores, or staple a twist-tie to the structure and fasten the vine with it. Japanese beetles and leaf spot diseases can severely damage Boston ivy plantings. Control the Japanese beetles with Tempo or Sevin or Orthene (acephate). Treat the leaf spot with maneb or zyban. Follow label directions carefully.

ADDITIONAL INFORMATION
Ivy will stick to brick walls and other masonry, as well as to wooden fences and aluminum siding. The adhesive pads from the plant are impossible to remove. Ivy does look wonderful growing up the side of a building, but it is not good for the structure. Rather than allowing the vine to cling to the building, construct a support of wire mesh or netting for the plant to grow on. It will protect the structure, and if there is a need to remove the vine for repairs or painting, the support can be cut loose and reinstalled when the work is done.

ADDITIONAL SPECIES, CULTIVARS, OR VARIETIES
Parthenocissus quinquefolia, Virginia creeper, is closely related to Boston ivy. It has leaves with 5 leaflets and is a more aggressive plant. It is commonly found in the woods and abandoned places. It grows over fences and rockpiles and will climb trees to 50 or 60 feet. It can become weedy in the garden, rooting where it touches the ground. Virginia creeper is a handsome plant where there is room for it. Its fall color is outstanding. It is one of the first plants to change color in fall. Crimson red, it can be seen climbing even to the tops of tall trees.

Clematis

Clematis × jackmanii

Zones: All
Size: 5 to 15 feet
Blooms: June until frost
Flower Colors: Red, white, yellow, purple,
     violet-purple, rose, pink, blue
Type: Deciduous

Light Requirement:

*F*lowers of the clematis are among the most beautiful in the garden. Although they are undeniably gorgeous, these vines are conspicuously absent from most gardens in Illinois. This is possibly due to their reputation for being difficult to grow. In fact, they are relatively easy to grow if given a proper location and some support. Clematises do require attention to detail. As the old adage says, they need a warm top and cool bottom. This means planting them where they get full sun or filtered shade, in a cool, moist soil. In the hottest parts of the state, some relief from the intense midday sun is helpful to keep them flowering. A mulch to keep the soil cool is probably helpful as well. Much of the literature insists that these plants must be grown in an alkaline soil with a pH of 7.0 to 7.5. We have seen plants growing in soils that were decidedly acidic, but we have also seen them in Illinois soils that have a pH of nearly 8.0. These plants grow on roadside mailboxes where they are baked by the sun and the soil is hot and dry. They may not look too good sometimes, but they hang on, and they do flower. One apparent problem with growing clematis is figuring out where to put it; evidently, many people think it must go on trellises. Actually, it can go anywhere any other vine can be grown. It can be grown on a fence, up the side of the garage, on a pile of rocks, over an arbor, or over the swing. I'm not sure why this plant is considered "different."

WHEN TO PLANT
Clematis can be planted in spring, or all summer from containers.

WHERE TO PLANT
Plant on anything that will support them. Soil should be deep and well drained but moist. The pH should be neutral or a little above.

Plant in full sun or partial shade (full shade will result in fewer flowers). Some of the most beautiful clematis plants I've seen were growing on a split rail fence at a horse farm . . . an unlikely place. Displaying a plant every couple of yards, they literally covered the fence for hundreds of feet.

HOW TO PLANT
Prepare the soil by spading it over and adding organic matter. Make sure the drainage is adequate. Set the plants at the depth they were growing in the nursery. Plants are available in containers, or as bare-root plants from mail-order catalogs. Soak the ground thoroughly after planting to settle the soil around the roots.

CARE AND MAINTENANCE
These plants will need some temporary support to keep them off the ground as they are becoming established; a bamboo stick will suffice. Once they begin to grow, the permanent support can be used. Water the plants during dry weather. Pruning is the key to keeping clematis blooming. The plants are divided into two kinds, those blooming on stems that grew the previous year (old wood), and those that bloom on stems growing the current year (new wood). Plants blooming on old wood usually bloom in midspring. Prune them when they finish flowering. Remove spent blooms, and reduce the length of the stems to force new growth. Those blooming on new wood can be pruned in early spring before growth begins. They should be cut back severely to force vigorous growth.

ADDITIONAL INFORMATION
Clematis vines support themselves by twisting, and with leaf petioles that fold over any support. A fungal disease is devastating to clematis plants in wet seasons, especially in wet soils. *Ascochyta* leaf spot and stem rot will kill plants at the soil line. Treat with wettable sulfur. Spray the foliage and stems every week as long as wet weather lasts. Improve drainage if needed.

ADDITIONAL SPECIES, CULTIVARS, OR VARIETIES
There are far too many kinds of clematis to describe in this text. The *Jackman Group* is the most popular; many of the largest and most colorful cultivars belong to this group. One of the most complete descriptions of the clematis is provided by Michael A. Dirr in *Manual of Woody Landscape Plants*, 4th Edition, pp. 218-222. For those interested in these special plants, they are worth looking up. Sweet autumn clematis, *C. terniflora*, is a naturalized plant in Illinois. It produces fragrant, 1-inch flowers from August until frost.

Climbing Hydrangea

Hydrangea anomala petiolaris

Zones: All
Size: 60 to 80 feet in height with adequate support
Blooms: Late June
Flower Color: White
Type: Deciduous

Light Requirement:

*C*limbing hydrangea is considered by some to be *the best vine*. That may be a bit of an overstatement, but it is indeed a fine plant. It is not for the timid, however. It will grow to an immense size, easily reaching the tops of 6-story buildings. The plant clings by means of aerial rootlets. It will cling tenaciously, and will destroy a wood or old masonry surface if allowed to get a good hold. It is essential that some means of support be provided for this plant. It is a woody vine, and the weight of a mature plant will be surprising, especially if it comes tumbling down and must be raised and resupported. This vine does not adhere closely to the wall supporting it but stands out, some-times shelf-like, creating greater relief than the flat effect of Boston ivy, for instance. The attractive foliage is a glossy dark green. as well, The red exfoliating bark is interesting in winter. Climbing hydrangea flowers with fragrant 6-inch clusters of lacy blooms. The outer flowers of the cluster are showy and white, and the blooms are held away from the foliage on long stems.

WHEN TO PLANT

Most climbing hydrangeas are container-grown; they are best planted in spring, but may be planted all season with care. (The roots are slow to recover from injury.)

WHERE TO PLANT

Plant in a rich, moist, well-drained soil. The plants will grow in full sun, but in exposed locations they may be winter-injured by severe winter weather. They will grow in full shade, but will be slower to develop.

How to Plant

Prepare the soil by spading, incorporating organic matter. Dig the planting holes the same depth and twice as wide as the containers in which the plants were grown. Carefully remove the plants from the containers to avoid injuring the roots. Set the plants at the same depth they were growing in the nursery. If the soil in the containers is a light artificial mix, either shake some of it off the roots or get extra from the nursery and mix it with the soil that will go back into the planting hole. This will create a gradual change from the soil on the plant to the soil around it. (Planting an artificial mix directly into a loam soil will create an interface through which water, air, and roots will not move.)

Care and Maintenance

The climbing hydrangeas are slow to recover from transplanting— make sure they have enough water, but be careful not to drown them.

Additional Information

Give some thought to developing a support for these beautiful vines. Some masonry structures will support them without trouble, but wooden structures may not. Make sure your building will not be damaged by these plants before you invest the time and money required to get them started. The plants can climb trees without harm unless they encircle them, risking girdling. They can climb utility poles, but they may be damaged by linemen if there is a need to climb the pole.

Additional Species, Cultivars, or Varieties

After being classified as *Hydrangea petiolaris* for as long as a century, this plant has been relegated to subspecies status. *H. anomala* is another vine hydrangea, with narrower leaves, and reported to be less hardy than *H. a. petiolaris*.

Dropmore Honeysuckle

Lonicera sempervirens × hirsuta 'Dropmore Scarlet'

Other Name: *Lonicera × brownii*
  'Dropmore Scarlet'
Zones: All
Size: Twining to 20 feet
Blooms: June to August
Flower Color: Red
Type: Deciduous

Light Requirement:

*D*ropmore honeysuckle is a twining vine that produces fragrant red flowers throughout the summer months. This plant climbs by twisting around its supporting structure. It is a vine that can be used as an accent in any garden—it is not so aggressive that it can't be kept under control. Dropmore can be trained quite easily with a little pruning and some tying of stems to get it started. As is true of many of the honeysuckles, this one leafs out early with attractive foliage, one of the earliest plants to show color in the spring. The flowers are spectacular and continue for much of the summer. The fragrance is particularly noticeable on a warm, still evening. The fragrance attracts both hummingbirds and hawk moths. Fruit is produced in fall—it is a bright-red berry, quite nice when plentiful. Some seasons they are abundant; others, they are sparse or nonexistent.

WHEN TO PLANT

Dropmore honeysuckle is best planted in spring; the plants are available in 5-gallon cans. Containerized plants may be planted throughout the season if care is taken not to injure the roots.

WHERE TO PLANT

Plant in full sun or light shade in a moist, well-drained soil. Use on fences, on trellises, on banks, over low piles of rocks in the garden—any place that can display the flowers. As a groundcover, the plants will make a tangle that needs to be pruned vigorously to keep it in some semblance of order. These plants will grow well in the shade, but there they will flower sparsely or sometimes not at all.

How to Plant

Dig the planting holes as deep and twice as wide as the containers. Set the plants at the same depth they were growing in the containers. Roots are slow to recover from transplanting. Space the plants so that they have room to grow. Usually one plant to a trellis is sufficient, and one plant every 5 feet on a fence should be enough.

Care and Maintenance

Pruning is the major maintenance chore associated with these honeysuckles; it should be done as soon as the plants have finished flowering. Remove overly long stems, and shoots going in the wrong direction. Removal of the oldest canes all the way to the main stem will stimulate vigorous new growth. This plant flowers on old wood, so vigorous growth will increase the chances of flowers. Aphids have been problems with the *sempervirens* honeysuckles. Control them with acephate (Orthene), following label directions.

Additional Information

'Dropmore' honeysuckle is sometimes listed as *Lonicera* × *brownii* 'Dropmore'. It was introduced by F. L. Skinner of Dropmore, Manitoba, and is the hardiest of all the vining honeysuckles.

Additional Species, Cultivars, or Varieties

Several vining honeysuckles have found use in the landscape industry. Some are so invasive that they have been relegated to the "noxious weed" category. Hall's honeysuckle is one of these. At one time *L. japonica* 'Halliana' was used widely as a groundcover to stabilize banks, but it is no longer being used, and some states have outlawed its use. *L. sempervirens* cultivars are good vines, some with colors and flower sizes comparable to 'Dropmore Scarlet'.

VINES

English Ivy

Hedera helix

Zones: All
Size: To 90 feet
Blooms: September or not at all
Flower Color: Green, inconspicuous
Type: Evergreen

Light Requirement:

*E*nglish ivy is a beautiful vine, the plant most people envision as ivy. If well supported, this plant can climb as high as the support allows, reportedly 90 feet in some cases. This vine is especially good for shaded spots in the garden. It prefers to be protected from winter sun, and will remain evergreen. Flowers are produced only on the "adult" plants. "Adults" are usually the tallest vines, and the flowers are at the top. English ivy has been cultivated for hundreds of years. It mutates freely, and literally thousands of selections have been made, usually for leaf size, color, or shape, or local adaptations. Some of these selections are strictly Southern adaptations. Some selections made in the North have resulted in hardier cultivars that will tolerate our Illinois winters. These plants are well suited for growing on masonry walls, on fences, up trunks of trees, or on the sides of buildings. They can be enticed to cover arbors and pergolas. English ivies climb and cling by means of aerial rootlets, and they will hold tenaciously. They may damage a wood or old masonry surface if allowed to get a good hold. It is essential that some means of support be provided for them. The plants are woody vines, and the weight of a mature plant will be surprising, especially if it comes tumbling down and must be raised and resupported.

WHEN TO PLANT

English ivy is available at garden centers in pots. It is best planted in spring so the plants can become well established before they must stand the rigors of an Illinois winter.

WHERE TO PLANT

Growing best in shade, English ivy needs protection from sun, especially in winter. It prefers a cool, rich, well-drained soil, but will tolerate almost any situation. It tolerates dry sites when well established. It tends to be shallowly rooted.

HOW TO PLANT

Plants are sold in pots or flats. Prepare the planting area by tilling or cultivating, incorporating organic matter if the soil is heavy. Set plants at the same depth they grew in their containers. Space them 12 inches or more apart along the wall or other support, depending on how quickly you need cover. If the plants were grown in a light, artificial soil mix, shake as much of it as you can off the roots before planting. If it is left on the roots, the plant may be unable to grow out of the mix into the surrounding soil. Plants in such a condition will wilt easily and will never become established.

CARE AND MAINTENANCE

English ivy plants are slow to start, but they will grow rapidly once established. Pruning will be necessary to remove old and damaged wood; old plants will develop woody trunks up to 5 inches in diameter. The largest plants will lose lower leaves, leaving the lower part of a wall bare. Setting new plants into the planting every few years and systematically removing the oldest plants will assure continuing healthy vines.

ADDITIONAL INFORMATION

English ivy is susceptible to a number of problems. Aphids and mites can be troublesome, but insecticidal soap will control both. Leaf spot diseases develop in wet seasons; use triforine or maneb fungicides where needed. Follow directions on the label. Root rots will develop in wet sites. Provide adequate drainage, and water thoroughly but infrequently. Significant plant losses may occur where ivy plantings adjoining lawns are watered continuously by a sprinkler system.

ADDITIONAL SPECIES, CULTIVARS, OR VARIETIES

Many selections of ivy have been made for Illinois conditions. 'Bulgaria' was selected by the Missouri Botanic Garden for cold tolerance and ability to stand droughty conditions. 'Thorndale' has larger leaves and will tolerate severe winters such as those of 1976 and 77.

Japanese Wisteria

Wisteria floribunda

Zones: All
Size: 20 to 30 feet depending on the size of the support
Blooms: Spring
Flower Colors: Pink, purple, white
Type: Deciduous

Light Requirement:

isteria is one of the loveliest flowering vines. The plants have been cultivated for centuries in the Orient, where hundred-year-old plants are not uncommon. This is a stout vine that climbs by twisting around its support. The twist always turns clockwise. If grown as a tree form, wisteria develops a twisted trunk that may be several inches in diameter. Wisterias are heavy and will pull down inadequate structures. When I was a youngster, our family had a home with a large porch festooned with wisteria. The plant was supported on heavy wires securely fastened into the concrete structure. I remember how heavy the plant was when it was necessary to remove it for painting. It took many of us to lift it back into place. Our wisteria bloomed profusely every spring, with a heady fragrance that filled the evening air.

WHEN TO PLANT

Plant wisteria in spring from containers. It establishes easily.

WHERE TO PLANT

These vines will grow up anything if given the chance. They look lovely growing up a tree, but they will eventually strangle it. Train wisteria on fences, arbors, pergolas, and porches where a support system has been devised. Wisteria does best in full sun and any good garden soil. It does need good drainage, and it must have sufficient water during flowering time.

HOW TO PLANT

Wisterias are available in 5- or 6-gallon containers. Dig the planting hole the same depth and twice the diameter of the container, and set the plant at the same depth it was growing. Water thoroughly to settle the soil. Wisteria plants are large; a plant every 10 to 20 feet along a support will be more than adequate.

CARE AND MAINTENANCE

Pruning to keep the plant in bounds is essential. Cut back vigorous growth to only 3 or 4 buds immediately after flowers drop. Remove any suckers from the bottom of the plant. Most cultivars are grafted onto seedling rootstocks, and shoots which arise from the roots will not be typical of the type. Some wisterias are very difficult to get to flower. Excessive vegetative growth is usually the cause of this. Fertilize cautiously with nitrogen; unless the plant is obviously deficient of nitrogen, it is better not to use any. Potassium fertilizer counteracts nitrogen's effects (excessive vegetative growth). Phosphorus fertilizer will sometimes stimulate flowering. Plants usually begin flowering 3 to 5 years after being planted. If blooming does not start, deeply cultivate the plant to sever surface roots. This will shock the plant into reduced vegetative growth and may cause it to bloom. Plants in full sun will usually develop the excess stored sugars needed for blooming sooner than plants in shade.

ADDITIONAL INFORMATION

Do not overstimulate wisteria plants with nitrogen or they will never bloom.

ADDITIONAL SPECIES, CULTIVARS, OR VARIETIES

Japanese wisteria plants must be bought as named cultivars. Seedling plants may not flower. There are many cultivars, and your local nursery will carry good ones for your area. *Wisteria sinensis*, Chinese wisteria, is a similar plant with more compact blooms. It is not as hardy, but has been grown in this part of the country successfully.

Trumpet Vine

Campsis radicans

Other Name: Trumpet Creeper
Zones: All
Size: 30 feet or more
Blooms: Summer
Flower Colors: Red, orange, yellow
Type: Deciduous

Light Requirement:

Trumpet vine is an aggressive hardy plant that will grow over anything in its way. It is a native American plant, perfectly able to handle the typical Illinois weather. It is naturalized in various places in the Midwest, where it is able to dominate its environment. It spreads by means of suckering from roots, or from root segments left in the ground. Trumpet vine makes a dense cover on fences, trellises, and pergolas, or as a screen on a staunch support. It will climb trees, but its flowers are often high up and hard to see. The vine climbs by means of root-like holdfasts. These holdfasts are not strong. The vines are very heavy, and they will break loose from their support in storms. They may need tying to keep them attached. Their bright flowers are the primary reason for growing trumpet vines. The flowers are trumpet-shaped, three inches long, and one and one-half inches wide at the mouth. Colors are mostly red or orange; some cultivars have been selected for floral color and size.

WHEN TO PLANT

Planting trumpet vine in spring or fall is probably best. Containerized plants may be planted all season. This plant is so vigorous that it can be planted any time plants can be acquired.

WHERE TO PLANT

Plant in any soil. Trumpet vine will grow in sand, clay, cinders, or garden soil. The pH is not important. It grows best in sun or light shade. The plant will grow in shade, but flowering will be diminished. Use these plants where quick cover is needed on fences, as screening, or to cover utility poles, retaining walls, ornamental arbors, or trellises. Avoid planting trumpet vine where its aggressive character will allow it to invade other plantings, such as in perennial gardens.

HOW TO PLANT

Dig the planting holes the same depth and twice as wide as the ball of the plant. Set the plant at the depth it was growing in the nursery. Water the plant well following planting to settle the soil around the roots.

CARE AND MAINTENANCE

It is extremely important to gain control over this plant from the beginning. If it is allowed to get a head start, it will be difficult to control, and there will be a tangle of strong vines to unwind. The plant is vigorous enough without fertilizing. Pruning is the key to handling trumpet vine. It flowers on new wood, the stems growing during the current season. Prune old canes to a few buds in fall after leaves have dropped, or in spring. You will be surprised at how fast the vine grows to a large size each year. If the plant is cut back severely every spring, it can be controlled, and blooming will be enhanced. Deadheading the blooms will prolong the flowering well into late summer. Many insects and diseases will reside on these plants, but the plants are so vigorous they will outgrow the pests.

ADDITIONAL INFORMATION

When describing trumpet vine's growth rate, one author suggested that you "keep your legs moving when in the vicinity of this plant." The gorgeous flowers are attractive to hummingbirds.

ADDITIONAL SPECIES, CULTIVARS, OR VARIETIES

Catalogs of Illinois nurseries list the cultivars red 'Flamenco', yellow 'Flava', and glowing red 'Crimson Trumpet'. A related hybrid, C. × *tagliabuana* 'Mme. Galen', is somewhat tamer, but it may not be as hardy as the more common trumpet creeper.

Wintercreeper

Euonymus fortunei

Zones: All
Size: Scrambling 40 to 50 feet up a structure
Blooms: Early summer
Flower Color: Green, inconspicuous
Type: Evergreen to semi-evergreen

Light Requirement:

intercreeper is a strong vine that will climb walls, fences, trees, and posts; it will easily reach the top of a two-story house. This plant is a true vine, climbing by means of aerial rootlets which attach strongly to the support. Wintercreeper is one of only a few evergreen vines that will tolerate Illinois winters. If growing in an exposed situation, it will turn light green or yellow for the winter. Some years the leaves are dropped if conditions are too severe. The stems of the plant generally remain viable in such years, and refoliate normally the next spring. The best of the wintercreepers for vining is *E. f.* 'Vegetus'. It has medium-green foliage and is a vigorous plant once it has become established.

WHEN TO PLANT

Wintercreeper transplants easily, but it is best transplanted in spring. This will allow it to become established before contending with a tough Illinois winter.

WHERE TO PLANT

Tolerating full sun, wintercreeper is also perfectly at home in shade. Wintercreeper isn't particular about soils as long as it doesn't stand in water. These plants are well suited for growing on masonry walls, on fences, up trunks of trees, or on the sides of buildings. They can be enticed to cover arbors and pergolas.

HOW TO PLANT

Euonymus plants are grown in quart- to 5-gallon-sized containers, and as balled-and-burlapped plants. The hole for planting should be no deeper than the depth of the ball of the plant, and at least twice as wide. Set the plant in the planting hole and replace half the soil. Fill the hole with water. (Remove the burlap from a balled-and-burlapped plant, and stuff it down in the hole.) Replace the remaining soil, and fill the hole with water again. Make a saucer around the plant with any remaining soil. Space the plants 3 to 5 feet apart.

CARE AND MAINTENANCE

Wintercreeper will benefit from annual pruning in spring, removing any winter-damaged branches. Cutting at least some branches to force renewed growth is helpful. These vines may be cut to a few buds on a branch, and will regrow vigorously. These plants are susceptible to several insects and diseases. Crown gall causes large growths on the stems and roots and can kill the plants. Mildew and anthracnose disfigure leaves. Water early in the day and keep moisture off the leaves. Black vine weevils eat notches out of the margins of leaves and feed on the roots. Euonymus scale is the most damaging. Spray with acephate about the time catalpas are in bloom to control it. Repeat 2 or 3 times. Follow label directions carefully. Applying a balanced fertilizer as the leaves begin to develop in spring will aid in recovery from winter damage.

ADDITIONAL INFORMATION

There are hundreds of wintercreeper selections. The ones with yellow leaves are sick-looking when used as vines. They appear to be chlorotic except when viewed quite closely. Use the good green kinds for vines. The 'Vegetus' cultivar will produce abundant fruit in certain situations. The fruit is pink and orange, and quite showy in those years when numerous. These plants will encircle trees as they climb. Be careful not to let this happen, or the trees may be girdled years later. A large sugar maple along the North Shore (Cook County) suffered this fate. Even though wintercreeper is easy to transplant, it is slow to begin vining. Be patient.

ADDITIONAL SPECIES, CULTIVARS, OR VARIETIES

Many cultivars of wintercreeper are available, but not all are suited to vining. Be sure to let your supplier know the use you intend for the plant. Some are better suited for use as groundcovers.

Wildflowers

*T*HEY POKE THEIR HEADS THROUGH THE SOD on the first warm day of spring: birdsfoot violets, spring beauties, pasque flowers. The Illinois woodlands and prairies burst forth with a palette of color, as they have each spring for millennia. The progression of blooms continues through the season with goldenrod, rattlesnake master, Joe-Pye weed, and the towering sunflowers. These are the wildflowers of our state. They bloom by the roadside and in abandoned fields, woodlots, and vacant lots.

In the past, few American gardeners noticed these plants—the flowers were nice, but they were just weeds, and they were not thought to belong in the garden. Maybe they were too common. In Europe, gardeners did notice, and the weeds became garden flowers. And now, almost as if shaken awake, we have begun to notice them too. These weeds have become treasured wildflowers, and they are appearing in gardens all over America.

In truth, many of them have been in our gardens for years. We called them perennials: gaillardia, coneflower, larkspur, columbine, and others. Many are unaware that these are the same plants as those that grow along the road.

Wildflowers are being planted in gardens, restored prairie lands, urban woodlands, parks, and nature centers . . . and once again, along roadsides. This renewed interest in wildflowers has come none too soon. The wildflowers' diminishing habitat is being replaced by planned plantings. Once again the prairie is blossoming with the flowers that should always have been there.

A huge development northwest of Chicago is landscaped mostly with wildflowers. Rural estates are being planted as prairie. The forest preserve district of Lake County is developing and maintaining many acres of wildflower plantings. Those who build golfcourses are helping, too, as they develop natural areas on the courses.

Wildflowers are unique garden flowers because they require so little work. They are well adapted to the climate and to the soils.

Chapter Eleven

Even disturbed soils will support wildflowers if there is some drainage.

Many wildflowers are available in garden centers and nurseries; these plants are often the same ones sold as perennials. Some are cultivars. If allowed to grow untended in the natural garden, they will revert to their species forms. Phlox will do this in a couple of seasons or so; the seeds they drop are no longer hybrids like those their parents grew from. Sometimes the species are not quite as colorful as the cultivars, but you will find they are more resilient, and may persist in difficult circumstances better than their hybrid relatives.

Wildflower nurseries and specialists are to be found all over Illinois, and a prairie plant association is flourishing here as well. Restored prairie and preserved woodlands are good places to learn about wildflowers. They have certain needs that determine where they do best. Once those needs are met, the wildflowers do just what they are intended to do . . . grow.

There are two general types of wildflowers, those that grow in the open prairie, and woodland plants. Some will grow in the transition area between the two. There are annual and biennial wildflowers, but the ones in this book are perennials. Some reseed themselves as well.

Wildflowers can be collected in the wild; areas scheduled for development are good sources. When you notice a site scheduled for development, get in touch with the developer for permission to collect some of the plants. Roadsides where plants are going to be sprayed with herbicide or mowed are also good sources. And fellow gardeners may have extras when dividing their plants.

If you collect or buy plants, be sure not to stray too far from home. Some wildflowers are native to large areas of North America, and while these plants all look the same, they may be quite local in their adaptations. Plants grown from seed collected in central Texas where summers are hot and winters mild may not survive in Elizabeth, Illinois, where summers are moderate and winters can be character-builders.

You will find that if you select the right wildflower, it will grow without much trouble, flowering happily year after year.

Black-eyed Susan

Rudbeckia hirta

Zones: All
Size: 3 feet
Blooms: June to September
Flower Colors: Golden-yellow petals
(ray flowers) around a brown disk

Light Requirement:

*B*lack-eyed Susans are among the most popular wildflowers. They bloom throughout the summer, providing an unusually long floral display. These are flowers of the tallgrass prairie, and they welcomed settlers as they moved west. The American natives were already making use of these plants before the settlers arrived. The Forest Potawatomi made a tea from the roots and used it as a cure for colds, and they boiled the disk flowers with other kinds of herbs to make a yellow dye. Settlers soon discovered the benefits of these plants, learning to prepare a tea from the leaves as a stimulant and diuretic. More than one species of *Rudbeckia* grows as a wildflower. *R. serotina* and *R. laciniata* are found in old pastures and prairie remnants throughout the state. *R. hirta pulcherima* is included in wildflower seed mixes. Some of these plants are considered weedy and *R. serotina* is reported to be rather aggressive. Unless these flowers are grown in a small, confined garden, their aggressive nature should not be a disadvantage. Some black-eyed Susans are incorporated into prairie seed mixes. Being sure which kinds are being sold is often difficult. Most seed mixes list only *R. hirta* and *R. subtomentosa*, the sweet black-eyed Susan. *Rudbeckia hirta* is a short-lived perennial, or it may be biennial. It self-sows and should maintain itself in the wildflower garden.

WHEN TO PLANT
Potted plants are available for planting throughout the season. Seed can be sown in fall or spring.

WHERE TO PLANT
Plant in open areas with full sun on well-drained soils. These plants will tolerate dry weather better than they will wet soils.

368

HOW TO PLANT

The seed may be sown in a small nursery bed. Set the seedlings in the garden when large enough to handle. In prairie plantings, the seed may be broadcast in combination with other wildflower seeds. Prepare the soil by tilling to a 4- to 6-inch depth. Plants may be set into the loosened soil by hand, spacing them about a foot apart. Seed can be broadcast and raked down into the soil an inch or so, or plant the seed in shallow furrows and cover lightly.

CARE AND MAINTENANCE

Black-eyed Susan, like most wildflowers that are perfectly adapted to their surroundings, needs no care. Perennial cultivars of black-eyed Susan can be divided in spring or fall.

ADDITIONAL INFORMATION

These lovely plants are especially attractive to butterflies. *Rudbeckia* is named for Olaf Rudbeck and his son, both Scandinavian botanists.

ADDITIONAL SPECIES, CULTIVARS, OR VARIETIES

A related species, the prairie coneflower (*R. nitida*) is grown as a garden perennial. Large black-eyed Susan (*R. grandiflora*) and annual black-eyed Susan are sometimes included in prairie seed mixes.

Blue Boneset

Eupatorium coelestinum

Other Name: Mist Flower
Zones: All
Size: 2 to 4 feet tall
Blooms: Late summer, fall
Flower Colors: Violet-blue

Light Requirement:

This is a wildflower of late summer that grows in waste places and prairie restorations. It is a plant that should be in every wildflower garden. It is easy to handle because of its relatively short height, and it has a good blue color. Blue boneset is adapted to well-drained, somewhat dry, soils and low fertility. Under such conditions it stays in bounds and does not fall over in storms. In moist, fertile soils it is more vigorous, producing more and larger blooms. Under these conditions it will tend to lodge and will spread very quickly. In a naturalized planting with other prairie plants, and where soils are dry and low in fertility, this plant will stay shorter and be easier to control. Dividing every year or two will keep it under control. Blue boneset has been introduced as a perennial garden flower, and it has a place in the cutting garden as well. It will need to be staked to keep it from lying down. Growing it in full sun and keeping it on the dry side will help. Its flowers are good for cutting; the fluffy violet-blue flowers are borne in flat-topped clusters on long stems.

WHEN TO PLANT

Blue boneset can be planted from seed scattered in fall, or from divisions made in early spring.

WHERE TO PLANT

Plant in full sun or partial shade. A moist, well-drained soil is best, but this plant is undemanding, and any good soil will suffice. For a prairie planting, the existing soil will be satisfactory, and the plant will exist in damaged or reconstructed soils as well. Plant in the garden away from valuable perennials which may be invaded by the blue boneset.

HOW TO PLANT

Seeds may be sown in a small nursery bed. Set the seedlings in the garden when large enough to handle. The seed may be broadcast in combination with other wildflower seeds in prairie plantings. Clear the area of any introduced grasses and broad-leaved weeds. The soil may be tilled for seeding. Divisions are planted at the same depth they were growing. Each clump should have several old stems and some well-developed roots. Set the clumps at least 3 feet apart; they will spread.

CARE AND MAINTENANCE

Blue boneset requires very little maintenance. In a natural setting, there will be no care required. Burning to eliminate old tops and invading weedy plants may be advantageous. In the garden, pinch or cut back during the summer to increase the numbers of shoots and flowers. Deadhead to keep the plants blooming longer, well into fall.

ADDITIONAL INFORMATION

In the northern part of the state, these plants may suffer some winterkill, which may help to keep the plants from spreading too quickly. The blue flowers blend well with the yellows and whites of hardy mums blooming at the same time. In some catalogs, blue boneset is listed as hardy ageratum.

ADDITIONAL SPECIES, CULTIVARS, OR VARIETIES

A vegetatively propagated selection sold as 'Wayside Variety' is shorter and more compact, according to its listing. Several other *Eupatoriums* are valuable in the wildflower garden.

Bluestem

Andropogon sp.

Zones: All
Size: 2 to 10 feet, spread to 3 feet
Blooms: August through September
Flower Colors: Green to bronze or purplish

Light Requirement:

The bluestems are plants of the prairie. Big bluestem was the dominant grass of the great prairies that extended through Illinois to the Great Plains. This must have been a magnificent sight, miles and miles of waving grasses as high as a horse's head. There are still big bluestem stands in prairie remnants, and along railroad rights-of-way. Big bluestem grows into big clumps and will develop into a dense sod. Big bluestems spread (slowly) by rhizomes and by seed. The root systems can be extensive and will grow down several feet into a deep soil. Little bluestem is found in the sand dunes along Lake Michigan and in dry prairie remnants, often with big bluestem but on lighter ground. It is a bunch grass, an intermediate plant between the tall grasses and the short grasses of the drylands. In the sand dunes, it forms clumps, turning brown and lasting through the winter. It grows to about 3 feet tall in scattered bunches, so flowering plants will grow with it. The little bluestem prairie is more colorful than the tallgrass prairie. The leaves of the bluestem plants are blue-green, and the stems are bluish at the joints. The flower is green or tinged bronze or purplish.

WHEN TO PLANT

Bluestems can be divided, or seed may be sown in spring. Plants are sold in containers and can be planted at any time during the season, the earlier the better.

WHERE TO PLANT

Plant in the garden where there is plenty of room, or in naturalized areas. The soil should be well drained, but any garden soil will suffice. Full sun is preferred.

How to Plant

The seeds may be sown in a small nursery bed. Set the seedlings in the garden when they are large enough to handle. Seed may be broadcast in combination with other wildflower seeds in prairie plantings. For prairie seeding in seed mixes, prepare the area by disking or tilling. Sow the seed, and drag to cover it lightly; or conservation-drill the seed. As a constituent of a mix, the seed is often hydroseeded in prairie plantings. In the garden, dig planting holes the same depth as the plant ball and twice as wide. Set the plants at the same depth they were growing. Divided clumps should be reset at the same depth they grew. Water the plants to settle the soil around the roots. Seeded areas may be irrigated to get the seed to germinate.

Care and Maintenance

Once the plants are established, they need very little watering. Plants should be cut down in fall or late winter before new growth begins. Divide garden plants when they become too crowded.

Additional Information

Early settlers in this part of the country quickly learned that the best corn grew on big bluestem land. The top corn-producing areas of the United States are, to this day, former bluestem prairie lands. Settlers were taught medicinal uses for the roots and leaves of the bluestem plants. Roots were boiled to make a tea for the treatment of urinary problems. Other unusual treatments were used for undetermined ailments.

Additional Species, Cultivars, or Varieties

Several *Andropogon* species grow in Illinois. Besides big bluestem (*A. gerardii*) and little bluestem (*A. scoparius*), you can find broom sedge (*A. virginicus*) and silver beard grass (*A. saccharoides*). These are incorporated in some prairie seed mixes offered by specialists; neither is commonly listed by wildflower nurseries. Big bluestem and little bluestem grasses may be seen at the Chicago Botanic Garden, Morton Arboretum, and other locations throughout the state.

Butterfly Weed

Asclepias tuberosa

Zones: All
Size: 3 feet tall, half as wide
Blooms: Late spring to midsummer
Flower Colors: Orange, also yellow or red

Light Requirement:

*B*utterfly weed is aptly named. It is one of the plants sought by butterfly enthusiasts (our grandchildren among them), because its bright colors attract butterflies. This is a member of the milkweed family, which is noted for its appeal to butterflies. Common milkweed is the favorite host for the monarch butterfly; butterfly weed is attractive to fritillaries, among others. Butterfly weed is a plant native to Illinois and is found along roadsides and in other waste places. It is a plant of dry, infertile soils; in a garden it will prosper from the improved soil conditions, but is not invasive, and even though it will grow larger, it will not fall over. Once established, this plant is just about indestructible. It is a plant that beginning gardeners can grow without fear; you can't kill it. Small, first-year plants are shallowly rooted and may be heaved out of the ground the first winter. This doesn't seem to hurt them. Just push them back down and they will grow as though nothing has happened. The plants grow deep taproots, but they will spread with time. Division of large plants is difficult because of the taproot; smaller plants divide and are moved more easily.

WHEN TO PLANT
Root cuttings or seed may be planted in early spring. Potted plants may be set in the garden at any time during the season.

WHERE TO PLANT
Plant in full sun in any good garden soil (these plants can be planted in almost any kind of soil except a swamp—the deep taproots cannot survive in soggy soils). Butterfly weed may be grown in the perennial garden or naturalized in prairie plantings. It can also be planted in a butterfly garden among other plants, or in the cutting garden. It is excellent for fresh floral arrangements, and its flowers can be dried as well. It is especially attractive planted in groups along driveways or rustic walkways, much as daylilies are used.

How to Plant

The seeds may be sown in a small nursery bed. Rub the fluff off the seeds and sow them in prepared soil. Set the seedlings in the garden when they are large enough to handle. In prairie plantings, the seed may be broadcast onto prepared soil; disk or till to prepare a seedbed. The seed is short-lived, so be sure you buy new seed. Dig holes for containerized plants the same depth as the plant ball and twice as wide. Set divisions at the same depth they were growing before. Water to settle the soil.

Care and Maintenance

No insect or disease pests will seriously affect butterfly weed. The plants may benefit from a mulch in winter after the ground has frozen. Apply a 4- to 6-inch layer of straw to keep the plants from freezing and thawing all winter. Avoid using insecticides that may harm the butterflies.

Additional Information

The name *Asclepias* is from the Greek god of healing, Asklepios.

Additional Species, Cultivars, or Varieties

Many milkweeds grow wild in Illinois, but butterfly weed is the only one that has wide acceptance as an ornamental. 'Gay Butterflies' is supposedly a cultivar selected for red and yellow flowers, but it is usually orange. Seedling plants vary in flower color. The reds and yellows are less common, so naturally they are the ones everyone wants. Swamp milkweed, *A. incarnata*, is a 4-foot-tall plant with crimson, pink, or white flowers. It grows in wet soils around water features or ponds and attracts hordes of butterflies. It is sometimes listed as red milkweed

Goldenrod

Solidago sp.

Zones: All
Size: 2 to 6 feet tall
Blooms: Midsummer to late fall
Flower Color: Yellow

Light Requirement:

*G*oldenrod is a flower of late summer, offering its golden blooms as the season is winding down. It mixes well with the purple of asters and the ripening ornamental grasses. More than 2 dozen goldenrods grow in Illinois, but only a few are commercially available. There are some cultivars and some hybrids that have better form and color than the species. Much of the hybridization has been done in Europe, where these plants are much more popular than they are here. For the wildflower purist, there are many species that can be grown in the garden or in prairie plantings. We can, of course, always enjoy the goldenrods that we find growing along the roadsides and in other undisturbed places. In fact, if you come across a plant that attracts you in the wild, it could be moved to your garden with little difficulty. (It is a good idea to ask permission if it is on someone else's property.) If you feel guilty, take only half the clump. As far as I know, there are no endangered goldenrods.

WHEN TO PLANT

Goldenrod can be started from seed sown in fall or spring. Divide plants in spring before growth begins. Containerized plants can be planted at any time during the season.

WHERE TO PLANT

Goldenrods grow in any soil of average fertility and decent drainage, in full sun or partial shade. Higher fertility will result in taller, weaker plants. These plants are suited to the perennial border and the cutting garden. Naturalized clumps are attractive along pathways; they combine well with other wildflowers blooming at the same time in naturalized areas. Some species are adapted to woodlands with light shade.

How to Plant

Seed may be sown in naturalized settings. Several goldenrods are often included in wildflower mixes. Disk or till the soil, and broadcast or drill the seed. The seeds may be sown in a small nursery bed. Once established, goldenrod reseeds itself easily. Set the seedlings in the garden when large enough to handle. Plant divisions or container-grown plants at the same depth they were growing before. Dig the planting holes the same depth and twice as wide as the plant balls. Space the plants 1¹/₂ to 2 feet apart in groups. The taller kinds will tend to support each other if closely planted.

Care and Maintenance

Once established in the garden, goldenrod requires little care. The garden's higher fertility will encourage vigorous growth, and division will be necessary every few years.

Additional Information

Before you move a plant of unknown habits into your flower garden, try it in another location. Some are quite rambunctious and they could take over. If you plant it where you can watch it, it can be killed off if it tries to assume control. The taller kinds can be kept under control in the garden by cutting them back to a foot or so tall in early summer. They will bush out, shorter, with more flowers. Goldenrod is still suffering from the reputation that it causes hayfever. This idea was disproved many years ago, but it persists. Hayfever is most often due to the pollen of ragweed, not goldenrod. Prairie plantings of goldenrod profit from occasional burning.

Additional Species, Cultivars, or Varieties

Hybrid goldenrods are mostly from England, where they were developed in the '40s. One recent United States introduction is 'Golden Fleece', 18 inches tall and spreading. Old field goldenrod, *S. nemoralis*, and stiff goldenrod, *S. rigida*, are common in prairie seed mixes. *S. graminifolia*, hairy grass-leaved goldenrod, will grow in wet areas. Elm-leaved goldenrod, *S. ulmifolia*, grows well in light shade.

Jack-in-the-Pulpit

Arisaema triphyllum

Zones: All
Size: 1 to 2 feet tall, half as wide
Blooms: Spring
Flower Colors: Green spathe with brown
stripes on underside

Light Requirement:

Jack-in-the-pulpit is a favorite woodland plant, eagerly sought out each spring by nature lovers as a true sign that spring is here. It is a plant of the moist woods. I can still remember the croaking of frogs, a sound closely associated with finding the first Jack-in-the-pulpits in the spring. The floor of the woods covered with its umbrella-like leaves is almost like a jungle. Filtered sunlight through the leafing-out trees . . . the songs of birds . . . what more could a person want? Well, back to reality! Spring is a wonderful time outdoors in Illinois. Jack-in-the-pulpit is strictly a moist shade plant. If you have an area where nothing will grow because of the shade and wetness, Jack may solve your problem. Once these plants are happy, they will proliferate and become more attractive each year. They can cover an area with their big leaves, and if kept moist will last all summer. Jack-in-the-pulpit is a member of the arum family. It grows from a corm deep in the ground. Two leaves on long petioles grow from the corm. As they reach full size, a third stalk appears between them. It bears the pulpit-shaped structure called a spathe. The flowers are on a spike called a spadix. This is Jack, or as it is sometimes called, "the preacher." Plants of the arum family all have similar flowers and spathes. Calla lily, Anthurium, even philodendron and dumbcane, all have similar flowers. Another feature of these plants is the high concentration of calcium oxalate crystals in them. That is what makes the dumbcane dumb— if you taste it, it will numb your tongue so you can't talk. Native Americans processed the roots of the Jack-in-the-Pulpit so they could eat it. Don't try this yourself unless you know how.

WHEN TO PLANT

Jack-in-the-pulpit can be started from seeds sown in the fall as soon as they are collected. Plants may be dug up and moved in spring just as the shoots appear and before the leaves emerge.

WHERE TO PLANT

Jack-in-the-pulpits must be planted in moist soil. They can stand filtered or full shade. Use them in shade gardens, on the north sides of buildings where it stays dark and moist, in woodland gardens, or next to shaded water features.

HOW TO PLANT

Seed is collected in fall as the berries turn red. The berries are attractive to birds, so get there early. Squeeze the berries open to get the seeds, and sow them immediately outdoors where you want them; or stratify the seeds in moist sphagnum moss for 2 months, and sow them indoors under lights. Germination takes 3 weeks. Set the plants out when the soil is dry enough to work. The corms are deeper than you think, so be careful not to cut the top off without the corm—take a big clump of soil. Wear gloves to handle the corms, or the calcium oxalate crystals will get into your skin and make you itch.

CARE AND MAINTENANCE

Once in place, Jack-in-the-pulpits do not like to be disturbed. Leave them alone. There are no pest problems associated with these plants.

ADDITIONAL INFORMATION

Jack-in-the-pulpit is disappearing from many of its former haunts because of development and drying out of low areas.

ADDITIONAL SPECIES, CULTIVARS, OR VARIETIES

There are no other species of Jack-in-the-pulpit. *A. dracontium* is 'Green Dragon', another plant of moist areas. It has a leaf with many leaflets, and a long, yellow, whip-like spathe.

Joe-Pye Weed

Eupatorium purpureum

Zones: All
Size: Up to 7 feet tall, half as wide
Blooms: Late July to September
Flower Color: Purple

Light Requirement:

*J*oe-Pye weed is such an unusual name that it is difficult to forget it. Most people remember the name long before they can recognize the plant. According to legend, Joe-Pye was a Native American herb doctor in the Massachusetts Bay Colony. He used this plant to cure fevers. The plant is still used in parts of Appalachia for some disorders. This is a plant that is too big for many gardens, but where there is room and where it can be kept under control it will provide quite a display of purple blooms. It goes well with the goldenrod and rudbeckia that are in bloom at the same time.

WHEN TO PLANT

Joe-Pye weed is planted from seed sown in fall, or from divisions in spring. Container-grown plants may be planted at any time during the season.

WHERE TO PLANT

This is a plant found at the edges of wetlands and other wet places. It will tolerate drier places but may scorch. It can be planted in full sun or semi-shaded sites. Use it in a wide border, with ornamental grasses, in naturalized areas, at the edges of woods, or near water features. It is a woodland plant that will prosper in woods that have been burned off to reduce the underbrush.

HOW TO PLANT

Sow seeds in fall after they are released by the plant, or in spring. For prairie restoration and sowing a seed mix, prepare the soil by disking or tilling. Spread the seed or drill it, covering it lightly. The seeds may be sown in a small nursery bed. Set the seedlings in the garden when large enough to handle. Clumps can be dug up and divided in spring. The roots are tough and fibrous; divide the clumps in half or in quarters. Dig planting holes the same depth as the balls of the plants or the clumps. Set the plants at the same depth they were growing. These plants will need to be watered to keep from wilting the first season after planting.

CARE AND MAINTENANCE
Joe-Pye weed requires little care. If it is planted in a dry place, it will grow if watered in dry weather. Prairie plantings will benefit from the burning which eliminates the old tops and may stimulate seed germination.

ADDITIONAL INFORMATION
Joe-Pye weed can be grown in a small garden if it is cut down to 2 feet in June. It will respond with a lower, bushy plant and many flowers. A fellow gardener keeps a plant at about 4 feet in his small backyard English garden. The leaves of this plant give off a pleasant vanilla-like fragrance when crushed. They can be dried and used in potpourri.

ADDITIONAL SPECIES, CULTIVARS, OR VARIETIES
These plants were popularized in Great Britain while ignored here. They are just too common here, growing along roadsides—but the recent popularity of native plants has sparked interest in this plant as a garden flower. Nurseries are propagating and selling Joe-Pye weeds as perennials. These plants are probably *E. maculatum* 'Atropurpureum'. They have more flowers in their clusters than the *E. purpureum*. 'Gateway' is smaller and has mauve flowers on purple stems.

May Apple

Podophyllum peltatum

Other Names: Mandrake
Zones: All
Size: 1 to 1¹/₂ feet high and wide
Blooms: May
Flower Color: White

Light Requirement:

May apple is a plant of the moist woodlands. It grows from a large rootstock, appearing in early spring as one or two large umbrella-like leaves. The leaves are deeply cut with as many as six or eight lobes. This is a familiar plant to anyone who frequents the woods. The flowers appear beneath the leaves and are hard to see unless a leaf is lifted. The name May apple refers to the fruit that appears in midsummer. The plants are poisonous.

When to Plant

Divisions can be planted in late summer or spring. It is very difficult to kill May apples. I have dug them up and planted them in our yard in midsummer. They wilt for a few days, then resume growing as if they had never been moved.

Where to Plant

May apple can be grown in the shade garden. In fact, this is a very vigorous plant, and it will spread if not confined. It competes well with grass, growing out of a shaded area into the sunny lawn if given the chance. It is a valuable plant where other things will not grow. It can be used well in a shady area surrounded by concrete walks or driveways, and is especially good on banks. Shady slopes around buildings are impossible to keep sodded, and May apples have been used successfully in these situations. It can be combined with taller ferns for a pleasing contrast in texture. Few plants are as well adapted to a naturalized woodland setting as is the aggressive May apple.

How to Plant

Plant divisions in holes dug the same depth and twice as wide as the plant balls. Set the divisions at the same depth they were growing before. Backfill the holes and water to settle the soil around the roots. On banks or among tree roots, where planting is difficult, mulch them with shredded bark, and water until they have become established. If necessary, a few rocks will hold the plants in place until they take root. The berries may be collected as they ripen and the seeds rubbed out. Sow them immediately; they will germinate the next spring.

CARE AND MAINTENANCE

Once established, May apples need no care. Remove the large leaves after they ripen in fall, or burn off the area in spring. If the plants begin to grow out of their situation, remove them by digging up the wayward plants and disposing of them. No diseases or insect pests are known to affect May apples—they are as trouble-free as any garden plant can be.

ADDITIONAL INFORMATION

May apple was used for medicinal purposes by Native Americans and early settlers. It was recommended as a treatment for snakebite and as a cathartic. Modern medicine has extracted from it a resin that is effective in treating some kinds of skin problems and is reported to have anti-tumor properties. The fruit loses its toxicity as it ripens, and pioneers used the berries for preserves.

ADDITIONAL SPECIES, CULTIVARS, OR VARIETIES

There are no varieties or selections of May apple.

Milkweed

Asclepias sp.

Zones: All
Size: 5 feet tall, spreading 2 feet
Blooms: July and August
Flower Colors: Pale pink to rose-purple

Light Requirement:

*M*ilkweeds are beautiful plants when in bloom. It is interesting to watch the seedpods as they open in fall, releasing their fluffy parachutes into the wind. The flowers are good for cutting, and the pods are wonderful in dried arrangements. As youngsters, we collected milkweed pods of *Asclepias syriaca*, common milkweed, for the fluff which was then being used as a substitute for kapok in life jackets. The milky sap was being tested for use as a rubber substitute. Milkweeds attract butterflies; the flowers are sources of nectar for them. The black-and-yellow larvae of monarch butterflies feed on the foliage of common milkweeds. These are large plants with fleshy leaves, so the feeding of a few of these insects does little to harm their looks. In our neighborhood, a few milkweeds grow in alleys, vacant lots, and other unmowed places. We always stop to see if monarchs are feeding, or whether we might be lucky enough to find one of their green-and-gold chrysalises. A neighbor rears monarchs for demonstrations at the local library and is constantly searching for milkweed plants to collect leaves to feed his brood. There are fewer each year. Red milkweed, *A. incarnata*, is a plant from the edges of prairie potholes where water persisted until well into summer. It is so wide-ranging in its adaptation that it will grow in fairly dry, alkaline soils as well.

WHEN TO PLANT

Milkweed crowns can be planted in spring or fall. Sow seeds as they develop in late summer.

WHERE TO PLANT

Plant in moist soil in full sun. These are large plants, so locate them at the back of the garden or in naturalized areas next to water features, ponds, or streams. Start a butterfly garden with milkweed and other inviting species.

How to Plant

Specialty wildflower growers start these plants in pots. Set the crowns at the same depth they were growing in their containers. The seeds may be sown in a small nursery bed. Rub the fluff off the seeds, and sow them in prepared soil. Set the seedlings in the garden when large enough to handle. The seed may be broadcast in combination with other wildflower seeds in prairie plantings. Drag the area to cover the seeds lightly. The plants will develop slowly, taking 2 seasons or more to flower. Red milkweeds are difficult to divide because they develop taproots and don't spread. They can be transplanted, but be sure to dig deep enough to minimize root damage. Common milkweed will spread and is easier to transplant from root divisions.

Care and Maintenance

Milkweeds are completely self-sufficient. Aphids are common on the plants, but are usually controlled naturally by ladybugs. Don't spray or dust the plants or the butterfly larvae will be killed.

Additional Information

Milkweeds get their name from the sap, which is milky-white. *Asclepias* comes from the name of the Greek god of medicine, Asklepios.

Additional Species, Cultivars, or Varieties

There are many milkweeds native to Illinois. Some wildflower growers have added "improved" cultivars to their plant lists, but I wonder if we can improve on plants that have adapted over the millennia to survive in their ecosystems. For the wildflower purist, only the species will suffice.

Prairie Phlox

Phlox pilosa fulgida

Zones: All
Size: 15 to 30 inches tall
Blooms: April to June
Flower Colors: Pink, rose, violet

Light Requirement:

*P*rairie phlox is a delightful plant that blooms in mid- to late spring. It is similar to many other phlox cultivars and species with its heads of dainty blooms on tall, unbranched stems. Prairie phlox is a more delicate flower than perennial garden phlox, *P. paniculata*. It has fewer flowers in its heads, and its colors tend to be more pastel, not as bright as the garden kinds. This flower is included in prairie plant seed mixes and used on many reclaimed sites. It is used on berms and in prairie plantings throughout the state. Some roadside plantings by the Illinois Department of Transportation have included prairie phlox. Prairie plantings in large industrial sites, such as the Sears Prairie Stone development in Northern Illinois, are brightened by these flowers in spring. This phlox is a plant of dried soils and will tolerate some drought. It will grow where the soils are moister, but not in soggy soils. Prairie phlox grows in many flower gardens; it is not as spectacular as garden phlox, but it does not require as much care. Hybrid garden phlox, if allowed to drop seed, will revert to the species. Prairie phlox grows the same from dropped seed as it does from divisions. In fact, gardeners who start with garden phlox sometimes end up with plants very similar to prairie phlox after a few years.

WHEN TO PLANT
Seed is available from suppliers of prairie or wildflower seeds, and in prairie-seed mixes. Seed may be collected as it develops and before the capsules pop open. Divide plants in spring or late fall.

WHERE TO PLANT
Plant prairie phlox in full sun in a well-drained soil. Use them in the border, the wildflower garden, or in naturalized prairie plantings.

HOW TO PLANT

Sow seed in fall as soon as it is collected, or in spring, in prepared soil. They may be sown in a small nursery bed. Prepare the soil by disking or tilling. Cover the seed lightly. Set the seedlings in the garden when large enough to handle. Plant divisions at the same depth they were growing. Dig the planting holes as deep and twice as wide as the rootball of the plant.

CARE AND MAINTENANCE

Once established, prairie phlox requires no care. In prairie plantings, burning every few years will prevent invasion by introduced species and woody plants, and it will stimulate the growth of native plants.

ADDITIONAL INFORMATION

Prairie phlox attracts butterflies. Many kinds of phlox have upper stems that are covered with a sticky material thought to prevent non-pollinating insects from getting to the flowers.

ADDITIONAL SPECIES, CULTIVARS, OR VARIETIES

Phlox divaricata is a woodland plant that is more common in gardens than prairie phlox. Some cultivars are available from nurseries. The species is a native wildflower. It is about a foot high, and forms colonies in the forest preserves and neighboring turfgrass areas. *Phlox pilosa* is sand prairie phlox. It inhabits sandy soils but will grow in moist soils as well. It is indistinguishable from *P. pilosa fulgida* to all but the most experienced eye.

Purple Coneflower

Echinacea purpurea

Zones: All
Size: 2 to 4 feet
Blooms: June to October
Flower Colors: Purple with a brown
  cone in the center

Light Requirement:

*P*urple coneflower, *Echinacea pallida*, is a native of our Illinois prairie. It was thought to be endangered earlier in this century. The popularity of the purple coneflowers in perennial gardens has reduced the chance that the plants will disappear, but native examples of it are increasingly rare. Two purple coneflowers were once widespread throughout Illinois: common, *E. pallida*, and broad-leaved, *E. purpurea*. For all practical purposes, they are both plants of drier soils and will grow in wildflower plantings. They are adapted to the small or large wildflower garden and are quite tidy in their habits. Rarely is a distinction made between them in seed catalogs. Restored prairie plantings often include purple coneflowers because they are reliable and provide interesting form and color for several weeks in summer. They are adapted to our heavy, often alkaline soils and the vagaries of precipitation in our typical summer. Once established, they can stand drought and will keep on blooming. Purple coneflower grows from a large root system. It is a sturdy plant, but it does not spread aggressively.

WHEN TO PLANT
Seeds of purple coneflowers may be sown in the fall or in spring. Divisions or started plants may be planted in early spring.

WHERE TO PLANT
Plant in naturalized areas or wildflower gardens, in full sun or light shade. Soils may be light or heavy, but they must be well drained. These are upland plants and will not survive in wet soils.

HOW TO PLANT
The seeds may be sown in a small nursery bed. Set the seedlings in the garden when they are large enough to handle. For seeding in a

prairie seed mix, prepare the soil by tilling or disking. Drill or broadcast the seed and drag to cover it lightly. Set divisions at the same depth they were growing before. Planting slightly high is preferred to planting too deeply.

CARE AND MAINTENANCE
The plants should be watered thoroughly after planting, and during the first season if there is extended dry weather. Seeded plantings will rarely need watering once the plants are up and growing. Prairie plantings will benefit from burning every few years to reduce competition from introduced species and woody plants. Most prairie plants respond to burning with increased vigor and floriferousness.

ADDITIONAL INFORMATION
Purple coneflowers are components of most prairie restoration seed mixes. The history of this plant includes many medicinal uses. Native Americans of the plains used ground roots as poultices for snake bite, bee stings, or dog bites, and they chewed root shavings for toothaches. The juice contains a topical anesthetic and was used by early settlers for relief from the pain of burns. There is still some interest in the medicinal properties of these plants.

ADDITIONAL SPECIES, CULTIVARS, OR VARIETIES
Both species of *Echinacea* seem to be sold as one. In the wild, it is possible to make the distinction based in the shape of the leaves. Some hybridization has been done to make the plant more civilized for perennial gardens. The species probably comes true from seed. *E. angustifolia* is another species native to the Great Plains.

Trillium

Trillium sp.

Other Names: Wake Robin
Zones: All
Size: Up to 18 inches tall
Blooms: Spring
Flower Colors: Red, white

Light Requirement:

*T*rilliums are immediately identifiable to almost everyone. They are distinctive with their single stem growing from a bulb. The stem is topped with a whorl of three leaves and a colorful flower with three petals. In some deciduous woodlands, the ground is covered with these lovely blooms in spring, just before the leaves in the canopy close out the sunlight. Trilliums are easy to grow in the wildflower garden. Plant them and leave them alone. They do not like to be disturbed; picking the flowers will remove the leaves that are necessary for replenishing the bulbs. Those picked plants will not bloom the next spring, and may not survive the winter. Trilliums in the wild have been the targets of plant collectors, and some populations have been destroyed. This is particularly true in forest preserves where the flowers have been picked. Try to keep the leaves on the plants as long as possible in spring. The longer they last, the better your chances of having plenty of flowers the following year.

WHEN TO PLANT

Sow seed outdoors in summer as soon as the seed is ripe. Potted plants may be set out in early spring. Bulblets can be collected after the tops die down in summer. Trilliums often do not transplant well.

WHERE TO PLANT

You can plant trilliums in moist woodlands that have a deep, humusy soil. Filtered sunlight is preferred, as it will allow the best replenishing of the bulbs.

HOW TO PLANT

Sow seed in a prepared bed outdoors. Collect the seed as berries begin to ripen, but before they split. Check the seeds in a few berries, and collect them as soon as they turn dark. Sow them immediately.

If they dry out, they will not germinate. The seeds will germinate over the next 2 years. Move the bulbs to permanent locations after the tops dry down in late summer. Plants will flower in 2 or 3 years.

Space the plants 2 feet apart. They are especially attractive in masses on the forest floor, or as specimens of the white-flowered species in the shade garden. Locate them where the absence of leaves later in the summer will not be noticed.

CARE AND MAINTENANCE
If these plants are in a spot that dries out in summer, make sure they get watered as long as the leaves are still green. Trilliums usually grow where there is a lot of litter from fallen leaves. In the garden, mulch them with compost to keep the soil cool and moist. There are no insect or disease pests that affect trilliums.

ADDITIONAL INFORMATION
Trilliums have been used in folk medicine for centuries. Native Americans used them to treat arthritis. They pounded the joint with a stick imbedded with needles, and rubbed a tea of powdered roots into the affected area.

ADDITIONAL SPECIES, CULTIVARS, OR VARIETIES
At least eight species of trillium grow wild in Illinois. Several are rare. The most common, and easiest to get for wildflower gardens, are the white large-flowered trillium (*T. grandiflorum*), and red trillium (*T. recurvatum*). These plants are available from specialty wildflower growers. Large-flowered trillium is a treasure, with flowers sometimes 4 inches across. Seed may be collected from wild populations of some of the other species.

Virginia Bluebells

Mertensia virginica

Zones: All	**Light Requirement:**
Size: To 2 feet	
Blooms: March to May	
Flower Color: Blue	

*V*irginia bluebells are welcome spring visitors that add something different to the garden. They bloom at the same time as many of the spring-flowering bulbs. Virginia bluebells are inhabitants of the moist, deciduous woods. They emerge, bloom, and dry down before the trees completely leaf out. This allows them to replenish the overwintering tubers. If grown in dark areas, they tend to thin out and may disappear. The ideal situation is a moist soil with plenty of organic matter, and filtered light as they bloom. Since these plants disappear in the garden in early summer, don't plant masses of them where a void will be noticed. They work very well with later-developing plants such as some of the ferns or hostas; these are late enough that they will not compete with the bluebells for light, and they will cover the bare spots well later in the season.

WHEN TO PLANT

Seed may be collected in spring as the fruits ripen. Tubers can be dug after the tops of the plants die down in early summer. They are offered for sale along with spring bulbs in fall.

WHERE TO PLANT

Plant in filtered shade where soils are cool and moist, shaded rock gardens, perennial borders, naturalized woodlands, or shaded grassy areas that are not mowed. These plants are often seen in forest preserve savannas, where the grasses do not compete early and scattered trees provide shade.

HOW TO PLANT

Plant divisions in late summer or fall. Existing plants may be divided and moved in fall. Set them at the same depth they were growing before. The seeds may be sown in a small nursery bed. Set the seedlings in the garden when large enough to handle. The seed may be broadcast in naturalized woodland plantings.

CARE AND MAINTENANCE

No diseases or insect pests seriously affect Virginia bluebells. If the plants are growing in an area that tends to dry out, apply compost to cool the soil and help maintain moisture.

ADDITIONAL INFORMATION

These plants will develop sizable crowns, but they usually spread by means of dropped seeds. Beds will enlarge in favorable areas. If the tops are cut down before they ripen, the plants will decline and die out. Although these plants are difficult to situate in the garden because they disappear quickly, they are so delightful while they last that it is worth the effort. Splendid naturalized plantings of Virginia bluebells pop up in unexpected places, usually deciduous woods. If hiking in the spring, don't be surprised if you see some of these delightful flowers in semi-open woodlands.

ADDITIONAL SPECIES, CULTIVARS, OR VARIETIES

No related species are available in Illinois, and the literature does not list any cultivars.

Wild Columbine

Aquilegia canadensis

Zones: All
Size: 2 to 3 feet tall
Blooms: April to July
Flower Colors: Red and yellow

Light Requirement:

*W*ild columbines have distinctive flowers with small red-and-yellow petals surrounded by red sepals, each ending in an elongated spur. These flowers are borne on nodding stems in spring and early summer. They tend to grow in the shade for the most part, and not in clumps. It is more common to see a few of them in one place. They don't compete well with grasses and other more vigorous plants. They are perfectly capable of growing in cracks in cliffs and can be seen doing just that in Starved Rock State Park. There are some growing like this in the Galena area, too. It is unlikely that there is a cliff in your garden, but wild columbine can do very well in a rock garden. This plant is one of the parents of the hybrid columbines grown in perennial gardens. All columbines are attractive to hummingbirds, butterflies, and moths, which feed on their nectar.

WHEN TO PLANT

Columbines can be grown from seed sown in midsummer. Plants may be divided in fall after the foliage begins to ripen.

WHERE TO PLANT

Plant in dappled sun or shade, though full sun will be tolerated. Use in rock gardens, wooded areas, and shaded wildflower gardens. Soil should be well drained, or even poor.

HOW TO PLANT

The seeds may be sown in a small nursery bed. Set the seedlings in the garden when they are large enough to handle. The seed may be broadcast in combination with other wildflower seeds in naturalized plantings. Winter stratification is needed to break dormancy. Plants will flower the second season. Divisions may be made or plants from containers planted in fall or early spring. Once established, wild columbines will maintain themselves by reseeding. Hybrid columbines may revert to the species if allowed to reseed.

CARE AND MAINTENANCE
Wild columbines require little care. Leaf miners will damage the foliage, but in naturalized plantings there is no need to control this pest. Garlic mustard, a weed, occupies the same kind of environment as does wild columbine; it will take over the planting if not controlled.

ADDITIONAL INFORMATION
Native Americans used the crushed seeds as a headache powder.

ADDITIONAL SPECIES, CULTIVARS, OR VARIETIES
Wild columbine is the only species indigenous to Illinois. Introduced cultivars that have reverted can be seen in old farmsteads and abandoned pastures, or wherever they were planted and abandoned.

Wild Geranium

Geranium maculatum

Zones: All
Size: 18 to 24 inches tall
Blooms: April to June
Flower Colors: Rose-lavender, pink

Light Requirement:

*T*he flowers of this springtime favorite seem to pop up overnight in wooded areas and along roadsides with the first nice spring weather. The flowers are rosy to pink and have delicate darker veins and five wide, nearly crepe-like petals. The leaves are finely cut, similar to those of some of the fragrant pelargoniums. Wild geraniums are among the more common of the woodland spring flowers. They are often found with blue phlox.

WHEN TO PLANT

Wild geraniums can be started from seed, or divisions can be made in early spring.

WHERE TO PLANT

Plant in moist woodlands, shaded wildflower gardens, or tree-lined roadside plantings in any average soil. While these are woodland plants, they are commonly seen growing along roadsides, just beyond the mowed strip, where they are in full sun much of the day.

HOW TO PLANT

The seeds may be sown in a small nursery bed. The addition of organic matter to improve moisture retention and soil structure is beneficial. Set the seedlings in the garden when they are large enough to handle. Divisions should be planted at the same depth they were growing and each clump should have several eyes. Set the clumps at least 3 feet apart. They will spread. In naturalized settings, the plants will reseed themselves and develop sizable beds.

CARE AND MAINTENANCE

Wild geraniums are essentially trouble-free. Garlic mustard has invaded naturalized plantings; it will squeeze these plants out unless controlled.

ADDITIONAL INFORMATION

Wild geraniums are much more tolerant of sites than some think. They are found in wet places and on fairly dry slopes. They grow in full shade and in full sun. In the sun, they do better if the soil has some moisture. The seeds are borne in capsules that split open, scattering the seeds some distance from the plants. This ensures the planting will spread. As is true of many native wild plants, geranium was used for medicinal purposes by Native Americans and early settlers. They used it as an astringent and for other various treatments. The plant has a high tannin content and was also used for tanning hides.

ADDITIONAL SPECIES, CULTIVARS, OR VARIETIES

Only one geranium is listed in the catalogs of wildflower seed companies. There are several wild geraniums that grow in Illinois. Some of these are introduced European species. The garden "geranium" is not a true geranium, but a *Pelargonium*.

SOURCES

Bibliography

American Horticultural Society, The, Christopher Brickell, ed., *Encyclopedia of Garden Plants*, Macmillan Publishing Company, NY.

Dirr, Michael A., *Manual of Woody Landscape Plants*, Stipes Publishing Co., Urbana, IL, 4th Edition, 1990.

Hill, May B., *Grandmother's Garden: The Old-Fashioned American Garden*, Henry N. Abrams, Inc., New York, 1995.

Holmes, Roger, ed., *Taylor's Guide to Ornamental Grasses*, Houghton Mifflin Company, Boston, New York, 1997.

Reddell, Rayford Clayton, *The Roses Bible*, Harmony Books, New York, NY, 1994.

Runkel, Sylvan T. and Alvin F. Bull, *Wildflowers of Illinois Woodlands*, Iowa State University Press, 1994.

Runkel, Sylvan T. and Dean M. Roosa, *Wildflowers of the Tallgrass Prairie: the Upper Midwest*, Iowa State University Press, 4th Edition, 1994.

Still, Steven M., *Manul of Herbaceous Ornamental Plants*, Stipes Publishing Co., Urbana, IL, 4th Edition, 1994.

Swink, Floyd and Gerold Wilhelm, *Plants of the Chicago Region*, Indiana Academy of Science, 4th Edition, 1994.

INDEX

Index

Index

Index

Index

Index

404

Index

Index

ABOUT THE AUTHOR

*J*AMES A. FIZZELL is best known as the "Staff Horticulturist" on Chicago's WGN radio where he has answered gardening questions for more than 35 years. Television viewers will recognize Fizzell as the congenial host of the Garden Street U.S.A. direct TV show.

As the president of James A. Fizzell & Associates, the author provides consulting services to the commercial horticulture industry. Fizzell's projects include such important landmarks as Wrigley Field, home of the Chicago Cubs, Chicago's O'Hare and Midway airports, and the Chicago Park District.

For nearly 30 years, the author served as the northeastern Illinois horticulturist with the University of Illinois Extension service. In that capacity, Fizzell wrote gardening columns for 200 newspapers in the Midwest, and hundreds of articles for horticultural trade publications.

Fizzell holds two degrees in horticulture from the University of Illinois. The esteemed horticulturist has received many honors including the prestigious Linnaeaus award by the Chicago Horticulture Society for lifetime service to horticulture. The author's contributions include his instrumental role in developing the Master Gardener Program in Illinois, and in forming the Illinois Landscape Contractors Association and the Illinois Arborist Association.

The author and his wife, Jane, enjoy gardening at their northern Illinois home on Garden Street.

ILLINOIS GARDENING ONLINE

www.coolspringspress.com

Now available, exclusively for Illinois gardeners!

To serve the needs of today's gardeners, Cool Springs Press has created one of the most advanced home pages in America devoted exclusively to gardening. It offers expert advice on how to make Illinois gardening more enjoyable and the results more beautiful.

Consult the Cool Springs Press home page for monthly information from the *Illinois Gardener's Guide.* Keep up-to-date with Illinois gardening on the Internet.

– LOCALIZED GARDENING CALENDAR FOR THE MONTH

– SELECTED "PLANT OF THE MONTH"

– DISCUSSION ROOM FOR CONVERSATION AND ADVICE, JUST FOR ILLINOIS GARDENERS

www.coolspringspress.com